Rick Leinecker

SAMS
Teach Yourself
Visual J++ 6
in 21 Days

SAMS

A Division of Macmillan Computer Publishing
201 West 103rd St., Indianapolis, Indiana, 46290 USA

Sams Teach Yourself Visual J++ 6 in 21 Days

Copyright © 1999 by Sams

International Standard Book Number: 0-672-31351-0

Library of Congress Catalog Card Number: 98-86423

Printed in the United States of America

First Printing: November 1998

00   99   98   4   3   2   1

Trademarks

All terms mentioned in this book that are known to be trademarks or service marks have been appropriately capitalized. Sams cannot attest to the accuracy of this information. Use of a term in this book should not be regarded as affecting the validity of any trademark or service mark.

Warning and Disclaimer

Every effort has been made to make this book as complete and as accurate as possible, but no warranty or fitness is implied. The information provided is on an "as is" basis. The authors and the publisher shall have neither liability or responsibility to any person or entity with respect to any loss or damages arising from the information contained in this book.

EXECUTIVE EDITOR
Tim Ryan

ACQUISITIONS EDITOR
Jeff Taylor

DEVELOPMENT EDITOR
Jon Steever
Gus Miklos

MANAGING EDITOR
Patrick Kanouse

SENIOR EDITOR
Elizabeth A. Bruns

PRODUCTION EDITOR
Carol L. Bowers

COPY EDITOR
Cheri Clark

INDEXER
Bruce Clingaman

PROOFREADER
Kim Cofer

TECHNICAL EDITOR
Andrew Fritzinger

SOFTWARE DEVELOPMENT SPECIALIST
Adam Swetnam

INTERIOR DESIGN
Gary Adair

COVER DESIGN
Aren Howell

LAYOUT TECHNICIAN
Susan Geiselman

Contents at a Glance

Contents

About the Author

Rick Leinecker is a software developer and an instructor at Rockingham Community College. Among his recently published books are *The Visual C++ 5 Power Toolkit*, *The Visual C++ 6 Bible*, *The Visual J++ Bible*, and *The Windows 98 Programming Bible*.

You'll find many of his software titles on the retail shelves including Championship Chess, Bicycle Spades and Hearts, and Trump Castle. In addition to games, he writes imaging software, including an add-on library called ImageObject for Visual C++, Visual Basic, and Visual J++.

You can check out Rick's Web site at www.infinitevision.net or send him email at ivt-rcl@interapth.com.

When Rick isn't writing books and software or teaching, he's making music. He sings in several groups, plays guitar and horn, and sometimes acts as musical director for the Rockingham County Theater Guild.

Tell Us What You Think!

As the reader of this book, *you* are our most important critic and commentator. We value your opinion and want to know what we're doing right, what we could do better, what areas you'd like to see us publish in, and any other words of wisdom you're willing to pass our way.

As the Executive Editor for the Java team at Macmillan Computer Publishing, I welcome your comments. You can fax, email, or write me directly to let me know what you did or didn't like about this book—as well as what we can do to make our books stronger.

Please note that I won't have time to help you with technical problems related to the topic of this book, and that due to the high volume of mail I receive, I might not be able to reply to every message.

When you write, please be sure to include this book's title and author as well as your name and phone or fax number. I will carefully review your comments and share them with the author and editors who worked on the book.

Fax: 317-817-7070

E-mail: java@mcp.com

Mail: Tim Ryan, Executive Editor
            Java Team
            Macmillan Computer Publishing
            201 West 103rd Street
            Indianapolis, IN 46290 USA

Acknowlegements

I've enjoyed working with the staff at Macmillan Computer Publishing. They've all been quite professional. They're also real people who are easy to work with, and made my job as an author much easier. Not all editors are this way. (I nicknamed a previous editor at another company "Atilla the Hun.") I appreciate the staff at Macmillan. Jon Steever was at the development helm, and he deserves applause for a job well done.

Marcy Pyrtle deserves the most credit for getting me through this project. She took my tape recorded babblings, and converted them into prose that made sense. Thanks for the help! Musicians can do more than play and sing. They can be downright smart when they need to be.

Lastly, I want to thank my family for letting me put activities off as they constantly heard "just let me finish this section I'm working on." Three children who want to swim and inline skate during the summer, who are as understanding as they were, deserve a pat on the back. Maybe next summer I won't be writing a book.

Introduction

Visual J++ is an important addition to software developers' tools. You can use it to create amazing Java applets for Web sites. These applets can take static HTML and bring it to life with animations, professional-looking user interfaces, and real-time display based on current data. Besides Java applets, Visual J++ gives you a viable alternative to using Visual C++ and Visual Basic for building applications. Visual J++ is a truly object-oriented language. For this reason, many software developers who are more comfortable with object-oriented approaches will choose it for their programming tasks.

I've tried to give you the information you need in this book yet keep it free of boring and overly technical discussions. Many authors throw the kitchen sink into every example, and it's hard to pick out the code that's related to the topic at hand. To avoid this situation, I keep examples simple and limit them to the current topic.

I've created a section on my Web site that will contain updates and answers to questions that readers send me. You can find the section if you go to www.infinitevision.net and follow the links to Books and then Learn Visual J++ 6 in 21 Days.

Feel free to email me at ivt-rcl@interpath.com. Remember, though, I'm a software developer and I might be in the middle of a project! During these times, I'm very busy. I can usually answer emails in a day or two, but during crunch times it might be closer to a couple of weeks.

Who Should Read This Book?

This book covers everything you need to bring you from no experience to a point at which you'll easily be able to create applications and applets with Visual J++. As a matter of fact, if you are conscientious and read one chapter each day, you'll amaze yourself at how good you'll get at Visual J++ programming.

Here's who should read this book:

- Web developers who want to jumpstart their sites by creating Java applets.
- Programmers who feel comfortable with object-oriented programming and want to use Visual J++ to develop applications.
- Developers who like some of the things Visual J++ has to offer, such as easy imaging and image-processing methods.
- Programmers who want to take advantage of the explosion in distributed computing and participate in Web-based solutions.

- Those who are going to teach Visual J++ for a class or seminar and want an organized approach to covering the material.

If you find yourself in any of these categories, this book is for you.

What This Book Contains

This book contains 21 days' worth of lessons—one lesson per day. Each chapter is designed to be read in a single day. It's like a course in Visual J++ that you can read and study on your own time and at your own pace.

This is not a reference book that's full of lists and dry class and method descriptions. It attempts to be like a friendly instructor who wants you to learn how to program with Visual J++. For lists and class and method descriptions, you can use the online help. You'll find that for learning Visual J++, though, the discussions in this book are clear and easily understood.

I start by teaching you introductory topics you need, such as how to create and edit projects. Then, you'll learn the basics of user-interface objects, such as editable text fields and menus. A section on graphics comes next—this is my personal favorite! Then, you'll learn some of the nuts and bolts of Visual J++ programming in an elements section that covers topics such as exceptions and strings. The last section covers more advanced topics, such as ActiveX controls and how to use J/Direct.

What You Need in Order to Begin

The main thing you'll need is Visual J++ 6. If you bought Visual Studio 6, you have a copy. You can also download a copy from Microsoft's Web site. To download a copy of Visual J++, go to www.microsoft.com/VisualJ. Then, follow the links to the Visual J++ download page.

If you're developing Java applets, you can run them on your local computer. But it's helpful to have a Web site to which you can upload applets and test them in a live environment.

Your 21 Days at a Glance

Day 1 gets you started. You'll learn about the Visual J++ environment, and how to create and build projects. You'll create and build two programs to get you going.

Day 2 teaches you about the Java language. You'll learn about variables, control statements, and expressions. This all-important chapter gives you the knowledge you need in order to understand the syntax of Java.

Day 3 shows you how to make your applets live on the Web. You'll learn about Web directory structure and HTML tags for applets.

Day 4 shows you how to debug Visual J++ programs. This might be one of the most important topics in the book because it will help you figure out what's wrong when something doesn't work.

Day 5 introduces windows. On this day you'll learn how to create and manipulate windows. You'll also learn about window events. Finally, you'll learn about some important object-oriented topics, such as classes and method overriding.

Day 6 shows you how to create and use menus. At the end of Day 6 you'll have no trouble using these important user-interface items.

Day 7 shows you how to create and use user-interface components in Visual J++ applets. Items such as combo boxes, list boxes, and editable fields are covered in full detail.

Day 8, similar to day 7, shows you how to create and use user-interface components in Java applications. Handling events generated by these items is also covered in detail.

Day 9 shows you how to create dialog boxes in Visual J++ applications and interact with them from the main program. Visual J++ makes dialogs a snap, and this chapter teaches you how.

Day 10 starts the graphics section. You'll learn about fonts and text. How to create fonts of different sizes and colors. How to center text in a window.

Day 11 shows you how to draw to your program's window. Lines, rectangles, ovals, and the like are all covered.

Day 12 is about images. Visual J++ makes loading and using images easy. This chapter brings you through the methods for applications and applets.

Day 13 teaches you about image processing. It's an important subject, especially if it reduces the number of files on a Web server and the amount of data that must be sent over the phone line to users.

Day 14 might be your favorite. It covers animation—most developers really enjoy this topic. You might get creative and build some great animation programs.

Day 15 covers the all-important topic of exceptions. This might be a new topic to many readers, making this chapter all the more important.

Day 16 deals with the topic of mouse input. You'll learn how to get and receive mouse events.

Day 17 teaches you how to create and use threads. It's a fairly advanced subject but one that all Visual J++ programmers will eventually need.

Day 18 covers the topic of strings. Strings are used in almost every part of Visual J++ programming, and this chapter covers the topics thoroughly.

Day 19 teaches you about stream I/O. You'll learn how to read from disk files and how to copy files.

Day 20 is about ActiveX. This buzzword crops up in just about every article about Windows computing. And this chapter gives you the know-how to understand and make use of the concepts.

Day 21 covers an advanced but important topic: J/Direct. This feature was added to Visual J++ to give programmers greater power and flexibility.

Conventions Used in This Book

This book uses different typefaces to differentiate between code and regular English, and also to help you identify important concepts.

- Actual code is typeset in a special monospace font.
- *Italic* highlights terms when they first appear in the text and is sometimes used to emphasize important points.

Note

Note boxes give you information that is especially important. Sometimes they provide extra information that helps you understand a topic better.

Tip

Tips give you ways to make something better or make a process easier.

Caution

Warnings indicate something you should be aware of to avoid malfunctions or problems.

INPUT The Input icon marks the beginning of a section of source code that gives an example of something talked about in the text.

OUTPUT The Output icon marks a section that describes or shows a screen shot of a program in operation.

ANALYSIS The Analysis icon marks the beginning of a section in which a program is analyzed. These sections are important for your understanding of the topic.

NEW TERM When new terms are introduced in the text, many times they'll show up with a New Term icon.

WEEK 1

At a Glance

- Getting Started: The Visual J++ Environment
- Java Language Fundamentals
- Making Applets Live On the Web
- Debugging Java Applets and Applications
- Windows
- Menus
- Applet User Interface Controls

1

2

3

4

5

6

7

DAY 1

Getting Started: The Visual J++ Environment

We're going to get started today learning about Java and Visual J++. It's an important introduction that will give you some background and explain some Java fundamentals. Java is a fairly new language that you see just about everywhere you look. And Microsoft's Visual J++ is a tool that lets you create Java applets and applications from a great integrated development environment (IDE).

Today you'll get started. In this lesson, you'll do all the following:

- Learn about Java
- Learn about Visual J++
- Create your first Visual J++ applet
- Learn about the order in which Java methods are executed
- Create your first Visual J++ application
- Learn where to find information on the Web

Mastering this chapter will give you a good understanding of what Java is, and of how Visual J++ is used to create Java applets and applications.

Java and Visual J++

I'm going to start with some background. First you'll read about the attributes of Java that make it unique. Then you'll learn about how Visual J++ makes it easy to develop Java applets and applications.

The Power of Java

Java programs can be embedded in HTML pages and downloaded by Web browsers to bring live animation and interactivity to Web clients.

The power of Java isn't limited to Web applets. Java is a general-purpose programming language. It has full programming features and can be used to develop standalone applications. Java is inherently object-oriented. Although many object-oriented languages began strictly as procedure languages, Java was designed to be object-oriented from the start. Object-oriented programming (OOP) is currently a popular programming approach that replaces the traditional procedural programming techniques.

 Note   Although Java and Visual J++ started out as an Internet application language, Microsoft is now advancing Visual J++ as a real alternative for Windows application development. With Visual J++ 6, you can write applications that take advantage of the Windows operating system.

One of the central issues of software development is how to reuse program components. Object-oriented programming provides great flexibility, modularity, clarity, and reusability through method abstraction, class abstraction, and class inheritance—all of which you'll learn about by using Visual J++.

Inheritance is a key element to the success of Visual J++. You can create a class that's derived from another class. With the new class, you get everything the base class has to offer free—with no effort. In no time flat, you can create classes that offer great functionality. All you have to do is add your own custom methods and variables, and voilà—you have a new, more useful, more powerful class.

Encapsulation is another OOP feature that Visual J++ provides. The concept is simple: encapsulate functionality and data neatly into a class. It prevents what we programmers call spaghetti code, in which everything is interwoven with everything else. I've had to

1

jump into too many projects in which the code was exactly what encapsulation is meant to avoid—interwoven spaghetti!

Limitations of the Web

Although the World Wide Web was a great leap forward in accessing information, it was static in nature. The pages and sites that made up the bulk of the Web were nothing more than still images and text with the occasional audio blurb. They were, by nearly all accounts, lifeless.

Here's why: Early Web browsers simply accessed and displayed Web content. All the Web content was defined by the Hypertext Markup Language (HTML). The HTML standard is relatively new. And although HTML will eventually support truly dynamic content, such as animation and streaming audio that's automatically presented to the user, it currently does not. At the moment, dynamic media presentation is handled by add-ons, plug-ins, ActiveX controls, CGI scripts, and Java applets.

NEW TERM The term *HTML* is used throughout this book. Every browser loads in HTML files from Web servers to display content. Sometimes, though, the HTML files are generated dynamically by the servers and don't really exist as files on a server.

Before Java, truly interactive content on the Web was practically nonexistent. Real interactivity goes way beyond merely typing information and waiting for a reply, or having a customized page generated for your personal viewing pleasure. Before Java, you could click on text and image links to navigate around the sea of information, but that was about the extent of it. There really wasn't a means for truly interacting with the user.

Solutions for the Web with Java

The Web has become a different world altogether with the addition of Java, whose most fundamental contribution is platform-independent access to executable content. To the uninitiated, that phrase might seem a bit obscure. But that's exactly what's at the heart of Java.

As for the executable content, well, that's where Java really explodes with potential. Executable content allows the Web to deliver software programs to the user, programs that execute when they arrive and actually do something. Before Java, the ordinary Web user merely clicked on a graphic or link and accessed the information to which it pointed. This was static, in the sense that nothing was going on except the click and the subsequent access of the linked information.

Because embedded Java programs are automatically downloaded and executed on the user's computer, dynamic content immediately becomes possible. The most obvious example is the use of animation through Java. Web pages embedded with little pieces of animation are pretty popular, because animation is an effective way of grabbing attention. Although animated GIFs offer simple frame animation, Java animations offer more advanced functionality, such as user interactivity, adaptive behavior, and on-the-fly image alteration.

The Introduction of Visual J++ 6

On March 11, 1998, Microsoft announced Visual J++ 6. The new version of Visual J++ offers a fast way for Java developers to build and deploy high-performance, data-driven client/server solutions for Windows and the Web.

Note Microsoft skipped Visual J++ versions 2–5. This was so that the version number of Visual J++ would match those of the other development languages found in Visual Studio. It's more a marketing decision than a development decision. Visual Interdev experienced the same version jump as Visual J++.

Visual J++ 6 still has the great things that version 1.0 and 1.1 had. It's a powerful and easy-to-use development tool for Java programs. It still has a Database Wizard, an ActiveX Wizard, a CAB Toolkit, and a Digital Signature Toolkit.

In addition to what's in the earlier versions, Visual J++ 6 supports the Windows Foundation Classes (WFC). WFC is an object-oriented framework designed to provide easy access to the full power of the Windows platform, enabling developers to build high-performance, native Windows-based applications using the Java programming language. WFC is built on the high-performance J/Direct API architecture, which provides access to the full array of Windows APIs and can be more than twice as fast as other native access mechanisms for Java.

Visual J++ 6 also features an updated and fully customizable rapid application development (RAD) integrated development environment, based on the popular Visual Basic IDE. Two-way visual design tools, IntelliSense technology to provide on-the-fly syntax and parameter information, advanced cross-language and remote debugging capabilities, scalable data access, and one-button application deployment make Java development fast and easy.

Highlights of the Visual J++ Environment

I can't tell you every single thing about the Visual J++ IDE in this chapter—mainly because I would need about 1,000 pages to cover it all. You'd also get pretty bored because the IDE is so easy to use that much of it requires no explanation. But this

1

section will show you some of the more important areas and get you jump-started in using the Visual J++ IDE.

Getting Help

The first thing you need to know is how to get help. Although Visual J++ is relatively easy to use, it's impossible to memorize all the interfaces, classes, methods, and fields. I don't even try—I just make sure that I can get to the online help anytime I have a question.

Begin by selecting Help, Search from the menu. This action will bring up the Microsoft System Developer Network (MSDN) program as shown in Figure 1.1.

FIGURE 1.1

The MSDN program comes up when you need help.

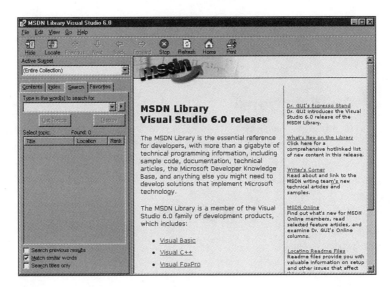

Notice that the Search tab is selected by default. When you enter a search term with this tab selected, MSDN will search the entire contents of its help database. This can create a large list, which you must then look through.

I almost never enter a search term with the Search tab selected. I've found it most convenient to select the Index tab. As I type the term for which I'm searching, the closest match is shown in the list. This works best when you're looking for an interface, a class, or a method.

Tip

Select the Index tab when you want to find an interface, a class, a method, or a field. If what you're looking for doesn't show up there, you'll have to select the Search tab and enter your search term.

Navigating Your Source-Code Windows

There are two ways I find easiest to navigate to different source-code files that are part of my project. My first choice is to double-click on the source-code module in the Project Explorer window. My next choice (which requires a little more effort) is to select the Window menu and then select the source-code module I want to edit.

If you have a file that's not part of your project, such as when you load some code from another project, you'll almost always use the Window menu to go to that source code. That's because it won't be found in the Project Explorer window if it's not part of your project.

Build Options

Right away, you'll need to know how to build your projects. Figure 1.2 shows the Build menu and its entries. Notice that the Build Configuration menu entry has a submenu that lets you specify a Debug or Release build.

FIGURE 1.2

The Build menu offers you the choices you need in order to build your projects.

To build the project, compiling only modules in which the source code is newer than the compiled byte code, you select the Build, Build menu option. This compiles only the modules you've edited since the last build.

To rebuild the entire project regardless of how current the source code is, select Build, Rebuild.

To change to a Debug build or a Release build, use the Build Configuration menu entry.

Project Settings

At various times you might want to change your project's settings. To do this, select Project, Project Properties. The entry isn't actually called Project Properties; it's named after the current project. For instance, if your project is named MyProject, you'll see MyProject Properties as the last entry in the Project menu.

For applications, the Project Properties dialog box lets you edit information such as what the executable file will be named, which kinds of compile options you want to use, and the output type.

For applets, the Project Properties dialog box lets you edit information such as what will be used to load the applet (usually Internet Explorer) as shown in Figure 1.3, CLASSPATH information, and output filenames.

FIGURE 1.3

The Project Properties dialog box allows you to set things such as which program will be used to launch your applets.

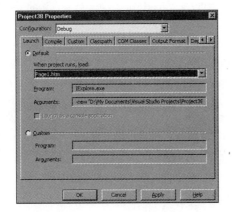

Creating Your First Applet

Note

Visual J++ uses Internet Explorer 4.0 (IE) in many ways. First and foremost, IE is the interpreter that's invoked when your applets run. It also serves as the debugger host. Also important is Visual J++'s use of the embedded Web browser control (as seen in the QuickView tab of the HTML editor), which requires shdocvw.dll, an integral part of IE. When you install Visual J++, it looks to see whether you have IE installed and, if so, which version. Before even installing Visual J++, it tries to install IE.

You can get updates for IE from www.microsoft.com.

1. Start by running Visual J++. The New Project dialog box will appear. This makes it easy for you to create a new project or load an existing project. To create a new project, make sure that the New tab is selected.

2. You'll see two Explorer-style windows. In the left window will be two upper-level folders: Visual J++ Projects and Visual Studio. Open the Visual J++ Projects folder.

3. Inside of the `Visual J++ Projects` folder, you'll see three folders. Each of these represents one of the categories of programs you can create with Visual J++. The `Applications` folder contains choices that let you create applications. These applications aren't for deployment on Web pages; they're more like applications you'd build in Visual Basic and Visual C++. The next folder, named `Components`, contains choices with which you can build components such as ActiveX controls. The third and last folder is named `Web Pages`. In this folder you'll find the choice we'll use for creating an applet destined for a Web page. Open the folder.

4. In the `Web Pages` folder, you'll have two choices: `Applet on HTML` and `Code-behind HTML`. It's the `Applet on HTML` choice we're interested in. The other choice, `Code-behind HTML`, creates a COM object that's hosted on an HTML page.

5. Now, name the project Hello1, as shown in Figure 1.4. For the entire book, I'll refer to a directory named `VJProjects`. It's off the root of my D drive. This will make it easier for me to find my project files, and it will also make it easier for you to understand my instructions if I consistently use the `VJProjects` directory. Finally, click the OK button and the project will be created.

Note

Throughout the book, I'll use applets and applications to teach you how to develop with Visual J++. Sometimes applets are a better way to teach you, and sometimes applications are better. I'm going to use whichever makes the explanation the clearest and easiest to understand.

FIGURE 1.4

Name this "Applet on HTML" project Hello1.

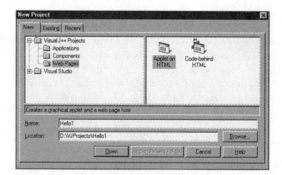

Congratulations! You've just created your first Visual J++ project. Let's test it. First, you have to compile the applet. To do this, select Build, Build. In several seconds (unless your machine is extremely slow), the applet will be compiled.

Now you can run it by selecting Debug, Start, pressing the F5 key, or pressing the Ctrl+F5 key combination. The applet itself doesn't actually run. Instead, Internet Explorer runs and loads the HTML file that Visual J++ created. When Internet Explorer interprets the HTML file, it finds that it has to load and execute the applet. It does this, and you see the applet appear inside of Internet Explorer. To run the applet (inside of Internet Explorer), select Debug, Run. You'll see something similar to what's shown in Figure 1.5.

FIGURE 1.5

When the applet runs, it shows you a single line of text. This text is part of the default source code that Visual J++ creates.

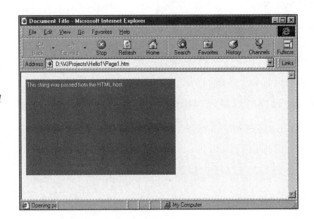

Visual J++ names all the default .java files Applet1.java, and all the default .htm files Page1.htm. However, it's more convenient to have the startup .java and .htm files named the same thing as the project. For instance, in my opinion the Hello1 project should create startup files named Hello1.java and Hello1.htm.

For the remainder of the book, I'll rename all applet startup files with the same name as the project (such as Hello1.java and Hello1.htm for the Hello1 project). But you'll need some instructions on how to do this:

1. In the Project Explorer window, right-click on Applet1.java.

2. When the pop-up menu appears, select Rename.

3. Rename to Hello1.java.

4. Make sure that the Hello1.java source code is opened in the source-code window. (You can double-click on Hello1.java to open it.)

5. Find the two occurrences of Applet1 in the Hello1.java file and replace them with Hello1.

6. In the Project Explorer window, right-click on Page1.htm.

7. When the pop-up menu appears, select Rename.

8. Rename to Hello1.htm.

9. Make sure that the Hello1.htm source code is opened in the source-code window. (As with the Hello1.java file, you can double-click on Hello1.htm to open it.)

10. Make sure that the Source tab is selected in the source-code window.

11. Find all occurrences of Applet1 in the Hello1.htm file and replace them with Hello1.

12. Rebuild the applet by selecting Build, Build.

Now we must display the famous message that all Visual J++ programmers should start off with: Hello Visual J++ World. Make sure that the Hello1.htm file is opened in the source-code window and that the Source tab is selected. You'll see a line that looks just like the following:

```
<param name=label value="This string was passed from the HTML host.">
```

Edit this line that so that our new message will be displayed. The newly edited line will look like the following:

```
<param name=label value="Hello Visual J++ World.">
```

Note When you make changes to the HTML file, you don't have to recompile. You do, however, have to recompile when you make changes to the Java source code.

When you click on the Quick View tab, the new message will be displayed in the applet window. Our applet source code is shown in Listing 1.1, and the HTML code is shown in Listing 1.2.

LISTING 1.1 THE JAVA SOURCE CODE FOR THE HELLO1 APPLET

```
1    // Hello1.java
2
3    import java.awt.*;
4    import java.applet.*;
5
6    /**
7     * This class reads PARAM tags from its HTML host page and sets
8     * the color and label properties of the applet. Program execution
9     * begins with the init() method.
10    */
11   public class Hello1 extends Applet
12   {
```

```
13      /**
14       * The entry point for the applet.
15       */
16      public void init()
17      {
18          initForm();
19
20          usePageParams();
21
22          // TODO: Add any constructor code after initForm call.
23      }
24
25      private     final String labelParam = "label";
26      private     final String backgroundParam = "background";
27      private     final String foregroundParam = "foreground";
28
29      /**
30       * Reads parameters from the applet's HTML host and sets applet
31       * properties.
32       */
33      private void usePageParams()
34      {
35          final String defaultLabel = "Default label";
36          final String defaultBackground = "C0C0C0";
37          final String defaultForeground = "000000";
38          String labelValue;
39          String backgroundValue;
40          String foregroundValue;
41
42          /**
43           * Read the <PARAM NAME="label" VALUE="some string">,
44           * <PARAM NAME="background" VALUE="rrggbb">,
45           * and <PARAM NAME="foreground" VALUE="rrggbb"> tags from
46           * the applet's HTML host.
47           */
48          labelValue = getParameter(labelParam);
49          backgroundValue = getParameter(backgroundParam);
50          foregroundValue = getParameter(foregroundParam);
51
52          if ((labelValue == null) || (backgroundValue == null) ||
53              (foregroundValue == null))
54          {
55              /**
56               * There was something wrong with the HTML host tags.
57               * Generate default values.
58               */
59              labelValue = defaultLabel;
60              backgroundValue = defaultBackground;
61              foregroundValue = defaultForeground;
62          }
```

continues

LISTING 1.1   CONTINUED

```
63
64          /**
65           * Set the applet's string label, background color, and
66           * foreground colors.
67           */
68          label1.setText(labelValue);
69          label1.setBackground(stringToColor(backgroundValue));
70          label1.setForeground(stringToColor(foregroundValue));
71          this.setBackground(stringToColor(backgroundValue));
72          this.setForeground(stringToColor(foregroundValue));
73      }
74
75      /**
76       * Converts a string formatted as "rrggbb" to an awt.Color object
77       */
78      private Color stringToColor(String paramValue)
79      {
80          int red;
81          int green;
82          int blue;
83
84          red = (Integer.decode("0x" +
            ➥paramValue.substring(0,2))).intValue();
85          green = (Integer.decode("0x" +
            ➥paramValue.substring(2,4))).intValue();
86          blue = (Integer.decode("0x" +
            ➥paramValue.substring(4,6))).intValue();
87
88          return new Color(red,green,blue);
89      }
90
91      /**
92       * External interface used by design tools to show properties of
         ➥an applet.
93       */
94      public String[][] getParameterInfo()
95      {
96          String[][] info =
97          {
98              { labelParam, "String", "Label string to be displayed" },
99              { backgroundParam, "String", "Background color, format
                ➥\"rrggbb\"" },
100             { foregroundParam, "String", "Foreground color, format
                ➥\"rrggbb\"" },
101         };
102         return info;
103     }
104
105     Label label1 = new Label();
106
```

```
107    /**
108     * Initializes values for the applet and its components
109     */
110    void initForm()
111    {
112        this.setBackground(Color.lightGray);
113        this.setForeground(Color.black);
114        label1.setText("label1");
115        this.setLayout(new BorderLayout());
116        this.add("North",label1);
117    }
118 }
```

Visual J++ creates HTML code for you whenever an applet project is created. You can see the HTML code for our program in Listing 1.2.

LISTING 1.2 THE HTML CODE FOR THE HELLO1 PROJECT

```
1    <HTML>
2    <HEAD>
3    <TITLE>Hello1 Program</TITLE>
4    </HEAD>
5    <BODY>
6
7    <!-- Insert HTML here -->
8        <applet
9            code=Hello1.class
10           name=Hello1
11           width=320
12           height=200 >
13           <param name=label value="Hello Visual J++ World.">
14           <param name=background value="008080">
15           <param name=foreground value="FFFFFF">
16       </applet>
17
18   </BODY>
19   </HTML>
```

What Comes First

One of the first things you'll need to learn is in which order the common Java methods are executed. These common methods are ones that can be overridden in your applet classes. It's important because you might be expecting things to be initialized when you hit the constructor code, and they're blowing up your applet with millions of divide-by-zero exceptions. Knowing the order will allow you to do everything in the proper sequence and avoid initialization and setup pitfalls.

NEW TERM   *Overriding* methods is a way in which classes that extend other classes can use their own method rather than the method that's part of the class from which they're extended. This is explained in more detail in Day 5's chapter, "Frame Windows."

Member Variable Declarations

The first thing most applet classes have are variable and class declarations. When variable declarations come first, this makes it easier for others to understand the program. This is because they don't have to scan through the source code to find the variables. For this reason, it's recommended that you place variables at the beginning of the applet class. Local variables are the obvious exception. They still have to be in the method that declares and uses them.

Variable initialization can be done at the same time as the declaration. You can set integer values or allocate a class. Following are some examples of legal initializations:

```
int x = 0;
int y = 0;
int horizontal = 0, vertical = 0;
String str1 = new String();
String str2 = new String( "This is my string" );
```

If you're declaring variables at the beginning of the class, you can't then assign them with regular code. In fact, you can't just stick code in the applet—code must be within a method. Here are some examples of declarations with legal and illegal initialization code:

```
public class ThreadedHelloWorld extends Applet implements Runnable
{
  int x, y;

  x = 2;     // ILLEGAL-not in a method
  y = x * 4; // ILLEGAL-not in a method

  public void InitXY()
  {
    x = 2;     // LEGAL-in a method
    y = x * 4; // LEGAL-in a method
  }

}
```

Constructors

Seasoned C++ programmers are probably looking for a constructor in which they can initialize their variables. Java provides one, probably for us old C++ salts. The constructor is named after the applet. For our Hello1 applet it would be a method named Hello1(). Although some might not agree (personal habits vary widely), the constructor is a good place in which to initialize variables. Assigning values to variables in the constructor and declaring variables at the top of the applet separates them for clarity and gives you one place to check when things aren't what they should be.

Note

All Java classes might or might not have constructors—it's up to the programmer who creates the class. When a class is instantiated, such as when it's created from a program that's going to use the class, the first method that's called is the constructor (unless the class has no constructor). These methods are called constructors because they're technically part of the class construction process.

Here's what the beginning of an applet with applet variable declarations and variable initialization in the constructor would look like:

```
public class Hello1 extends Applet
{
    int x, y;
    int nHorizontal, nVertical;

    // Hello1 Class Constructor
    //--------------------------------------------------------
    public Hello1()
    {
        x = 5;
        y = 20;
        nHorizontal = x * 2;
        nVertical = y * 3;
    }

    // Place other methods here.
}
```

The `init()` Method

The next of the common methods that will be called is the `init()` method. The `init()` method is called by the Virtual Machine when an applet is first loaded or reloaded. Use this method to perform whatever initialization your applet needs, such as initializing data structures, loading images or fonts, creating frame windows, setting the layout manager, or adding user interface components.

The `init()` method is where most programs retrieve parameters. Actually, Visual J++ creates startup code inside of the `init()` method that calls a method named `usePageParams()`. The `usePageParams()` method loads and processes all the HTML parameters. The `usePageParams()` method is not an override of a method. It's just a convenient method that Microsoft's Visual J++ adds.

The start() Method

In a multithreaded applet, the start() method comes next in the sequence of events. It's in this method that the main applet is created and started. You can add your own code in this method, but you'll need some basic things. Following is a bare-bones start() method for a multithreaded applet:

```
public void start()
{
    if( m_Params == null )
    {
        m_Params = new Thread( this );
        m_Params.start();
    }
    // Place additional applet start code here
}
```

The run() Method

After the start() method is called, the thread begins execution. The program will remain in the run() method until an interruption is detected. In the run() method, repaint() and sleep() are usually called. For most applets, repaint() won't need to be called every time you go through the loop. You'll most likely call the repaint() method only when the applet's display will change as a result of something your program's code has done.

The value passed to the sleep() method determines the amount of time the applet waits before executing the code in the run() method. Its value is in milliseconds. If the value passed to sleep() is 1000, the sleep() method waits one second before returning control to the applet. If the value is 500, it waits a half second before returning control. A good default value is 50. A bare-bones run() method follows:

```
public void run()
{
    while( true )
    {
        try
        {
            // Do stuff here
            Thread.sleep(50);
        }
        catch (InterruptedException e)
        {
            // Place exception-handling code here in case an
            //        InterruptedException is thrown by Thread.sleep(),
            //            meaning that another thread has interrupted
                        this one
```

```
            stop();
        }
    }
}
```

The `stop()` Method

When the applet is interrupted, usually by the browser going to another site, the `stop()` method is called. The thread is destroyed, and you have the opportunity to perform additional steps you might want to take for applet cleanup. Here's a bare-bones `stop()` method:

```
public void stop()
{
    if( m_Params != null )
    {
        m_Params.stop();
        m_Params = null;
    }
    // Place additional applet stop code here
}
```

The `destroy()` Method

The `destroy()` method is called automatically when the applet is terminated. It's still a good place to put all of your cleanup code because all the exit code will be organized in one place. For this reason, your `stop()` method should call `destroy()` after the thread is stopped. You can avoid any code except for the call to `destroy()` in the `stop()` method.

You might have some difficulty because `destroy()` might not be executed as early in the cleanup process as you'd like. A good example from my own programming is a situation in which I have sockets that are open. The applet is far more robust when the sockets are closed immediately as users exit the applet. If there's any kind of delay in closing the sockets, users can actually come back to the HTML page and rerun the applet. If the sockets are slow to close, the newly instantiated applet will fail when it tries to open these sockets that haven't yet closed.

It's okay to explicitly call this method.

Creating Your First Application

It's time to create an application using Visual J++. Your application will be in the form of a compiled .EXE. Whereas the applet we created was loaded into Internet Explorer and then executed, the compiled application doesn't require Internet Explorer.

Compiled Visual J++ applications are normally very small. This is because they don't contain the runtime code that's necessary for the application to run. So how does the application actually run when you execute the .EXE file? The compiled Visual J++ application almost immediately executes a program named WEXESTUB.EXE. This is part of the redistributable Visual J++ files. This program in turn invokes the Java Virtual Machine in such a way that it executes the byte code of the compiled application.

Note

The Java Virtual Machine is the software that resides on Java-aware computer systems that interprets Java byte code. It's something you won't have to worry about as a Visual J++ programmer. Just write your programs and assume that Java-aware computers all have a functioning Virtual Machine.

You might ask yourself why Visual J++ would go through all that trouble. It might seem as though spawning an extra .EXE and then invoking the Java Virtual Machine is a lot of trouble. And you run the risk of encountering problems with both. What if WEXESTUB.EXE is missing or damaged, or what if the Java Virtual Machine is somehow missing?

All of these are good questions. But the fact is, Java has always relied on another application to correctly execute. Browsers such as Netscape and Internet Explorer are how users have executed Java for years. And the Java Virtual Machine has always been a required element of that. So it's not too unusual that a similar system is part of executing Visual J++ applications.

These small applications take up less space—probably about a tenth the size of what a self-contained application would be. That size reduction is not trivial when you're talking about installing to someone's hard drive. Installation files will be smaller, and this might be very important if the installation files are downloaded from the Web.

Another good reason to rely on the Java Virtual Machine is that as it's updated, the applications run better and faster. The applications don't change, just the Java Virtual Machine does. So application developers benefit when users upgrade to a newer version of the Java Virtual Machine without having to deploy another version of their application.

Tip

If a small number of users are experiencing unexplained behavior when they encounter one of your applets on the Web, suggest that they upgrade to a newer version of their browser. The newer version will invariably contain a newer version of the browser's Virtual Machine. In most cases, this step will fix the problem.

Now to create the application. If you've just started Visual J++, the New Projects dialog box will open. If Visual J++ is already running, select File, New Project and the New Projects dialog will appear.

This time, we'll select `Applications` in the `Visual J++ Projects` folder. As you can see in Figure 1.6, there are three application choices: Windows Application, Console Application, and Application Wizard. We'll choose Windows Application.

FIGURE 1.6

For this project, you'll select Windows Application from the Applications category.

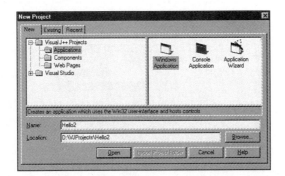

Name your project Hello2. As you can see in Figure 1.6, the directory in which I'm creating the project is `VJProjects\Hello2`. Click the OK button and the project will be created.

After the project is created and you double-click on `Form1.java` in the Project Explorer window, you'll see the default form in the center of the screen, as shown in Figure 1.7. This is a canvas on which you can add items from the toolbox by dragging and dropping.

FIGURE 1.7

The default form appears after your project has been created.

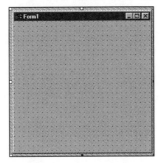

Let's start off by adding a label to the form. In the toolbox, select Label. Move the mouse inside of the form, and you'll notice that the mouse cursor changes shape, indicating that you're ready to put a label on the form. Point the mouse to the location at which you'd like the upper-left corner of the label to appear, and hold down the left mouse button. While holding down the left mouse button, draw the mouse down and to the right until the label is the desired size. You can always change the label's size and position with the mouse.

After the label is placed on the form as shown in Figure 1.8, you'll notice that the Properties window changes to the properties of a label. The list contains quite a few properties, all of which change the appearance of the label. The one we're going to change now is the text property. Click in the text property field and change the text to Hello Visual J++ World. As you type, the label in the form will change.

FIGURE 1.8

Labels are easy to add to Visual J++ applica- tion forms.

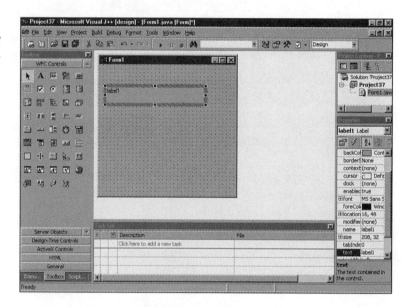

Compile the application by selecting Build, Build. Then select Debug, Run. Your appli- cation will appear, displaying your Hello Visual J++ World message.

By now you're probably wondering where the source code is for the application. Visual J++ makes every effort to keep things visual so that developing applications is easy and intuitive. That's why you see the form and not the source code by default. But to see the source code in the editor is easy. Just double-click on the form (not the form that's exe- cuting as an application, but the form that's part of the Visual J++ editor).

Scroll down through the source code. You'll see the following lines as a result of adding the label from the toolbox:

```
label1.setLocation(new Point(20, 30));
label1.setSize(new Point(210, 40));
label1.setText("Hello Visual J++ World");
label1.setTabIndex(1);
this.setNewControls(new Control[] {
    label1});
```

Let's experiment. Go back to the form by double-clicking on `Form1.java` in the Project Explorer window. Then, click on your label so that its properties are shown in the Properties window. In the `font` property field, click on the button with the "..." label, and a font selector dialog will appear. Now, change the font size to 14 and click the OK button. Finally, edit the `location` property to a value of `10, 50`. Build the program and then go to the source code. The changes will be reflected in the source code, even though you didn't touch the source code. Your source code should look as shown next.

> **Note**
>
> The first line of code in the following code block, shown in bold, is what was added by Visual J++. It simply sets the font for the label.

```
label1.setFont(new Font("MS Sans Serif", -19));
label1.setLocation(new Point(10, 50));
label1.setSize(new Point(210, 40));
label1.setText("Hello Visual J++ World");
label1.setTabIndex(1);
this.setNewControls(new Control[] {
    label1});
```

Your application's label displays text that's larger than before. Now let's add another label below the existing one with text that says `Visual J++ is Cool`. When you rebuild your application, it will look something like the one in Figure 1.9.

FIGURE 1.9

Your application should look something like this one.

Resources on the Web

Information about Java and Visual J++ changes often. For that reason, it's a good idea to keep a list of references to Web sites that will keep you up on the latest information. This section gives you some recommended sites that have Java and Visual J++ information. Because Visual J++ is relatively new, there are many more sites that are generic Java sites. It's rare that you'll find a site dedicated 100% to Visual J++.

www.microsoft.com/visualj/

This is the most authoritative site for Visual J++. It covers Visual J++ features and what's coming up in future versions of Visual J++. There's even a section that shows you how to get started by creating the basic project types.

One thing I found especially interesting here is Microsoft's explanation of its Visual J++ strategy. Microsoft talks about unifying the programming model for applications and the Web using WFC. It talks about Dynamic HTML with Visual J++. In short, the background information found at this site is well worth the time it takes to read through.

www.sun.com/java/

Sun is the original developer of Java. This site offers a wealth of information about the Java language. You can find out about Java hardware, Java software solutions, Java services, and embedded products. You'll find the Java Developers section especially useful. It caters to Java developers and offers insight into and information about Java classes.

An extensive set of white papers is available on the site. They cover everything from nitty-gritty Java information to design considerations from the user viewpoint. These white papers provide an unbelievable resource for Java developers.

www.developer.com/directories/pages/dir.java.html

This is the site that replaces the site that was formerly www.gamelan.com. It's a repository of thousands of Java applications, applets, and controls. This is where I come to get ideas. You'll see just about everything imaginable—everything from games to financial calculators.

For many of the programs, source code is available. This is an invaluable resource. You can use the source code to learn how to do some more advanced things in Java that aren't covered in books or references.

www.javasoft.com

This site is arguably the most authoritative site for Java technology. Besides the usual Java API reference and Java documentation, there's a wealth of valuable information. One section pertains to business and licensing. This is very informative if you want to take your Java programs to market. You'll learn about the legalities of the software business.

1

From time to time, JavaSoft sponsors contests. If you have a hot Java program, it's probably worth checking out. You might end up the winner.

www.javalobby.org

The Java Lobby consists of a group of people who share a common interest in Java software development and the advancement of Java standards and software. The main purpose of the Java Lobby is to represent the needs and concerns of the Java developer and user community to the companies and organizations that have influence in the evolution of Java. This site encourages all people who care about Java to stand together.

www.javaworld.com/javasoft.index.html

JavaWorld magazine is dedicated to fueling innovation for its readers. Among those who frequent the site are technology developers and enterprise managers who are planning, developing, and delivering real-world apps that are changing the way their companies do business daily. *JavaWorld*'s content helps readers understand and effectively use Java and related technologies.

www.jars.com

This site, as well as all the others mentioned, contains a ton of useful information for Java developers. This site differs, though, in that its major emphasis is rating Java applets on the Web. You might have visited sites that displayed a Jars top 10% logo. This is the site responsible for those awards.

After you've gotten good at Java development, you'll want to come back and have Jars rate your applets. You might turn out to be one of the top Java programmers and get a Jars top 1% rating!

Macmillan Computer Publishing's Java Resource Center

Here you'll find information about Java and Visual J++ books in print, links to interesting Java sites on the Web, and other useful information. You can get to the Java Resource Center by first visiting the main Resource Center page at http://www.mcp.com/resources. From there, choose the link titled Programming. From the Programming Resource Center page, follow the Java Resource Center link, and you're in.

Summary

In this chapter, you've learned about Java and Visual J++. You've gotten an introduction to Java and learned how Visual J++ makes developing Java easier. You learned how to create a Java applet and a Java application.

Right now is a good time to do some experimenting on your own. Go ahead and try some things. You'll learn far more by doing than by reading.

The review questions that follow will help you solidify your understanding of the material we've covered. Spend the time necessary to work through the questions.

Q&A

Q What's the difference between Java and JavaScript?

A They're two different animals. Although their names sound the same, the languages themselves are quite dissimilar. JavaScript is more like VBScript than Java, and Java is more like C++ than JavaScript.

Q What kind of World Wide Web limitations sparked the creation of the Java language?

A HTML is essentially static. The pages that made up the bulk of the World Wide Web are still images and text. Java was seen as a way to easily add dynamic content to the Web.

Q How do I create a Java applet with Visual J++?

A The first thing you'll need to do is make sure that the New Projects dialog box is opened. This should automatically happen when you first run Visual J++ (unless you have your options set to load the previous solution at startup). If Visual J++ is already running, you can simply select File, New Project.

Q How can I change the text that appears by default in applets?

A Just open the HTML source code. Find the parameter with the name of `label` (name=label) and a value of `"This string was passed from the HTML host."` (value="This string was passed from the HTML host."). Edit the value string so that it contains the text you'd like displayed.

Q Do I need to recompile when I change the HTML code?

A No. The HTML code is interpreted. That means the latest HTML code is read in and used. Applet code, on the other hand, is different. Java classes must be compiled. The compilation process converts the `.java` source code to what's known as byte code. Byte code is what interpreters such as Internet Explorer load in and execute. If you don't compile after a change to your `.java` source code, the source code is different, but not the byte code.

Q What's the difference between a Java applet and a Java application?

A A Java applet is byte code that's interpreted by something such as Internet Explorer. Applets are usually embedded in HTML pages and executed when browsers hit the pages. Java applications are collections of byte code that are wrapped in an .EXE file. The .EXE file runs a special program that causes the byte code to be interpreted by the Java Virtual Machine. Java applications can't be deployed in Web pages.

Q I don't know anything about programming. Can I expect to learn how to program with Visual J++ by reading this book?

A The first thing you might consider doing is getting a copy of *Teach Yourself Java 1.2 in 21 Days* (also published by Macmillan). This book systematically teaches all the concepts and techniques you need to know to program with Visual J++. If you conscientiously work your way through the book without skipping anything, you'll have a good basis for your Visual J++ programming. You will, however, be much better off if at the end of each chapter you spend some time experimenting with what you learned in the chapter.

Q I know a lot about HTML programming. Will that help me write with Visual J++?

A Any programming experience will help because many concepts carry over. Visual J++ is much more difficult than HTML, though, so don't expect it to be a cakewalk. Once again, if you're patient and work through this book systematically, you'll have very little trouble learning how to program with Visual J++.

Review Exercises

1. Create an applet with Visual J++. Change the message so that it says This is an applet created with Visual J++. Then change the size of the applet window that appears in the browser by editing the width and height parameters in the .htm file. Compile and run the applet.

2. Create an application with Visual J++. Add a label that says This is an application created with Visual J++. Add a second label that says I like Visual J++. Compile and run the application.

33

WEEK 1

DAY 2

Java Language Fundamentals

Today, you'll learn about the Java language. C and C++ programmers will be comfortable with the material because the syntax of Java and C/C++ are almost identical. If you're already comfortable with the Java language, or you're a competent C/C++ programmer, this chapter serves as a reference. If it's all new to you, this chapter makes an excellent tutorial.

We'll cover the basics of the Java language in a logical order. The following are the topics we'll cover today:

- Variables
- Expressions
- Program control
- Exceptions

Java Variables

Your programs need to store values. For instance, you might have a program that calculates the resistance of an electrical circuit based on the amperage and voltage. The user inputs the amperage and voltage, and the resistance is calculated. The amperage and voltage, though, need to be stored somewhere so that when the calculation is performed, the values that the user entered are available.

Not only do variables store values, but they also can be altered. You can multiply a value that's stored in a variable by 5, increment it, negate it, or perform any number of other operations.

Variables can control the flow of program execution and affect the overall state of a program. They are a fundamental part of programming languages; without them, you'd be hard-pressed to develop software.

Declaring Variables

Before you use a variable, you must declare it. A variable has two parts, the data type and the identifier:

```
type identifier;
```

The data type determines the legal range of values that a variable can contain, what operations can be applied to the variable, and how such operations are performed. For instance, an integer variable deals with whole numbers, and a double variable deals with floating-point numbers.

The identifier is used to associate a name with a variable. This gets confusing for some of my students. They think the name of a variable is `int`. It's not. The name is anything you want to give it such as `George`, `Sam`, or `Steve`. The `int` part of it has nothing to do with the name.

Any number of variables can be declared on a single line, each of the same type, as long as each identifier is unique and is separated from the others by a comma. A semicolon is used to signal the end of a variable declaration.

Here, an integer variable is declared and is given the name `horizontal`:

```
int horizontal;
```

Naming Variables

In Java, variable names commonly start with a lowercase letter. All other words that make up the variable are uppercase. For instance, you might have `leftCorner`, `rightSide`, or `niceBigValue`.

Many C++ programmers who program in Java are now adopting some of the Hungarian notation conventions. In this case, because the variable already starts with a lowercase letter, all the first words that make up the variable will begin with an uppercase character. Table 2.1 shows the basic numeric variables that observe this convention. Similarly named variables will be used throughout the book.

TABLE 2.1 BASIC NUMERIC VARIABLE NAMING CONVENTIONS USED THROUGHOUT THE BOOK

Declaration	Description
int nValue;	Integers can be preceded by an n or i character.
int iValue;	In this book, the n character is used for signed variables; i, for unsigned.
long lValue;	Longs are preceded by an l character.
double dValue;	Doubles are preceded by a d character.
String strData;	Strings are preceded by the str characters.

Member variables are usually preceded by m_, whereas local variables are not, as shown in Table 2.2.

TABLE 2.2 NAMING CONVENTIONS FOR MEMBER AND LOCAL VARIABLES

Declaration	Description
int m_nValue;	Integer member variable
String m_strData;	String member variable
int nValue;	Integer local variable
String strData;	String local variable

Some variables with single-character names are left as single characters if it's clear what they're being used for. Examples of this are variables named x, y and i. A variable named x almost always signifies the x value of a coordinate pair, and a variable named y almost always signifies the y value of a coordinate pair. A variable named i is almost always used as a local loop counter.

In the following example, several integer variables are declared, all on the same line:

```
int nHorizontal, nVertical, x, y, nMonths, nYears, nDays;
```

However, you could have broken the preceding declaration into several separate declarations:

```
int nHorizontal;
int nVertical;
```

```
int x;
int y;
int nMonths;
int nYears;
int nDays;
```

How you declare variables depends mainly on personal taste, although most programmers would choose the first example for ease of readability. You aren't required to place all variable names on the same line. You can spread them over several lines, if you want, as long as the last variable name is immediately followed by a semicolon:

```
int nHorizontal, nVertical,
    x, y,
    nMonths, nYears, nDays;
```

Notice how much more readable the preceding declarations are. With the variables grouped according to their purpose, it's easier for people reading the code to understand the variable organization. You should also notice that the second and third lines of the preceding example are indented so that it's easy to see that all three lines of the declaration are related.

Declaring Variable Types

Java variables fall into one of two categories: primitives and references to objects. This section discusses these two variable types.

Your programs will likely use various primitive variables. Any variable you declare of type byte, short, int, long, float, double, char, or boolean is a primitive variable. The following are examples of variable declarations for each primitive type:

```
byte x;
short nDaysInMarch;
int nCounter;
long lBacteriaCount;
float fAccountBalance;
double dExactBalance;
char cMiddleInitial;
boolean bQuit;
```

Reference variables are used to store references, or pointers, to objects. (Keep in mind that I'm not referring to pointers such as those used in C and C++ here, but simply the concept of pointing to an object in memory.) These objects can be class instances, class instances that implement interfaces, or arrays.

The following are examples of reference variable declarations for each type:

```
String strHelloString;  // Class instance.
AudioClip Music;  // Class instance of AudioClip, an interface.
int nHighScores[];  // Array of integers.
```

Initializing and Storing Values in Variables

After a variable has been declared, a value can be stored in it. This can be done either when a variable is declared—a process known as initialization (assigning a value to the variable)—or anytime after it has been declared. In either case, any value assigned to the variable must be of the same type as the variable itself.

These are examples of variables being initialized at the time of declaration:

```
byte x = 3;
short nDaysInMonth = 30;
int nCounter = 900;
long nBacterialCount = 12249123;
float fAccountBalance = 152.76;
double dExactBalance = 452.77;
char cMiddleInitial = 'R';
boolean bQuit = false;
String strHelloString = "Hello World";
AudioClip Music = getAudioClip( getCodeBase(), "hello.au" );
```

In each of the preceding examples, a value consistent with the variable's data type is assigned to it at the time of declaration. These variables have been initialized. From the moment the variables are created, they contain a value. Notice, however, that there is no example of an array being initialized.

Initializing an Array

In the case of arrays, each element can contain a value. If you declare an array to have a dozen integer elements, it can hold 12 different integers.

When an array is initialized, it's done in two steps. First you declare the number of elements the array will have. Then each element in the array is individually initialized, or set to a value (usually zero). Here is an example of how you would initialize an array of integers:

```
int nHighScores[] = new int[12]; // Declare for 12 integers.
for( short i=0; i<12; i++ )
    nHighScores[i] = 0; // Initialized each to zero.
```

As you can see, the for loop used previously also contains a variable declaration. You declare an index, i, that is used to access each element in the array. Before using i, you initialize it to zero, because the first element in every array is at position zero. After 12 iterations, each element in the array has been initialized to zero.

Caution

You can access a variable only within its scope. Because the first element of every array is at position zero, the scope of a 12-element array runs from 0 to 11. If you attempt to access a variable outside its scope, the compiler generates an error.

Every variable has an associated scope, which is the extent to which it can be used. The scope of a variable begins immediately where it is declared and ends with the closing brace (}) of the block of code in which it is declared.

In the following example, I use three local variables in a method: i, j, and, k. The variable i is in scope for the entire method. The variable j is in scope inside of the for loop, and the variable k is in scope within the if conditional.

```
public void Foo( void )
{
    int i;
    for( i=0; i<12; i++ )
    {
        int j;
        j = i * 8;
        if( j == 16 )
        {
            int k;
            k = j + i;
        }// End of scope for k.
        // Trying to access k here will result in a compiler error.
    }// End of scope for j.
    // Trying to access j here will result in a compiler error.
}// End of scope for i.
```

Variables that are declared as member variables of a class have a valid scope throughout the class. For instance, the Variables applet in Listing 2.1 has three member variables: m_nHorizontal, m_nVertical, and m_bButton. These variables can be accessed in any of the applet's methods.

LISTING 2.1   DECLARING VARIABLES IN THE VARIABLES APPLET

```
import java.applet.*;
import java.awt.*;
import java.awt.event.MouseListener;
import java.awt.event.MouseMotionListener;
public class Variables extends Applet implements Runnable
{
    private Thread     m_Variables = null;
```

```java
int m_nHorizontal, m_nVertical;
boolean m_bButton;

public void paint(Graphics g)
{
    g.drawString( "m_nHorizontal=" + m_nHorizontal,
        10, 20 );
    g.drawString( "m_nVertical=" + m_nVertical,
        10, 40 );
    g.drawString( "m_bButton=" + m_bButton,
        10, 60 );
}

public void start()
{
    if (m_Variables == null)
    {
        m_Variables = new Thread(this);
        m_Variables.start();
    }
}

public void stop()
{
    if (m_Variables != null)
    {
        m_Variables.stop();
        m_Variables = null;
    }
}

public void run()
{
    while (true)
    {
        try
        {
            repaint();
            Thread.sleep(50);
        }
        catch (InterruptedException e)
        {
            stop();
        }
    }
}

public class MyListener implements MouseListener
{
```

continues

LISTING 2.1   CONTINUED

```
public void mouseClicked( MouseEvent e )
{
    m_bButton = true;
}

public void mouseReleased( MouseEvent e )
{
    m_bButton = false;
}

}

public class MyMotionListener implements MouseMotionListener
{

    public void mouseDragged( MouseEvent e )
    {
        m_nHorizontal = e.getX();
        m_nVertical = e.getY();
    }

    public void mouseMoved( MouseEvent e )
    {
        m_nHorizontal = e.getX();
        m_nVertical = e.getY();
    }

}

}
```

This simple applet displays the mouse x and y coordinates. It also displays the status of the mouse button. Figure 2.1 shows the applet while it's running.

Suppose, though, that you declared the horizontal and vertical integers in the paint() method. If this were the case, the scope of these variables would be limited to the paint() method. Any attempt to access these variables outside of paint() would generate an error, because the variables can't be accessed outside of their scope. An example follows:

```
public void paint(Graphics g)
{
    int nHorizontal = 100, nVertical = 50;
    g.drawString( "nHorizontal=" + nHorizontal +
        "nVertical=" + nVertical, 10, 20 );
}
```

```
public class MyMotionListener implements MouseMotionListener
{

    public void mouseMoved( MouseEvent e )
    {
        nHorizontal = e.getX(); // ILLEGAL-attempt to access
                                // outside of scope.
        nVertical = e.getY();   // ILLEGAL-attempt to access
                                // outside of scope.

    }

}
```

FIGURE 2.1

The Variables applet shows the x and y coordinates of the mouse, along with the mouse button state.

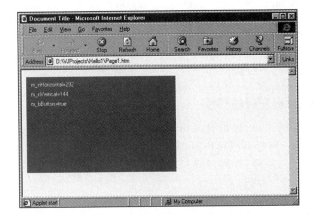

A special situation can occur in which a variable is hidden by the declaration of another variable with the same name. This happens if the second variable declaration happens within a subblock of code residing in the original variables immediately following the class signature, as in Listing 2.1. Clearly, the scope of these variables would be the entire class itself.

However, if you also declared m_nHorizontal and m_nVertical integer variables inside the paint() method, the original variables would be hidden from that method. In this case, any reference to the m_nHorizontal and m_nVertical variables inside paint() would refer to the variables declared in that method, as shown in the next code segment, instead of the original ones. (Avoiding this kind of mix-up is a major reason that member variables are named beginning with m_ and local variables are not.)

```
int m_nHorizontal, m_nVertical;
public void paint(Graphics g)
{
    int m_nHorizontal = 100, m_nVertical = 50;
    // Local variables of the same name.
```

```
    g.drawString( "m_nHorizontal=" + m_nHorizontal +
        "m_nVertical=" + m_nVertical, 10, 20 );
    // Uses the local variables declared here in paint(),
    // not the class member variables.
}

public class MyMotionListener implements MouseMotionListener
{

    public void mouseMoved( MouseEvent e )
    {
        m_nHorizontal = e.getX(); // Refers to the member variable, not
                                  // the local variable declared in paint().
        m_nVertical = e.getY();   // Refers to the member variable, not
                                  // the local variable declared in paint().
    }

}
```

Java Expressions

Expressions are statements that, when executed, result in a value. When programming, you use expressions all the time, sometimes without even realizing it. Java expressions are similar in syntax to those of C and C++. The following are examples of Java expressions:

```
65 + 5 // Produces a value of 70.
( i < 10 ) // Produces a true or false.
5 * 100 // Produces a value of 500
x = 25 - 5 // Subtracts 5 from 25 then stores in x
175 - 4 // Produces 171
```

Expressions are typically composed of several smaller expressions, or subexpressions, connected by operators. For instance, consider the following lines of code:

```
int x = 100, y;
y = ( x / 4 ) + 4;
```

The first line of code, in which the variables are declared, actually contains an expression in the assignment of 100 to the x variable. The integer literal 100 is an expression, albeit a simple one. When the compiler looks at this line, it sees something like "evaluate the expression to the right of the assignment operator = and place its value in the variable on the left." Because the expression is the integer literal 100, it evaluates to 100 and is then stored in the x variable. Pretty simple, yet it's an expression.

Now take a look at the next line. The complete expression would be this:

```
y = ( x / 4 ) + 3;
```

However, this expression is made up of several subexpressions. You might recognize one right off the bat:

```
x / 4
```

Although you'd be correct in assuming this to be a subexpression, there are even subexpressions inside this simple statement. The x variable is a subexpression that evaluates to 100, and the integer literal 4 is another subexpression that evaluates to 4. After each of these is evaluated and the division operation is performed, the result is 25. To this, the value 3 is added, another subexpression. And finally, the entire value (28) is placed inside the y variable. As you can see, there can be many levels of expressions, even in what appear to be simple statements.

Understanding Operators

Because Java expressions are typically made up of several subexpressions linked together by operators, it's important to understand exactly how operators work. Java supports both *unary* and *binary* operators. Unary operators are those that act on a single operand, whereas binary operators act on two operands.

The following example is an expression using the unary postfix increment operator. As you can see, it requires only the one operand (x, in this case):

```
x++;
```

And here is the functional equivalent to the preceding using the binary addition operator:

```
x = x + 1;
```

As you can see, the binary addition operator acts on two operands (x and 1). After the right side of the assignment operator is evaluated, the result is stored in the x variable on the left.

These two expressions do the same thing: they increase the value of x by one. However, a different operator is used in each case. In the first example, the unary operator ++ is used. In the second example, the binary addition operator + is used.

Evaluating Operator Precedence

Expressions are evaluated from left to right, according to the precedence of the operators in the expression. By following the precedence order, Java guarantees that a particular expression will produce the same results every time it is executed. For example, take into consideration the following example:

```
x = 15 + 3 * 2 - 14;
```

Without a precedence order, which subexpression is evaluated first? Is it 15 + 3, 3 * 2, or 2 - 14? And after the first subexpression is evaluated, which is next? Clearly, the value of the expression changes, depending on the order in which its subexpressions are evaluated.

If you couldn't rely on the order in which operations are performed, your programs would be about as consistent as the New York City subway system. Luckily, Java operators are arranged and executed in order of precedence. Table 2.3 lists all Java operators according to their precedence order. You'll see that I've placed parentheses first in this table. Parentheses aren't really operators because they don't perform an operation on data types, but they appear in the table nonetheless to emphasize that they're given top priority during evaluation.

TABLE 2.3 JAVA OPERATOR PRECEDENCE

Precedence	Associativity	Operator	Description
First		( )	parentheses (forcing order)
Second	R-to-L	++	pre/post increment (unary)
	R-to-L	- -	pre/post decrement (unary)
	R-to-L	!	logical complement (unary)
	R-to-L	~	unary bitwise logical negation
	R-to-L	+	addition (unary)
	R-to-L	-	subtraction (unary)
Third	L-to-R	* / %	multiplication, division, and remainder
Fourth	L-to-R	+ -	addition and subtraction
Fifth	L-to-R	<<	shift left
	L-to-R	>>	shift right (sign extension)
	L-to-R	>>>	shift right (zero extension)
Sixth	L-to-R	< <=	"less than" and "less than or equal to"
	L-to-R	> >=	"greater than" and "greater than or equal to"
	L-to-R	instanceof	"is the object an instance of this class?"
Seventh	L-to-R	==	equality
	L-to-R	!=	non-equality
Eighth	L-to-R	&	bitwise AND, boolean AND
Ninth	L-to-R	^	bitwise XOR, boolean XOR
Tenth	L-to-R	¦	bitwise OR, boolean OR
Eleventh	L-to-R	&&	AND (boolean conditional "short-circuit")

Precedence	Associativity	Operator	Description
Twelfth	L-to-R	||	OR (boolean conditional "short-circuit")
Thirteenth	R-to-L	?:	ternary conditional
Fourteenth	R-to-L	=	assignment
Fifteenth	R-to-L	+= -=	assignment (and operation)
		*= /= %=	

Because all operations are performed according to the precedence of the operators involved, Java expressions are evaluated in a predictable manner. Operations whose operators have the highest precedence are performed first, with lower-precedence operators following in sequence. When operations of the same precedence occur within the same expression, they are processed from left to right.

Now, return to the example:

```
x = 15 + 3 * 2 - 14;
```

Thanks to operator precedence, you can see that the expression evaluates in a specific order. The middle operation (3 * 2) is performed first, and then the next two operations are carried out from left to right:

3 * 2	produces 6, which is used in the next operation
15 + 6	produces 21, which is used in the next operation
21 - 14	produces 7, which is stored in the variable x

Forcing Operator Precedence

If you don't want the natural order of evaluation to be used, you can use parentheses to control the order of evaluation. For example, suppose you wanted the subexpression 2 - 14 to be evaluated first. You could ensure this by placing it inside of parentheses:

```
x = 15 + 3 * ( 2 - 14 );
```

In this case, the following sequence of steps is taken when the expression is evaluated:

2 - 14	produces -12, which is used in the next operation
3 * -12	produces -36, which is used in the next operation
15 + -36	produces -12, which is stored in the variable x

Because multiplication operators have precedence over arithmetic ones, this operation is performed after the subexpression inside parentheses. However, you could have added another pair of parentheses to force the multiplication operation to take place last:

```
x = ( 15 + 3 ) * ( 2 - 14 );
```

In this case, the subexpressions inside the parentheses are of the same precedence. As a result, they are carried out from left to right. This sequence of steps is as follows:

15 + 3   produces 18, which is used in the final operation

2 - 14   produces -12, which is used in the final operation

18 * -12   produces -216, which is stored in the variable x

And, of course, parentheses can be nested. You can, for example, group these three subexpressions by surrounding them with parentheses and adding another subexpression to the mix. Here are a few examples, each producing a different data type:

```
x = ( ( 15 + 3 ) * ( 2 - 14 ) ) + 1;   // Produces integer value
x = ( ( 15 + 3 ) * ( 2 - 14 ) ) + 1.2; // Produces a floating-point value
x = ( ( 15 + 3 ) * ( 2 - 14 ) ) > 1;   // Produces a boolean value
```

Performing Array Operations

When operations are performed on arrays, they return the value of a specific element in that array. However, unlike the data types dealt with thus far, an array element must be allocated using the new operator before it can be assigned to a variable:

```
int a = new int[15];
```

In the preceding example, an array of 15 integer elements is created and assigned to the variable a. After this operation has taken place, you can store and retrieve values in the array elements using the following syntax:

```
nArrayVariable[expression]
```

For example, each of the following lines of code accesses the same element in our array:

```
int x = 5, y = 2, z = 10; // Initialize variables.
a[10] = 82569;            // Store 82569 in the 11th element.
a[z] = 4370;              // Store 4370 in the 11th element.
a[x*y] = 1117911;         // Store 1117911 in the 11th element.
a[x+5] = 592;             // Store 592 in the 11th element.

int i;
i = a[10];                // Retrieve the 11th element.
i = a[x+5];               // Retrieve the 11th element.
i = a[100/z+1];           // Retrieve the 11th element.
i = a[a.length-5];        // Retrieve the 11th element.
```

In the preceding example, I used the instance variable length in the expression. Because a length returns the number of elements in the array, this is a valid expression.

If, in any case, an array index is negative or greater than the number of elements in the array minus one (which would be 14 in this example), an `ArrayIndex` `OutOfBoundsException` is thrown. Using the sample array, the following operations would cause an out-of-bounds exception:

```
a[x+2];       // Expression evaluates to 15
a[x*x];       // Expression evaluates to 25
a[a.length];  // Expression evaluates to 15
```

Array index values can be of byte, short, int, or event char types. However, array indexes of type long are not permitted. To use a long, it must be cast into the int type, as the following example shows:

```
long lMyLong = 10;
a[lMyLong]; // Illegal since it's a long.
a[(int)lMyLong]; // Legal since it's cast to an int.
```

Keep in mind that array indexing begins at zero. In this example, as with all arrays, the first element is accessed with an index value of zero: a[0]. Because there are 15 elements in this particular array (from index 0 to 14), the last element is referenced with an index value of 14: a[14].

In Java, a special operator exists that allows you to determine whether an object is an instance of a particular class, subclass, or interface. Using the instance of binary operator, you can test objects to compare them against a specific class or interface type:

```
if( theObject instance of className )
{
   // Do stuff...
}
```

Java Program Control

To direct the flow of program execution, Java supports several control-flow statements. These are similar to their C and C++ counterparts and look and act as you would expect. You'll take a look at each, beginning with the popular if statement.

if Statements

Java supports two types of if statements, both of which require the use of a Boolean expression. This is the syntax for the most basic if statement:

```
if( boolean expression)
{
    // Do some stuff here
}
```

Depending on the value of the Boolean expression, the body of the `if` statement might or might not be executed. If the expression evaluates to `true`, the body is executed. If the expression evaluates to `false`, the body of code is skipped.

Take, for example, the following statement:

```
if( x < 10 )
{
    System.out.println("The if block is being executed.\n" );
    System.out.println( "And the value of x is: " + x );
}
```

When the preceding statement is encountered, the Boolean expression is evaluated:

```
x < 10
```

The body of code following the `if` statement will execute only in cases in which `x` is less than `10`. If `x` is equal to (or greater than) `10`, the block of code is skipped, and program execution continues immediately after the closing brace (`}`).

This form of control flow is often called an `if-then` statement, because it follows the logic of "if the expression is true, then execute this body of code."

The second form of the `if` statement uses the keyword `else`, directing program execution along one of two distinct routes:

```
if( boolean expression )
{
    // Do stuff here
}
else
{
    // Or else do stuff here
}
```

If the Boolean value evaluates to `true`, the block of code immediately following that value is executed. If the expression evaluates to `false`, the `else` block is executed.

This form of control flow is often called an `if-then-else` statement, because it follows the logic of "if the expression is true, then execute this body of code, or else execute this one."

The preceding example looks like this, using the `if-then-else` statement:

```
if( x < 10 )
{
```

```
    System.out.println( "The if block is being executed.\n" );
    System.out.println( "And the value of x is: " + x );
}
else
{
    System.out.println( "The else block is being executed.\n" );
    System.out.println( "And the value of x is: " + x );
}
```

At any given time, only one of the preceding blocks of code will be executed. At no time will both be executed, because the value of the Boolean expression directs flow of execution in only one of two possible directions, not both.

An additional aspect of control can be added to the `if` statement using the following `else-if` construct:

```
if( boolean expression )
{
    // Do stuff here
}
else if( boolean expression )
{
    // Or maybe do stuff here
}
else
{
    // Or else do stuff here
}
```

Applying this to the earlier example, you can exercise more precise control over the flow of program execution:

```
if( x < 10 )
{
    System.out.println( "The if block is being executed.\n" );
    System.out.println( "And the value of x is: " + x );
}
else if( x == 15 )
{
    System.out.println( "The else block is being executed.\n" );
    System.out.println( "And the value of x MUST be 15" );
}
else
{
    System.out.println( "The else block is being executed.\n" );
    System.out.println( "And the value of x is: " + x );
}
```

2

Caution   Unlike if statements in C, Java if statement expressions must return a
Boolean value. In C, a value of 0 (zero) is treated as false and a value of 1 is
treated as true. This is not the case with Java, in which only Boolean expressions can be used in an if statement.

switch Statements

The switch statement is similar in nature to the if-then-else statement, although it
makes the programmer's job a lot easier when multiple else clauses are needed:

```
switch( expression )
{
    case constant1:
        // Do stuff if the expression evaluates to constant1
        break;
    case constant2:
        // Do stuff if the expression evaluates to constant2
        break;
    case constant3:
        // Do stuff if the expression evaluates to constant3
        break;
    default:
        // Do stuff here if the expression doesn't evaluate
        // to any of the explicit cases
        break;
}
```

Upon entering a switch statement, the expression is evaluated. The data type of the
expression must be char byte, short, or int. Boolean expressions aren't allowed,
although they are used in all other control-flow mechanisms.

The value of the expression is then converted to the int type, as are all the case constants. Beginning with the first case statement, the value of the expression is compared
to the value of the case constant. If the two values are equal, any code following the
colon is executed, until the break statement is reached. If the expression doesn't match
the case constant, it is compared to the next one. This process continues until the default
case is reached, at which point the code for this case is executed.

When a case is executed, the break statement is used to stop the flow of execution.
When a break statement is reached, execution stops immediately and resumes after the
closing brace (}) of the switch body. Because execution terminates when the first break
is encountered, the default case will be executed only if no match is found between the
value of the switch expression and all other cases.

The switch statement is particularly useful when multiple cases exist. If you were to try to write more than a half-dozen else clauses in an if-else statement, you'd find the process a bit tedious. It would be even more difficult to read the code. With a switch statement, however, the code is clean and easy to read. You can use as many cases as you need, without making a mess of the code. And if none of the cases matches the value of your expression, you can rely on the default case being executed.

Caution

Be certain to end each case with a break statement. If you don't, all cases following the matching one will be executed as well! This is an undesirable condition known as *fall-through*. You can avoid it by matching a break statement with every case.

Programming with Loops

Control-flow statements include a number of loops:

- while loops
- do-while loops
- for loops

Java while and do-while loops are identical to those in C:

```
while( boolean expression )
{
    // Do something
}

do
{
    // Do something
} while( boolean expression )
```

In the while loop, the Boolean expression is evaluated. The value of this expression determines whether the body of the loop is executed. If the expression evaluates to true, the loop is executed. If it's false, it does not. Each time through the body of the while loop, the expression is reevaluated. The loop continues until the expression evaluates to false:

```
int x = 0;
while( x++ < 10 )
{
    System.out.println( "The while loop is being executed.\n" );
    System.out.println( "And the value of x is: " + x );
}
```

In the preceding example, the body of the loop continues executing as long as x is less than 10. Because you increment the value of x by one (x++) in the expression itself, the loop is executed 10 times.

Note that the increment could have also taken place in the body of the loop itself, as shown here:

```
while( x < 10 )
{
    x++;
    System.out.println( "The while loop is being executed.\n" );
    System.out.println( "And the value of x is: " + x );
}
```

With the do-while loop, the body of the loop executes once before the expression is ever evaluated. This ensures that your loop code is executed at least once, regardless of how the expression evaluates. Here's an example:

```
do
{
    System.out.println( "The while loop is being executed.\n" );
    System.out.println( "And the value of x is: " + x );
} while( x++ < 10 );
```

As with the while loop, you could have incremented the expression inside the loop body rather than inside the expression:

```
do
{
    System.out.println("The while loop is being executed.");
    System.out.println( "And the value of x is: " + x );
    x++;
} while( x < 10 );
```

The while loop is by far the most popular of the two, although the do-while loop has the advantage of executing your code at least once.

Be sure to change your expression value either inside of the body of the while or do-while loop, or in the expression itself. If the value never changes, the expression always remains true and the loop executes indefinitely.

The for loop repeats program execution as controlled through a series, which terminates when a certain limit is reached. It continues looping until the specified limit is reached, at which point the loop is broken and execution resumes after the loop body:

```
for( expression; booleanExpression; expression)
{
    // Do something
}
```

The first expression initializes the loop variable. The second is a Boolean expression that specifies the limit. The third and final expression specifies how the loop variable is to change each time through the loop.

Consider the following example:

```
int x;
for( x=0; x<10; x++ )
{
    System.out.println( "The for loop is being executed.\n" );
    System.out.println( "And the value of x is: " + x );
}
```

The first expression, x=0, sets the loop variable to zero. The loop executes until the second expression, x<10, evaluates to `true`. And the final expression, x++, increments the loop variable by one every time through the loop.

Unlike C, Java supports the declaration of loop variables inside the initialization portion of the loop statement:

```
for( int x=0; x<10; x++ )
{
    System.out.println( "The for loop is being executed.\n" );
    System.out.println( "And the value of x is: " + x );
}
```

In this case, the scope of the loop variable is the loop itself. You're free to access x, as long as you do so in the body of the for loop. However, you can't use x outside of the closing loop brace (}), because anything outside the loop is beyond the scope of this variable.

break and continue Statements

In addition to the if, switch, while, and do-while control-flow constructs, Java supports two additional statements: break and continue. These are considered "jump" statements, because they allow the flow of program execution to branch out in directions not seen with the standard control-flow statements already discussed.

As you've seen, the switch statement uses the break statement to terminate a case's execution. However, those break statements were used without labels. Both break and continue can be used with an optional label, specifying exactly where the execution will be transferred. Without a label, break and continue behave exactly as they do in C.

Take a look at the following example of a labeled break statement in a switch occurring in a while loop:

```
int x = 0;
enterLoop:
while( x++ < 10 )
```

```
{
    System.out.println( "Inside the while loop, iteration: " + x );
    switch( x )
    {
        case 0: System.out.println( "Inside switch, x: " + x );
            break;
        case 1: System.out.println( "Inside switch, x: " + x );
            break;
        case 2: System.out.println( "Inside switch, x: " + x );
            break;
        default:
            if( x == 5 )
            {
                System.out.println("Break out of switch and while.");
                break enterLoop;
            }
            break;
    }
    System.out.println( "Out of switch, back in while loop." );
}
```

Each time through the while loop, the switch statement is encountered. Up until the time x is equal to 5, standard break statements are used to break out of the switch statement and back into the while loop. However, when x is 5, the line is executed:

```
break enterLoop;
```

When this happens, the break occurs not only for the switch statement, but also for the entire while loop! If this labeled break were not present, the while loop would execute 10 times. However, it executes only 5 times, because the labeled break kicks the flow of control out of both the switch and the while loop.

Whereas the break statement is used to break out of the loop, a labeled continue statement redirects the flow to the label itself.

Unlike break, the labeled continue statement transfers control of program execution to the iteration following the label:

```
int x = 0;
enterLoop:
while( x++ < 5 )
{
    System.out.println( "Inside the while loop, x: " + x );
    for( int i=0; i<10; i++ )
    {
        System.out.println( "Inside for loop, i: " + i );
        if( i == 5 )
        {
            System.out.println( "Out of for loop" );
            continue enterLoop;
```

```
        }
    }
    System.out.println( "Out of for loop, back in while." );
}
```

Here, I've created a `for` loop inside a `while` loop. Each time through the `while` loop, the `for` loop is executed until `i` equals 5, at which point program execution jumps out of the `for` loop and goes to the first statement inside the `while` loop:

```
System.out.println("Inside while loop, iteration: " + x);
```

When this happens, the final output line in the `while` loop isn't executed, because the flow of execution has been rerouted to its beginning. However, if I hadn't included a label, the `break` statement alone would have rerouted the execution to the first line of code following the `for` loop. In that case, the final output line would have been executed. In Java, there are actually four jump statements:

- `break`
- `continue`
- `return`
- `throw`

The `return` statement is used to return program execution to the caller of a code segment—for example, when a method has been invoked. At any point in the method, a `return` statement can return the flow of control to the caller of that method. The `throw` statement is used to signal a runtime exception, described in the next section, which interrupts the flow of program execution while a handler is sought to deal with that exception.

Java Exceptions

Java features a general-purpose error-processing system known as an *exception mechanism*. The exception mechanism is composed of two parts: throwing exceptions and catching them. To throw an exception means to signal an error, whereas to catch one is to trap and handle an error that was previously thrown. Exceptions provide a uniform approach to signaling and processing errors, removing much of the burden of traditional error processing.

The term *exception* is short for *exceptional event*. Exceptional events are those that disrupt the normal flow of program execution. C++ programmers will find Java's exception mechanism very similar to that of C++ and will be throwing and catching exceptions in no time. If you're a C programmer, you'll find learning to use Java's exception mechanism well worth the effort.

In languages other than Java, such as C, each function is responsible for signaling success or failure during execution. In many cases, this is done by returning an integer value that the caller can test. Generally, if the return value of a function is zero, the function is executed without error. If a nonzero value is resumed, an error might have occurred during execution.

However, not all routines return error codes, and those that do return them don't necessarily report errors in the same way. Some might return an error code, others might return a null value, and still others might set a global error variable. Such inconsistencies place a substantial burden on the programmer, who must learn the error-reporting mechanism employed by each routine and write the appropriate code to test for errors.

As a result, many programmers save time by testing only for errors generated by critical routines, not bothering with the others. In some cases, the programmer might not fully understand the routine in question and might handle errors incorrectly. In both cases, the integrity of the program suffers and error checking becomes a nuisance, if not a nightmare.

Using exceptions, Java provides developers with a consistent and relatively simple mechanism for signaling and dealing with errors. Exceptions provide methods with a way to stop program execution when an error is encountered, while allowing the method to notify its caller that a problem has occurred. If the caller chooses, it can ignore, or "duck," the exception, in which case the exception is passed down the call stack until it is dealt with. However, exceptions allow you only to temporarily pass the buck when an error is encountered, because you must deal with the error eventually.

Managing the Call Stack

A call stack is nothing more than the sequence of methods that have been invoked. For instance, if a method named drawShape() calls another method named drawCircle(), you have a pretty simple call stack. Here, you can see that drawShape() calls the drawCircle() method. The drawShape() method is said to be at the "bottom" of the stack, and drawCircle() is at the "top."

However, drawCircle() might invoke another method named draw(). This would then sit at the top of the call stack. And draw() might call another method, named paint(), as the call stack continued to grow. If an exception occurred in paint(), it could possibly be ignored by every method. As a result, the exception would be passed all the way down the call stack.

If an exception isn't handled by a method, it's passed down the call stack to the method below it. If none of the methods in the call stack catches the exception by the time it reaches the bottom, and the method at the bottom doesn't catch it either, the program is aborted!

Somewhere along the way, the exception will have to be caught and dealt with. If it isn't, the program will be aborted. If you try to write a Java program without catching an exception, the compiler warns you.

Caution

> In Java, all nonruntime exceptions must be caught or declared. If they are not, the compiler spits out an error message. If the compiler realizes that a nonruntime error hasn't been properly handled, it refuses to compile the code. When this is the case, you must either catch or declare the exception.

2

Throwing Exceptions

Before an exception can be caught, it must be thrown. Exceptions can be thrown by any Java code: your own code, code in the packages that come with the Java development environment, and code in packages written by others. Even the Java runtime system can throw exceptions that your programs must catch.

When an exception is thrown, the Java runtime system receives a signal that an error has been generated. Exceptions are thrown to flag errors, which is something you would do in your own programs to notify the system that an error has occurred. As soon as an exception is thrown, the runtime system searches for the matching `catch` clause to handle it.

Exceptions are thrown using the following Java syntax:

```
throw new AnyExceptionObject():
```

Regardless of what code raises an exception, it's always done via the `throw` statement. `throw` takes a single argument: a throwable object. Throwable objects are instances of any subclass of the `Throwable` class defined in the `java.lang` package. In the preceding example, you instantiated a throwable object:

```
new AnyExceptionObject()// instantiate throwable object
```

If you attempt to throw an object that isn't throwable, the compiler outputs an error message and refuses to complete the compilation process. Most exception objects you'll encounter are derived from the `Exception` class, the `RuntimeException` class, or the `Error` class. Each of these classes is a subclass of `Throwable` (`java.lang.Throwable`), and therefore produces objects (or is extended by other classes) that are considered throwable.

Consider for a moment the following method declaration:

```
public static int myDivide( int x, int y )
  throws ArithmeticException()
{
   if( y == 0 )
       throw new ArithmeticException();
   else return( x / y );
}
```

In the method signature, you declare this method as being capable of throwing the
`ArithmeticException`:

```
throws ArithmeticException
```

The Java language requires that methods either catch or declare all nonruntime exceptions they can throw. With the preceding line, you declare that your `myDivide()` method
throws the `ArithmeticException`, satisfying this requirement.

In cases in which you want to define your own methods, you simply create a new class
that is a subclass of `Exception`. Here is the same program, but using a custom exception:

```
class MyOwnException extends Exception
{

    public static int myDivide(int x, int y) throws MyOwnException
    {
        if( y == 0 ) throw new MyOwnException();
        else return( x / y );
    }
}
```

However, throwing exceptions is only half the battle. To write effective Java programs,
you must be able to catch exceptions as well.

Catching Exceptions

When an exception is thrown, the Java runtime system immediately stops the current
flow of program execution and looks for an exception handler to catch it. Searching
backward through the call stack, a corresponding handler is started with the method
where the error occurred.

The search continues down the call stack until a method containing an appropriate exception handler is found. The first handler encountered that has the same type as the thrown
object is the one chosen to deal with the exception.

If the exception travels all the way down the call stack with no handler catching it, the
program aborts execution. Typically, an error message is output to the terminal display in

such cases. This, of course, assumes that the exception is a runtime exception that can't be seen by the compiler.

Dividing a number by a variable that happens to be zero, accessing an array element using an index variable that is beyond the legal range, and accessing null objects and similar dynamic activities will all produce runtime exceptions that aren't recognized at compile time. As a result, the compiler can't force you to catch such exceptions, because it doesn't even realize that they exist. And in cases in which a runtime exception propagates to the bottom of the call stack, your program will be aborted.

To catch an exception, you must write an exception handler using the `try-catch` clause. For instance, suppose you wanted to use the original `myDivide()` method created earlier. To catch the exception that might result, you'd write the following `try-catch` clause:

```
try
{
    int y = myDivide( 10, 0 ):
}
catch( ArithmeticException e )
{
    System.out.println( "Whoops - there it is!" );
}
```

Handling Exceptions with `try-catch`

The first part of a `try-catch` clause, the `try` block, encloses those statements that might throw an exception. Here is the syntax of a typical `try` block:

```
try
{
    // Statements here might throw exceptions
}
```

The only code in the earlier example capable of throwing an exception is the `myDivide()` method. However, any number of legal Java statements that have the potential to throw an exception can be included in the `try` block. As you can see, I intentionally supply `myDivide()` with parameters that will cause an exception to be thrown. Specifically, the second integer passed to the method is zero.

If you had additional lines of code following `myDivide(10,0)`, they wouldn't be executed. Instead, `myDivide()` would throw an exception that would immediately stop program execution at that point, and would then drop into the `catch` portion of the `try-catch` clause.

Following the `try` block are one or more `catch` blocks you can use to trap and process exceptions. This is the `catch` block syntax:

```
catch( ThrowableClassName variable )
{
    // Handle the error here
}
```

Although I supplied only one `catch` block in the `myDivide()` exception handler, any number could have been provided. However, because the `myDivide()` method throws only one exception, you have to catch that one. In this example, I merely output a line of text to prove that the exception was indeed caught. In the case of multiple `catches`, the `try-catch` clause has the following syntax:

```
try
{
    // Do stuff here that might throw an exception
}
catch( ThrowableClassName1 variable )
{
    // Handle the exception that throws ThrowableClassName1
}
catch( ThrowableClassName2 variable )
{
    // Handle the exception that throws ThrowableClassName1
}
catch( ThrowableClassName3 variable )
{
    // Handle the exception that throws ThrowableClassName1
}
catch( ThrowableClassName4 variable )
{
    // Handle the exception that throws ThrowableClassName1
}
```

For instance, suppose `myDivide()` was capable of throwing two different exceptions. In this case, you would provide a `catch` block for each of the possible exceptions:

```
try
{
    int y = myDivide( 10, 0 );
}
catch( ArithmeticException e )
{
    System.out.println( "Have caught an ArithmeticException." );
}
catch( MyOwnException e )
{
    System.out.printin( "Have caught MyOwnException." );
}
```

The exception that is thrown is compared to the argument for each `catch` block in the order (the `catch` argument can be an object or an interface type). When a match is found, that `catch` block is executed. If no match is found, the exception propagates down the call stack, where it is compared against potential exception handlers until a match is found. And, as always, if no match is found, the program is aborted.

You can access the instance variables and methods of exceptions just as you can for any other object. With this in mind, you can invoke the exception's `getMessage()` method to get information on the exception—`getMessage()` is a method defined in the `Throwable` class:

```
System.out.println( e.getMessage() );
```

The `Throwable` class also implements several methods for dealing with the call stack when an exception occurs (such as `printStackTrace()`, which outputs the call stack to the display). The `Throwable` subclass you create can implement additional methods and instance variables. To find out which methods an exception implements, look at its class and superclass definitions.

Unlike C++, Java's `try-catch` clause supports the use of an optional `finally` block. If defined, this is guaranteed to execute, regardless of whether an exception is thrown. As a result, you can use it to perform any necessary cleanup operation (closing files and streams, releasing system resources, and so on) that your methods require before the flow of control is transferred to another part of the program. This is the syntax of the `finally` block:

```
finally
{
    // Statements here are executed before control transfers
}
```

In the context of the `myDivide()` example, a `finally` block might look like this:

```
try
{
    int y = myDivide( 10, 0 );
}
catch( ArithmeticException e )
{
    System.out.printin( "Have caught an ArithmeticException." );
}
catch( MyOwnException e )
{
    System.out.printin( "Have caught MyOwnException." );
}
finally
{
    System.out.printin( "cleaning up. . . " ) ;
    // Do any clean-up work here
}
```

Upon execution of the `finally` block, control is transferred out of the `try-catch` clause. Typically, whatever event caused the `try` statement to terminate (fall-through the execution of a `break`, `continue`, or `return` statement, or the propagation of an exception) dictates where the flow of control will resume.

The `finally` block could also execute a jump statement. This would cause another unconditional control transfer outside its block, or cause another uncaught exception to be thrown. In either case, the original jump statement is abandoned, and the new unconditional control transfer (or exception) is processed.

All jump statements (`break`, `continue`, `return`, and `throw`) transfer control unconditionally. Whenever one causes control to bypass a `finally` block, the control transfer pauses while the `finally` part is executed, and it continues if the `finally` part finishes normally.

Declaring Exceptions

Java requires that methods either catch or declare all non-runtime exceptions that can be thrown within the method's scope. This means that if a method chooses not to catch an exception, it must declare that it can throw it.

Sometimes, it's not a good idea to catch exceptions. For example, if you catch an exception deep down in the call stack, you might not know how or why your method is being called. What would you do with the exception after it was caught?

Because you don't know enough about what caused your method to be called, you might not be able to adequately handle the exception. In that case, it would be better to pass the exception back down the call stack; you should declare the exception rather than catch it.

To declare an exception, simply add the `throw` statement to your method signature, followed by the exception name. To declare more than one exception, separate each name by a comma.

Suppose, for example, that you wanted to define a new method that calls the `myDivide()` method created earlier. Instead of implementing an exception handler for `myDivide()` in your new method, you can declare the potential exceptions to pass them down the call stack:

```
public void myMath()
  throws ArithmeticException, MyOwnException
{
    // Do stuff here
}
```

Some programmers realize that it takes a lot less time to declare an exception than it does to write an appropriate exception handler, and they are often tempted to simply pass the buck rather than handle the exception. As a general rule, this is a bad idea. However, there are times when it is appropriate to declare an exception rather than handle it.

Summary

To use variables in programming, they must first be declared and initialized. If they aren't initialized, Java will do it for you. However, good programming style doesn't rely on auto-initialization.

Variable declaration consists of two parts: a data type and an identifier. Variable types are either primitives or references to objects. Once declared, a value is introduced to a scope, which can then be stored in a variable, provided that it is within the limits of the variable's type. Furthermore, expressions can be utilized to perform calculations and can also be used to store values.

Expressions make use of operators, which are the symbols (or group of symbols) a program uses to indicate a specific operation to perform (such as addition, multiplication, or division). Operators are evaluated in order of precedence, and as either left-to-right or right-to-left, depending on their associativity.

Control-flow statements, such as branching statements and loops, direct Java's program execution. In addition, exception handlers are used to control the flow of program execution when an exception is thrown. Java's exception mechanism is a general-purpose error-processing mechanism, which detects errors in code by throwing objects that disrupt the normal flow of program execution.

Q&A

Q How does a program store values?

A Programs store most values in variables. Not only do variables store values, but they can be altered as well. Variables can control the flow of a program's execution and affect the overall state of a program.

Q How do you declare variables?

A Variables must be declared before they're used. Variable declarations have two parts: the data type and the identifier. The data type determines the kind of data and the range of values a variable has. Examples of this are int, long, and double. The identifier is the name that the programmer gives a variable.

Q What does "variable initialization" mean?

A When variables are declared, they can be initialized with a starting value. Here are some examples of variable initialization:

```
int nWidth = 500;
int nHeight = 200;
boolean bQuit = false;
```

Q How is an array initialized?

A An array is initialized in two steps. First, you declare the number of elements the array will have. Then each element in the array is individually initialized. Here's an example:

```
int nValues[] = new int[25];
for( int i=0; i<25; i++ )
nValues[i] = i * 2;
```

Q What is meant by "variable scope"?

A Every variable has an associated scope. The scope is the extent to which the variable can be used. A variable's scope begins where it's declared, and ends with the closing brace (}) of the block of code it's in. You can access a variable only within its scope. Any attempt to access it outside of its scope generates a compiler error.

Q What are expressions?

A Expressions are statements that, when executed, result in a value. When programming, you use expressions all the time, sometimes without realizing it.

Q When you use a `for` loop, is there any way to get out of it before the count has finished?

A Yes, you can use the `break` statement. The `break` statement exits the current `for` loop and executes the next statement immediately after the end of the `for` loop.

Q Is it optional to catch exceptions?

A No. If a method throws an exception, your code must catch it. Otherwise, a compile error will occur.

DAY 3

Making Applets Live On the Web

Today, you'll learn how to make your Java applets live on a Web site. First, you'll learn about the HTML file and what you need to do to edit it. Next, you'll learn what the <APPLET> tag is and how to use it. Another thing you'll learn is how to get applets uploaded to your Web site.

Today's lesson is important for anyone writing applets for Web sites. Application developers who're writing programs that will run on standalone PCs can skip to Day 4's chapter, "Debugging Java Applets and Applications."

In this chapter, we'll cover these topics:

- The <APPLET> tag
- HTML applet attributes
- Class files
- CODEBASE
- Applet parameters

- Uploading to a Web server
- The Web server layout

For Web developers, this chapter contains skills that are essential for migrating Java applets from local development machines to live Web servers.

The <APPLET> Tag

The <APPLET> tag, used to embed Java applets in Web pages, is the mother of all non-standard tags. Depending on the applet you are embedding, and to what extent you choose to customize that applet for your page, the <APPLET> tag you must construct can be relatively simple or exceptionally complex.

The <APPLET> tag, like other compound tags, is composed of several parts. However, only a few of these parts are required. Whether or not you must provide anything other than the bare minimum depends entirely on the applet you are configuring. Some applets make heavy use of all parts of the <APPLET> tag; others need only the required parts.

The following code gives a simplified look at the four main parts of the <APPLET> tag:

```
<APPLET attributes>
applet-parameters
alternet-HTML
</APPLET>
```

Attributes

As with all tags, both standard and nonstandard, the applet tag begins with an opening tag. And like many other tags, the applet tag supports various attributes—information that is used to enhance the way the applet looks or acts when a browser runs it.

Attributes are keywords that tell browsers to do something special when they encounter a tag; in the case of the <APPLET> opening tag, this something is a bit more complex than with other tags. Although many opening tags consist of nothing more than a letter or two (<A>, <I>, <BR>, and so forth) and no attributes whatsoever, the <APPLET> tag is much more involved. Not only must you provide the initial part of the opening tag (<APPLET>), but you also must supply at least three attributes that together tell the browser the name of the applet and how much space the applet will take up when displayed:

```
<APPLET CODE="MyApplet" HEIGHT=100 WIDTH=200>
```

In this example, an applet named MyApplet has been specified. The CODE attribute of the opening tag identifies the file containing the applet. The HEIGHT and WIDTH attributes of the opening tag, on the other hand, are used to tell the browser how much space in the page the applet requires. In this case, the applet takes up 100 pixels in height and 200 pixels in width.

Notice that the name of the applet file, `MyApplet`, is surrounded by quotation marks, but the height and width values aren't. This is because the name of an applet file might contain spaces (for example, `Ticker Tape`), whereas numeric values never will (that is, the number one hundred is always represented by 100, not 10 0, 1 00, or even 1 0 0). Surrounding the name of the applet file with quotation marks ensures that the browser knows exactly what to look for, even if spaces are included with the name. For example, if you left off the quotation marks on an applet file named `Ticker Tape`, the browser would see only the first word. In this case, the browser would attempt to find the applet file named `Ticker` and would come up empty-handed.

> **Note**
>
> Case matters! When supplying the name of an applet file, be sure to type the name exactly, matching each letter case for case. For example, if an applet is named MyApplet, you must specify that name exactly in the CODE attribute. If you specify myapplet instead, the browser won't be able to find the applet!

3

ABOUT THE CLASS EXTENSION

Almost all applets are stored in files having a `.class` extension. This is a result of the compile process, the final step of which involves converting human-readable Java source code into machine-readable bytecode. When converted, the bytecode is stored in a file with the `.class` extension.

As a result, the MyApplet applet is really stored in a file named `MyApplet.class`. Although you're free to include the `.class` extension when specifying your applets, you don't have to. Java-aware browsers know to look for a file with that extension. You must, however, provide the extension if it's anything other than `.class`. Thus, the following opening applet tag is functionally equivalent to the one shown previously, although slightly more precise when it comes to the applet filename:

```
<APPLET CODE="MyApplet.class" HEIGHT=100 WIDTH=200>
```

At a bare minimum, all opening `<APPLET>` tags must contain the three attributes shown in the preceding examples: `CODE`, `HEIGHT`, and `WIDTH`. These are known as required attributes, as shown in Table 3.1, because you can't include applets in Web pages without them.

TABLE 3.1   REQUIRED APPLET ATTRIBUTES

Attribute	Description
CODE	Specifies the name of the applet class file
HEIGHT	Specifies the height of the applet in pixels
WIDTH	Specifies the width of the applet in pixels

In addition to the three required attributes, you can use various optional attributes to control how an applet appears in your pages. You can include these optional attributes, listed in Table 3.2, anywhere within the opening tag. I recommend, however, that you specify optional attributes after the three required ones to increase the readability of your HTML source code (the exception to this rule is CODEBASE, which should come before the CODE attribute if you use it).

It's time to show you a complete example for using the <APPLET> tag. The following HTML code shows you what an <APPLET> tag looks like for the MyApplet program:

```
<APPLET CODE="MyApplet" HEIGHT=100 WIDTH=200 ALT="This is a cool applet"
HSPACE=10 VSPACE=25>
```

TABLE 3.2   OPTIONAL APPLET PARAMETERS

Attribute	Description
ALIGN	Specifies where your applet is placed on the page in respect to the text around it; it can be one of the following nine alignments: left, right, top, text top, middle, absmiddle, baseline, bottom, and absbottom. The most common alignments (left, top, and right) are shown in Figure 3.1.
ALT	Specifies alternate text to be displayed by Java-savvy browsers that are incapable of executing the applet for whatever reason. Note that this text is seen only by Java-savvy browsers because it falls within the opening <APPLET> tag, which all non-Java browsers skip over. If you want to communicate with non-Java browsers, do so using alternate HTML. ALT helps not only those who are running browsers incapable of displaying Java, but also those who have turned the capability off because of limited horsepower. If you present a convincing argument, those users might be persuaded to turn the feature back on "just this once" to see your applet run.
CODEBASE	Specifies the base URL for your applet. The applet itself must be located relative to this URL. If CODEBASE isn't specified, the applet is expected to reside in the same directory as the Web page itself. We'll talk more about CODEBASE later.
HSPACE	Specifies the horizontal space surrounding your applets.
NAME	Specifies the symbolic name of your applet, allowing other applets embedded in the same page to locate your applet by name. This attribute is used only when applets on a page communicate with one another, something most applets don't do.
VSPACE	Specifies the vertical space surrounding your applet.

FIGURE 3.1

The most common alignments: left, top, and right.

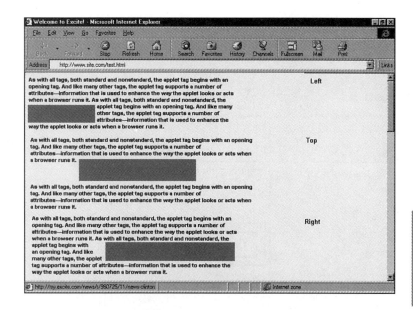

Tip

After you begin adding optional attributes to the mix, the opening tag can become quite difficult to read. To further increase the readability of your HTML source code, I recommend placing any optional attributes on their own line:

```
<APPLET CODE="MyApplet" HEIGHT=100 WIDTH=200
    ALT="This is a cool applet"
    HSPACE=10
    VSPACE=25>
```

The browser doesn't care how the tag appears, as long as it begins with < and ends with >. As a result, you can format your opening tag in any way you want.

CODEBASE

Under normal circumstances, the browser expects to find the applet file inside the same directory as the Web page itself. In this case, you must ensure that the applet file and Web page in which it is embedded share the same directory.

However, keeping the applet and the Web page in the same directory isn't always possible. What if the applet you want to embed in your page resides halfway around the world? In this case, it's physically impossible for your Web page and the applet to reside in the same directory. Figure 3.2 shows a picture of a hypothetical server that has three HTML pages. Each of these HTML pages uses two of the three applets that are stored in the Html/Applets directory.

FIGURE 3.2

*Three HTML pages,
each of which uses two
of the three applets
located in the*
Html/Applets
directory.

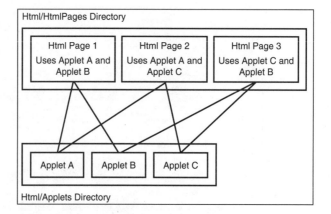

And what if you want a bunch of different pages on your Web site to use the same applet? What a profound waste of time and Web server space it would be to have to upload a copy of the applet into every directory containing a Web page that used it. A better idea would be to have the applet reside in a central location on your server, where all pages can get to it. But how?

Fortunately, the optional CODEBASE tag does just that. It allows you to specify a URL that points to the directory containing your applet. When a Java-savvy browser encounters the CODEBASE attribute, it automatically knows to look for the applet in whatever directory that attribute points to. The URL you supply for CODEBASE can point to a directory on your server, or one on any other server on the Web:

```
<APPLET CODEBASE="http://www.infinitevision.net/applets/"
    CODE="MyApplet" HEIGHT=100 WIDTH=200>
```

In this example, browsers won't look for the MyApplet applet inside the same directory as the Web page containing this <APPLET> tag. Instead, browsers expect the applet to be located on the Infinite Vision Technologies server, inside the applets directory.

The CODEBASE tag is particularly helpful when a number of pages on your site use the same applet. Rather than having multiple copies of the same applet scattered all around your server, you can place a single copy of the applet in one directory and specify the appropriate CODEBASE attribute in all pages. Not only does this take the headache out of creating these pages, because you no longer have to upload a copy of the applet for every page that uses it, but it also makes upgrading the applet a cinch—simply upgrade the single applet and you're done.

The URL you supply for CODEBASE can be either relative or absolute.

Applet Parameters

The second major part of the <APPLET> tag, applet parameters, is where you can really customize an applet. To make an applet look or act as you want it to, you use a special <PARAM> tag that has two of its own attributes: NAME and VALUE. Although not all applets are customizable, those that are allow you to supply information using one or more <PARAM> tags according to the following format:

```
<PARAM NAME="parameter name" VALUE="parameter value">
```

For example, an applet might allow you to provide a sound track that will play in the background when the applet is running. To tell the applet the name of the sound file to use and where that file is located, you could supply the following <PARAM> tag:

```
<PARAM NAME="sndTrack" VALUE="audio/rock/eagles.au">
```

In this example, the name of the parameter is sndTrack. The value associated with this parameter, audio/rock/eagles.au, is a relative URL leading to a sound file. Some applets might also accept an absolute URL for this parameter:

```
<PARAM NAME="sndTrack"
VALUE="http://www.infinitevision.net/audio/rock/beatles.au">
```

Because the author of an applet must write the programming code that allows the applet to deal with parameters, each applet is unique in the parameters it accepts. For example, another applet might also allow you to specify a sound track. However, depending on how it was written, it might not understand URLs at all. In this case, the applet might insist that the sound file reside in the same directory as the applet itself, meaning that you supply only a filename:

```
<PARAM NAME="music" VALUE="bluesSong.au">
```

Here, the applet just looks for the sound file named bluesSong.au, expecting to find it in the same directory in which the applet itself resides. Not only that, but the parameter name isn't sndTrack. Because the programmer decides which features you can customize, as well as the parameter names that correspond to these features, you'll find various names used for the same thing. Whereas this applet uses music as the parameter name corresponding to the file with a background sound track, others might use the name background, back music, sound_Track, sound, or just about anything else a programmer can think of.

Applets usually play sounds that are stored in the .au format. That's why each of the sound files specified here has the .au extension.

Good, Solid Values

Different applets might support any number of different parameters. It's not unusual, for example, to come across applets that support several different parameters, giving you great flexibility when it comes to configuring them. To supply more than one parameter, all you have to do is enter the parameters one after another.

A Marquee applet, for example, allows you to customize the text that scrolls across the screen. You can specify the font, style, and point size the text should appear in. All you have to do is provide a parameter tag for each:

```
<PARAM NAME="font_face" VALUE="Helvetica">
<PARAM NAME="font_size" VALUE=24>
<PARAM NAME="font_italic" VALUE="yes">
<PARAM NAME="font_bold" VALUE="no">
<PARAM NAME="marquee" VALUE="The text you are reading will scroll across
the screen">
```

You can customize the preceding applet in various ways, although you don't necessarily have to supply a parameter for each. Many applets supply a default if you don't bother to supply a parameter yourself. If, for example, you don't supply any information about the font, Marquee might use TimesRoman by default. Of course, it's up to the programmer whether an applet provides a default. Some applets force you to supply parameters; others are written to fall back on default values if you leave parameters out.

As the developer of Visual J++ programs, you must decide which parameters are and are not required. You'll be the one to determine which default parameters will be acceptable for a program's operation.

Just as with opening <APPLET> tag attributes, any parameter value that contains a space character (or many spaces) must be surrounded by quotation marks. Of course, when parameters require numeric values, you don't need to use quotation marks at all.

Multiple Values

Some applets don't stop at just one value being associated with a given parameter name. In many cases, you can supply several values at once. When this is possible, each value must be separated from the others so as not to confuse the applet. Typically, the ¦ character is used to separate the values:

```
<PARAM NAME="sounds" VALUE="eagles.au¦beatles.au¦bach.au">
```

In this case, the applet receives three sound files as one parameter. Not all applets accept multiple parameters, of course, but those that do insist that you separate each with a special character. Although the ¦ character is the most common, it's up to the developer of the applet to decide which character you must supply. As a result, don't be surprised to find commas, colons, semicolons, and even spaces used to separate multiple values:

```
<PARAM NAME="sounds" VALUE="eagles.au,beatles.au,bach.au">
<PARAM NAME="images" VALUE="shark.gif:pig.gif:tiger.gif">
<PARAM NAME="speeds" VALUE="100 355 23 0 535">
```

Alternate HTML

Following any parameter tags that you might use, but before the closing </APPLET> tag, there is a special area where you can supply what's known as alternate HTML. Here, you can enter any amount of HTML code you want; such code will be displayed only by non-Java browsers.

Although applets completely ignore alternate HTML, it's an important part of the <APPLET> tag nonetheless. Alternate HTML gives you an opportunity to create Web pages that are useful to users who view your pages regardless of the browser they happen to use. If you don't supply alternate HTML for non-Java browsers, you run the risk of alienating these users.

Although a carriage return between the last <PARAM> tag and the alternate HTML isn't necessary, it makes the code easier to read.

It's always a good idea to provide alternate HTML code for your applets whenever possible. Of course, there are some things applets do that you can't mimic with standard HTML (such as playing music). However, whenever it's possible to provide alternate HTML code that approximates an applet's visual appearance, you should do it so that users of both non-Java and Java powered browsers will benefit from your site.

The Closing Applet Tag

The fourth and final part of the <APPLET> tag brings the entire tag to a close. To properly form an <APPLET> tag, you must balance the opening tag with a closing </APPLET> tag. When the browser sees </APPLET>, it knows there is no more to the applet.

Although many applets are quite easy to use for users, others are extremely complex. The more parameters the applet expects, the harder it will be for the Web designer to use. The only way users know how to construct an appropriate <APPLET> tag for a given applet is to read the information that came with the applet. Be sure to include good documentation with your applets.

Making Applets Live

After you've created an applet, the chances are pretty good that you'll want to make it available to the entire Web population. To do this, you must upload the various files that make up the applet to a Web site and test them, to make sure that nothing breaks in the process.

To upload applets to a Web site, you must have the authority and the tools (such as an ftp tool) to do so. If the site you want to add the applet to is maintained by someone other than yourself, you'll have to obtain permission and perhaps even get the access passwords if you plan to upload the materials yourself. If you don't already have such authority, you can give the applet and the various files it uses to someone who will eventually perform the upload.

Obtaining WS_FTP

My preference in tools for doing the file uploads is WS_FTP. It's a great FTP tool that you can download from a Web site. The version that's downloadable is a trial version. If you decide to continue using it, you're expected to buy the full version.

To get a copy of WS_FTP, go to the Ipswitch Web site at `http://www.abraxis.com/ipswitch/Default.htm`. Besides getting the trial version, you'll be able to check out Ipswitch's entire line of products.

For the remainder of this chapter, the FTP program we'll use is WS_FTP. Before going any further, you might want to download the program and install it on your system.

Creating the Web Server Directory Layout

If this is the first time Java is being used at a site, it might be a good idea to create a directory structure that will contain the Java classes and other associated files such as audio and graphics files. This is pretty straightforward and will be similar to how the directory structure is set up on your local drive.

Make sure that you know in which directory the initial HTML file will be located. Many services require an index HTML file in a directory, and Web browsers that hit the site will automatically load this particular file. If your service has this requirement, you will probably want to place your Java files in this directory.

Connecting to the Server

If you have permission to upload files to a site on the Web, you're ready to get started.

After WS_FTP32 is installed, run it. The Session Properties dialog box, shown in Figure 3.3, will appear on top of the main program window.

In this dialog box, you'll enter information about the destination server, including its name (or IP address), your login name, and your password. If you have the Save

Password and Auto Save Config check boxes selected, the information will be saved and you can log in by simply selecting the server from a list.

FIGURE 3.3

The first thing you see when you run WS_FTP is the Session Properties dialog box.

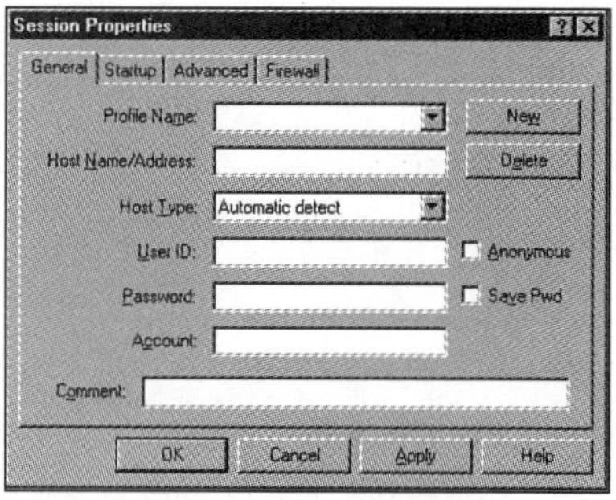

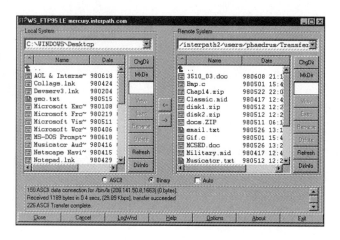

Fill in the Profile Name, Host Name, User ID, and Password fields. It's a good idea to make the Profile Name and Host Name the same to avoid ambiguity. With the information correctly entered, click the OK button and the program will try to log on to the server.

The left list box of WS_FTP's main window contains a listing of the current directory, even when you're not logged on to a server. When logged in, you'll see a directory listing in the list box on the right half of the screen, as shown in Figure 3.4. This shows only the names of the files and directories, not file and directory details. To get a listing of full file and directory information, click DirInfo in the right column of buttons.

FIGURE 3.4

The right list box contains a directory listing of the server to which you logged on.

You'll have to know how to find your directory on the server. Many ISPs have a directory structure that will make it hard to find your directory. Make sure that you have the documentation for your account. Although it might be cryptic (as is usually the case), it'll be your best bet of finding the directory. Other ISPs are more understanding and drop you right into your directory after you log on.

These are the steps for connecting to a server:

1. Run WS_FTP (the Session Profile dialog box will appear).
2. Enter information about the server such as the server name (or IP address), your login name, and your password.
3. Click the OK button and wait for WS_FTP to connect to the server.
4. In the list box on the left side of the WS_FTP window, navigate to the local directory you want to transfer from.
5. In the list box on the right side of the WS_FTP window, navigate to the server directory you want to transfer to.
6. Highlight the files you want to transfer and click the -> button.

Uploading the Applet

After you're connected, you can upload the files. I'll use a HelloWorld applet as an example. You must upload `HelloWorld.class` and `HelloWorld.html`. Not all three of these files (the `HelloWorld.html`, `HelloWorld.class`, and `HelloWorld.java` files) are necessary to run the Java program—only `HelloWorld.class` is required. You can upload `HelloWorld.java` if you want to offer the source code for download. Our example here will assume that you're uploading the `.java` source code so that users can download it.

The `HelloWorld.html` file is the HTML file that J++ created with some additional lines so that users can download the source code. Later in the chapter, we'll talk about incorporating this code into another HTML file, but for simplicity you'll use it as it was created and have your main HTML file upload `HelloWorld.html`.

Begin by navigating the left list box so that it shows all three HelloWorld files. Highlight them as shown in Figure 3.5 and then click the -> button.

The files will be uploaded to the server. Because the files are short and most modem connections are pretty fast, you won't see much more than a blink as the upload progress box appears during the upload. For longer files, the upload progress box will stay visible long enough for you to see it.

FIGURE 3.5

Highlight the files you want to upload and click the -> button.

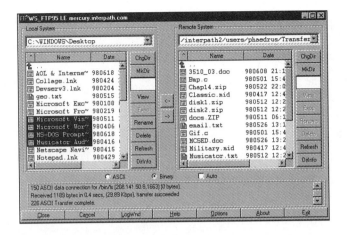

Caution

Most FTP client programs, such as WS_FTP, automatically detect the type of file you're uploading. For FTP uploads, a distinction is usually required between binary and text files. When a program automatically detects the file type, you don't have to worry about it; the correct settings will be used for the transfer.

But some FTP client programs might not have an automatic detection feature. If this is the case, you'll have to specify text for HTML files, and binary for .class files.

Editing the HTML File

Editing the HTML file is an easy way to change the position at which your applet appears. You can center the applet, justify it on the left side of the browser screen, or justify it on the right side of the browser screen. Many of the applets created in this book will have parameters that reside in the HTML file. Changing them will alter the behavior of the applet.

After the three HelloWorld files are on the server in the correct directory, the main HTML file must be edited so that users have the chance to bring up your applet. As mentioned earlier, the main HTML file on your Web server will probably have a special name such as index.html. There's a difference between writing an applet and testing it on a local machine, and uploading to a Web server and testing on the server. Details such as what the name of the default (main) HTML page is are important.

For now, you'll have the main HTML file bring up `HelloWorld.html`. Open your main HTML file in a text editor. Add the following line:

```
<h3><p>Run <a href=HelloWorld.html> <i>HelloWorld</a></h3><p>
```

A new line will appear when your browser opens the HTML at your site, as shown in Figure 3.6.

FIGURE 3.6

The line that was added to the HTML file causes Run HelloWorld *to show in the browser.*

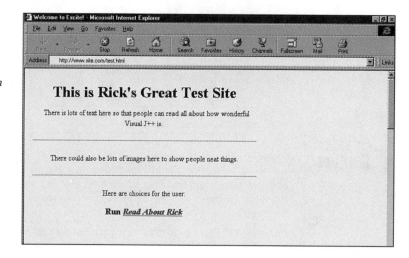

When you click on the HTML line, you'll see the HelloWorld applet run in your browser. The source code is available for viewing with a line at the bottom labeled "The source," as shown in Figure 3.7. All HTML files created by J++ make the source code available.

OFFERING YOUR SOURCE CODE FOR DOWNLOAD

Most people who want to take a look at your source code don't want to look at it from within a browser. They usually want to download it and look at it on their computers. For this reason, it's a good idea to include an archived version of the source code. The best way to do this is to zip the source code into a separate file. You can then add another line that offers zipped source code for downloading.

Zip the source code to a file named `HelloWorld.zip`. You'll need the latest version of WinZip that supports long filenames. It can be found at `http://www.winzip.com`.

By the way, WinZip can be downloaded and used free of charge for a limited time. If you use it after 30 days, you need to register it.

Add the following line to your `HelloWorld.html` file, and the archived source code will be available for downloading:

```
<a href=HelloWorld.zip>The source zipped.</a>
```

Now that you know how to make the changes in the HTML file for the HelloWorld applet, it's time to take a look at the complete file. Listing 3.1 has the HTML source code for the HelloWorld applet.

INPUT   **LISTING 3.1** THE COMPLETE HelloWorld.html FILE

```
1    <HTML>
2    <HEAD>
3    <TITLE>HelloWorld Test HTML Page</TITLE>
4    </HEAD>
5    <BODY>
6        <applet
7            code=HelloWorld.class
8            name=HelloWorld
9            width=320
10           height=200 >
11           <param name=label value="Hello Visual J++ World.">
12           <param name=background value="008080">
13           <param name=foreground value="FFFFFF">
14       </applet>
15
16   <hr>
17   <a href="HelloWorld.java">The source.</a>          } download
18   <a href="HelloWorld.zip">The source zipped.</a>
19
20   </BODY>
21   </HTML>
```

OUTPUT

FIGURE 3.7

Your applet runs from inside of your browser, and the source code is available for viewing.

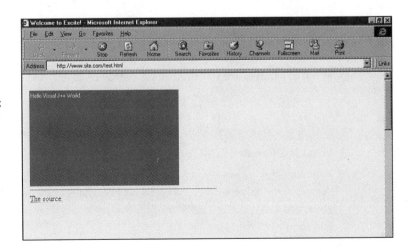

SUMMARY OF STEPS TO MAKE APPLETS LIVE

1. Connect to your server with an FTP program, such as WS_FTP32.
2. Upload HTML, Java, and Class files.
3. Edit the main HTML file by adding this:

```
<h3><p>Run <a href=HelloWorld.html>
        <i>HelloWorld</a></h3><p>
```

4. Test the file with your browser.

Summary

Uploading your applets to a Web server is an important part of the development process. It's one you need to be familiar with so that you can do it without a lot of aggravation.

Editing your HTML files is important too. The appearance of your Java program relies on your ability to edit the HTML file and correctly set the applet parameters.

A good tool to use for uploading files is WS_FTP. A trial version can be downloaded and used free of charge for a limited time.

Q&A

Q How do you indicate that a Java applet is to be embedded into a Web page?

A You use the <APPLET> tag in the HTML file. When a Java-aware browser sees the <APPLET> tag, it knows that anything that follows is part of a Java applet's attributes and its parameters.

Q What attributes are required in an <APPLET> tag?

A Three tags are required in an <APPLET> tag: CODE, HEIGHT, and WIDTH. CODE specifies the name of the applet class file. HEIGHT specifies the height of the applet window in pixels. WIDTH specifies the width of the applet window in pixels.

Q What is alternate HTML and why should you use it?

A Following any parameter tags you might use, yet before the closing </APPLET> tag, there is a special area where you can supply what's known as alternate HTML. Here, you can enter any amount of HTML code you want; such code will be displayed only by non-Java browsers.

Although applets completely ignore alternate HTML, it's an important part of the <APPLET> tag nonetheless. Alternate HTML gives you an opportunity to create Web pages that are useful to Web surfers regardless of the browser they happen to use. If you don't supply alternate HTML for non-Java browsers, you run the risk of alienating these users.

Q What information do you need for an FTP program so that you can connect to a Web site?

A The first thing you need to do is to make sure that you have a valid user account. This gives you permission to upload files to the Web server. For a program such as WS_FTP, you'll need to provide a username, a password, and the FTP server name (or IP address). This is the minimum information you'll need in order to connect to an FTP site. There might be additional required information if you must go through a proxy server to get to your space on the Web server. (Your site administrator can give you the information you need for connecting through a proxy server.)

Q Why would you want to make your Java source code available for download?

A Many Visual J++ and Java programmers enjoy fostering an attitude of sharing with other programmers. Practically every Visual J++ programmer has at one point relied on source code found on the Web to learn how to do something for a project.

Q Why do you have to use FTP to upload files to the Web?

A You can't use HTTP because it's a one-way transfer. Users can only get files using HTTP. To send files to a server, you must use a trusted protocol such as FTP that requires a login name and password. Other options include using programs such as PC Anywhere.

Review Exercises

1. Now that you know how to send your applets to the Web, create some and make them available to the public through your Web site.

2. Create three applets that simply show some distinct text onscreen. Upload them to your Web server into a directory named Applets. Create three HTML pages. Have each of the HTML pages load in two of the three applets. Make sure that they find the applets by specifying the CODEBASE.

DAY 4

Debugging Java Applets and Applications

The Visual J++ debugger might be as important as any other part of Visual J++. Debugging programs effectively is almost as important as writing good code—unless, that is, your code is always perfect. But for the rest of us competent-but-not-perfect programmers, the debugger gets us out of trouble more times than we can count.

In the early days of computers, the guys who wrote assemblers and compilers didn't think debuggers were necessary. They reasoned that if a person wrote the code, that person would know how it should work and wouldn't make any mistakes. That theory was soon shot to pieces. The same guys then wrote debuggers for their assemblers and compilers, much to the relief of software developers.

Today's lesson is divided into two sections. In the first section, you'll learn how to use the Visual J++ debugger. You'll learn about the debug windows and how to navigate through your code with the debugger. In the second part of the chapter, you'll learn hints and tips for effective debugging. This is no trivial matter because effective debugging requires some of the most difficult reasoning in software development.

In this chapter, you'll learn the following:

- How to prepare projects for debugging
- How to start a debug session
- How to step through a project with the debugger
- About the debugger windows
- How to set and use breakpoints
- How to effectively debug programs

If you can master all the techniques listed previously, you'll be equipped for the remainder of your Visual J++ journey. If you know how to use the debugger from the start, your development will be much easier and less frustrating because you'll know how to track down the errors that baffle others who don't rely on the debugger.

Preparing Projects for Debugging

You can compile projects in one of two ways: with debug code and without debug code. If you compile a project with debug code, the compiler inserts a lot of extra information into the compiled program file (whether it's an applet `.class` file or an application `.exe` file). This extra information is used by the debugger. Included is symbolic information that tells the debugger all the details about variables and classes. This is very important because during a debug session you're going to want to know about variables and what values are stored in them. Another very important classification of information that's stored relates the compiled bytecode to the source code. The debugger can look at this and know what line of bytecode goes with what line of source code. Knowing this allows the debugger to execute the program while displaying the correct source code.

Before starting a debug session, you must make sure that all modules of a program are compiled with debug code. Start by going to the Build menu. The Build Configuration menu item gives you two choices: Debug and Release. Debug obviously creates a program with embedded debug code. Release creates a program with no embedded debug code. Figure 4.1 shows how your project should be set so that it will compile debug code into the program.

FIGURE 4.1

Make sure that the Build Configuration is set to Debug before you build your project so that debug code is embedded into the compiled program.

If you're not sure that all the modules in your program have been compiled with debug code, it's a good idea to select Build, Rebuild. This step recompiles all modules in your project. After you're sure that all the modules have been recompiled with debug code, you can safely use Build, Build and have only out-of-date modules rebuilt.

Note

> It's not wise to upload class files with debug code to the Web, or even deploy them as applications. They contain a lot of extra information that release programs shouldn't have. As a general rule, the debug versions of programs are from two to four times as large as the release versions.

4

Starting a Debugging Session

You can start a debugging session in several ways. Let's first start by creating an application with which we'll explore the world of debugging. First, create a Windows Application project named LearnToDebug. Make sure that the Build Configuration has Debug selected. (This is the default, so it should be.) Now build the project by selecting Build, Build. Follow the steps listed here to create and build the program:

1. Select File, New Project. The New Project dialog box will appear.

2. Make sure that the New tab is selected in the New Project dialog box.

3. In the window in the left side of the New Project dialog box that has the Visual J++ Projects folder, open the applications folder.

4. In the window in the right side of the New Project dialog box, select Windows Application.

5. In the Name field, type `LearnToDebug`.

6. Click the Open button.

7. Select Build, Rebuild.

If you select Debug, Start, the program will execute inside of the debugger. The problem is that Start runs the program and stops only when a breakpoint is encountered. Because we just created and built this program, no breakpoints are set. If you've selected Start and the program is running, you can stop it by closing the application or by selecting Debug, End.

You might notice that the Start item in the Debug menu changes to Continue while the program is executing (even if it's stopped at a breakpoint).

With the program running, you can also select Debug, Break. The program will pause wherever it currently is. With the program paused, you can resume the program by selecting Debug, Continue.

The Start (Continue), End, and Break commands can be found in the Debug menu. There are also default shortcut keys you can use, as shown in Table 4.1.

TABLE 4.1   DEFAULT DEBUG KEYS

Shortcut Key	Action
F5	Start/Continue
Ctrl+F5	Start Without Debugging
Ctrl+Break	Break
Shift+F5	End
Ctrl+Shift+F5	Restart
Ctrl+F10	Run To Cursor
F11	Step Into
F10	Step Over
Shift+F11	Step Out
Ctrl+F9	Enable Breakpoint
Ctrl+Shift+F9	Clear Breakpoints
Ctrl+B	Breakpoint Dialog

Tip

> All the shortcut keys in Visual J++ can be changed. To change them, select Tools, Options, and the Options dialog box will appear. In the Environment category, select Keyboard—you'll see the keyboard category and commands lists. To change the shortcut keys for debugging, select Debug in the category list. The available options will appear in the commands list.

When you run an application in debug mode, Visual J++ invokes its debugger. But when you run an applet in debug mode, it first runs Internet Explorer, which in turn interacts with the debugger. Applets that are run in the debugger take anywhere from 15 seconds to three minutes to begin execution. That's because of the number of things Visual J++ and its components must do to get Internet Explorer and everything else running in debug mode.

Stepping Through a Project

By now you've probably selected Run and had the LearnToDebug application execute in the debugger. If you haven't, stop reading now and do it. This part is not too exciting, but we're ready now to get into the nitty-gritty of navigating through projects while in a debug session.

Step Into

The first command we'll try is the Step Into command. If Visual J++ still has the default shortcut keys, you can press F11. It's much easier than selecting Debug, Step Into.

Make sure that the program is not running, and then select Step Into (or press F11). You'll come to a line of source code in the LearnToDebug program that looks like the following:

```
Application.run(new Form1());
```

All of our applications will start with this line. The only exception will be if the form is named something other than Form1. For example, if you're debugging a program other than the LearnToDebug program, your form might be named MyGreatForm, in which case the first line would look like the following:

```
Application.run(new MyGreatForm());
```

Employ the Step Into command again and you'll find yourself at the Form1 constructor. If your program has anything that's initialized, you'll be able to step through that code here. Because we're working with a program that's been created by Visual J++, there is nothing here except a call to the initForm() method.

4

Your next use of Step Into brings you to the place that creates a new Container object. Pressing F11 again gets you into the `initForm()` method. Each time you press F11, you step through another line of code in the `initForm()` method until that method is completely executed. Then you return to the end of the `Form1` constructor. You get the idea—the Step Into command steps through your program one line of source code at a time.

End

Let's practice the End command. Select Debug, End or press Shift+F5. The application will no longer be in debug mode, and Visual J++ will return to its normal state. The only difference might be this: when the debugger stops at a line of source code, the source-code editor stays at that location. So if your source code showed the top of the `Form1` source-code module when you started debugging and you stop the debugger in the `initForm()` method, the source code you see when the debugger stops is the code in the `initForm()` method.

Step Over

The default shortcut key for the Step Over command is F10.

Let's say you don't want to fool around with stepping through the `initForm()` method. You know that everything in it works fine, and there might be a hundred lines of code by the time your application is developed. For that reason, the Step Over command was invented. You can step over an entire method (and methods which that method calls).

Make sure that the debugger isn't running. Execute a Step Into command, and you should see the first line of code. Use the Step Into command until the cursor is on the call to `initForm()` inside of the `Form1` constructor. The following source code shows you where to stop:

```
public Form1()
{
    // Required for Visual J++ Form Designer support
    initForm(); // Stop when the debug cursor is on this line.

    // TODO: Add any constructor code after initForm call
}
```

Instead of using Step Into, which you know will step you right into the `initForm()` method, use Step Over (you can use the F10 shortcut). Voilà! All the code in the `initForm()` method was executed, but you didn't have to walk through (or should I say drudge through) the code in the `initForm()` method.

Tip

Use the Step Over command whenever possible during your debug sessions. If you know that a method has no problems, there's no reason to waste time stepping through its code.

Step Out

Okay, you made a mistake and accidentally used Step Into one too many times. You're now on the first line of the `initForm()` method. All is not lost. Visual J++ has a very nice command called Step Out. It proceeds to the end of whatever method you're in and exits. The default shortcut key for this command is Shift+F11.

Run To Cursor

There's one last navigation command that will make your debugging easier: the Run To Cursor command. Let's say there's one line toward the `initForm()` method that's doing something strange. You want to run the program until you get to that line and see what's going on. This is easy. In your source code, click on the line at which you want the debugger to stop. Use the Run To Cursor command by selecting it from the Debug menu or pressing the default Ctrl+F10 key combination. Your program will execute and stop at the point where the cursor is.

Debug Windows

When you debug programs, you're going to rely on the tools that help you view the contents of variables. The values that are stored in variables determine the results of calculations and the flow of the program. That's why knowing what's in variables is at the crux of debugging.

This section shows you how to use the Visual J++ debug windows. Knowing how to use them properly will help you get the most out of them. And this will make your debugging sessions far more productive.

Before we get started, you'll need to add some variable declarations and assignments to the LearnToDebug project. At the top of the `Form1` class, add the following code and rebuild the application:

```
public class Form1 extends Form
{

    int m_nHorizontal = 50;
    int m_nVertical = 75;
    boolean m_bButton = false;
    double m_dValue = 4.5;
    String m_strText = "This is text";
```

The Watch Window

Start a debug session by pressing F11 until you get to the initForm() method. You'll notice that you step through the newly added code that declares and initializes variables.

By default, the Watch window is open when Visual J++ is in a debug session. If it's not, go to View, Debug Windows. One of the choices you'll see is Watch. If you select this option and you're in a debug session, the Watch window will open. You can look at variables in the Watch window. It displays the variable name, contents, and type.

Assuming you're in a debug session, here's how you add a variable to the Watch window. Type the variable name exactly as it appears in your source code in the Name column of the watch window. The variable's value and type will appear.

Try adding the m_nHorizontal variable to the Watch window. The value will be 50 and the type will be int. Your Watch window will look like the window shown in Figure 4.2.

FIGURE 4.2

You can easily add variables to the Watch window by entering the variable name in the Name column.

If you add a variable that doesn't exist, or a variable that's out of scope, you'll see Error: symbol 'xxxx' not found (xxxx being the name of the variable you typed). Remember: The scope of a variable begins immediately where it is declared and ends with the closing brace (}) of the block of code it is declared within. For more information, look back to the Scope section on Day 2, "Java Language Fundamentals."

The Locals Window

The Locals window displays the local variables and their values in the current stack frame. The current stack frame reflects the local variables, any parameters that have been passed to the method, and methods that have called this method. As the execution switches from procedure to procedure, the contents of the Locals window change to reflect the local variables applicable to the current procedure.

The Locals window is updated only when execution is stopped. Values that have changed since the last break are highlighted as shown in Figure 4.3.

FIGURE 4.3

The Locals window shows you the local variables in the current method.

In the Locals window you can change the current stack frame within the active thread by selecting it from the Context list. You can also drag a selected variable to the Immediate window or the Watch window. To edit a variable, double-click it. You can click the "+" or "-" to view or hide the member variables of an object variable or array. You can also use the keystrokes listed in Table 4.2 to view or hide member variables of the selected object or array or to move around in the Locals window.

TABLE 4.2   LOCALS WINDOW ACTIONS

Action	Keystroke
Collapse the member variables list	Left-arrow key
View the member variables	Right-arrow key
Toggle between hiding and viewing the variables	Enter
Move upward in the member variables list	Up-arrow key
Move downward in the member variables list	Down-arrow key
Move up an expanded list	Left-arrow key
Move down an expanded list	Right-arrow key

The Autos Window

The Autos window displays the values of all variables that are within the scope of currently executing procedures. Whereas the Locals window shows variables for a single thread, the Autos window shows variables for all threads. This window allows you to learn about the changes to a variable that might be caused by code executing on a different thread. A variable remains visible as long as it is in scope, reflecting any changes to its value. When the variable goes out of scope, it is removed from the Autos window.

In Figure 4.4, you can see the Autos window. It contains the global variables from our LearnToDebug applet.

FIGURE 4.4

The Autos window here contains the global variables we added to our LearnToDebug application.

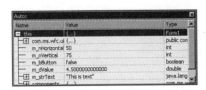

The Immediate Window

The Immediate window is used to enter expressions to be evaluated or executed by a development language. The rules for entering expressions and the behavior of the Immediate window are dependent on the Java language.

Start a debugging session and step into the initForm() method. In the Immediate window, type m_nHorizontal. On the next line, the value of 50 will be printed. This shows you that the value of m_nHorizontal is 50. That's not too useful, though, because we can see that information in the Watch window. But if you type m_nHorizontal * 8, the debugger prints 400 on the next line. You can just as easily type m_nHorizontal * m_nVertical for a value of 3750, as shown in Figure 4.5. The Immediate window is a great opportunity to evaluate expressions that will help you debug your program.

FIGURE 4.5

The Immediate window lets you evaluate expressions.

The Call Stack Window

The Call Stack window displays a list of all active procedures or stack frames for the current thread of execution. Active procedures are the uncompleted procedures in a process.

In the Call Stack window, you can change the active thread by selecting it from the threads list. You can also change the size of the column header by dragging its border to the right to make it larger or to the left to make it smaller. Double-clicking a row allows you to change the contents of the Locals window to correspond with the selected procedure. Change the size of a column by dragging the border of the column header to the right to make the column larger or to the left to make it smaller.

The threads list contains a list of all threads in the current process. Selecting a thread from the list gives the thread the focus in IDE. The list of threads is the same as the list that appears in the Threads window.

The Call Stack window won't be open by default. To open it, select View, Debug Windows, Call Stack.

Breakpoints

Breakpoints are places in the source code where you specify that the debugger must pause execution until you continue (by pressing F5, F10, F11, or any other navigation shortcut key). Breakpoints give you the opportunity to examine variables at a given point in the program. For instance, if somewhere in the calculateValue() method a variable is becoming negative when it should always be positive, you can set a breakpoint right before the variable is altered and watch what happens when its value changes.

To set a breakpoint, simply click in the gray margin of the source-code window. A small red circle will appear, indicating that a breakpoint is set at that location. You can also set a breakpoint wherever the cursor is by pressing the F9 key.

Clearing breakpoints is done the same way as setting them. Just click on the red breakpoint circle, and it will go away. You can also press F9 when the cursor is on a line with a breakpoint, and it will go away.

Okay, let's practice. Add the method given in Listing 4.1 to your LearnToDebug application, and then call it from your Form1 constructor after the initForm() method is called.

LISTING 4.1   A METHOD THAT WILL HELP YOU LEARN TO DEBUG

```
1    void practiceMethod()
2    {
3        int i, j, k;
4        int nValue = 0;
5        int nCalculate = 0;
6
7        for( i=0; i<10; i++ )
8        {
9            for( j=0; j<15; j++ )
10           {
11               for( k=0; k<15; k++ )
12               {
13                   nValue = i * j + k;
14                   if( j == 10 )
15                       nValue = -nValue;
16                   else if( j ==5 && i == 4 )
17                       continue;
18                   else if( k == 10 && i == 5 )
19                       break;
20               }
21           }
22           // Here is where we need to
23           // know the contents of nValue.
24           nCalculate = nValue - 1; // Set your breakpoint here.
25       }
26
27   }
```

4

There are three for loops in the preceding code. It would take a long time to step through the code. Because all we're concerned with is the value of nValue and the assignment to nCalculate, we simply have to set a breakpoint on the line indicated in the source code at line 25. Every time the debugger gets to line 25, program execution will be paused. After you examine the contents of nValue, you can use the Continue command (F5) to resume execution.

One point to note: At the line at which the breakpoint is set, the nCalculate variable hasn't been set. To allow this variable to be set, you'd have to single-step with the Step Into command (actually, Step Over would work also).

Tip

> In a situation like this, when there's no code following a variable assignment at which to set a breakpoint, you can add some code just so that you have the opportunity to set a breakpoint after the line nCalculate = nValue – 1; (line 25). In the preceding situation, I would add a local variable at the top named m and the code m = 0; below the nCalculate = nValue – 1; line (which would become line 26) so that there's a place to set a breakpoint after nCalculate is set.

After running through the program, you'll get values as shown in Table 4.3.

TABLE 4.3 VALUES DURING THE DEBUG SESSION

i	nValue	nCalculate
0	14	13
1	28	27
2	42	41
3	56	55
4	70	69
5	80	79
6	98	97
7	112	111
8	126	125
9	140	139

The Breakpoints Dialog Box

The Breakpoints dialog box shown in Figure 4.6 displays a list of all breakpoints in the current solution. To bring up the breakpoints dialog box, press Ctrl+B or select Debug, Breakpoints. You can use the Breakpoints dialog box to add a new breakpoint by name only. You can also enable, disable, or remove one or more existing breakpoints by pressing Ctrl and clicking on the breakpoint or breakpoints. And you can modify the properties of a breakpoint.

FIGURE 4.6

The Breakpoints dialog box offers an easy way to manage your breakpoints.

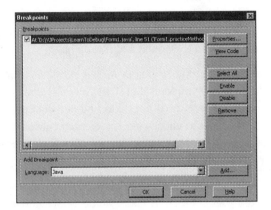

Several options are available in the Breakpoints dialog box. Table 4.4 shows the options.

TABLE 4.4 THE BREAKPOINTS DIALOG BOX OPTIONS

Option	Description
Breakpoints	Lists all the breakpoints in the current solution
Properties	Displays the Breakpoint Properties dialog box, where you can set the properties of the selected breakpoint
View Code	Closes the Breakpoints dialog box after saving the changes, and displays the selected breakpoint in the Text Editor window
Select All	Selects all the breakpoints in the Breakpoints list
Enable	Enables the selected breakpoints
Disable	Disables the selected breakpoints
Remove	Deletes the selected breakpoint or breakpoints

4

Debugging Tips

Knowing the Visual J++ debugger inside and out makes it easier to debug programs. But that's only part of what you need in order to debug Visual J++ programs. You need an approach to debugging that helps you get to the problem. You can spend hours chasing your tail trying to find a bug, but if you follow the suggestions presented next, you should better be able to avoid costly dead ends.

You can sometimes fix a bug and then find another bug related to the first or to the way you fixed it. When I fix a bug, I ask myself three questions to ensure that I've thought carefully about its significance. You can use these questions to improve productivity and quality every time you think you've found and fixed a bug.

The key idea behind these questions is that every bug is a symptom of an underlying process. You have to treat the symptoms, but if all you do is treat symptoms, you'll continue to see more symptoms forever. You need to find out what process produced the bug and then change the process. The underlying process that caused your bug probably is nonrandom and can be controlled after you identify what happened and what caused it to happen.

Before you ask the three questions, you need to overcome your natural resistance to looking carefully at the bug. Look at the code and explain what went wrong. Start with the observable facts and work backward, asking *why* repeatedly, until you can describe the pattern that underlies the bug. Often, you should do this with a colleague, because explaining what you think happened will force you to confront your assumptions about what the program is up to. Here's an example of such scrutiny:

> *It blew up because subscript* j *was out of range.*
>
> *Why?*
>
> j *was* 10 *but the top array subscript is only* 9.
>
> *Why?*
>
> j *is a string length, and the array origin is* 0; *so the last character in a string of length* 1 *is index* 0.

Look for additional surprises in the situation at the time the bug was found. Check key program variables at the point of failure to see whether you can explain their values. For example:

> *Why is the name null?*
>
> *Why was it trying to output an error message anyway?*

Keep notes of what you did and what happened. You need to know what is really going on, and this means keeping measurements and history.

When these steps are out of the way, you are ready to ask the first of the three questions.

Is This Mistake Somewhere Else Also?

Look for other places in the code where the same pattern applies. Vary the pattern systematically to look for similar bugs. Ask questions such as these:

Where else do I use a length as a subscript?

Do all my arrays have the same origin?

What would happen for a zero length string?

Try to describe the local rule that should be true in this section of the code but that the bug disobeyed; your search for this invariant[1] will help you see other potential bugs. This is the general thought pattern:

The starting offset plus the length, minus 1, is the ending subscript...unless the length is zero.

It's more productive to fix several bugs for every one you find. Trying to describe the bugs in general terms also raises your level of understanding about what the program is doing and helps you avoid introducing more bugs as you program.

What Next Bug Is Hidden Behind This One?

After you figure out how to fix the bug, you need to imagine what will happen after you fix it. The statement after the failing one might have a bug in it too, but the program never got that far before; or some other code might be entered for the first time as a result of your fix. Take a look at these untried statements and look for bugs in them. Think about this:

Would this next statement work?

While you're thinking about control flow is a good time to ask whether there are other unreached parts of the program. Ask yourself:

Are there combinations of features I've never tested?

It doesn't take much work to instrument a program so that you can check off as you execute its various parts; and it's often surprising how much of a program doesn't work at all after the builder says it's been tested. The thought process continues:

Can I make all the error messages come out in test?

Beware of making a change in one place that causes a bug somewhere else. A local change to some variable might violate the assumptions made further on in execution. For example, you might consider this:

> *If I just subtract 1 from* j, *the* move *statement later will try to move -1 characters when the string length is* 0.

If you've made a lot of changes to the program already, consider carefully whether adding another local fix is the right thing to do, or whether it's time to redesign and reimplement.

What Should I Do to Prevent Bugs Like This?

Ask how you can change your ways to make this kind of bug impossible by definition. By changing methods or tools, it's often possible to completely eliminate a whole class of failures instead of shooting the bugs down one by one.

Start by asking when the bug was introduced: when in the development life cycle could the bug have been prevented? You might think:

> *The design is OK; I introduced this bug in coding.*

Examine the reason for the bug in detail. Think about the process that was going on at the moment the bug was introduced, and ask how it could be changed to prevent the bug. For example:

> *Separate data types for offset and length would have caught this error at compilation time.*

> *Each text item could be output with a macro that hides the subscripting calculation. Then I can figure this out just once.*

Don't be satisfied with glib answers. Suppose your explanation for a bug is "I just forgot." How can the process be changed so that you don't need to remember? The language can be changed so that the detail you omitted is completely hidden, or your omission is detected and causes a compiler diagnostic. You could use a language preprocessor for this problem domain, or a clever editing tool that fills in defaults, checks for errors, or provides hints and rapid documentation. The bug might be a symptom of communication problems in the programming team, or of conflicting design assumptions that need discussion.

Consider the way the bug was found, and ask how it could have been found earlier. How could testing be made more air-tight? Could tests be generated automatically? Could inline checking code be added that would trap errors all the time? You might think these kinds of thoughts:

I should try a zero length string in my unit tests.

I could enable subscript checking and catch this sooner.

Systematic methods and automated tools for compilation, build, and test are always worth creating. They pay for themselves quickly, by eliminating long debugging and fact-finding sessions.

Applications of the Technique

Make a habit of asking the three questions every time you find a bug. You don't even have to wait for a bug to use the three questions.

During design and implementation review, each comment you get can be treated with the three questions. Review comments are the result of an underlying communication process that you can improve. If you feel that a reader's comment on a specification is wrong, for example, you might ask what kept your document from being understood, and how you can communicate better with the reviewer.

THREE APPROACHES TO DEBUGGING

I have three approaches to debugging. I use each of them at different times. Deciding which method to use is more black art than logical reasoning—at least for me. I have an intuition about it that serves me well. I'm also ready at any moment during a debugging session to change my approach.

THE WISHFUL-THINKING APPROACH

The wishful-thinking approach is the easiest approach to debugging. If it works, it's the fastest way to arrive at a solution. It's also the least effective. But it's where most of us start when we first try to debug applications. I still use it if I feel that the solution is something trivial—especially if I think it's something more along the lines of a typographical error in the code that I'll spot pretty quickly.

Here's how you do it. Run the debugger. Set a breakpoint in the code ahead of where you suspect the problem is located. Then step into methods or step over them. Step over methods you're sure are okay, and step into methods you're not sure about.

As you do this, your mind can't help doing a mental simulation of the code execution while the debugger is in operation. When I use this method of debugging, 90% of the time I find the problem when I'm getting close to the code with the error. It's because as I get close, I realize in my mind what's wrong. It's almost as if the debugger is nothing more than a crutch to force my mind to carefully simulate the code's execution.

4

Tip

> Use the wishful-thinking approach to debugging when your program is relatively small, or when you think the problem is fairly trivial. This approach will save you time if the bug is easy to find, but it will be a big waste for bugs that are hard to find.

THE SPLIT-THE-DIFFERENCE APPROACH

Have you ever played the game in which someone thinks of a number, and you have a certain number of guesses to determine the number? Let's say you're guessing a number from 1 to 100. The wisest approach is to guess 50. Then if it's above 50, you guess 75. If it's below 75, you guess halfway between 50 and 75—63. And the game goes on like this. Basically, you're splitting the difference by guessing a number that's midway in the range into which the target number falls. At least that's how the logicians suggest playing that game. You might have a bolder strategy.

This split-the-difference method is similar to the numbers guessing game. You start off with the given information. You know that everything is fine at a certain point, but you're sure it's not fine at this other point. Okay, you have a range of source code in which you know the problem occurs.

Start off by splitting the difference. Set a breakpoint halfway into the code. When the debugger stops at your breakpoint, examine all the variables. Is everything okay? If there are no detectable problems, chances are that the error occurred later. If the problem has surfaced, it was in the first half of the code.

Now that you know in which half of the code the problem occurred, clear the breakpoint you've set, and set a breakpoint in the middle of that code. Then restart the program. You proceed with this process, narrowing the area in which the error occurs. Finally, when you get a manageable piece of code, step through it and find the exact line at which the error occurs.

Tip

> Use the split-the-difference approach to debugging if you feel that the error will be somewhat difficult to find. It's also recommended if your program is of a medium to large size.

THE ASSUME-NOTHING APPROACH

The assume-nothing approach to debugging is my last resort. It's the most rigorous approach to debugging, and it takes the most time. You still have to identify the block of code in which the error occurs before you start. If this is the entire program, so be it—that's the block of code you'll have to work with.

Here's how it works. Let's say you have a method. Somewhere in that method, a variable is becoming negative when it should always be positive. Start by commenting out all the code and recompiling. To comment out source code, just place two / characters at the beginning of each line of code. Two methods follow. The first method is normal; the second one has all the lines of source code commented out:

```
private void initForm()
{

    this.setBackColor(Color.CONTROL);
    this.setLocation(new Point(0, 0));
    this.setSize(new Point(300, 300));
    this.setTabIndex(-1);
    this.setTabStop(true);
    this.setText("Form1");
    this.setAutoScaleBaseSize(13);
    this.setClientSize(new Point(292, 273));
    this.addOnClick(new EventHandler(this.Form1_click));
}

private void initForm()
{

//    this.setBackColor(Color.CONTROL);
//    this.setLocation(new Point(0, 0));
//    this.setSize(new Point(300, 300));
//    this.setTabIndex(-1);
//    this.setTabStop(true);
//    this.setText("Form1");
//    this.setAutoScaleBaseSize(13);
//    this.setClientSize(new Point(292, 273));
//    this.addOnClick(new EventHandler(this.Form1_click));
}
```

With all the source code in your method commented out, you know for certain that the variable can't become negative. Rebuild the program and run the debugger. Make sure that the variable never becomes negative. If it does, the problem is elsewhere. If it never becomes negative, you're correct in assuming that the problem is in your method.

Now, add back lines of code to the method by uncommenting them. Try adding one line of code at a time. Sometimes you can't and you have to add two or three lines. Each time you uncomment lines of code, rebuild the application and run the debugger. When you finally add the code that makes the variable become negative, you've found the problem.

This example is actually pretty trivial compared to some situations I've encountered. Still, though, it shows you how to implement the assume-nothing approach to debugging.

4

Tip

Use the assume-nothing approach to debugging as a last resort. It takes the most time but is the most systematic when you need to find an error that's difficult to uncover.

Good Design Can Prevent the Need for Debugging

You now know how to use the Visual J++ debugger. These skills will help you get the most out of the debugger. But there's more to debugging than knowing which key to press and which window to watch. You need to develop a systematic approach to debugging programs. A random or haphazard technique will waste time and produce intermittent results.

Design Your Program Carefully

It might sound strange to talk about program design in a chapter about debugging. But if you think about it, it's not strange at all. A properly designed program will prevent more bugs than you'll ever know and will make the debugging process easier when the need arises.

If you're a software developer in a company that has several developers, somewhere along the way someone will reuse some of your code or inherit your project. That person will have no chance of understanding your program, especially when it comes to debugging, if it's not properly designed.

Organize Your Program Well

Principle number one: organize your program into easily understood chunks. I once took over a project from a developer who was long gone from the company. He used a method named `redrawScreen()`. This is easy enough to understand. My guess at first glance was that this method redraws all information on the screen. I couldn't have been more wrong. Although the first couple of lines redrew the screen, the rest of the huge method did stuff such as checking a user's database connection, calculating variables that had nothing to do with the screen redraw, and checking the state of some hardware peripherals.

This method should have never included anything except the screen redraw code because it was called `redrawScreen()`. The extra couple of minutes it would have taken the programmer to create separate methods for the unrelated code would have been well worth it. Not only would he have had an easier time debugging the program, but I would have had an easier time understanding it as well.

I'm not just whining to have an easier time. When a program is easier to debug, it saves time. And this translates into a monetary value for the employers of software developers. Anything a developer can do to save time in the long run is good. I know what the pressure of a deadline is like. But don't use sloppy techniques, even if something is due tomorrow.

Let's take a look at a simple example. Consider the following code:

```
int m_nVolts, m_nAmps = 2, m_nOhms = 200;
int m_nSpeed, m_nDistance = 120, m_nTime = 2;
double m_dKinetic, m_dMass = 5.0, m_dVelocity = 3.0;

public void mainProgram()
{

    // Do stuff here.

    calculateStuff();

    // Do stuff here.

}
public void calculateStuff()
{

    // Calculate volts.
    m_nVolts = m_nOhms * m_nAmps;

    // Calculate speed.
    m_nSpeed = m_nDistance / m_nTime;

    // Calculate kinetic energy.
    m_dKinetic =
        ( m_dMass * m_dVelocity * m_dVelocity ) / 2;

}
```

The main program code calls a single method, which then makes three different calculations. This is a simple example, so it might appear okay on the surface. But consider how it would look if the three calculations were complicated, maybe a hundred lines of code each. And what if this program wasn't the trivial example that it is, but instead a program of ten thousand lines of code?

Your program all of a sudden develops a problem. It's incorrectly calculating kinetic energy. To debug this, you have to step into the `calculateStuff()` method. Now, instead of strictly debugging the kinetic energy calculations, you're mixed up with two other calculations.

The situation gets even more mixed up when you declare local variables, maybe just some temporary counter and scratch variables, and use them for all three calculations. There's a principle of object-oriented programming called encapsulation. It's one of the cornerstones of object-oriented programming. In a strict sense, encapsulation means separating the implementation details from the abstraction. This is what we want to do— separate the three calculations so that they are by themselves. This technique makes them easier to understand and far easier to debug.

The following change to the preceding poorly designed example follows:

```
int m_nVolts, m_nAmps = 2, m_nOhms = 200;
int m_nSpeed, m_nDistance = 120, m_nTime = 2;
double m_dKinetic, m_dMass = 5.0, m_dVelocity = 3.0;

public void mainProgram()
{

    // Do stuff here.

    calculateVolts();
    calculateSpeed();
    calculateKinetic();

    // Do stuff here.

}

public void calculateVolts()
{

    // Calculate volts.
    m_nVolts = m_nOhms * m_nAmps;

}

public void calculateSpeed()
{

    // Calculate speed.
    m_nSpeed = m_nDistance / m_nTime;

}

public void calculateKinetic()
{

    // Calculate kinetic energy.
    m_dKinetic =
        ( m_dMass * m_dVelocity * m_dVelocity ) / 2;

}
```

Make Each Class and Method Easy to Understand

Sure, you're the programmer—you're going to understand. But how about the poor guy six months from now who gets assigned a modification to your program? Do you want him to have to come to you for explanations? Or, how about you yourself six months from now? If you're anything like me, in six months you've worked on so many other things that you've forgotten many of the details regarding how the project works.

Here's how you can avoid the problem: make every class, every method, and every variable easy to understand. Just how are you going to do that? Here's a list of suggestions:

- Name methods according to exactly what they do. A method that performs screen updates should be named updateScreen(). If it does another thing such as make a beep sound, rename the method to updateScreenAndBeep().

- Name variables according to exactly what they're for. A variable that holds the count of the number of times the user has clicked the left mouse button should be named leftMouseButtonClicks. If it's an integer (which it should be), it should be named nLeftMouseButtonClicks. If it's a member variable, it should be named m_ nLeftMouseButtonClicks.

- Add source-code comments whenever it's necessary to understand the code. I don't mean only if it's necessary for you to understand the code right after you've written it. I mean if you think that anyone who looks at your code would have trouble understanding it. Furthermore, I've had many instances in which I was working on a difficult method that I just couldn't get right. I've found that if I started adding source-code comments as I went, my thinking process cleared up and the method was much easier to write.

- Indent your source code so that it's easy to see how the logic flows. For instance, after an if statement, all source code should be indented an additional tab until the end of what's contained in the if clause.

Read Your Source Code and Simulate It Mentally

Before you run the debugger, run your mental debugger. It's far better for you to discover the problem by following the program's execution. You can simulate what the program does in your mind and follow the code just as if you were running the debugger.

Why would this approach be better than running the debugger? Because you gain more value as the developer by mentally simulating the execution of the program. You can better understand exactly how the code works when you follow the code through in your mind.

The next thing you must do is watch the variables. Be aware of their initial values and where their values change. Keep tabs on the more important ones, especially the ones you suspect are involved in the unwanted behavior.

Summary

In this chapter, you've learned what a debugger is and why it's so important to software development. You've learned how the Visual J++ debugger works.

The navigation commands such as Step Into and Step Over are important things to know when you use the debugger, and they were all covered. The debug windows are important too, and familiarity with them is essential to good debugging.

Effective debugging techniques were discussed. Besides knowing how to use the debugger, you need to know how to think through the processes.

Q&A

Q How can you make sure that a project has been compiled for debugging?

A Go to the Build, Build Configuration menu item. Make sure that Debug is selected. If you're not sure whether all the modules have been compiled for debugging, select Build, Rebuild so that all the modules are recompiled.

Q How can you step through a program with the debugger?

A You can use several different commands. The Step Into command (F11) lets you step through source code one line at a time. The Step Over command (F10) lets you step through source code while stepping over any methods that are called.

Q How can you view the contents of variables while debugging?

A The best way is with the Watch window. Class variables and local variables can be added to this window. Variables you've added will display their values (contents) and their types. Local variables are best viewed in the Locals window.

Q What is the Immediate window for?

A This window allows you to evaluate expressions in immediate mode. For example, you might want to see the value of a variable or evaluate an expression with variables. Things such as nMyVariable * 5 can be evaluated.

Q What's in the Call Stack window?

A The Call Stack window displays a list of all active procedures or stack frames for the current thread of execution.

Q How are breakpoints used?

A Breakpoints can be set anywhere in your program. When the debugger gets to a line of source code at which a breakpoint is set, it pauses execution of the program until you stop debugging or continue execution.

Q Why is debugging so important to Visual J++ development?

A Even though you designed the software and wrote the code, you might have missed some important factors that will cause your program to malfunction. This happens to the best of software developers.

Q Are there additional approaches to debugging that haven't been mentioned in this chapter?

A The are probably as many ways to approach debuggings as there are Visual J++ programmers. Although this chapter presented some systematic approaches to debugging, your best bet is to develop your own approach that fits your way of thinking.

Review Exercises

1. Create a program. Declare some global variables and assign them values. Declare some local variables in the `init()` method and assign them some values. Start the debugger and step into the `init()` method. Use the Watch window to view the contents of the variables.

2. Restart the program you created for the first exercise. Step into the `init()` method. In the Immediate window, obtain the value of one of your variables by typing the variable name and then pressing Enter. Then type another variable (making sure it's a number) and multiply it by 5. The Immediate window should correctly evaluate the expression *variable* * 5.

3. Open the LearnToDebug program. Set a breakpoint in the `initForm()` method. Start the program and watch it stop at the breakpoint you set.

DAY 5

Windows

Java has a rich set of classes that help you build graphical user interfaces. You can use these various classes, such as Frames, Panels, Labels, Buttons, TextFields, TextAreas, List boxes, Choice menus, and menus, to construct user interfaces. These classes are grouped into packages, and these packages are all part of what's known as the Abstract Windowing Toolkit (AWT).

The AWT classes provide a platform-independent interface to develop visual programs and graphical user interfaces. For each platform on which Java runs, the AWT components are automatically mapped to the platform's specific components. This mapping enables the user applications to be consistent with other applications running on the specific platform. For instance, a Java user interface on Windows 95 looks the same as other Windows 95 applications. But the same program might look slightly different when it's running on a Macintosh. Today, we'll learn the AWT concepts. Specifically, we'll be talking mostly about the Frame class. We'll cover these topics:

- The Frame class
- A Java class's tutorial
- Class inheritance
- Extending classes

- The super() method
- Frame class events
- Programs that use the Frame class
- The this keyword
- Garbage collection in Java

Creating Windows with the Frame Class

A Frame is a top-level window with a title and a border. Normally, Frame windows appear initially above the main applet window. To create and use a frame requires very little. The following source code shows how to create and show a Frame window:

```
// Declared global to the applet.
Frame m_MyFrame;

// Created in the init() method.
m_MyFrame = new Frame( "MyFrame Window" );
m_MyFrame.setVisible( true );
```

The Frame class actually has two constructors. The one I've used in the preceding example takes one argument—a string. This string becomes the title of the Frame window. The other kind of Frame constructor doesn't take any arguments, and the Frame window won't have a title. However, you can add a title later if you want with the setTitle() method.

One of the problems with the source-code example I just gave is that the size of the Frame window will be a width of 0 and a height of 0. For that reason, it's always a good idea somewhere before the window is made visible to use the setSize() method. The setSize() method lets you specify the width and height of the Frame window that will appear. The following example shows how to use the setSize() method to set a Frame window to have a width of 200 and a height of 200:

```
m_MyFrame.setSize( 200, 200 );
```

INPUT Okay, now it's time to build an entire applet that creates a Frame window and displays it. Listing 5.1 shows a simple applet that creates and displays a Frame window that's titled MyFrame Window.

LISTING 5.1 THE MYFRAMEWINDOW APPLET

```
1    import java.awt.*;
2    import java.applet.*;
3
```

```
4    public class Applet1 extends Applet
5    {
6      Frame m_MyFrame;
7
8        public void init()
9        {
10           m_MyFrame = new Frame( "MyFrame Window" );
11           m_MyFrame.setSize( 200, 200 );
12           m_MyFrame.setVisible( true );
13       }
14
15   }
```

OUTPUT When you compile and run the program, you'll see a Frame window appear as shown in Figure 5.1. Now suppose you want to close the window. Normally, you would click the upper-right corner of the menu or use the system menu to select Close, but the window isn't closed in either case because you haven't yet added the capability to your program to close the window. We'll show you how to do that later today when we talk about frame events.

FIGURE 5.1

This program creates and displays a Frame window.

Note

You might look through the MSDN Help and see methods you might want to use, but they're marked *deprecated*. Deprecated means that these are older Java API methods. In Java 1.1, new methods were introduced to fix interface or implementation bugs. Old deprecated methods will be supported in the short term for Java 1.0, but your programs won't compile. When the browsers find these methods in older applets, they interpret them just fine.

5

There are two methods that belong to the Frame class that you might find useful. The first one is the setResizable() method. This lets you set the resizable flag, which determines whether the frame is resizable. It takes a single argument. The following line of code makes a Frame window nonresizable:

```
m_MyFrame.setResizable( false );
```

Another method you might find useful is the setTitle() method. This changes the title text of the Frame window. One reason why this might be especially useful is that at different times during your program's execution, you might want to change the title on the Frame window to give users different information. The following example shows how to use the setTitle() method to set the title of the Frame window to new text:

```
m_MyFrame.setTitle( "This is a new title!" );
```

If you look through the MSDN online help at the Frame class, you'll notice that it doesn't really have many methods of its own. There are still methods, though, that the Frame class has at its disposal. The reason it has additional methods it can use is that Frame is an extension of Window, Window is an extension of Container, Container is an extension of Component, and Component is an extension of Object. Therefore, the Frame class inherits all methods from these classes above. We'll talk more about inheritance shortly, but for now, we'll go ahead and show you how to set a background color for a Frame class. You can use the following line of code to set the Frame class to red:

```
m_MyFrame.setBackground( Color.red );
```

Note

Sometimes it's confusing to know the difference between a Component's setForeground() method and a Graphics class's setColor() method. First of all, these methods do the same thing. They set the foreground color to the value of a parameter. The difference is in where you use them. If you're trying to set the color of a Component, use the setForeground() method. If you're in a paint() method and you want to draw in a certain color with one of the Graphics class's methods, use the setColor() method.

We'll talk a lot about the Graphics class and the Color class during Day 10, "Fonts and Text," and Day 11, "Drawing." For now, it's important to note that for a Component (or in this case the extended Frame class), you'll use setBackground().

Defining Java Classes

Classes function like blueprints that define the attributes and behaviors that objects have after they've been created or instantiated. When a program creates an object, it creates an instance of an object's class. Therefore, the word *instantiate* is used interchangeably with the word *create* in regard to objects.

NEW TERM   The term *instantiate* means to make an instance of an object's class.

Declaring Classes

The declaration of a class in Java has a specific syntax. The following code describes the full syntax for the declaration of a Java class:

```
[modifiers] class Identifier [extends SuperClass]
    [implements Interface {, Interface}]
{
    class body
}
```

Note

In the preceding code you might notice two unfamiliar terms: extends and implements. These terms are discussed later in this chapter. Note, too, that the items in brackets are optional.

Normally, the classes you create won't have modifiers, and in many cases they won't extend or implement anything. The following example shows you the simplest kind of class declaration, in which we name a class SomeItem, and then put whatever sort of code and data in it that we need:

```
class SomeItem
{
    body of class
}
```

Declaring Instance Variables

Instance variables apply to the individual objects that are instantiated from a class. Instance variables are declared within a class definition but outside the body of any methods. An instance variable can be of any type and can be initialized in its declaration. The following code declares the m strType and m_nLength instance variables:

```
class SomeItem
{
    String m_strType = "Lamp Shade";
    int m_nLength = 100;

}
```

If not explicitly initialized, instance variables are assigned default initial values: 0 for number types, false for booleans, and null for objects. To make an instance variable constant, you start its declaration with the keyword final. Any final variables must be initialized. The following code declares the m_strType and the m_nLength variables as final:

```
class SomeItem
{
    final String m_strType = "Lamp Shade";
    final int m_nLength = 100;

}
```

Notice that if either one of these `final` variables were not initialized, the compiler would generate an error.

 Tip

> Many Visual J++ programmers are also Visual C++ programmers. If you're going to be programming in C++ as well as J++, remember to initialize variables you declare in both languages. This is good programming practice, and it helps to ensure that you don't forget to initialize your C++ variables. Because C++ does not initialize variables for you, the habit of explicitly initializing variables can save you a lot of debugging time.

Using Class Variables

Class variables are similar to instance variables except that they apply to all the objects instantiated from a class. Only one value per each class value can exist, regardless of how many objects have been created. Class variables exist even if no instances of a class exist. They are the equivalent of static members in C++. Not surprisingly, class variables are declared using the `static` modifier. The following example shows how to declare a static string. This string will be the same for all instantiations of this class.

```
class SomeItem
{
    static String m_strType = "Lamp Shade";
    final int m_nLength = 100;

}
```

A static variable can be accessed via its class name, as shown in the following line of code:

```
SomeItem.m_strType = "Other Lamp Shade";
```

Declaring Methods

All class methods, except for constructors, must have a return type. This return type can be of any fundamental data type or object. Methods that don't return anything must be declared with a return type of `void`. The following code describes the syntax for the declaration of a Java method:

```
ReturnType MethodName( type arg1, type arg2. ... )
{
    body of the method
}
```

Java class methods can have an optional parameter list. The parameter list records type and name pairs separated by commas. All parameter passing in Java is done by value.

> **Note**
>
> When objects are passed to a method, a value representing the object's reference is passed. This process makes it possible for the target method to modify the contents of the object. It is very important to remember, however, that you can't change the value of a fundamental data type, such as int or float, in the target method.

I've created a class that has two methods. The first method takes one argument that is an integer. It returns an integer. The second method takes two strings as arguments. It puts them together and returns a string that's a combination of the two strings that were passed in. The class I've created with these two methods is shown here:

```
class SomeItem
{
    int m_nMultiplier = 15;

    // This method takes one integer argument and returns an integer.
    public int getMultiple( int nNumber )
    {

        return( m_nMultiplier * nNumber );

    }

    // This method takes two Strings as arguments and returns a String.
    public String concatenate( String strOne, String strTwo )
    {
        String strEntire;

        strEntire = strOne + strTwo;

        return( strEntire );
    }


}
```

5

Overloading Methods

In Java, overloaded methods can be defined with the same name, but the methods must have different parameter lists. This is known as method overloading. Methods can be overloaded by the type or number of their parameters. Overloading a return type is not supported. When a method is invoked, Java tries to match the method name and parameter list used in the call with the predefined version of the method. I've created a new class called SomeOtherItem. It has two methods, both of which are named concatenates. The first of these takes two strings as arguments. It combines them and returns the entire string as the return type. The second concatenate() method takes two arguments; but whereas the first one is a still a string, the second one is an integer. The method then takes both of these and combines them into a single string and returns that string. When you're using this class and you call the concatenate() method and pass it two strings, it already knows which of these two methods to use. If you call a concatenate() method and you have the first argument as a string and the second argument as an integer, again it knows which of these two methods to call and will use the appropriate method.

The following class shows two concatenate() methods that are overloaded:

```
class SomeOtherItem
{

    // This method takes two Strings as arguments and returns a String.
    public String concatenate( String strOne, String strTwo )
    {
        String strEntire;

        strEntire = strOne + strTwo;

        return( strEntire );

    }

    public String concatenate( String strOne, int nTwo )
    {
        String strEntire;

        strEntire = strOne + nTwo;

        return( strEntire );

    }

}
```

Declaring Constructors

When you declare a class in Java, you can declare constructors for the class. Constructors are methods that perform the required initializations for each new instance of a class. Java constructor methods have the same name as the class to which they belong. They don't return anything. They can take zero or more parameters, and they can be overloaded. Pretty cool, huh?

Constructors are used to ensure that all new objects are created in a valid initial state. Because Java objects are always created from the heap, object constructors are called only in conjunction with a new keyword. In fact, it is illegal to call a constructor at any time other than when creating an object with a new keyword.

For example, the following code shows a legal constructor call, and an illegal constructor call:

```
SomeOtherItem Item;

Item = new SomeOtherItem(); // SomeOtherItem()
[ccc]constructor is called here legally.

Item.SomeOtherItem(); // SomeOtherItem()
[ccc]constructor is called illegally here.
```

All Java classes have constructors. If you do not declare a constructor, the compiler automatically creates a default constructor for you. Java guarantees that all data members are initialized as we said before, and that all uninitialized data members are assigned default values.

Constructors can call other constructors in the same class, or constructors in its superclass. Calls to other constructors must be the first statement in any constructor. If no other constructor of the superclass is invoked, the default constructor of the superclass is called automatically. We'll talk a little bit more about the super() method later.

Creating and Destroying Objects

You can create an object in Java by placing the new keyword in front of a call to the object's class constructor. This operation allocates memory for the object, calls the constructor that follows the new keyword, and returns a reference to the newly created and initialized object. The Java environment keeps track of all memory allocations and automatically frees memory when a resource is no longer needed. You never need to delete an object's memory as you do in other languages.

Comparing Objects

Java provides two operators for comparing objects: the equality (==) and the inequality (!=). These operators test whether two object references refer to the same object. Because Java does not have an operator overloading function, you can't change the behavior of the equality operators. If you want to compare the contents of two objects, you have to write a method of your own to perform this function. The Java Object class, from which most of your classes will be extended, provides an equals method you can override. The Object class's equals() method compares two object references, like the equality operator.

Copying Objects

The Java Object class provides a clone() method that can be used to create copies of objects. The default implementation of this method creates a clone by performing a bitwise copy of the original object. This bitwise copy might or might not be the appropriate thing to do for any given class.

NEW TERM   A *bitwise* copy of an object is allocated and then copied bit by bit. Although a completely new object is created, the original object is copied, including its references to other objects.

Cloning objects that contain only pure data types is simple. You must be careful, however, when cloning objects that reference other objects. The default clone() method does not make copies of the referenced objects. The cloned object references the same objects that are referenced by the original object.

Using Inheritance

Java supports inheritance, the capability of a class to inherit attributes and behaviors from its parent, or superclass. The extends keyword is used to establish an inheritance relationship between a subclass and a superclass. We're going to start this section with a simple example. I've created an entire applet. Within this applet is the declaration for a class called Shape. The Shape class has three methods. The first method, the draw() method, simply draws just the shape. The second method, the setPosition() method, takes two integer arguments: the new x and y positions for the shape. The third method, the movePosition() method, takes two arguments: the distance to move the x coordinate, and the distance to move the y coordinate. Listing 5.2 shows this applet, and Figure 5.2 shows this applet running.

INPUT **LISTING 5.2** THE SHAPE APPLET

```
1    import java.awt.*;
2    import java.applet.*;
3
4    public class Applet1 extends Applet
5    {
6        // Declare and create the Shape object.
7        Shape m_Shape = new Shape();
8
9        // The applet's paint method in which the Shape
10       // draw method will be called.
11       public void paint( Graphics g )
12       {
13           m_Shape.draw( g );
14       }
15
16       // The Shape class.
17       public class Shape
18       {
19           // Declare and initialize the x and y coordinates.
20           int m_nX = 20, m_nY = 20;
21
22           public void draw( Graphics g )
23           {
24               // Set for red.
25               g.setColor( Color.red );
26               // Draw a rectangle at m_nX, m_nY.
27               g.drawRect( m_nX, m_nY, 50, 30 );
28               // Set for green.
29               g.setColor( Color.green );
30               // Draw an oval at m_nX, m_nY.
31               g.drawOval( m_nX, m_nY, 50, 30 );
32           }
33
34           public void setPosition( int x, int y )
35           {
36               // Set the x position.
37               m_nX = x;
38               // Set the y position.
39               m_nY = y;
40           }
41
42           public void movePosition( int dx, int dy )
43           {
44               // Move the x position.
45               m_nX += dx;
46               // Move the y position.
47               m_nY += dy;
```

5

continues

LISTING 5.2 CONTINUED

```
48              }
49          }
50
51      }
```

OUTPUT

FIGURE 5.2

This applet merely draws a shape to its window.

ANALYSIS Let's talk about the nitty-gritty details of this applet, because we're going to be using this to learn about inheritance. It's important that you understand everything in the applet. Line 7 is the declaration and creation of the Shape object. This object can be used anywhere in the Applet1 class, but we use it just in the paint() method.

Line 13 simply calls the Shape object's draw() method. Because all the attribute data (position, color, and so on) is encapsulated in the Shape class, the draw() method doesn't need anything more than the Graphics class. The shape() method already knows how to draw and knows where to draw.

Line 17 is where the Shape class declaration starts. Notice that in line 20, two variables are declared and assigned a value of 20 so that the shape will draw by default to a position at (20,20).

At line 22, the draw() method begins. It takes a single argument, as we said before, which is the Graphics class to which it will draw. Line 25 sets the drawing color to red. Line 27 draws a rectangle. Notice that the rectangle is drawn to the x and y coordinates that were initialized to 20. The rectangle it draws has a width of 50 and a height of 30. At line 29, the drawing color is set to green. At line 31, an oval is drawn that will be inside of a bounding rectangle—the same as the rectangle drawn in line 27. At line 34, the setPosition() method begins. This is a really straightforward method that simply sets the class's x and y position to a new x and y position that is passed in. At line 42, the movePosition() method starts. This is different from the setPosition() method because you can move a shape over or downward, relative to its current position. For instance, if you input movePosition(5,5), the object would be moved 5 pixels to the right of its current position, and 5 pixels down from its current position. That's pretty much all you need to know about this applet and the Shape class. Now, onward and upward!

We're going to add another class to the applet we created. This class, though, will be an extension of the Shape class. We'll name the new class BetterShape. After line 49 in the applet, we're going to add the new class. The source code for the new class follows:

```
public class BetterShape extends Shape
{

    public void centerShape()
    {
        Dimension dm = getSize();
        int nNewX, nNewY;
        nNewX = ( dm.width / 2 ) - 25;
        nNewY = ( dm.height / 2 ) - 15;
        setPosition( nNewX, nNewY );
    }
}
```

Because the new BetterShape class extends the Shape class, it gets all the methods and attributes of the Shape class. For instance, although you can't see a draw() method in the declaration of the BetterShape class, it has one. It has one because it extends the Shape class, which already has a draw() method.

We're now going to go back to the applet, and at line 7, where we declare a Shape object, we'll change that to a BetterShape object. We also have to let the operator know what kind of object we're creating: a BetterShape object. The following line of code shows how we'll change the applet so that instead of a Shape object, we're creating a BetterShape object:

```
BetterShape m_Shape = new BetterShape();
```

If you compile and run this applet, it won't look any different than when you compiled it and ran it before. That's because, for all practical purposes, nothing has changed except that the BetterShape class has one extra method that the Shape class does not have. That extra method is the centerShape() method.

Because the BetterShape object extends the Shape object, it not only has its own new method, which is the centerShape() method, but also has everything the Shape class has to offer. We're going to make a simple change to the applet now that will utilize the centerShape() method. In the applet, find line 13. Before line 13, insert a call to the BetterShape object's centerShape() method. The following line of source code shows how to do it:

```
m_Shape.centerShape();
```

Now, when you run your applet, the shape will be centered inside the applet's window as shown in Figure 5.3. Every time you resize the applet window, the shape will center itself within the applet window, no matter what the size of the applet window.

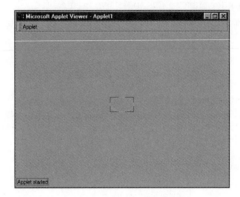

Using the `Super()` Method

In Java terminology, the existing class is called the superclass. The class derived or extended from the superclass is called the subclass. Sometimes a superclass is referred to as a parent class, or a base class, and a subclass is referred to as a child class, an extending class, or a derived class. You can reuse or change the methods of superclasses. You can add new data and new methods in the subclasses. Subclasses usually have more functionality than their superclasses.

The `super()` method refers to the superclass of a class in which the `super()` method appears. This method can be used in two ways: to call a superclass constructor or to call a superclass method.

Calling Superclass Constructors

The syntax to call a superclass constructor is as follows:

```
super( parameters );
```

In the `BetterShape` class, for example, the `super()` method can be used to call the `Shape` class's constructor. Anytime you use the `super()` method in the constructor, it has to appear in the first line of the constructor, and it is the only way to invoke a superclass's constructor.

Caution Java requires the super() method to appear first in the constructor, even before data fields. It also requires using the keyword super to call the superclass's constructor.

Calling Superclass Methods

The keyword super can be used to reference a method other than the constructor in the superclass. The syntax can look like this:

```
super.method( parameters );
```

It is not always necessary to use the super keyword if you're calling one of the superclass's methods. If the subclass does not have a method matching the same name, all you have to do is call the superclass method you want to use. If, however, both the superclass and the subclass have methods of the same name, don't worry. From within the subclass method (or anywhere, really), you can make a call to the superclass's method by inputting super.method() as shown in the preceding example.

Calling with the `this` Keyword

The keyword super is used to reference superclasses. Occasionally, you need to reference the current class. Java provides another keyword, this, for referencing the current object. Use of the this keyword is analogous to use of super. For instance, in the preceding section we talked about calling super.method. You can also call this.method(), or you can access this.method() to call methods in the current class. The following syntax line shows how to use the this keyword to call a method in the current class:

```
this.method( parameters );
```

5

Creating a Program That Uses an Extended Frame Class

We're going to keep things simple! We're going to create an applet that declares a class called MyFrame. The MyFrame class is extended from the Frame class. It doesn't do anything more than add its own paint() method. You can use this paint() method, then, to draw anything you want in the Frame window. The source-code listing for this applet is given in Listing 5.3. You can see the applet running in Figure 5.4. Note that if you look at the figure, you'll see two windows: the Main applet window and the Frame window, which is above the applet window.

INPUT   LISTING 5.3   THE MYFRAME APPLET

```
1    import java.awt.*;
2    import java.applet.*;
3
4    public class Applet1 extends Applet
5    {
6        // Declare and create the MyFrame object.
7        MyFrame m_MyFrame = new MyFrame( "My Frame" );
8
9        public void init()
10       {
11           // Set the size of the window.
12           m_MyFrame.setSize( 200, 200 );
13           // Make the window visible.
14           m_MyFrame.setVisible( true );
15       }
16
17       public void paint( Graphics g )
18       {
19           // Draw to the applet window.
20           g.drawString( "Drawing to the applet", 20, 20 );
21       }
22   // Declare a new class that extends the Frame class.
23       public class MyFrame extends Frame
24       {
25           public MyFrame( String s )
26           {
27               // Call the Frame constructor.
28               super( s );
29           }
30
31           public void paint( Graphics g )
32           {
33               // Draw to the Frame window.
34               g.drawString( "Drawing to the frame", 20, 50 );
35           }
36
37       }
38
39   }
```

Listening for Frame Class Events

Earlier today, we talked about the problem of the Frame window not closing when you
clicked the Close button. To respond to events such as the user clicking the Close button,
we must create a class inside of the Frame class that will listen for such events. The class

we create will extend the WindowAdapter class. (And you were wondering why we spent time today talking about classes and how to extend them!) After we declare this, we can override the windowClosing() method and do whatever we want, which is to close our window. Now the last step! Inside of the Frame class's constructor, call the addWindowListener() method and add the extended WindowAdapter class.

OUTPUT

FIGURE 5.4

An applet that's using an extended Frame *class.*

These are the steps necessary to listen for frame window events:

1. In your Frame subclass, declare a class that extends the WindowAdapter class.
2. In the WindowAdapter class, override any methods you want to respond to.
3. Somewhere in the Frame subclass, use the addWindowListener() method to add your new class so that it will receive messages as they come in.

Seven different events are available to you when you have a class that's extended from the WindowAdapter class. They are windowActivated(), windowClosed(), windowClosing(), windowDeactivated(), windowDeiconified(), windowIconified(), and windowOpening() methods. Table 5.1 shows you all these methods.

TABLE 5.1 THE WindowAdapter CLASS'S EVENTS

Name	Description
windowActivated()	This event is triggered when the window gets the focus.
windowClosed()	This event is fired after the window is closed.
windowClosing()	This event is triggered in response to a user's request to close a window, such as clicking the Close button.
windowDeactivated()	This event is triggered when the window loses the focus.
windowDeiconified()	This event is not available on all platforms. It's triggered when users attempt to minimize the window.

continues

TABLE 5.1   CONTINUED

Name	Description
windowIconified()	This method is also not available on all platforms. It's triggered when users attempt to unminimize the window.
windowOpening()	This event is triggered when a window is first opened.

You need to remember one more thing when you're trying to get events from Frame windows. You need to import Java.AWT.event (line 3 in Listing 5.4). To create the example in Listing 5.4, I simply took the preceding example and followed the three steps for event handling. Notice that in line 3, I imported Java.AWT.event. Also notice that in line 32, I made a call to the addWindowListener() method. This is what actually adds the WindowListening class to the event cue. Now look at line 42. This is where my WindowListening class begins. The only method I'm listening for is the windowClosing() method, which starts at line 45. You can see at line 48 that the window's visibility is set to false, which hides it. Then the applet sets the parent class's m_MyFrame variable to null. Now, when you click the Frame window's Close button, it will actually close.

LISTING 5.4   THE MYFRAME APPLET INCORPORATES THE THREE STEPS FOR HANDLING EVENTS

```
1    import java.awt.*;
2    import java.applet.*;
3    import java.awt.event.*;
4
5    public class Applet1 extends Applet
6    {
7        // Declare and create the MyFrame object.
8        MyFrame m_MyFrame = new MyFrame( "My Frame" );
9
10       public void init()
11       {
12           // Set the size of the window.
13           m_MyFrame.setSize( 200, 200 );
14           // Make the window visible.
15           m_MyFrame.setVisible( true );
16       }
17
18       public void paint( Graphics g )
19       {
20           // Draw to the applet window.
21           g.drawString( "Drawing to the applet", 20, 20 );
22       }
23
24       // Declare a new class that extends the Frame class.
```

```
25      public class MyFrame extends Frame
26      {
27          public MyFrame( String s )
28          {
29              // Call the Frame constructor.
30              super( s );
31
32              addWindowListener( new WL() );
33          }
34
35          public void paint( Graphics g )
36          {
37              // Draw to the Frame window.
38              g.drawString( "Drawing to the frame", 20, 50 );
39          }
40
41          // Our window listener class.
42          public class WL extends WindowAdapter
43          {
44              // Override the windowClosing() method.
45              public void windowClosing( WindowEvent e )
46              {
47                  // Hide the window.
48                  setVisible( false );
49                  // Set the parent class to null.
50                  m_MyFrame = null;
51              }
52          }
53
54      }
55
56  }
```

5

THE Import STATEMENT

The import statement tells the compiler to include existing Java programs in the current program. In the case of the preceding applet, we imported Java.AWT, Java.applet, and Java.AWT.event. You can use the operations in Java.AWT.event in your program instead of rewriting the code. This is an example of software reusability; that is, the program is written once and is used by many other people without being rewritten.

Java code is organized into packages and classes. Classes are inside packages, and packages are libraries of Java code that contain all kinds of operations ready for you to import and use. Java provides standard libraries such as Java.AWT that come with a compiler.

Collecting the Garbage

Previous languages such as Lisp and Smalltalk implemented their languages in such a way that programmers could ignore memory deallocation. The developers of languages such as Lisp and Smalltalk felt that the language should be able to determine what is no longer useful, and get rid of it. In relative obscurity, these pioneering programmers developed a whole series of garbage collectors to perform this job, each getting more sophisticated and efficient as the years went by.

Finally, now that the mainstream programming community has begun to recognize the value of this automated technique, Java can become the first really widespread application from the technology these pioneers developed. Imagine that you're a programmer in a C-like language. Each time you create something dynamically in such a language, you're completely responsible for tracking the life of that object throughout your program, and mentally deciding when it will be safe to deallocate it. This can be quite a difficult task, because any of the other libraries or methods you called might have squirreled away a pointer to the object, unbeknownst to you. When it becomes impossible to know, you simply choose never to deallocate the object, or at least wait until every library and method call involved has completed, which can be nearly as long.

The uneasy feeling you get when writing such code is a natural, healthy response to what is inherently an unsafe and unreliable style of programming. If you have tremendous discipline, you can (in principal) survive this responsibility without too many mishaps, but memory problems are the leading cause of software failure and software bugs today. That's why companies such as NuMega, who published BoundsChecker, make so much money. Their products help programmers track down these memory allocation errors.

Summary

Frame windows are a powerful tool in making programs more flexible and communicative. They can underscore special information you want brought to users' attention, or they can hold information that's somehow different than what's in your main program.

There's just about no end to what you can do with Frame windows if you get creative. Go ahead and do the review exercises to really get up to speed!

Q&A

Q How is a constant variable declared in Java?

A A constant variable is declared as a `final` variable.

Q How do you compare two objects for equality?

A If the object properly implements the `equals()` method, the `equals()` method must be used. The (==) operator can be used, however. This operator only checks to see whether both variables are referencing the same object instance.

Q What can you do with a `Frame` class after you have created it if you have not extended it into your own class?

A Not much! You can use a few of the `Frame` class's methods, such as `setTitle()` and `setSize()`, but you won't be able to intercept any kinds of events or override any of the `Frame` class's methods, such as the `paint()` method.

Q Why is garbage collection in Java so important?

A Because the leading causes of program bugs and program failures are memory allocation and overrun bugs. Not having to worry about deallocating memory saves Visual J++ programmers a huge headache. In addition, it prevents many, many bugs from creeping into their programs.

Q Why would I ever want to overload methods? Why wouldn't I want to just write separate methods that take different parameters?

A The reason is that if methods perform the same functions, they should be named the same thing (for program clarity) even if they do different things. For instance, the `concatenate()` method does the same thing whether it takes two strings or a string and an integer as arguments. The minute you start renaming these methods depending on which arguments they take, you confuse their meaning and make the program less obvious and less straightforward.

Exercises

5

1. Create an applet. In the applet, declare and create a `Frame` class. In the applet's `init()` method, call the Frame's `setVisible()` method, and set the frame visibility to `true`.

2. Create an applet. In the applet, create your own class that extends the `Frame` class. In your extended `Frame` class, declare a constructor that calls the superclass's claim constructor. (If you're unclear on how to do this, refer to the example in Listing 5.3.) After you've done that, add a `paint()` method to your new class. Inside the `paint()` method, display some text at a coordinate of (50,50) so that you know you've actually drawn to your Frame window when the applet runs.

3. Take the applet you just wrote, and inside the extended `Frame` class, create another class that extends the `WindowAdapter` class. Inside this `WindowAdapter` class, add a `windowActivated()` method. Inside the `windowActivated()` method, change the Frame window's text so that every time the window is activated, the Frame window's text changes and you can tell that the Frame window caught the `windowActivated()` event and responded to it.

DAY 6

Menus

Today, you'll learn how to add menus to your programs. The two types of menus I'll teach you to add are pull-down menus and pop-up menus. Menus are different for applets and applications. You'll learn how to add menus for both.

Today you'll learn about the following:

- How to create menus
- How to respond to menu events in applets
- How to perform advanced menu operations, such as disabling menu choices
- How to create menus for applications
- How to respond to menu events in applications
- Advanced menu methods in applications
- A demo program
- How to create and respond to pop-up menus in applets
- How to create pop-up menus and respond to events in applications

Menus are one of the most common user-interface items that programs have. They give users a clear, easy, and understandable way to interact with a program.

Creating Applet Menus

In this section, you'll learn how to create menu bars and menu items for applets. When you do this, though, you need to have created a Frame window. It's to the Frame windows that you'll add the menus. You can't add menu bars to normal applet windows. Before we go too much further, I'd like to review the basic creation and showing of a Frame window, because we'll be using that knowledge throughout this entire section. The following example shows how we'll be creating our Frame windows, setting the size, and then making them invisible. Before we set the size of the Frame window and set it to visible, we'll do all our menu stuff as shown in the source code comment with the init() method.

```
Frame m_Frame = new Frame( "Menu Tester" );

public void init()
{
    // Here's where we'll do our menu creation stuff...

    m_Frame.setSize( 300, 200 );
    m_Frame.setVisible( true );
}
```

The first thing we'll do is to create a MenuBar object. The MenuBar constructor takes no arguments. It simply creates an empty MenuBar object. The following line shows how to do this:

```
MenuBar menu = new MenuBar();
```

After your MenuBar is created, you need to add it to the Frame window using the Frame class's setMenuBar() method. The following example shows how to do that for the MenuBar we just created:

```
m_Frame.setMenuBar( menu );
```

If all you did was create a frame, create an empty menu bar, and then add a MenuBar to the Frame, you wouldn't see a whole lot when you ran your program. In your Frame window where you would normally expect to see a menu bar, you'd see just a thin gray object about three pixels high. That's because there would be nothing in your menu bar—no menu bar items and no menu entries. You can see what I'm talking about in Figure 6.1. Notice that something does appear where the menu bar should be, but it's barely visible.

FIGURE 6.1

The empty menu bar is barely visible.

I'm going to clarify something before we go any further. I will refer to the entire structure that goes along the top of the Frame window as the menu bar (the class that contains
it is the MenuBar class). Each item you see in the menu bar, such as File, Options, or
Actions, I'll call a menu item. Each menu item will contain what I call menu entries. For
instance, if you take a look at your Visual J++ IDE, you'll see the menu bar. In the menu
bar, before you pull down any menu, you'll see the items File, Edit, View, Project, Build,
Debug, Tools, Window, and Help. These are the menu items. When you click on one of
these items, you will see what I'll refer to as menu entries. So if you click on the File
menu item, you'll see the entries New Project, Open Project, Close All, and so forth. If
you click on the Edit menu item, you'll see the menu entries Undo, Redo, Cut/Copy, and
so forth.

Now that we've got the menu bar created, we need to add menu items. To create menu
items ourselves, we use the Menu class. There are three Menu class constructors. The first
constructor takes no arguments. The second one takes an argument with a string that
specifies the label. This is the one we'll be using while we get you up to speed on
menus. The third constructor takes a third argument, which is a Boolean flag that indicates whether the menu is a tear-off menu.

There are two steps, then, to adding menu items to your menu bar: create a Menu object
and then add the Menu object to your menu bar. The following example creates and adds
three menu items to the menu bar:

```
// menu is an already-instantiated MenuBar object
Menu file = new Menu( "File" );
menu.add( file );
Menu options = new Menu( "Options" );
menu.add( options );
Menu actions = new Menu( "Actions" );
menu.add( actions );
```

You might be wondering whether you must add the menu items to your menu bar before
you call the Frame class's setMenuBar() method. The answer is no. You can either create
the menu bar, add all the menu items, and then call the Frame's setMenuBar() method,
or create the menu bar, call the Frame class's setMenuBar() method, and then add all
your menu items. Either way is fine.

6

To complete the picture, we need to add menu entries to our menu items. It's easy to do. You simply use the Menu class's add() method to add the menu entries. The add() method takes a single string argument. This string argument will be the label of your menu entry. There's one other add() method that takes a menu item as an argument. We won't talk about that right now, though. The following example shows the resulting code after we've added menu entries to the three menu items that we created in the preceding step:

```
// menu is an already-instantiated MenuBar object

Menu file = new Menu( "File" );
menu.add( file );
file.add( "Open" );
file.add( "Close" );

Menu options = new Menu( "Options" );
menu.add( options );
options.add( "Set to Red" );
options.add( "Set to Green" );
options.add( "Set to Blue" );

Menu actions = new Menu( "Actions" );
menu.add( actions );
actions.add( "Go Home" );
actions.add( "Go to Work" );
```

After we've added the menu entries, the program will look complete. The menu bar will have the three menu items, and each menu item will have menu entries. You can see the program running in Figure 6.2.

FIGURE 6.2

With the menu items and the menu entries added, this program looks complete.

The following steps sum up how to create and add menus to frame windows:

1. Create a MenuBar object.

2. For each menu item, create a Menu object and use the MenuBar's add() method to add this Menu object.

3. For each Menu object, add the menu entries with the add() method.

4. Use the Frame class's setMenuBar() method to add the populated menu bar to the frame window.

Handling Applet Menu Events

The biggest problem with everything we've talked about so far is that we haven't mentioned menu events or handled them. This section discusses how to handle menu events so that we can perform many tasks that our program requires when a user makes a menu selection.

The first thing we need to do even before handling the menu events is handle the frame event when the user tries to close the frame. In the preceding chapter, the way we solved this problem was to create a new Frame class that extended the Frame class. In this new Frame class, we created a new class that extended the WindowAdapter class. Inside of the extended WindowAdapter class, we could then handle the window closing event. For more details, either review Day 5, "Windows," or wait until we do the analysis of Listing 6.1.

To handle the menu events, we first need to create a class that implements the ActionListener interface. Then, inside this new class, we add the actionPerformed() method. The actionPerformed() method is where all the menu events will come when a menu event has been triggered. The following example shows our new class that implements the ActionListener interface, and how it contains an actionPerformed() method that lets us handle the menu events:

```
public class MyListener implements ActionListener
{
    public void actionPerformed( ActionEvent ae )
    {
        if( ae.getSource() instanceof MenuComponent )
        {
            // Handle your menu events here…
        }
    }
}
```

Using a Menu in an Applet

I've created an entire program that simply creates a Frame object and then creates a menu that's added to this frame. To keep things simple and recognizable, I use all the previous examples to build this program. See Listing 6.1.

INPUT   **LISTING 6.1**   AN APPLET THAT USES A MENU IN A FRAME WINDOW

```
1    import java.awt.*;
2    import java.applet.*;
3    import java.awt.event.*;
```

continues

LISTING 6.1   CONTINUED

```
4
5    public class Applet1 extends Applet
6    {
7
8        // Create the MyFrame object.
9        MyFrame m_Frame = new MyFrame( "Menu Tester" );
10
11       Label m_lLabel = new Label( "No actions..." );
12
13       public void init()
14       {
15           m_Frame.add( m_lLabel );
16
17           MyListener Listener = new MyListener();
18
19           // Create the MenuBar object.
20           MenuBar menu = new MenuBar();
21
22           // Create the file Menu object and add menu entries.
23           Menu file = new Menu( "File" );
24           menu.add( file );
25           file.add( "Open" );
26           file.add( "Close" );
27           file.addActionListener( Listener );
28
29           // Create the options Menu object and add menu entries.
30           Menu options = new Menu( "Options" );
31           menu.add( options );
32           options.add( "Set to Red" );
33           options.add( "Set to Green" );
34           options.add( "Set to Blue" );
35           options.addActionListener( Listener );
36
37           // Create the actions Menu object and add menu entries.
38           Menu actions = new Menu( "Actions" );
39           menu.add( actions );
40           actions.add( "Go Home" );
41           actions.add( "Go to Work" );
42           actions.addActionListener( Listener );
43
44           // Use the setMenuBar() method to tell the Frame
45           // class what MenuBar to use.
46           m_Frame.setMenuBar( menu );
47
48           // Set the Frame size and make it visible.
49           m_Frame.setSize( 300, 200 );
50           m_Frame.setVisible( true );
```

```
51
52          }
53
54          public class MyListener implements ActionListener
55          {
56              public void actionPerformed( ActionEvent ae )
57              {
58                  if( ae.getSource() instanceof MenuComponent )
59                  {
60                      m_lLabel.setText( "The '" + ae.getActionCommand()
                        ➥+ "' menu entry was selected." );
61                  }
62              }
63          }
64
65          public class MyFrame extends Frame
66          {
67              MyFrame( String s )
68              {
69                  super( s );
70
71                  // Add the extended WindowAdapter class.
72                  addWindowListener( new WL() );
73              }
74
75              // Our window listener class.
76              public class WL extends WindowAdapter
77              {
78                  // Override the windowClosing() method.
79                  public void windowClosing( WindowEvent e )
80                  {
81                      // Hide the window.
82                      setVisible( false );
83                      // Set the parent class to null.
84                      m_Frame = null;
85                  }
86              }
87          }
88  }
```

OUTPUT When the program runs, the label will inform you that no action has taken place so far. Every time you make a menu selection, however, the label will reflect the menu selection you have made. You can see the program running in Figure 6.3.

FIGURE 6.3

*This program shows
you which menu entry
you've selected.*

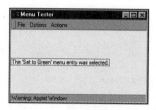

ANALYSIS Let's discuss this program's source code now. To make the explanations more
clear, I don't always cover things in sequential order.

At line 9, I create a frame window. The frame is not built from a straight Frame class; it's
built from my extended Frame class beginning at line 65. If you skip down to line 65,
you'll see a class declared called MyFrame that extends Frame. Notice that there's a single
constructor that takes a string. This constructor first calls the super() and then calls the
addWindowListener() method so that the frame window will get window messages. In
the MyFrame class at line 76, you'll see that we declare a class named WL that extends the
WindowAdapter class. At line 79 we override the windowClosing() method to catch any
window closing events. If you want to handle other window events, you then have to add
other methods. Examples of other window events you might want to handle would be
windowActivated() and windowOpened(). For more information on additional window
events you can handle, refer to Day 5.

Now look back up to line 17. This is where we create the listener. The listener is what
we'll use to catch the menu events. Notice, though, that we don't use a standard
ActionListener interface; we have to declare a class that implements the
ActionListener interface. If you'll look at line 54, you can see a very short class named
MyListener that implements the ActionListener class. At line 56, you'll see that we've
overridden the actionPerformed() method. It's here that the program will come when a
menu event is triggered.

Now back to line 20. Here, we create our MenuBar object. In lines 23–27, we create our
File menu, add the File menu to the MenuBar object, add two menu entries (the Open and
Close entries), and add the newly created Listener class to this Menu object. Lines
30–35 do the same thing for the Options menu. The Options menu is created, it's added
to the MenuBar object, its menu entries are added, and then it's told about the
ActionListener. The last operations in the menu creation area (lines 38–42) create and
add the Actions menu. You'll see at line 46 that we use the Frame class's setMenuBar()
method to add the MenuBar object to the frame window. Finally, at lines 49 and 50, we
set the frame window's size and make it visible. After that, throughout the program for
every menu event that is handled, at line 60 we set the label text to reflect the menu
value of the menu item that has been selected.

Creating Menus in Applications

It's a lot easier to create menus in applications than it is to create menus in applets. The reason is that all you have to do in an application is select the Menu control and place it on your form.

When you first put the Menu control on your form window, it will appear at the top of the form window, and you'll see the text Type Here where the first menu item will go. This is shown in Figure 6.4.

FIGURE 6.4

This form shows an empty menu control that has been added.

It took me a while to get good at editing the menu item text and the menu entries. Where it says, Type Here, click the mouse and you can type the menu item text. If you press either Tab or the right-arrow key, the focus goes to the next menu item, and you can then type the text for that menu item. If you want to go ahead after you've typed the menu item text and type the menu entries, you'll notice that below each menu item for which you've entered text, you'll see a Type Here label. If you just select that and type your menu entry, the menu entry will be created with whatever text you type. This would be a really good time for you to create an application and put a Menu control on the application's form to practice adding menu items, adding menu entries, and then going back to edit them. Adding a blank Menu control to your form doesn't add very much code to it—in fact, it adds only two lines of code. The following line shows how I added a Menu control to my form and created the Menu control:

```
MainMenu mainMenu1 = new MainMenu();
```

Then, the Menu control added the menu to the form. The following example shows how the Menu control added the menu to the form:

```
this.setMenu(mainMenu1);
```

If, however, you add all the menu items and menu entries, a significant amount of code is added to your program. Including the two lines of code I just showed you, by adding

6

three menu items having two, three, and two entries respectively, I added 36 lines of code to my form's source code. When my program runs, it doesn't look much different than the previous program I created that was an applet. Figure 6.5 shows my form with a functioning menu that has been added.

FIGURE 6.5

This program shows a form with a functioning menu added.

Adding Menu Events in Applications

Adding event-handler methods to applications for menu entries is very easy. To do this, select the menu entry you want to generate an event handler for. You do this in the Form window by just single-clicking on the menu entry. In the Properties window, be sure that it's set to events. You do this by clicking the button that has the lightning bolt on it. You'll see three events. The first event is the click event. This is triggered when the menu event is selected. The pop-up event is triggered before the containing menu is displayed. The select event, which is the one you'll be interested in, is triggered when the menu event is selected. With the menu entry for which you want to generate the event selected, double-click on the select event. An event handler for that menu goes immediately to the source code for that handler.

This is how you add event handlers for application menu entries:

1. Make sure that the Form window is in view.

2. Select the menu entry you want to generate an event for by single-clicking on it.

3. Make sure that the Properties window is set for events. Do this by clicking the event button.

4. Double-click on the select event and the handler will be created. You'll immediately see the source code for the handler after you've done this.

Presenting a Sample Application Program

I've taken all the previous examples for applications' menus and created a sample program. This program performs exactly what the applet program performed. There are three menu items: File, Options, and Actions. Each one of them has some menu entries. The program then responds to the menu event and displays text in a label so that you know which menu entry was selected.

INPUT   The program's source code is shown in Listing 6.2.

LISTING 6.2   A SIMPLE PROGRAM THAT USES A MENU AND RESPONDS TO MENU EVENTS

```
1    import com.ms.wfc.app.*;
2    import com.ms.wfc.core.*;
3    import com.ms.wfc.ui.*;
4    import com.ms.wfc.html.*;
5
6    /**
7     * This class can take a variable number of parameters on the command
8     * line. Program execution begins with the main() method. The class
9     * constructor is not invoked unless an object of type 'Form1' is
10    * created in the main() method.
11    */
12   public class Form1 extends Form
13   {
14       public Form1()
15       {
16           // Required for Visual J++ Form Designer support
17           initForm();
18
19           // TODO: Add any constructor code after initForm call
20       }
21
22       /**
23        * Form1 overrides dispose so it can clean up the
24        * component list.
25        */
26       public void dispose()
27       {
28           super.dispose();
29           components.dispose();
30       }
31
32       private void menuItem4_click(Object source, Event e)
33       {
34           label1.setText( "File/Open was selected" );
35       }
36
```

continues

6

LISTING 6.2   CONTINUED

```
37      private void menuItem5_click(Object source, Event e)
38      {
39          label1.setText( "File/Close was selected" );
40      }
41
42      private void menuItem6_click(Object source, Event e)
43      {
44          label1.setText( "Options/Set to Red was selected" );
45      }
46
47      private void menuItem7_click(Object source, Event e)
48      {
49          label1.setText( "Options/Set to Green was selected" );
50      }
51
52    private void menuItem8_click(Object source, Event e)
53      {
54          label1.setText( "Options/Set to Blue was selected" );
55      }
56
57      private void menuItem9_click(Object source, Event e)
58      {
59          label1.setText( "Actions/Go Home was selected" );
60      }
61
62      private void menuItem10_click(Object source, Event e)
63      {
64          label1.setText( "Action/Go to Work was selected" );
65      }
66
67      /**
68       * NOTE: The following code is required by the Visual J++ form
69       * designer. It can be modified using the form editor. Do not
70       * modify it using the code editor.
71       */
72      Container components = new Container();
73      MainMenu mainMenu1 = new MainMenu();
74      MenuItem menuItem1 = new MenuItem();
75      MenuItem menuItem2 = new MenuItem();
76      MenuItem menuItem3 = new MenuItem();
77      MenuItem menuItem4 = new MenuItem();
78      MenuItem menuItem5 = new MenuItem();
79      MenuItem menuItem6 = new MenuItem();
80      MenuItem menuItem7 = new MenuItem();
81      MenuItem menuItem8 = new MenuItem();
82      MenuItem menuItem9 = new MenuItem();
83      MenuItem menuItem10 = new MenuItem();
84      Label label1 = new Label();
```

```
85
86      private void initForm()
87      {
88          menuItem4.setText("Open");
89          menuItem4.addOnClick(new EventHandler(this.menuItem4_click));
90
91          menuItem5.setText("Close");
92          menuItem5.addOnClick(new EventHandler(this.menuItem5_click));
93
94          menuItem1.setMenuItems(new MenuItem[] {
95                                  menuItem4,
96                                  menuItem5});
97          menuItem1.setText("File");
98
99          menuItem6.setText("Set to Red");
100         menuItem6.addOnClick(new EventHandler(this.menuItem6_click));
101
102         menuItem7.setText("Set to Green");
103         menuItem7.addOnClick(new EventHandler(this.menuItem7_click));
104
105         menuItem8.setText("Set to Blue");
106         menuItem8.addOnClick(new EventHandler(this.menuItem8_click));
107
108         menuItem2.setMenuItems(new MenuItem[] {
109                                 menuItem6,
110                                 menuItem7,
111                                 menuItem8});
112         menuItem2.setText("Options");
113
114         menuItem9.setText("Go Home");
115         menuItem9.addOnClick(new EventHandler(this.menuItem9_click));
116
117         menuItem10.setText("Go to Work");
118         menuItem10.addOnClick(new EventHandler
            ➥(this.menuItem10_click));
119
120         menuItem3.setMenuItems(new MenuItem[] {
121                                 menuItem9,
122                                 menuItem10});
123         menuItem3.setText("Actions");
124
125         mainMenu1.setMenuItems(new MenuItem[] {
126                                 menuItem1,
127                                 menuItem2,
128                                 menuItem3});
129         /* @designTimeOnly mainMenu1.setLocation(new Point(0, 8)); */
130
131         this.setText("Form1");
132         this.setAutoScaleBaseSize(13);
```

6

continues

LISTING 6.2   CONTINUED

```
133            this.setClientSize(new Point(292, 273));
134            this.setMenu(mainMenu1);
135
136        label1.setLocation(new Point(8, 48));
137        label1.setSize(new Point(272, 24));
138        label1.setTabIndex(1);
139        label1.setTabStop(false);
140        label1.setText("No action...");
141
142        this.setNewControls(new Control[] {
143                          label1});
144    }
145
146    /**
147     * The main entry point for the application.
148     *
149     * @param args Array of parameters passed to the application
150     * via the command line.
151     */
152    public static void main(String args[])
153    {
154        Application.run(new Form1());
155    }
156 }
```

OUTPUT   When the program runs, you'll see a menu with the three menu items. Each time you select a menu entry, the label in the Form window will show what you just selected, as shown in Figure 6.6.

FIGURE 6.6

This application has a menu with three items in response to the menu entry events.

ANALYSIS   At line 32, the event handler for the first menu item's first menu entry can be seen. The menu event handlers go all the way through line 65; there's one event handler for each menu entry. Line 73 shows where the Main menu is created. Lines

74–83 show where the menu items are created. As you can see in lines 88–128, a lot of source code was added to create and populate the menu.

Some methods that you might find very useful are available in applications. The first is the `setChecked()` method. This allows you to either check or uncheck a menu entry. The following example shows how to turn on a check for a menu item:

```
menuItem1.setChecked( true );
```

It's also going to be important at times to gray out your menu entries. You do this by setting its enabled flag to `false`. The method to use is the `setEnabled()` method, which takes a single Boolean argument. The following example shows how to gray out a menu item by using the `setEnabled()` method with an argument of `false`:

```
menuItem1.setEnabled( false );
```

Adding Pop-Up Menus in Applets

It's easy to add pop-up menus in your applets. The `Popup` class offers pretty much all you need in order to do this. You first need to create the `Popup` object. The following example shows how to do just that:

```
Popup m_Popup = new Popup();
```

Then, you have to add the pop-up entries. You use the `Popup` class's `add()` method to do this. The following three lines of source code show how to add three menu entries to a pop-up menu:

```
m_Popup.add( "Canvas to Red" );
m_Popup.add( "Canvas to Green" );
m_Popup.add( "Canvas to Blue" );
```

Finally, you have to add your pop-up to a component. In the following example, I've created a button and then added a `Popup` object to it:

```
Button button = new Button( "Test Popup" );
button.add( m_Popup );
```

6

INPUT I've created a simple program, shown in Listing 6.3, that attaches a pop-up menu to a button. To handle the button event and show the pop-up menu when the button was pressed, I had to extend my `Button` class. This topic is covered in detail on Day 7, "Applet User Interface Controls," so for now I'll just mention it without explaining it in-depth.

LISTING 6.3   THIS PROGRAM SHOWS HOW TO ATTACH A POP-UP MENU TO A BUTTON

```
1    import java.awt.*;
2    import java.applet.*;
3    import java.awt.event.MouseListener;
4    import java.awt.event.*;
5
6    public class Applet1 extends Applet
7    {
8        PopupMenu m_Popup = new PopupMenu();
9
10       public void init()
11       {
12           m_Popup.add( "Canvas to Red" );
13           m_Popup.add( "Canvas to Green" );
14           m_Popup.add( "Canvas to Blue" );
15
16           MyButton button = new MyButton( "Test Popup" );
17           button.add( m_Popup );
18           add( button );
19       }
20
21       public class MyButton extends Button
22       {
23           MyButton( String s )
24           {
25               super( s );
26               enableEvents( AWTEvent.ACTION_EVENT_MASK );
27           }
28
29           public void processActionEvent( ActionEvent ae )
30           {
31               m_Popup.show( this, 0, 0 );
32           }
33       }
34
35   }
```

OUTPUT   When the program runs, you'll see a single button in the applet window. When you click the button, a pop-up menu with three choices will appear.

Summary

Adding pull-down menus to your programs is a fundamental part of providing users the kind of user interface they're accustomed to. It's not that hard with Visual J++. The classes that let you attach menus to Frame windows are straightforward and easy to use. And responding to menu events in Visual J++ applications is almost trivial.

Q&A

Q Can you add a menu to an applet window?

A Not to the main applet window. You must create a Frame window first. You can add a menu bar to a Frame window in an applet.

Q How do you create a menu bar to add to an applet Frame window?

A Here are the steps: First, create a `MenuBar` object. Then, for each menu item you want, create a `Menu` object. When you create the `Menu` objects, you'll want to specify the text in the menu constructor. For each menu item, you'll need to add the menu entries. The menu entries are the text that will appear under the menu items. You simply use the `Menu` class's `add()` method to add the menu entries. You then use the `MenuBar`'s `add()` method to add the menu items to it. Finally, after the entire menu is created, use the Frame window's `setMenuBar()` method to add the menu bar to the Frame window.

Q How do you respond to menu events in applets?

A You have to declare a new class that implements the `ActionListener` interface. You then need to override the `actionPerformed()` method that will catch all the menu events. Then, you must use the `Menu` class's `addActionListener()` method to add the `ActionListener` class you created.

Q How do you create a menu in an application?

A You simply display your Form window, select the `Menu` control in the Toolbox, and then place a `Menu` control on the Form window. After you've added a window to your application's Form window, you can add menu items and menu entries.

Q How do you create a menu event handler for an application?

A You select a menu entry you want to create an event handler for. You double-click on that menu entry, or in the Property window with the event button selected, double-click on the click event. You then are brought directly to the source code for the event handler for that menu entry.

Q Not all applets that you see on the Web use menus. When would it be advisable to create menus for your applets on the Web?

A The first problem with using menus in applets on the Web is that you must have a frame window that comes out on top of your main applet window. So for starters, you have to ask yourself whether having a frame window is what you want for your program. If it is, menus might be a good choice. If it's not, you won't want to use pull-down menus. If you decided that frame windows are okay for your applet, you must ask yourself whether you need to present some sort of a well-organized

6

set of actions to your users. If the answer is yes, go ahead and implement pull-down menus. If the answer is no, don't.

Q When would you ever use pop-up menus?

A Pop-up menus are common in desktop Windows applications. We normally call them context menus. They're good for when users want more information about something in the window, or when you need to offer specific actions for some item in the window.

Review Exercises

1. Create an applet with a frame window. Make sure that you handle the frame window's close event. Create a menu with four items. In each item, add at least two or three entries. Add the menu to the frame window, compile the program, and run it to see what it looks like. After you're satisfied that the program looks the way you want it, add the event handler for the menu events. Display in the frame window enough information so that the users can see what they've selected after they have selected it.

2. Create an application. Put a menu in the form. Add at least four items to the form's menu, and add at least two or three entries to each menu item. Add click event handlers for each of the menu entries. Then display text in the form window when each of the menu entries is selected.

DAY 7

Applet User Interface Controls

Today you'll learn about the user interface controls you can use when you create applets. These controls are all extended from the Component class, so they inherit all the Component class methods. These controls are all windows; but unlike Frame windows in the normal applet window, you won't be drawing to these windows. Instead, these controls have their own graphical representation that adopts the look and feel of the operating system in which they're running. On one hand, this approach saves you from having to adapt to multiple platforms and manage the details of implementing controls on the various platforms. On the other hand, you have less control on these graphical objects.

Today, you will learn about the following topics:

- The Button control
- The Checkbox control
- The Checkbox group control
- The Choice control

- The ListBox control
- The TextField control
- The TextArea control
- The Label control

After you create a component, you add it to a window. After you've added a control to a window, you'll want to interact with it. There are several ways of doing this, and we'll talk about all of them in this chapter.

The Button Control

A button is one of the most common user interface components. A button can be constructed with a text string, and it has the capability to trigger a user event when it's pressed.

Constructors

You can create button objects in two ways. The first method uses the Button constructor that takes a text string. The following example shows how to do this:

```
Button Button1 = new Button( "Button Text" );
```

The second way to create a button object is by simply calling the Button constructor that takes no argument. Later, you'll have to use the Button class's setLabel() method to give the button some sort of text. I've created a simple example that shows how:

```
Button Button2 = new Button();
Button2.setLabel( "Button Text" );
```

Handling Events

You can handle button events in two ways. The first method is by extending the Button class, enabling events in the extended Button class, and overriding the processActionEvent() method to perform the tasks you want. The following line of source code shows how to enable events in your Button class. I usually call this method from my extended Button class's constructor.

```
enableEvents( AWTEvent.ACTION_EVENT_MASK );
```

The next thing you need to do is to add a processActionEvent() method to your extended Button class. The first thing you'll do inside the processActionEvent() method is to perform the many tasks you'll need to take care of; the last thing you'll do in this method is to call the super.processActionEvent() method. The following example shows what you'd add to your extended Button class to handle Action events:

```
public void processActionEvent( ActionEvent ae )
{
    // Perform your tasks here...
    super.processActionEvent( ae );
}
```

The second way of handling `Button` events is to attach one or more `ActionListeners` to the button. To do that, create an object that implements the `ActionListener` interface. Put the action to be taken in the `actionPerformed()` method, and then associate it with a button using the `addActionListener()` method. The following example shows how to create a class that implements the `ActionListener` interface:

```
public class MyListener implements ActionListener
{
    public void actionPerformed( ActionEvent ae )
    {
        if( ae.getSource() == Button1 )
        {
            // Perform task here for Button1...
        }
    }
}
```

After you've added the class that implements the `ActionListener`, for each button that you want to handle `ActionEvents`, you need to use its `addActionListener()` method. The following example shows how to do this:

```
Button1.addActionListener( new MyListener() );
```

INPUT   I created a program, shown in Listing 7.1, that adds three buttons to the applet window. I then created a class in the applet that extends the `Button` class. I enabled events and then added a `processActionEvent()` method. So the way I'm handling the events in this sample program is the same as the first approach to handling events that I described earlier.

LISTING 7.1   THE BUTTONDEMO PROGRAM SHOWS AN EXTENDED Button CLASS THAT HANDLES THE EVENTS

```
1   import java.awt.*;
2   import java.applet.*;
3   import java.awt.event.*;
4
5   public class Applet1 extends Applet
6   {
7       String m_strDisplay = "No buttons have been pressed.";
8
```

continues

7

LISTING 7.1   CONTINUED

```
9     MyButton m_Button1 = new MyButton( "First Button" );
10    MyButton m_Button2 = new MyButton( "Second Button" );
11    MyButton m_Button3 = new MyButton( "Third Button" );
12
13    public void init()
14    {
15        add( m_Button1 );
16        add( m_Button2 );
17        add( m_Button3 );
18    }
19
20    public void paint( Graphics g )
21    {
22        g.drawString( m_strDisplay, 20, 120 );
23    }
24
25    public class MyButton extends Button
26    {
27        String m_strText;
28
29        MyButton( String s )
30        {
31            super( s );
32            enableEvents( AWTEvent.ACTION_EVENT_MASK );
33            m_strText = s;
34        }
35
36        public void processActionEvent( ActionEvent ae )
37        {
38            m_strDisplay = "The '" + m_strText + "' was pressed";
39            getParent().repaint();
40            super.processActionEvent( ae );
41        }
42    }
43
44 }
```

OUTPUT   When the program runs, you'll see three buttons at the top of the window. There's a text string below them that tells you which button has been pressed. When the program first runs, it tells you that no buttons have been pressed, but by pressing any of the buttons, you cause the text string in the window to change. Figure 7.1 shows the program running within Internet Explorer.

FIGURE 7.1

*The first ButtonDemo
program.*

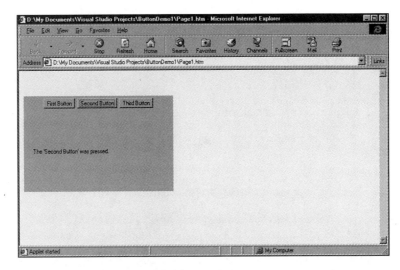

ANALYSIS The extended `Button` class is named `MyButton`. Its declaration begins at line 25. The constructor just takes a string like the normal `Button` constructor. The first thing that happens inside of a constructor is that it calls the `super()` method. The next thing it does is call the `enableEvents()` method. As I said earlier, you must call this method in order for the extended `Button` class to handle events. The last thing that the `Button` constructor does is store the button text so that we can use it later when we display which button was pressed.

At line 36, the `processActionEvent()` method begins. It's this method that handles the events. The first thing that happens in the method is that it sets the display string so that the next time the applet window is repainted, you'll see which button was pressed. The next thing it does is to cause its parent, which is the Main applet window, to repaint. The last thing it does is call the `super.processActionEvent()` method.

Now, notice back at lines 9, 10, and 11 that instead of creating normal button objects, we're creating `MyButton` objects. We do this because we need to use the extended `Button` class to handle the events.

There's another way of handling the `Button` events, as mentioned earlier. I've written a second program, shown in Listing 7.2, that has an identical appearance to the first program but implements the `Button` event handling differently. Why would you need two different ways to handle `Button` events? Well, it depends on the program you're writing and what's easier for you. In certain circumstances one way will be easier, and in other circumstances the other way might be more to your liking.

7

INPUT **LISTING 7.2**   THIS BUTTONDEMO PROGRAM SHOWS HOW TO IMPLEMENT THE
actionListener INTERFACE

```
1   import java.awt.*;
2   import java.applet.*;
3   import java.awt.event.*;
4
5   public class Applet1 extends Applet
6   {
7       String m_strDisplay = "No buttons have been pressed.";
8
9       Button m_Button1 = new Button( "First Button" );
10      Button m_Button2 = new Button( "Second Button" );
11      Button m_Button3 = new Button( "Third Button" );
12
13      MyListener Listener = new MyListener();
14
15      public void init()
16      {
17          m_Button1.addActionListener( Listener );
18          m_Button2.addActionListener( Listener );
19          m_Button3.addActionListener( Listener );
20          add( m_Button1 );
21          add( m_Button2 );
22          add( m_Button3 );
23      }
24
25      public void paint( Graphics g )
26      {
27          g.drawString( m_strDisplay, 20, 120 );
28      }
29
30      public class MyListener implements ActionListener
31      {
32          public void actionPerformed( ActionEvent ae )
33          {
34              if( ae.getSource() == m_Button1 )
35              {
36                  m_strDisplay = "The 'First Button' was pressed.";
37                  repaint();
38              }
39              else if( ae.getSource() == m_Button2 )
40              {
41                  m_strDisplay = "The 'Second Button' was pressed.";
42                  repaint();
43              }
44              else if( ae.getSource() == m_Button3 )
45              {
46                  m_strDisplay = "The 'Third Button' was pressed.";
47                  repaint();
```

```
48                    }
49              }
50        }
51
52   }
```

OUTPUT This program will look exactly like the first `ButtonDemo` program. When it first runs, you'll see that no button has been pressed, but each time you press a button, the text will change and you'll see which button was pressed.

ANALYSIS The first thing we'll look at in this sample program is line 30. We've created a class that implements the `ActionListener` interface. In line 32, you can see that we've added an `actionPerformed()` method. It will be to this method that all the `Button` events will go. Inside the `actionPerformed()` method, we used the `Action` event `getSource()` method to find out which button was pressed. After determining which button was pressed, we change the display string text, and then we repaint the applet's window so that users see which button was pressed. Notice that in lines 9–11, we create standard `Button` objects. In line 13, notice that we create a `MyListener` class. Remember that the `MyListener` class is our newly created class that implements the `ActionListener` interface. We're going to use this `MyListener` class for each of the buttons. Look at lines 17, 18, and 19. In these lines, we're telling the `Button` objects to use the `ActionListener` we created. After we've done this, all the `Button` actions will go to the `MyListener` class.

The Checkbox Control

The `Checkbox` user interface component has two states: `true` (or selected) and `false` (or deselected). `Checkbox` components trigger user events when selected and deselected. When more than one `Checkbox` appears within a container, they can either be independently selected or be exclusive of each other. For `Checkbox` controls to be exclusive of each other, they must all belong to the same group. Only one `Checkbox` component in a group can be selected at a time. The `Checkbox` components in a group are usually referred to as radio buttons. In Java, you can give `Checkbox` components the behavior of radio buttons by associating each component with another object by `Checkbox` group. We'll talk about the `Checkbox` group later in the next section.

Constructors

The `Checkbox` control has four different constructors you can use. The first one takes no arguments, and constructs a `Checkbox` initialized to `false` with no label text. If you use this constructor, you can set the `Checkbox`'s text by using the `setLabel()` method at a

7

later point. The following example shows how to create a `Checkbox` by using a constructor that takes no arguments:

```
Checkbox cb = new Checkbox();
```

The second `Checkbox` constructor takes a single argument, the `Checkbox` label text. This `Checkbox` initializes to a `false` state. The following example shows how to create a `Checkbox` control with this constructor:

```
Checkbox cb = new Checkbox( "My Checkbox" );
```

The third `Checkbox` constructor takes three arguments. The first argument is the `Checkbox` label text, the second argument is a `Checkbox` group object into which this `Checkbox` will belong, and the third argument is the initial state in this `Checkbox`:

```
Checkbox cb = new Checkbox( "My Checkbox", groupObject, true );
```

The fourth and final `Checkbox` constructor takes two arguments. The first argument is a string that sets the `Checkbox`'s text. The second argument determines the `Checkbox`'s starting initial state. Here's an example:

```
Checkbox cb = new Checkbox( "My Checkbox", true );
```

Checkbox Events

There are two ways of handling `Checkbox` events. Both of these are similar to the way we handle `Button` events. The first way is to extend the `Checkbox` class and handle the events in the extended `Checkbox` class itself. There are essentially three steps involved in doing this. The first step is to create a class of your own that extends the `Checkbox` class. Step number two is to add a constructor to your extended `Checkbox` class in which you call the `enableEvents()` method. Unlike what we did with the `Button` class, we won't specify an `ACTION_EVENT_MASK` mask, but we will specify an `ITEM_EVENT_MASK`. The following line shows how to do it:

```
enableEvents( AWTEvent.ITEM_EVENT_MASK );
```

The last thing you'll do is add a `processItemEvent()` method to your extended class. Inside your `processItemEvent()` method, you'll first take care of whatever tasks you want to perform. Then, you'll call the `super.processItemEvent()` method. The following simple example shows the method you need to add:

```
public void processItemEvent( ItemEvent ie )
{
    // Perform your tasks here...
    super.processItemEvent( ie );
}
```

The second option for handling Checkbox events is to attach one or more ItemListeners to the Checkbox. To do that, create a new class that implements the ItemListener interface. Put the task to be taken in the itemStateChanged() method. Then associate the newly created class with a check box by using the addItemListener() method. The following source code shows how to create your own class that implements the ItemListener interface. It has the itemStateChanged() method added.

```
public class MyListener implements ItemListener
{
    public void itemStateChanged( ItemEvent ie )
    {
        if( ie.getSource() == m_Checkbox )
        {
            // Perform tasks here for the checkbox that was selected.
        }
    }
}
```

The next example shows how to add the ItemListener to your Checkbox control:

```
m_Checkbox.addItemListener( new MyListener() );
```

Many times your program will use check boxes and you won't want to handle the events. As a matter of fact, most of the time you won't want to handle the events. All you'll want to do is use the Checkbox getState() method to find out how the Checkbox is set, and use that information to perform whatever actions your program needs to perform.

Sample Programs

I've created two sample programs to show how to add check boxes to an applet, and how to handle the events. The first program extends the Checkbox class and lets the extended class handle the events. The second program adds an ItemListener and lets a new class (which implements the ItemListener interface) handle the events.

INPUT   The source code for the first check box demo program follows in Listing 7.3.

LISTING 7.3   THE FIRST CHECKBOXDEMO PROGRAM SHOWS THE EXTENDED Checkbox CLASS

```
1    import java.awt.*;
2    import java.applet.*;
3    import java.awt.event.*;
4
5    public class Applet1 extends Applet
6    {
7        String m_strDisplay = "No events";
8
```

continues

LISTING 7.3   CONTINUED

```
9        Checkbox m_Checkbox1 = new Checkbox( "One" );
10       Checkbox m_Checkbox2 = new Checkbox( "Two" );
11       Checkbox m_Checkbox3 = new Checkbox( "Three" );
12       MyCheckbox m_Checkbox4 = new MyCheckbox( "Four" );
13       MyCheckbox m_Checkbox5 = new MyCheckbox( "Five" );
14       MyCheckbox m_Checkbox6 = new MyCheckbox( "Six" );
15
16       public void init()
17       {
18           add( m_Checkbox1 );
19           add( m_Checkbox2 );
20           add( m_Checkbox3 );
21           add( m_Checkbox4 );
22           add( m_Checkbox5 );
23           add( m_Checkbox6 );
24       }
25
26       public void paint( Graphics g )
27       {
28           g.drawString( m_strDisplay, 20, 100 );
29       }
30
31       public class MyCheckbox extends Checkbox
32       {
33           String m_strText;
34
35           MyCheckbox( String s )
36           {
37               super( s );
38               m_strText = s;
39               enableEvents( AWTEvent.ITEM_EVENT_MASK );
40           }
41
42           public void processItemEvent( ItemEvent ie )
43           {
44               m_strDisplay = "'" + m_strText + "' was just pressed. ";
45               getParent().repaint();
46               super.processItemEvent( ie );
47           }
48
49       }
50
51   }
```

OUTPUT When the program runs, you'll see six check boxes and some text in the window that indicates the last action or event. Check boxes one, two, and three don't produce any events. Check boxes four, five, and six do produce events. You can see the program running within Internet Explorer in Figure 7.2.

FIGURE 7.2

This program generates and handles events for check boxes four, five, and six, and shows what the last event was in the applet window.

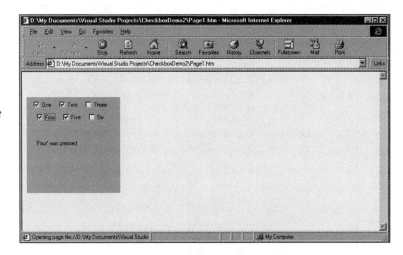

ANALYSIS The most important thing you should notice about the program source code is line 31, where the declaration for the MyCheckbox class is found. The MyCheckbox class extends Checkbox, and the reason we've extended Checkbox is so that we can handle the Checkbox events inside the extended Checkbox class. Notice that at line 35, we've implemented our own constructor that takes a string. If we wanted to use any of the other constructors, such as the ones that take two and three arguments, we would have to implement additional constructors. However, for this simple program, the only constructor we'll need is the one that takes a String argument. Notice at line 39 that we're enabling the ITEM_EVENT_MASK. Also, at line 42, we've added the processItemEvent() method to which all events will go. Looking back up at lines 9, 10, and 11, we're creating three simple check boxes. Lines 12, 13, and 14 show we're creating three more check boxes through our extended Checkbox class. Already you can see that the first three check boxes will not be able to handle events, whereas the fourth, fifth, and sixth check boxes will. Lines 18–23 simply add all six check boxes to that container.

INPUT And now comes the second sample program, shown in Listing 7.4, in which we create a class that implements the ItemListener interface.

7

LISTING 7.4 THE SECOND CHECKBOXDEMO PROGRAM USES AN `ItemListener` TO HANDLE Checkbox EVENTS

```
1   import java.awt.*;
2   import java.applet.*;
3   import java.awt.event.*;
4
5   public class Applet1 extends Applet
6   {
7       String m_strDisplay = "No events";
8
9       Checkbox m_Checkbox1 = new Checkbox( "One" );
10      Checkbox m_Checkbox2 = new Checkbox( "Two" );
11      Checkbox m_Checkbox3 = new Checkbox( "Three" );
12      Checkbox m_Checkbox4 = new Checkbox( "Four" );
13      Checkbox m_Checkbox5 = new Checkbox( "Five" );
14      Checkbox m_Checkbox6 = new Checkbox( "Six" );
15
16      MyListener Listener = new MyListener();
17
18      public void init()
19      {
20          m_Checkbox4.addItemListener( Listener );
21          m_Checkbox5.addItemListener( Listener );
22          m_Checkbox6.addItemListener( Listener );
23          add( m_Checkbox1 );
24          add( m_Checkbox2 );
25          add( m_Checkbox3 );
26          add( m_Checkbox4 );
27          add( m_Checkbox5 );
28          add( m_Checkbox6 );
29      }
30
31      public void paint( Graphics g )
32      {
33          g.drawString( m_strDisplay, 20, 100 );
34      }
35
36      public class MyListener implements ItemListener
37      {
38          public void itemStateChanged( ItemEvent ie )
39          {
40              if( ie.getSource() == m_Checkbox4 )
41              {
42                  m_strDisplay = "'Four' was pressed.";
43                  repaint();
44              }
45              else if( ie.getSource() == m_Checkbox5 )
46              {
47                  m_strDisplay = "'Five' was pressed.";
```

LISTING 7.4   CONTINUED

```
48                    repaint();
49                }
50                else if( ie.getSource() == m_Checkbox6 )
51                {
52                    m_strDisplay = "'Six' was pressed.";
53                    repaint();
54                }
55          }
56      }
57
58  }
```

OUTPUT   When this program runs, it will look identical to the earlier program. Check boxes one, two, and three will generate no events, whereas check boxes four, five, and six will generate events. The text string in the applet window will show the last event that was handled.

ANALYSIS   Once again, we'll start about halfway down the program with the analysis because it's very important. At line 36, we declare our own class, named MyListener, which implements the ItemListener interface. At line 38, we add the itemStateChanged() method. This is where all the events will go when they are triggered. Inside the itemStateChanged() method, we use the Item event's getSource() method to find out which instantiated object triggered the event. We make a comparison, and depending on which one triggered the event, we respond by displaying the event to the window. Lines 9–14 show where we create the six check boxes that we add to the applet window. They're all normal Checkbox objects; none of them is an extended Checkbox object. In line 16, we instantiate one of the MyListener classes. In lines 20–22, we add the ItemListener by using the addItemListener() method to check boxes four, five, and six. Just as in the earlier program, you can see that there's no way that check boxes one, two, and three will handle events because we don't add the ItemListener to them. Finally, lines 23–28 simply add the check boxes to the applet.

Checkbox Groups

If you combine check boxes into a Checkbox group, you'll get check boxes with a different look. Whereas check boxes are normally square, the Checkbox groups (usually referred to as "radio buttons") are normally round. Besides the difference in appearance, they function differently. After you add check boxes into a Checkbox group, only one of the check boxes can be selected at a time.

7

Constructors

There is only one Checkbox group constructor. It takes no arguments. The following line of code shows how to create a Checkbox group:

```
CheckboxGroup group = new CheckboxGroup();
```

Before we go on, though, let's revisit the Checkbox constructors. There's a Checkbox constructor that's especially meant for creating check boxes that will be grouped together. It takes three arguments: a string, a Checkbox group, and an initial state. If you specify an initial state of true for more than one check box in a group, the last one for which you specify true will be shown as selected.

Grouping Check Boxes

Checkbox groups handle no events on their own. However, the check boxes that are grouped into them handle events in the exact same manner as was described in the preceding section. There's absolutely no difference in event handling for check boxes, whether they're in a group or not.

Here are the steps to creating check boxes and associating them all in a group:

1. Create a Checkbox group object.
2. Create all the Checkbox objects that will be grouped.
3. In the Checkbox constructor, give it these items:
   - The Checkbox label
   - The group to which it will belong
   - The initial state of that particular check box

The following short example shows how to group three check boxes:

```
CheckboxGroup group = new CheckboxGroup();
Checkbox Checkbox1 = new Checkbox( "One", group, true );
Checkbox Checkbox2 = new Checkbox( "Two", group, false );
Checkbox Checkbox3 = new Checkbox( "Three", group, false );
```

Sample Program

Because handling events for check boxes that are grouped in a Checkbox group is exactly the same for check boxes that are not in a group, the purpose of this example is not to show you how to handle events, but to show you how to group the check boxes together.

I've taken the first sample program from the Checkbox section and altered it so that the first three buttons are grouped together and the last three buttons are grouped together. This altered program is given in Listing 7.5.

INPUT No substantive change to the event-handling code was made. Therefore, check boxes one, two, and three will not trigger any events, but check boxes four, five, and six will.

LISTING 7.5   A MODIFIED PROGRAM SHOWING HOW TO GROUP CHECK BOXES

```
1    import java.awt.*;
2    import java.applet.*;
3    import java.awt.event.*;
4
5    public class Applet1 extends Applet
6    {
7      String m_strDisplay = "No events";
8
9      CheckboxGroup m_Group1 = new CheckboxGroup();
10     CheckboxGroup m_Group2 = new CheckboxGroup();
11     Checkbox m_Checkbox1 = new Checkbox( "One", m_Group1, true );
12     Checkbox m_Checkbox2 = new Checkbox( "Two", m_Group1, false );
13     Checkbox m_Checkbox3 = new Checkbox( "Three", m_Group1, false );
14     MyCheckbox m_Checkbox4 = new MyCheckbox( "Four", m_Group2, true );
15     MyCheckbox m_Checkbox5 = new MyCheckbox( "Five", m_Group2, false );
16     MyCheckbox m_Checkbox6 = new MyCheckbox( "Six", m_Group2, false );
17
18     public void init()
19       {
20           add( m_Checkbox1 );
21           add( m_Checkbox2 );
22           add( m_Checkbox3 );
23           add( m_Checkbox4 );
24           add( m_Checkbox5 );
25           add( m_Checkbox6 );
26       }
27
28     public void paint( Graphics g )
29       {
30           g.drawString( m_strDisplay, 20, 100 );
31       }
32
33     public class MyCheckbox extends Checkbox
34       {
35           String m_strText;
36
37           MyCheckbox( String s, CheckboxGroup group, boolean state )
38             {
```

continues

7

LISTING 7.5   CONTINUED

```
39                    super( s, group, state );
40                    m_strText = s;
41                    enableEvents( AWTEvent.ITEM_EVENT_MASK );
42            }
43
44        public void processItemEvent( ItemEvent ie )
45        {
46            m_strDisplay = "'" + m_strText + "' was just pressed. ";
47            getParent().repaint();
48            super.processItemEvent( ie );
49        }
50
51    }
52
53  }
```

OUTPUT   When the program runs, as shown in Figure 7.3, you'll notice right away that the check boxes have a different appearance. When you start clicking on the check boxes, you'll also notice that their behavior is very different. Because the first three check boxes are grouped together, only one of those first three can be selected at once. The same holds true for the fourth, fifth, and sixth check boxes. You'll also see the text string in the applet window change only when you select fourth, fifth, and sixth radio-button check boxes.

FIGURE 7.3

This program groups check boxes together.

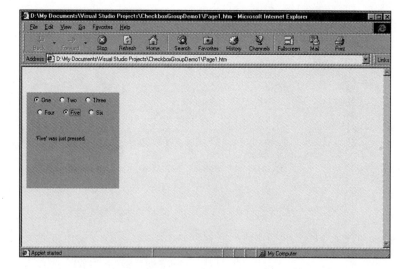

ANALYSIS There aren't many differences between the source code for this program and that for the first check box sample program, but notice that lines 9 and 10 create two Checkbox groups. Then notice that lines 11, 12, and 13 use the Checkbox constructor that takes three arguments, one of which is the group to which the check box will belong. Lines 14, 15, and 16 call the MyCheckbox constructor that also takes three arguments, one of which is the group to which this Checkbox belongs. Remember that previously the constructor took only a single argument—the label String. You'll notice in line 37 that we had to modify the constructor.

So now, not only does it take a String, but it also takes a Checkbox group in an initial state. Lines 20–25, as always, have the Checkbox controls to the applet; and line 33, as before, is where the declaration of the extended Checkbox class begins.

The Choice Control

The Choice control generates the drop-down list. This is similar to what Windows programmers know as a combo box. Choice control allows one item to be selected at a time. An event is triggered when an item is selected. Choice control does not have sorting capabilities; therefore, items are positioned in the Choice list in the order in which they were added.

Constructors

There is only one constructor for a Choice control. It takes no arguments. The following example shows how to create a Choice control:

```
Choice choice = new Choice();
```

After a Choice control has been created, you use the addItem() method to add choices to the Choice controls list. The following example shows how to add a Choice control and add three items to this list:

```
Choice choice = new Choice();
choice.addItem( "Selection One" );
choice.addItem( "Selection Two" );
choice.addItem( "Selection Three" );
```

Choice Events

As with most controls that you can add to applets, you can handle events for Choice controls in two ways. The first way is to create your own class that extends the Choice control class. Inside this class, you add your own processItemEvent() method. This processItemEvent() method is what catches all the triggered events. In your extended class's constructor, though, you must call the enableEvents() method and specify

7

ITEM_EVENT_MASK. A simple example of a class that extends the Choice class follows. Notice that it has the constructor that calls the enableEvents() method, and that it adds its own processItemEvent() method.

```
public class MyChoice extends Choice
{
    MyChoice()
    {
        super();
        enableEvents( AWTEvent.ITEM_EVENT_MASK );
    }

    public void processItemEvent( ItemEvent ie )
    {
        // Perform tasks here...
    }
}
```

The second way of handling Choice events is to create your own class that implements an ItemListener interface. Then, you use the Checkbox's addItemListener() method to add your newly created class that extends the ItemListener interface. The following example shows how to create a new class that implements the ActionListener class. Inside this class, an itemStateChanged() method was added. It's inside of the itemStateChanged() method that you'll perform your event handling.

```
public class MyListener implements ActionListener
{
    public void itemStateChanged( ItemEvent ie )
    {
        // Perform tasks here.
    }
}
```

Of course, you'll have to use your Choice control's addItemListener() method to add your newly created class. Without doing this, the class that implements the ActionListener interface will never get any events. The following example shows how to do this:

```
Choice choice = new Choice();
choice.addItemListener( new MyListener() );
```

Sample Programs That Handle Choice Control Events

I've created two programs that show how to use both methods to handle Choice control events. The first program, seen in Listing 7.6, extends the Choice class and lets the extended Choice class handle the events. The second one creates a class that implements the ActionListener interface.

INPUT
LISTING 7.6 THIS SAMPLE PROGRAM EXTENDS THE Choice CLASS TO HANDLE Choice CONTROL EVENTS

```
1   import java.awt.*;
2   import java.applet.*;
3   import java.awt.event.*;
4
5   public class Applet1 extends Applet
6   {
7   String m_strDisplay = "No events.";
8
9   MyChoice m_Choice = new MyChoice();
10
11    public void init()
12    {
13        m_Choice.addItem( "Selection One" );
14        m_Choice.addItem( "Selection Two" );
15        m_Choice.addItem( "Selection Three" );
16        add( m_Choice );
17    }
18
19    public void paint( Graphics g )
20    {
21        g.drawString( m_strDisplay, 20, 100 );
22    }
23
24    public class MyChoice extends Choice
25    {
26        MyChoice()
27        {
28            super();
29            enableEvents( AWTEvent.ITEM_EVENT_MASK );
30        }
31
32        public void processItemEvent( ItemEvent ie )
33        {
34            m_strDisplay = "'" + getSelectedItem() + "' was selected.";
35            getParent().repaint();
36        }
37    }
38
39  }
```

OUTPUT When the program runs, you'll see a single Choice control in the window, as well as a text string that displays the last event that was handled. Figure 7.4 shows the program running within Internet Explorer.

7

FIGURE 7.4

This program responds to Choice *events by extending the* Choice *class.*

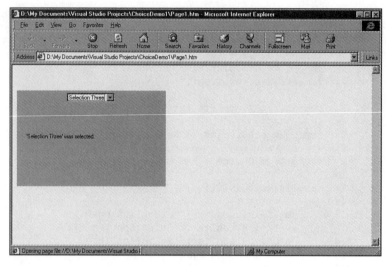

ANALYSIS The first thing I'd like to point out in this simple program is at line 24, where a new class that extends the Choice class is declared. Inside of the constructor, at line 29, the Choice class enables item events. At line 32, the Choice class adds a processItemEvent() method. Inside this method is where events are responded to. Now back up to line 9. This is where the Choice control is created. Lines 13, 14, and 15 show where the three different selections are added via the addItem() method. Finally, at line 16, the Choice control is added to the applet.

INPUT The second program in this section shows how to handle Choice events by creating a class that implements the ItemListener interface. The source code is given in Listing 7.7.

LISTING 7.7 THIS SAMPLE PROGRAM CREATES A CLASS THAT IMPLEMENTS THE ActionListener INTERFACE

```
1    import java.awt.*;
2    import java.applet.*;
3    import java.awt.event.*;
4
5    public class Applet1 extends Applet
6    {
7      String m_strDisplay = "No events.";
8
9      Choice m_Choice = new Choice();
10
11     MyListener Listener = new MyListener();
12
13     public void init()
```

```
14   {
15     m_Choice.addItemListener( Listener );
16     m_Choice.addItem( "Selection One" );
17     m_Choice.addItem( "Selection Two" );
18     m_Choice.addItem( "Selection Three" );
19     add( m_Choice );
20   }
21
22   public void paint( Graphics g )
23   {
24     g.drawString( m_strDisplay, 20, 100 );
25   }
26
27   public class MyListener implements ItemListener
28   {
29     public void itemStateChanged( ItemEvent ie )
30     {
31       m_strDisplay = "'" + m_Choice.getSelectedItem()
       ➥+ "' was selected.";
32       repaint();
33     }
34   }
35
36 }
```

OUTPUT   This program will look exactly like the first sample program in this section.
When you make a selection with the Choice control, the text string in the applet
window will show you the event that was handled.

ANALYSIS   The important thing to note in this program is at line 27. A new class is created
that implements the ItemListener interface. Inside this class, at line 29, the
itemStateChanged() method is added. Within the itemStateChanged() method, the
event is handled. Now if you'll look back at line 9, where the Choice control was created, we use the normal Choice control, not the extended Choice control of the earlier program. At line 11, we create the Listener class. At line 15, we tell the Choice object
which listener to use by using the addItemListener() method. Lines 16–18 show where
we add the Selection items to the Choice control. Line 19 is where we add the Choice
control to the applet.

Tip

It's not always necessary for Choice controls to handle events. You might be
interested only in what selection has been made at certain times throughout
your program's execution. For instance, let's say you want to do something,
and at that time you need to know where the selection is set. All you need
to do is call the Choice control's getSelectedIndex() method, which returns

7

an integer, or the `Choice` control's `getSelectedItem()` method, which returns a string. In this way, you can save yourself a lot of code if it's not necessary for your program to handle `Choice` control events.

The List Control

The `List` control displays a number of selected items in a multiline list box. The number of rows to be displayed in a list can be specified in the constructor. The list can be defined to enable the user to select one item at a time or more than one item at a time. The `List` component triggers user events when items are selected or deselected.

Constructors

There are two `List` constructors. The first one takes no arguments and simply creates a new scrolling list initialized with no visible lines and no multiple selections. The following example shows how to create a `List` that takes no arguments:

```
List list = new List();
```

The second `List` constructor takes two arguments. The first argument specifies the number of visible lines that will be in the control. The second argument specifies whether multiple selections are allowed. The following example shows how to create a `List` control that has 10 visible lines and allows multiple selections:

```
List list = new List( 10, true );
```

List Control Events

You have two ways of handling `List` control events. They are very similar to the previous methods for the other controls we've mentioned. The first method involves extending the `List` control. In the extended class's constructor, you have to call the `enableEvents()` method to allow your extended class to catch item events. You also need to make sure that you have a `processItemEvent()` method. It's in the `processItemEvent()` method that you'll get the event notifications. I've created a short example that extends the `List` class. In this example, I've chosen to implement both constructors so that I can use either one for my program.

```
public class MyList extends List
{
    MyList()
    {
```

```
        super();
        enableEvents( AWTEvent.ITEM_EVENT_MASK );
    }

    MyList( int nLines, boolean bMultiselect )
    {
        super( nLines, bMultiselect );
        enableEvents( AWTEvent.ITEM_EVENT_MASK );
    }

    public void processItemEvent( ItemEvent ie )
    {
        // Perform tasks here...
    }

}
```

The second method is to create a class that implements the AddListener interface. Inside of this class, you'll need to be sure to add an itemStateChanged() method. The short source-code example that follows shows how to declare this class. You'll also have to remember to use the addItemListener() method from your List class so that it knows which ItemListener to use.

```
public class MyListener implements ItemListener
{
    public void itemStateChanged( ItemEvent ie )
    {
        // Perform tasks...
    }
}
```

Sample Programs

In this section, I've created two sample programs, showing different ways to handle List events. The first sample program extends the List class and lets the extended List class handle the event. The second sample program creates a class that implements the ItemListener interface and lets this handle the events.

INPUT This first program is the one that extends the List control. The source code for it is given in Listing 7.8.

LISTING 7.8 THIS PROGRAM HANDLES List EVENTS BY EXTENDING THE List CONTROL

```
1   import java.awt.*;
2   import java.applet.*;
3   import java.awt.event.*;
4
```

7

continues

LISTING 7.8   CONTINUED

```
 5    public class Applet1 extends Applet
 6    {
 7        String m_strDisplay = "No event.";
 8
 9        MyList m_List = new MyList( 10, false );
10
11        public void init()
12        {
13            m_List.addItem( "Selection One" );
14            m_List.addItem( "Selection Two" );
15            m_List.addItem( "Selection Three" );
16            add( m_List );
17        }
18
19        public void paint( Graphics g )
20        {
21            g.drawString( m_strDisplay, 20, 170 );
22         }
23
24        public class MyList extends List
25        {
26            MyList()
27            {
28                super();
29                enableEvents( AWTEvent.ITEM_EVENT_MASK );
30            }
31
32            MyList( int nLines, boolean bMultiselect )
33            {
34                super( nLines, bMultiselect );
35                enableEvents( AWTEvent.ITEM_EVENT_MASK );
36            }
37
38            public void processItemEvent( ItemEvent ie )
39            {
40                int nStateChange = ie.getStateChange();
41                if( nStateChange == ItemEvent.SELECTED )
42                {
43                    m_strDisplay = "'" + getSelectedItem()
               ➥+ "' was selected.";
44                    getParent().repaint();
45                }
46            }
47
48        }
49
50    }
```

OUTPUT When the program runs, you'll see a list box that contains three items. Each time you select an item, the text string in the applet window shows the one you selected. Figure 7.5 shows the program running from within Internet Explorer.

FIGURE 7.5

This program responds to List *events.*

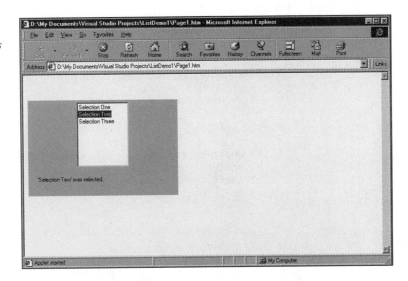

ANALYSIS As with the other programs, I'd like to direct your attention to a point about halfway down the source code. Take a look at line 24. This is where the new class that extends the List class begins. Notice that at line 26 there's a constructor that takes no arguments, and at line 32 there's a constructor that takes two arguments. These match both constructors of the List class. Also notice that in each of these constructors, a call to the enableEvents() method was made. In line 38, you'll find the processItemEvent() method. Notice that the first thing you do in this method is get an integer that represents the stateChange(). This could be selected or deselected, but for now we'll focus only on the selected stage. Looking up now to line 9, we create the List object that was extended from the List class. Lines 13, 14, and 15 show where we add the selections to List control, and line 16 is where we add the List control to the applet.

INPUT This second sample program creates a class that implements the ItemListener interface. It then uses the addItemListener() method for the List control so that the List control knows where to send its events. The source code for this program is given in Listing 7.9.

7

LISTING 7.9 THIS PROGRAM USES A CLASS THAT IMPLEMENTS THE `ItemListener` INTERFACE TO HANDLE List EVENTS.

```
1    import java.awt.*;
2    import java.applet.*;
3    import java.awt.event.*;
4
5    public class Applet1 extends Applet
6    {
7        String m_strDisplay = "No event.";
8
9        List m_List = new List( 10, false );
10
11       public void init()
12       {
13           m_List.addItemListener( new MyListener() );
14           m_List.addItem( "Selection One" );
15           m_List.addItem( "Selection Two" );
16           m_List.addItem( "Selection Three" );
17           add( m_List );
18       }
19
20       public void paint( Graphics g )
21       {
22           g.drawString( m_strDisplay, 20, 170 );
23       }
24
25       public class MyListener implements ItemListener
26       {
27           public void itemStateChanged( ItemEvent ie )
28           {
29               if( ie.getStateChange() == ItemEvent.SELECTED )
30               {
31                   m_strDisplay = "'" + m_List.getSelectedItem()
                     ➥+ "' was selected.";
32                   repaint();
33               }
34           }
35       }
36
37   }
```

OUTPUT   This program will look exactly like the first List sample program. When you make a selection, the display string in the applet will tell you what selection you just made.

ANALYSIS   At line 25 of the source code, you'll see that we created a new class that implements the `ItemListener` interface. In this class, at line 27, we added an itemStateChanged() method. It's inside this method that we handled the events. Now back up to line 9. You'll notice we created a normal List control, not an extended List control. Line 13 is where we add the Listener class to the List control with the addItemListener() method. Lines 14, 15, and 16 show where we add the List selections, and line 17 is where we add the List control to the applet.

The TextField Control

The TextField control enables the user to enter information into a text field. TextField controls can be created as empty or with an initial string. These controls can be defined to have an initial number of columns. If you don't define an initial number of columns, the layout manager can use the TextField component's initialTextValue() method to determine the TextField component's appropriate length.

Constructors

The TextField control has four constructors. The first constructor constructs the new text field and takes no arguments. The following source code shows how to create a TextField argument with this constructor:

```
TextField tf = new TextField();
```

The second constructor allows you to specify the number of columns for a text field. This is important when you want the text field to be a certain size. The following example shows how to create a TextField object that is 25 columns wide:

```
TextField tf = new TextField( 25 );
```

The third TextField constructor takes a single argument: a string that is in the text field when it first appears. The TextField will be created with enough columns to accommodate the text string that's been passed to the constructor. The following example shows how to create a text field with an initial string of "Hello World":

```
TextField tf = new TextField( "Hello World" );
```

The last constructor takes both a string and the number of columns that specify how wide the text field will be. The following source code creates a text field with an initial string of "Hello World" and a column width of 25:

```
TextField tf = new TextField( "Hello World", 25 );
```

As with the other components that we've talked about thus far, you have two ways of handling events in a TextField object. In the case of a TextField object, by far the easiest way to extend is to create a new class that extends the TextField class. TextFields trigger four types of events: focus events, keyboard events, text events, and action events.

7

The difference between keyboard events and text events is that text events are generated only when the setTextMethod() is called programmatically. I've created an example that shows how to extend the TextField class so that you can catch focus events, keyboard events, and action events. Unlike the other examples, this one is not so simple. I've also included only one constructor in my extended class. It's the constructor that takes a string as an argument. If you want the class that you extend to be flexible, you'll have to have all four kinds of constructors that the TextField class has. Inside of my extended class, I add a processKeyEvent() method, a processActionEvent() method, and a processFocusEvent() method. Any one of these three methods can be triggered by events that my extended TextField class triggers. The source code for my extended class follows:

```
public class MyTextField extends TextField
{

    MyTextField( String s )
    {
        super( s );
        enableEvents( AWTEvent.ACTION_EVENT_MASK |
            AWTEvent.FOCUS_EVENT_MASK | AWTEvent.KEY_EVENT_MASK );
    }

    public void processKeyEvent( KeyEvent ke )
    {
        if( ke.getID() == ke.KEY_RELEASED )
        {
            // Respond to keypress here...
        }
        super.processKeyEvent( ke );
    }

    public void processActionEvent( ActionEvent ae )
    {
        // Handle the action event here...
        super.processActionEvent( ae );
    }

    public void processFocusEvent( FocusEvent fe )
    {
        if( fe.getID() == fe.FOCUS_GAINED )
        {
            // Respond to focus here..
        }
        super.processFocusEvent( fe );
    }

}
```

Sample Program

Because we've really focused only on one method of handling TextField events, we're going to limit ourselves to one sample program. This sample program extends the TextField class and allows it to handle the events. You can see the source code for this sample program in Listing 7.10.

LISTING 7.10   THIS PROGRAM USES A CLASS THAT EXTENDS THE TextField CLASS

INPUT

```
1    import java.awt.*;
2    import java.applet.*;
3    import java.awt.event.*;
4
5    public class Applet1 extends Applet
6    {
7        String m_strDisplay = "No event.";
8
9        MyTextField tf = new MyTextField( "Hello TextField!" );
10
11       public void init()
12       {
13           add( tf );
14       }
15
16       public void paint( Graphics g )
17       {
18           g.drawString( m_strDisplay, 20, 150 );
19       }
20
21       public class MyTextField extends TextField
22       {
23
24           MyTextField( String s )
25           {
26               super( s );
27               enableEvents( AWTEvent.ACTION_EVENT_MASK |
28                   AWTEvent.FOCUS_EVENT_MASK | AWTEvent.KEY_EVENT_MASK );
29           }
30
31           public void processKeyEvent( KeyEvent ke )
32           {
33               if( ke.getID() == ke.KEY_RELEASED )
34               {
35                   m_strDisplay = "The key released was "
                     ➥+ ke.getKeyChar() + ".";
36                   getParent().repaint();
37               }
38               super.processKeyEvent( ke );
```

7

continues

LISTING 7.10 CONTINUED

```
40
41        public void processActionEvent( ActionEvent ae )
42        {
43            m_strDisplay = "There was an action event.";
44            getParent().repaint();
45            super.processActionEvent( ae );
46        }
47
48        public void processFocusEvent( FocusEvent fe )
49        {
50            if( fe.getID() == fe.FOCUS_GAINED )
51            {
52                m_strDisplay = "The focus was gained.";
53                getParent().repaint();
54            }
55            else if( fe.getID() == fe.FOCUS_LOST )
56            {
57                m_strDisplay = "The focus was lost.";
58                getParent().repaint();
59            }
60            super.processFocusEvent( fe );
61        }
62
63    }
64
65 }
```

OUTPUT   When the program runs, you'll see a single text field that's initialized with the
value of "Hello TextField!". If you click inside the text field with the mouse,
you'll see a message that says focus was gained. If you click outside the text field with
the mouse, you'll see a message that says focus was lost. If you edit the text field, you'll
see each figure you type appear in the display string that's telling you which actions are
being handled. If you press the Enter key, you'll see that an action event was triggered.
Figure 7.6 shows the program running within Internet Explorer.

ANALYSIS   This time, I'll go in sequential order through the source code instead of skipping
to a point halfway down the example. Looking at line 9, you can see that this is
where the extended TextField class was created. Notice that the constructor takes a single string argument. This is the only constructor we've implemented. At line 13, the
TextField object is added to the applet. Line 21 is where the extended class begins.
Notice that at line 24, the one and only constructor begins. Pay attention to line 27. It's at
this line where we enable the events. Notice that we're enabling three separate event
types: action events, focus events, and key events. At line 31, the method that handles
key events can be seen. It's the processKeyEvent() method. At line 41, the method that

handles action events, the processActionEvent() method, can be seen. Lastly, at line 48, the method that handles focus events can be seen—the processFocusEvent() method.

FIGURE 7.6

This program handles events for a TextField *control.*

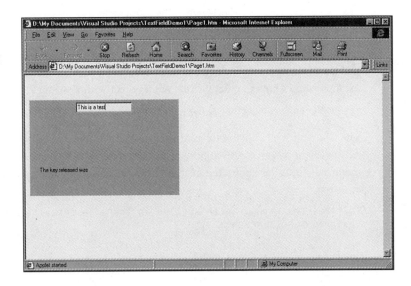

The TextArea Control

The TextArea control can contain multiple lines of text. Like the TextField control, TextArea controls can be created empty or with an initial string. TextArea controls can be defined with an initial number of rows and columns. The TextArea control inherits most of its functionality from the Text control.

Constructors

There are five constructors for creating TextArea controls. The first constructor takes no arguments and creates an empty TextArea control. The following example shows how to do this:

```
TextArea text = new TextArea();
```

The second constructor lets you create a text area and specify the number of rows and columns. It takes two integer arguments, the first one being the number of rows you want, and the second one being the number of columns you want. The following example lets you create a text field of 25 rows and 45 columns:

```
TextArea text = new TextArea( 25, 45 );
```

7

The third constructor takes a single argument. That argument is a string. When created, this string will be displayed in the text area. The following example lets you create a text area with a string in it:

```
TextArea text = new TextArea( "Hello there TextArea!" );
```

The fourth constructor takes three arguments. The first argument is the string that will be initially placed in the text area. The second argument is the number of rows you want, and the third argument is the number of columns you want the text area to have. The next example shows how to create a `TextArea` object with a string, 25 rows and 45 columns:

```
TextArea text = new TextArea( "Hello there TextArea!", 25, 45 );
```

The fifth and final constructor is almost identical to the preceding one we discussed, except that it adds a fourth argument that determines how the text area's scrollbars are managed. Table 7.1 shows the available values. Following is an example of the final constructor:

```
TextArea text = new TextArea( "Hello there TextArea!", 25, 45,
TextArea.SCROLLBARS_NONE );
```

TABLE 7.1   AVAILABLE SCROLLBAR VALUES FOR TEXT AREAS

Value	Description
SCROLLBARS_BOTH	Have both vertical and horizontal scrollbars.
SCROLLBARS_VERTICAL_ONLY	Have only vertical scrollbars.
SCROLLBARS_HORIZONTAL_ONLY	Have only horizontal scrollbars.
SCROLLBARS_NONE	Allow no scrollbars.

Events

`TextAreas` do not generate action events. They do, however, generate keyboard, focus, and text events. These events are handled exactly in the same way as `TextField` events.

The `Label` Control

The most basic user interface control is the `Label`. The `Label` is a text string that is usually used to indicate the name of other user-interface components. `Label` components can be assigned an arbitrary text string and alignment attribute. After a label has been created, the text string and alignment can be queried and modified.

Constructors

Three constructors are available when you create `Label` controls. The first constructor takes no arguments. The next example shows how to create a label using this constructor:

```
Label label = new Label();
```

Normally, though, when you create a label, you tell it what text to use. The second label constructor takes a single argument, which is a string. This is the string that will be displayed in the label. The next example shows how to create a label with the text `"Hello Label"`:

```
Label label = new Label( "Hello Label" );
```

The last way to create a `Label` control is with a constructor that takes two arguments. The first argument is a string that determines the text that will be in the label, and the second argument is the alignment. Three alignment types are available: `label.LEFT`, `label.CENTER`, and `label.RIGHT`. The following example shows how to create a label with the text `"Hello Label"` and an alignment of `LEFT`:

```
Label label = new Label( "Hello Label", Label.LEFT );
```

Events

Mouse and keyboard events are generated for labels, but no selection or action events are. It's rare that you'll need to handle events from labels. Java 1.0 did not even have this capability.

Sample Program

This section just presents a simple program that displays four labels, all with different alignments. The source code is given in Listing 7.11.

INPUT   **LISTING 7.11**   THIS SIMPLE PROGRAM SHOWS SIMPLE LABEL ALIGNMENTS

```
1    import java.awt.*;
2    import java.applet.*;
3
4    public class Applet1 extends Applet
5    {
6
7        public void init()
8        {
9            Label label1, label2, label3, label4;
10           label1 = new Label( "        Label 1        " );
11           label2 = new Label( "        Label 2        ", Label.LEFT );
```

continues

7

LISTING 7.11   CONTINUED

```
12          label3 = new Label( "        Label 3        ", Label.RIGHT );
13          label4 = new Label( "        Label 4        ", Label.CENTER );
14
15          Font font = new Font( "Helvetica", Font.BOLD, 25 );
16          label2.setFont( font );
17          label3.setFont( font );
18          label4.setFont( font );
19
20          add( label1 );
21          add( label2 );
22          add( label3 );
23          add( label4 );
24
25      }
26
27  }
```

OUTPUT   When the program runs, you'll see four labels in the applet window, as shown in Figure 7.7. The first one uses the default text and the default alignment. The next three use a larger font with a left alignment, right alignment, and center alignment.

FIGURE 7.7

This program displays text in Label controls with different alignments.

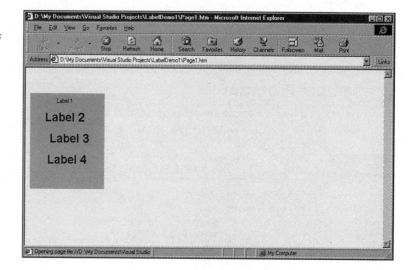

Summary

Java provides the functionality required to implement cross-platform Java applets with sophisticated and interactive user interfaces. The Advanced Windowing Toolkit contains many interface components. These can be placed within containers via the add() method. A great deal of your Java programming will contain and include these Java interface components.

Q&A

Q How many ways are there to handle Button events?

A There are two ways. One approach is to extend the Button class, call the enableEvents() method, and add a processActionEvent() method to the class for handling the events. Another approach is to create a class that implements the ActionListener interface. Using the addActionListener() method to add an instantiation of the newly created class that implements the ActionListener interface will then cause the new class's actionPerformed() method to get called whenever an action event is triggered.

Q How can you use check boxes without handling Checkbox events?

A Anytime you want to get the state of a check box, simply call the getState() method. If it returns true, the check box is selected; false, the check box is not selected.

Q How many constructors does the Choice control have?

A One. The Choice control's only constructor takes no arguments. To add selectable items to a Choice control, you have to use the addItem() method.

Q How do you make check boxes act like radio buttons such that only one simultaneous selection in the group is allowed?

A You must first create a CheckboxGroup control. Then when you create the Checkbox controls, use the constructor that accepts a CheckboxGroup object as an argument. All the check boxes that are placed into this CheckboxGroup will be grouped together in a radio-button family.

Q What's the different between an Edit control and a TextArea control?

A An Edit control contains a single line of editable text. A TextArea control contains multiple lines of text.

Q When would you want to not handle events for user-interface controls?

A When you have no action that must be performed during an event. A good example of this is a Checkbox control. You might only need to know what the user has selected when you go to perform a task. In this case, you can simply use the getState() method to find out whether the check box is selected or deselected.

7

This approach requires far less code than is required to handle Checkbox events. On the other hand, if you need to take some action when the user clicks on a check box, you'll have to handle the Checkbox events.

Q What happens if you don't use the `add()` method to add these controls to the applet's window?

A Nothing. The controls will not be displayed to users, and they won't have the ability to interact with the control.

Q Can I write my own custom controls and use them rather than the controls discussed in this chapter?

A Sure, if you want to work harder than you have to and not provide cross-platform look and feel. First of all, it's hard to write a control. Second, the beauty of these controls is that they fit the platform on which they're running.

Exercises

1. Create an applet and create a class that extends the Button class. In the constructor, call the `enableEvents()` method with the `AWTEvent.ACTION_EVENT_MASK` argument. Add a `processActionEvent()` method to your extended class. Then add a label at the top of the applet into which you'll alert users to events that your extended class handled. Add three buttons to the applet, but create them from your extended Button class. In the `processActionEvent()` method, set the label text so that users know what event you just handled. Compile and run the program.

2. Create an applet and create a class that extends the Checkbox class. Make sure that the extended class calls the `actionEvent()` method with the `AWTEvent.ITEM_EVENT_MASK` argument, and that the class has a `processActionEvent()` method. Create a CheckboxGroup. Create three Checkboxes from your extended class. Make sure that you've added a constructor that takes a CheckboxGroup object. Then, when you create the Checkboxes from your extended class, use the constructor that lets you give it the CheckboxGroup object. When a Checkbox event is triggered, update a label in the window to show the user what event you just handled.

WEEK 2

At a Glance

- Application Controls
- Dialogs
- Fonts and Texts
- Drawing
- Images
- Image Processing
- Animation

8

9

10

11

12

13

14

DAY **8**

Application Controls

There's a big difference between adding controls to applets and adding controls to applications. When you add controls to applets, you have to manually type the code, figure out the size, and adjust the properties of the controls. In applications, there's a toolbox that already contains all the controls. You simply drag these controls onto your form, and the code for the control is automatically added to your program. You can also edit the properties of these application controls very easily with the Properties window.

Today, we'll cover these topics:

- `Label`, `Edit`, and `RichEdit` controls
- `Button` controls, including `CheckBox` and `RadioButton` controls
- `ComboBox`, `ListBox`, and `CheckedListBox` controls
- `ListView` and `TreeView` controls

We'll talk about each of these controls, and then we'll group them and create some sample programs to demonstrate how to use them.

Label, Edit, and RichEdit Controls

These three controls are grouped together because they all deal with text presentation to users and text input from users.

Label Control

Label controls are encapsulated by the Label class. These controls display a string of text that the user cannot edit. You can use a label to display status information about your program. You can also use a Label control to identify a control that doesn't itself have a built-in label. When a Label control gets the focus, it passes that focus on to the next control in the tab order. Therefore, a Label control never actually gets and keeps the focus. Here's the icon from the toolbox that represents a Label control.

To use a Label control, simply click on it in the Toolbox window and drag it over to your form. When it's on your form, you can resize it and move it around. When a Label control is on the form and it's selected, you'll notice that the Properties window shows all the properties for that label. At least half of these properties are stock properties that pretty much come with any control. An example of two stock properties that most controls have is backColor and foreColor. The one property you'll end up changing most is the font property. If you click in the Edit field of the font property, you'll see a small button with an ellipsis come up. If you click this, it brings up the file selector dialog box, which allows you to set the font for this control. The textAlignment property is also very important. To change the text that's in the label, you edit the text property. One of the most interesting properties I've found is the cursor property. This allows you to set the cursor type that the mouse cursor will change to when the mouse enters the area that the label occupies.

When you first change the label, go back to the source code and look for the declaration of your label. It's in the gray area that you can't edit, but you can view it. The declaration for your label should be right above the initForm() method. The next line of source code shows the declaration of your first label when you add it:

```
Label label1 = new Label();
```

Other source code must also be added for this label. A label with default properties has five methods added: the setLocation(), setSize(), setTabIndex(), setTabStop(), and setText() methods. However, these won't be added to your source code until you close the Form window and reopen it. That's the way it works! So if you add a label (or any other control, for that matter) to your form and you don't see source code before the control, just close the window and reopen it. Then watch your source code magically appear.

8

The following example shows the source code that was added after I closed my form and opened it again:

```
label1.setLocation(new Point(32, 32));
label1.setSize(new Point(176, 48));
label1.setTabIndex(0);
label1.setTabStop(false);
label1.setText("label1");
```

The Label class has methods that match the label properties you can see in the Properties window. For instance, there's a getAutoSize() method, which gets the Boolean value indicating whether the size of the control automatically adjusts and the fonts change. That matches the autoSize property that you'll see in the property window when a label is selected. So somewhere in the Label class you can see labels that match all the properties. If, however, you don't see a method in the Label class that matches the property, you might have to check the control superclass that has methods that the Label and other controls inherit.

Many events are available to Label controls. In the Properties window, click on the icon that looks like a lightning bolt.

When you click the Events button in the Properties window, you see a new list. All the properties available to that control are shown. To add a handler for the event you want, simply double-click on the event name, and the event is added to your source code.

Let's try a simple experiment. Add a mouseEnter() event and a mouseLeave() event. You'll immediately see the source code for both of them in your form source code. In the mouseEnter() event handler method, we'll set the foreground color of the label to aqua. In the mouseLeave() event handler method, we'll set it back to black, which is the default color. The following source code shows both examples:

```
private void label1_mouseEnter(Object source, Event e)
{
    label1.setForeColor( Color.AQUA );
}

private void label1_mouseLeave(Object source, Event e)
{
    label1.setForeColor( Color.BLACK );
}
```

Go ahead and compile and run the program. As you move the mouse into the label area, the text changes to an aqua color. As you move the mouse outside the label area, the text changes to black.

Edit Control

The Edit control is encapsulated into an Edit class. This control is a rectangular control into which users can enter text. Here's the icon for the Edit control you'll find in the Toolbox:

As with the Label control, the Properties window lists many stock properties that are common to most controls. Still, some properties are noteworthy and are ones you'll use fairly often.

The first of these properties is the acceptsReturn property. You'll use this for multiline Edit controls. This indicates whether return characters are accepted as input. The next property you'll find interesting is the acceptsTab property. This is also for multiline Edit controls. It indicates whether tab characters are accepted as input. Another property that might make your life easier is the characterCasing property. When this is set to true, all characters that are typed are entered as either all uppercase or all lowercase, depending on where you have the control set. One property that might intrigue you (although you might not use it very often) is the passwordChar property. When this is set to true, the characters displayed are asterisks, as all password fields normally are. The last property I want you to take note of is the word wrap property. This is for multiline Edit controls. It indicates whether lines are automatically word-wrapped.

When you first add an Edit control to your form and bring your form back up, you have added four lines of code that set some minimal properties. The methods that are called are the setLocation(), setSize(), setTabIndex(), and setText() methods. You can see the source code that was added by default:

```
edit1.setLocation(new Point(32, 120));
edit1.setSize(new Point(176, 20));
edit1.setTabIndex(1);
edit1.setText("edit1");
```

The Edit control has many of its own methods, and most of these methods correspond to the actual properties in the Property window. The Edit class inherits many methods from the Control class. The two methods that are most commonly used are the getText() method and the setText() method. These are methods in the Control class. The following example shows how to get the text from an Edit control:

```
String strText;
strText = edit1.getText();
```

With your Edit control selected in the Form window, click the Events button in the Properties window. You'll see a whole list of the events that are available for the Edit control.

INPUT Now, let's create a program. The first thing we'll do is add a `textChanged()` event handler in the control. Click on the `textChanged()` event. Then go to that method and edit it so that it looks like the following example:

```
private void edit1_textChanged(Object source, Event e)
{
    label1.setText( edit1.getText() );
}
```

When the program runs, every time you press a key or the edit text changes, the label above the `Edit` control also changes. This program is shown in Figure 8.1.

OUTPUT

FIGURE 8.1

The label text changes every time the edit text changes.

RichEdit Control

The `RichEdit` control is encapsulated in a `RichEdit` class. The `RichEdit` control is a control that contains formatted text. It supports font selection, boldface, and other type attributes.

This control makes it a snap to create text editors and simple word processors. I remember the days in the mid-1980s when it was a big deal just to get word wrap to work in a DOS edit box. Now, the `RichEdit` control makes it a no-brainer to do word wrap with different fonts and text attributes, and it all works seamlessly in your application. Here is the `RichEdit` icon that appears in the Toolbox window:

Quite a few properties are associated with the `RichEdit` control. It has some of the same properties that are important to the `Edit` control, such as the `acceptsReturn` property and the `acceptsTab` property. Yet it adds a few additional ones that are specific to the `RichEdit` control. Some of the more interesting ones are the `rightMargin` property, which defines the right margin of the `Edit` control, and the `selProtected` property, which turns the contents of the currently selected text on and off.

Because the `RichEdit` control is so much more complicated than the `Label` and `Edit` controls, it needs to set more properties from the start to function properly. A total of six lines of source code are added to the program by default when you add a RichEdit control to your program. The following source code shows the default lines of code that have been added:

```
richEdit1.setFont(Font.DEFAULT_GUI);
richEdit1.setForeColor(Color.WINDOWTEXT);
richEdit1.setLocation(new Point(16, 16));
richEdit1.setSize(new Point(264, 192));
richEdit1.setTabIndex(0);
richEdit1.setText("richEdit1");
```

There are a few methods of note. These methods are ones you might find very useful and turn to often. The first one is the find() method. This searches the text in the RichEdit control for a given string. Another important method is the getCellText() method. This returns the currently selected text of a RichEdit control. If no characters are selected, it returns a string of zero length. The loadFile() method loads a file in RichText format into a RichEdit control.

Button, CheckBox, RadioButton, and GroupBox Controls

These four controls are grouped together because they are similar in nature. Buttons allow users to make quick selections, check boxes allow users to set items on and off, and radio buttons allow users to set items to one of several preset values. Group boxes allow you to group radio buttons into families.

Button Control

A Button control is encapsulated into a Button class. These are labeled buttons. The application can cause some connection to happen when the button is pressed. Here's the icon for a Button control:

Most of the properties available to buttons are either stock properties or ones that are easy to figure out, but one of great interest is the dialogResult property. This tells you what result clicking the button will produce. The choices you have are OK, cancel, abort, retry, ignore, yes, and no. Those results will all be for dialog boxes, if the button happens to be placed in a dialog box.

After you've added your Button control to the form, clicked the form, and opened it up again, you'll see that four lines of code were added to initialize the Button control. These four lines of code that were added to my control are shown in the next example:

```
button1.setLocation(new Point(32, 24));
button1.setSize(new Point(72, 24));
```

```
button1.setTabIndex(0);
button1.setText("Button One");
```

The Button class is extended from the Control class. It inherits all the methods and fields of the Control class. One very interesting method, though, that you might end up using in the Button class is the performClick() method. This generates a click event for the button simulating a click by a user. The event list for a button contains the event handlers you would expect: click, mouse move, mouse enter, mouse leave, and so forth. However, the one you'll use most often is the click event. I've created a program that has two buttons. Above both buttons is a label. For each button, I've added a click event handler. If you remember, it's easy to do this. All you do is select your Button control on the form, causing the Properties window to change to reflect the properties for that window; click the events button in the Properties window; and then double-click on the click event. This automatically adds source code to the click event handler. After I did this, in each click handler, I added text that changed the label so that it showed which button had just been pressed.

INPUT   The complete source code for this program is given in Listing 8.1.

LISTING 8.1   THIS PROGRAM HAS TWO BUTTONS, EACH OF WHICH HAS A CLICK EVENT HANDLER

```
1    import com.ms.wfc.app.*;
2    import com.ms.wfc.core.*;
3    import com.ms.wfc.ui.*;
4    import com.ms.wfc.html.*;
5
6    /**
7     * This class can take a variable number of parameters on the command
8     * line. Program execution begins with the main() method. The class
9     * constructor is not invoked unless an object of type 'Form1' is
10    * created in the main() method.
11    */
12   public class Form1 extends Form
13   {
14       String m_strText = "";
15
16       public Form1()
17       {
18           // Required for Visual J++ Form Designer support
19           initForm();
20
21           // TODO: Add any constructor code after initForm call
22       }
23
24       /**
25        * Form1 overrides dispose so it can clean up the
```

continues

LISTING 8.1 CONTINUED

```
26        * component list.
27        */
28       public void dispose()
29       {
30           super.dispose();
31           components.dispose();
32       }
33
34       private void Form1_click(Object source, Event e)
35       {
36
37       }
38
39       private void button1_click(Object source, Event e)
40       {
41           label1.setText( "Button One has been pressed." );
42       }
43
44       private void button2_click(Object source, Event e)
45       {
46           label1.setText( "Button Two has been pressed." );
47       }
48
49       /**
50        * NOTE: The following code is required by the Visual J++ form
51        * designer.  It can be modified using the form editor.  Do not
52        * modify it using the code editor.
53        */
54       Container components = new Container();
55       Button button1 = new Button();
56       Button button2 = new Button();
57       Label label1 = new Label();
58
59       private void initForm()
60       {
61           this.setText("Form1");
62           this.setAutoScaleBaseSize(13);
63           this.setClientSize(new Point(292, 273));
64           this.addOnClick(new EventHandler(this.Form1_click));
65
66           button1.setLocation(new Point(32, 96));
67           button1.setSize(new Point(72, 24));
68           button1.setTabIndex(0);
69           button1.setText("Button One");
70           button1.addOnClick(new EventHandler(this.button1_click));
71
72           button2.setLocation(new Point(128, 96));
73           button2.setSize(new Point(72, 24));
```

```
74          button2.setTabIndex(1);
75          button2.setText("Button Two");
76          button2.addOnClick(new EventHandler(this.button2_click));
77
78          label1.setLocation(new Point(48, 24));
79          label1.setSize(new Point(144, 24));
80          label1.setTabIndex(2);
81          label1.setTabStop(false);
82          label1.setText("No button has been pressed.");
83          label1.setTextAlign(HorizontalAlignment.CENTER);
84
85          this.setNewControls(new Control[] {
86                          label1,
87                          button2,
88                          button1});
89      }
90
91      /**
92       * The main entry point for the application.
93       *
94       * @param args Array of parameters passed to the application
95       * via the command line.
96       */
97      public static void main(String args[])
98      {
99          Application.run(new Form1());
100     }
101 }
```

OUTPUT When the program runs, you'll see a label that says, "No button has been pressed." Two buttons appear below that. If you press Button One, the label changes to say, "Button One has been pressed." If you press Button Two, the label changes to say, "Button Two has been pressed." You can see this program running in Figure 8.2.

FIGURE 8.2

This program has two buttons, each of which handles a click event.

ANALYSIS Notice the button1_click() method at line 39. It doesn't do much; it simply sets the label text so that the label says, "Button One has been pressed." At line 44, the button2_click() method can be found. This method also doesn't do very much except to set the label text so that users can see that Button Two has been pressed. At line 66, you can see that the default methods are inserted so that the button will be minimally functional. At line 72, the methods needed so that the second button will be functional are added. Lastly, at line 78, you can see that the methods needed to make the Label control functional have been added.

CheckBox Control

A CheckBox control is encapsulated in a CheckBox class. These check boxes are labeled boxes that are selected or unselected. The check box icon is shown as it appears in the Toolbox:

The checkedProperty property lets you determine whether the initial state is checked or unchecked. Another property you might find useful is the threeState property. This controls whether the check box supports the indeterminate state.

As usual, when you add a control to your form, some default code is added to make your check box minimally functional. Here's the source code that is added:

```
checkBox1.setLocation(new Point(40, 32));
checkBox1.setSize(new Point(120, 32));
checkBox1.setTabIndex(0);
checkBox1.setText("First Checkbox");
```

The two methods you'll probably use most will be the getChecked() method, which retrieves a Boolean value that indicates whether the check box is selected, and the setChecked() method, which sets a Boolean value that indicates whether the check box is selected. The event you'll probably use more than any other event is the checkState Changed() method. I've created a program that has a check box that handles this event. In the event, I've simply set the text of a label in my form so that I know that the check box state has been changed. The source code for my checkStateChanged() method follows:

```
private void checkBox1_checkStateChanged(Object source, Event e)
{
    label1.setText( "The state of checkBox1 was changed." );
}
```

RadioButton Control

A RadioButton control is encapsulated in a RadioButton class. This control is a small circle that has the given text displayed next to it, typically to its right. The control highlights the circle and sends a message to its parent window when the user selects the button. The control removes the highlights and sends a message when the button is next selected. The RadioButton icon that appears in the Toolbox is shown here:

The two properties you'll want to pay special attention to are the checked property, which lets you set the initial state of the button either on or off, and the textAlign property, which lets you determine whether the text is to the left or right of the button.

Four lines of code are added each time you put a radio button on your form. The following example shows the default code that was added to my program when I added a single radio button directly to the form:

```
radioButton1.setLocation(new Point(40, 48));
radioButton1.setSize(new Point(80, 32));
radioButton1.setTabIndex(1);
radioButton1.setText("radioButton1");
```

The Button class has two methods you will use most frequently. The first is the getChecked() method. This retrieves a Boolean value that indicates whether the button is checked. The second, the setChecked() method, sets the button to either true or false. A true value makes the button checked; false makes it unchecked. The event you will most likely rely on will be the check changed event. The check changed event is triggered whenever the checked property changes value. If you're adding radio buttons directly to the form, all of these radio buttons will be part of the same group, so their parent will be the Form window. So if you add 10 radio buttons to the form, or 20, or 30, or 40, only one of those radio buttons will be selectable at any given time.

GroupBox Control

The problem with adding radio buttons to the Form window is that every radio button you add to the Form window is part of the same group. You need a way to separate radio buttons into different groups. The way you'll do this is by using a GroupBox class.

The GroupBox control is encapsulated into the GroupBox class. This is a rectangle that contains other controls, and in this case, we'll be using them to contain radio buttons. A group box has a border around it and displays the caption for the group in the upper-left corner of the group box.

Besides visually setting a group of controls apart from another group of controls, a group box affects the behavior of the controls contained within. For instance, when we added radio buttons to the form, they were all in the same group. You could click only one at a time. But if you put a group box on the form and then add radio buttons within that group box, any radio buttons that were already on the form will not be affected by those radio buttons that are inside of the group box. The radio buttons inside of the group box become their own group. Only one of them can be selected at a time. Their behavior is completely independent from radio buttons that are either on the form or in other group boxes. Here's the GroupBox icon as it appears in the Toolbox:

Probably the only property in the GroupBox control you'll be interested in is the text property. This allows you to change the label text that appears in the upper-left corner of the group box.

When you add a GroupBox control to your form, five lines of default code are added. These lines of code are called the setLocation(), setSize(), setTabIndex(), setTabStop(), and setText() methods. They are shown in the following example:

```
groupBox1.setLocation(new Point(24, 128));
groupBox1.setSize(new Point(176, 72));
groupBox1.setTabIndex(3);
groupBox1.setTabStop(false);
groupBox1.setText("First Group");
```

The only method you'll probably end up using with group boxes is the setText() method. Even this you probably won't use very often, because it will be rare for you to change the title text in a group box during program execution. Although several events are available to group boxes, it will be a rare occasion when you use them.

ComboBox, ListBox, and CheckedListBox Controls

These three controls are grouped together because they offer a list of choices to users. The three are similar in function, and in many cases, your choice will just depend on your personal preference or the situation in which you find yourself.

ComboBox Control

ComboBox is a list box combined with a Static Text control or an Edit control. The list-box portion of the control can be displayed at all times, or it can drop down when the user clicks the drop-down arrow. Shown here is the ComboBox icon as it appears in the Toolbox:

In the Properties window, you should take note of several things. The first one is the items property. This allows you to add text strings to the selection list of a combo box. All you have to do is click the button with the ellipsis, and it brings up a string list editor dialog box that allows you to enter text selections for your combo box. The next property you'll probably want to note is the sorted property. This determines whether the combo box is sorted alphabetically. The style property controls the appearance and functionality of a combo box. The choices are simple: drop-down and drop-down list.

As with all other controls, when you put a ComboBox control on your form, some default source code that initializes the combo box is added. The following example shows a combo box that I added to my program:

```
comboBox1.setLocation(new Point(32, 48));
comboBox1.setSize(new Point(168, 21));
comboBox1.setTabIndex(1);
comboBox1.setText("");
```

Some of the methods you'll find important are the addItem() method, which lets you add an item to the combo box; the findString() method, which finds the first item in the combo box that starts with a specified string; the getSelectedIndex() method, which retrieves the zero-based index of the currently selected item in the combo box; and the getSelectedText() method, which retrieves the text for the currently selected item. These methods will be the ones you use most frequently. With your combo box selected on the form, you can find the events available for a combo box by clicking the lightning-bolt button in the Properties window. Of these events, the one I use most often is the selectedIndexChanged() event. If you double-click on it, it generates a method in your program that you can use. The following source code shows a method I created for my program that gets whatever text has been selected in a combo box and sets the label text of the Form window to reflect the selected text:

```
private void comboBox1_ selectedIndexChanged(Object source, Event e)
{
    label1.setText("The selected item is " + comboBox1.getSelectedItem() );
}
```

ListBox Control

The ListBox control is encapsulated in a ListBox class. This displays a list from which the user can select one or more items. The ListBox control icon as it appears in the Toolbox window is shown here:

The most important properties you'll be interested in with the ListBox control start with the items property. The items property is just like the items property in a combo box. When you click the small button with the ellipsis, it brings up the string box editor dialog box. You can use this dialog box, then, to add any selection strings to your list box that you want. The multiColumn property might also be important to you. This determines whether values should be displayed in columns horizontally. Also, as with the combo box, the sorted property is one you might find important too.

When you add the list box to your form, five default methods are added to your source code. These default methods set up the control so that it has basic functionality. These five methods are shown in the next example:

```
listBox1.setLocation(new Point(32, 96));
listBox1.setSize(new Point(168, 108));
listBox1.setTabIndex(2);
listBox1.setText("listBox1");
listBox1.setUseTabStops(true);
```

Some of the methods you found useful in the ComboBox control, you'll find useful in the ListBox control as well. The addItem() method is important. This adds an item to the list box. The findString() method operates the same way as the findString() method of the combo box. It finds the first item in the list box that starts with a specified string. The getSelectedIndex() method returns the zero-based index of the currently selected item in a single selection list box. The getSelectedIndices() method contains an integer array containing the zero-based indices of all currently selected items. If you call this method in a single selection list box, it returns an array containing a single element. If there are no selected items in the list box, it returns an empty array. The setSelected() method selects or clears a selection for the specified item in a multiple selection list box. The ListBox control has many events you'll find useful. The one I use most frequently is the selectedIndexChanged() method. This is the event that's fired whenever the selectedIndex property for this control changes. The following example shows a method I added to my program that takes the item that was selected in a list box and displays it in a label on my form:

```
private void listBox1_selectedIndexChanged(Object source, Event e)
{
    label1.setText( "The selected item is " + listBox1.getSelectedItem() );
}
```

CheckedListBox Control

The CheckedListBox control is encapsulated in the CheckedListBox class. These controls display a list box containing items accompanied by check boxes that can be selected or cleared. The icon for the CheckedListBox control is shown here:

The CheckedListBox control offers two properties you'll want to note. The first one is the CheckOnClick property. This determines whether the check box should be toggled on the first click of an item. The second property to take note of is the threeDCheckBoxes() property. This property indicates whether the checked values should be shown as flat or 3D check marks.

When you add a check box to your form, six lines of source code are generated to set the default properties of your checked list box. They are shown in the following example:

```
checkedListBox1.setLocation(new Point(216, 104));
checkedListBox1.setSize(new Point(72, 68));
checkedListBox1.setTabIndex(3);
checkedListBox1.setText("checkedListBox1");
checkedListBox1.setIntegralHeight(true);
checkedListBox1.setItems( new Object[]{} );
```

The methods of most interest include the getCheckedIndices() method. This method returns an integer array that contains the zero-based indices of all items with selected check boxes. The getItemChecked() method returns a zero-based index of the item whose check box state you want to examine. The setItemChecked() method takes two arguments. The first argument is the index of the item whose check box state you want to set, and the second argument is the value that indicates the current state of the check box. The CheckedListBox control has most of the same properties that the ComboBox and the ListBox controls have. The one I use most often is the selectedIndexChanged() event.

INPUT   I've written a program that combines a combo box, a list box, and a checked list box into one form. Listing 8.2 shows the event handlers for this program.

LISTING 8.2   THIS PROGRAM SHOWS THE EVENT HANDLERS THAT USE A COMBO BOX, A LIST BOX, AND A CHECKED LIST BOX CONTROL

```
1    private void listBox1_selectedIndexChanged(Object source, Event e)
2    {
3        label1.setText( "The selected item is " +
         ➥listBox1.getSelectedItem() );
4    }
5
6    private void checkedListBox1_selectedIndexChanged(Object source,
     ➥Event e)
7    {
8        label1.setText( "The selected item is " +
         ➥checkedListBox1.getSelectedItem() );
9    }
10
11   private void comboBox1_selectedIndexChanged(Object source, Event e)
12   {
13       label1.setText( "The selected item is " + comboBox1.getText() );
14   }
```

OUTPUT   When the program runs, you'll see the three selection controls and a label at the top of the form that shows what selection you just made. The program is shown running in Figure 8.3.

FIGURE 8.3

This program combines a combo box, list box, and checked list box all on one form.

ListView and TreeView Controls

The icon for the ListView control is shown here:

There are several properties you'll want to pay close attention to here. One property is the alignment property. This determines how items are aligned within the ListView control. The fullRowSelect property determines whether all subitems are highlighted within the item when they're selected. As with some of the other controls that have an items property, the items property for the ListView control lets you add the items you want to appear in your ListView control.

When you add a ListView control to your form, four lines of source code are added to set the default ListView control properties. These are shown in the following example:

```
listView1.setLocation(new Point(32, 16));
listView1.setSize(new Point(208, 112));
listView1.setTabIndex(0);
listView1.setText("listView1");
```

You'll find various methods in the ListView class to fulfill your programming needs. The getSelectedItems() method returns an array of currently selected list items. The insertItem() method takes four arguments. The first argument is an index for a new item you want to insert. The second argument is a string containing the text for the new item. The third argument is an integer that will be an index into the image list for this item. The fourth and final argument is an integer that will be a handle to external data to be stored by this item.

The ListView control has most of the same events that other controls have. There are, though, two events that are different for this control. The itemActivate event occurs when an item is activated. The itemDrag event occurs when the user begins dragging an item.

The `TreeView` control is encapsulated in a `TreeView` class. This control displays a generic Windows `TreeView` control. Here's the icon that appears in the Toolbox for the `TreeView` control:

 The `TreeView` control has various important properties that are different. The first and most interesting is the `dock` property. The `dock` property is in the Properties window. When you click the small button, it brings up a window displaying the docking options. These docking options are displayed graphically, as shown in Figure 8.4.

FIGURE 8.4

The dock *property graphically shows the options available to you.*

Another property you'll find important is the `hotTracking` property. This determines whether nodes give feedback when the mouse is moved over them. The `showLines` property lets you set whether lines will be displayed between sibling nodes, and between parent and child nodes. The `showPlusMinus` property lets you determine whether plus/minus buttons are shown next to parent nodes. The `showRootLines` property lets you set whether lines are displayed between root nodes.

When a `TreeView` control is added to your form, four lines of default source code are added to your program. They are shown in the following example:

```
treeView1.setLocation(new Point(48, 168));
treeView1.setSize(new Point(120, 72));
treeView1.setTabIndex(1);
treeView1.setText("treeView1");
```

Now let's look at some of the more important methods in the `TreeView` control. The `getSelectedNode()` method gets the currently selected node in the `TreeView` control. The `insertNode()` method inserts a node into the `TreeView` control. It inserts it as a root node at the specified position. There are various very important events for a `TreeView` control. The first one is the `afterExpand` event. This happens when a node has been expanded. The `afterLabelEdit` event is triggered when the text of a node has been edited by the user. The `afterSelect` event happens when a selection has been changed. The beforeCollapse event occurs when a node is about to be collapsed. The beforeExpand event takes place when a node is just about to be expanded.

HScrollbar and VScrollbar Controls

In this section, I'm going to talk about these two controls together. The HScrollbar control is encapsulated in an HScrollbar class, and the VScrollbar control is encapsulated in a VScrollbar class. Both of these controls can be placed on a form. They allow users to scroll an item. The icons for the HScrollbar control (on the left) and the VScrollbar control (on the right) are shown here:

Both controls have the same properties. The first property you'll want to take note of is the largeChange property. This lets you set the change and position of the thumb when the user clicks in the scrollbar area or uses Page Up or Page Down. Corresponding to this is the smallChange property. This lets you set the change and position of the thumb when a user clicks on one of the up- or down-arrow keys, or uses the up- or down-arrow key on the keyboard.

Four lines of source code appear on your scrollbar when you put one on your form. They are found in the following example:

```
HScrollBar1.setLocation(new Point(16, 232));
HScrollBar1.setSize(new Point(200, 16));
HScrollBar1.setTabIndex(1);
HScrollBar1.setText("HScrollBar1");
```

The event I primarily use for scrollbars is the scroll event. When the scrollbar triggers this event, it gives you as an argument a ScrollEvent class. This ScrollEvent class can be used to determine what happened to trigger the scroll event. Normally, I don't use it to get the exact event (whether it was a largeChange or a smallChange event). I use the newValue member variable of the ScrollEvent class just to find out what the position of the scrollbar will be. The method that handles my scrollbar event is shown in the following example. As I mentioned before, what I'm interested in regarding the ScrollEvent class is the newValue member variable.

```
private void HScrollBar1_scroll(Object source, ScrollEvent e)
{
    m_nXOffset = e.newValue;
    invalidate();
    update();
}
```

INPUT   I've created an entire program that uses a horizontal scrollbar and a vertical scrollbar. Text is drawn inside of the form window, and depending on the position of both scrollbars, this text is drawn at different x and y coordinates. The source code in Listing 8.3 shows this entire program.

LISTING 8.3   THIS PROGRAM USES A HORIZONTAL AND A VERTICAL SCROLLBAR TO DETERMINE A POSITION AT WHICH IT WILL DRAW TEXT

```
1   import com.ms.wfc.app.*;
2   import com.ms.wfc.core.*;
3   import com.ms.wfc.ui.*;
4   import com.ms.wfc.html.*;
5
6   /**
7    * This class can take a variable number of parameters on the command
8    * line. Program execution begins with the main() method. The class
9    * constructor is not invoked unless an object of type 'Form1' is
10   * created in the main() method.
11   */
12  public class Form1 extends Form
13  {
14
15      int m_nXOffset = 0, m_nYOffset = 0;
16
17      public Form1()
18      {
19          // Required for Visual J++ Form Designer support
20          initForm();
21
22          // TODO: Add any constructor code after initForm call
23      }
24
25      /**
26       * Form1 overrides dispose so it can clean up the
27       * component list.
28       */
29      public void dispose()
30      {
31          super.dispose();
32          components.dispose();
33      }
34
35      private void Form1_click(Object source, Event e)
36      {
37
38      }
39
40      private void Form1_paint(Object source, PaintEvent e)
41      {
42          Font font = new Font( "Times Roman", (float)
            ➡55.0, FontSize.PIXELS );
```

continues

LISTING 8.3 CONTINUED

```
43          e.graphics.setFont( font );
44          e.graphics.drawString( "This is line one.",
            ➥m_nXOffset + 20, m_nYOffset + 50 );
45          e.graphics.drawString( "This is line two.",
            ➥m_nXOffset + 20, m_nYOffset + 100 );
46      }
47
48      private void HScrollBar1_scroll(Object source, ScrollEvent e)
49      {
50          m_nXOffset = e.newValue;
51          invalidate();
52          update();
53      }
54
55      private void VScrollBar1_scroll(Object source, ScrollEvent e)
56      {
57          m_nYOffset = e.newValue;
58          invalidate();
59          update();
60      }
61
62      /**
63       * NOTE: The following code is required by the Visual J++ form
64       * designer.  It can be modified using the form editor.  Do not
65       * modify it using the code editor.
66       */
67      Container components = new Container();
68      Label label1 = new Label();
69      HScrollBar HScrollBar1 = new HScrollBar();
70      VScrollBar VScrollBar1 = new VScrollBar();
71
72      private void initForm()
73      {
74          this.setText("Form1");
75          this.setAutoScaleBaseSize(13);
76          this.setClientSize(new Point(231, 249));
77          this.addOnClick(new EventHandler(this.Form1_click));
78          this.addOnPaint(new PaintEventHandler(this.Form1_paint));
79
80          label1.setLocation(new Point(8, 8));
81          label1.setSize(new Point(224, 16));
82          label1.setTabIndex(0);
83          label1.setTabStop(false);
84          label1.setText("Scrollbar Demo");
85          label1.setTextAlign(HorizontalAlignment.CENTER);
86
87          HScrollBar1.setLocation(new Point(16, 232));
88          HScrollBar1.setSize(new Point(200, 16));
```

8

```
89          HScrollBar1.setTabIndex(1);
90          HScrollBar1.setText("HScrollBar1");
91          HScrollBar1.addOnScroll(new ScrollEventHandler
            ➥(this.HScrollBar1_scroll));
92
93          VScrollBar1.setLocation(new Point(216, 32));
94          VScrollBar1.setSize(new Point(16, 192));
95          VScrollBar1.setTabIndex(2);
96          VScrollBar1.setText("VScrollBar1");
97          VScrollBar1.addOnScroll
            ➥(new ScrollEventHandler(this.VScrollBar1_scroll));
98
99          this.setNewControls(new Control[] {
100                         VScrollBar1,
101                         HScrollBar1,
102                         label1});
103      }
104
105      /**
106       * The main entry point for the application.
107       *
108       * @param args Array of parameters passed to the application
109       * via the command line.
110       */
111      public static void main(String args[])
112      {
113          Application.run(new Form1());
114      }
115 }
```

OUTPUT When the program runs, you'll see two lines of text appear in the Form window. Every time you move the horizontal or vertical scrollbars, you'll see the position of the text that's drawn in the form window changed. Figure 8.5 shows this program as it is running.

FIGURE 8.5

This program shows the horizontal and vertical scrollbars determining the position at which the text is drawn.

ANALYSIS The first thing you want to take a look at is line 15, where we see that there are two member variables to this class that keep track of the x and y offset to which the two lines of text will draw. At line 40 is the `form1_paint()` method. The first thing that happens here is that a new font is created. For more information about creating and using fonts, refer to Day 10, "Fonts and Text." At lines 44 and 45, the two strings are drawn into the form window. They use the x and y opposite variables. Now, notice at line 48 the start of the `HScrollbar` control's `scrollEvent()` method. The x offset variable is set to the new value, and the window is invalidated, then updated. At line 55, the `VScrollbar` control's `scrollEvent()` starts. It also simply takes the new value from the `ScrollEvent` class and sets the y offset variable to this value. It invalidates and then updates the window. Line 69 is where the `HScrollbar` control is declared and created, and line 70 is where the `VScrollbar` control is declared and created. At line 87, the `HScrollbar` control's properties are set. At line 93, the `VScrollbar` control's properties are set.

Toolbar and StatusBar Controls

These two controls are found in many Windows programs. Toolbars normally appear at the top of an application window, and they provide users with an easy way to perform functions by offering them buttons for one-click operations. Status bars usually are at the bottom of an application window, and they offer an easy way to show users the status of different application items.

Toolbar Control

The `Toolbar` control is encapsulated in the `Toolbar` class. This control allows users to easily perform functions in an application. Here's the Toolbar icon that appears in the Toolbox:

Several properties are important for toolbars. The first that you'll see is the `appearance` property. This controls whether the toolbar will have a normal appearance (which is 3D) or a flat appearance. The next property is the `buttons` property. This is a collection of toolbar buttons that make up the toolbar. When you click the small button with the ellipsis in it, the toolbar button editor appears. Then, in the status bar box, you can add your toolbar buttons.

When you add a `Toolbar` control to your form, four lines of default code are added that initialize the control with some default properties. These four lines of code are shown in the next example:

```
toolBar1.setSize(new Point(292, 22));
toolBar1.setTabIndex(0);
```

```
toolBar1.setDropDownArrows(true);
toolBar1.setShowToolTips(true);
```

Most of the methods available in the `Toolbar` class correspond to toolbar properties. Examples of this are the `getAutoSize()` method, the `getBorderStyle()` method, and the `getAppearance()` method.

But with toolbars, you'll be mostly interested in the events. The two events you'll use more often than any others will be the `buttonClick` event and the `buttonDropDown` event. The `buttonClick` event is triggered whenever a button in the toolbar is clicked by the user. The `buttonDropDown` event is triggered whenever a button in the drop-down style is pressed.

StatusBar Control

Status bars are areas that are usually displayed at the bottom of an application window. Status bars are used by applications to display various kinds of status information. Here's the StatusBar icon that appears in the Toolbox:

Two properties are the most important for status bars. The first one is the `dockControl`. As with the `dockControl` for the toolbar, when you select this property, a visual representation of possible docking positions comes up. You can then use this to select a docking position. Another important property is the `panels` property. When you click the small button with the ellipsis in it, the status bar editor dialog appears. In this, you can add any status bar panels that you want. The next property you'll want to pay attention to is the `showPanels` property. It lets you designate whether the status bar displays panels or whether it displays a single line of text.

When you add a status bar to your form, five lines of code that set the `StatusBar` control's property to default values are added for you. You can see them in the next example:

```
statusBar1.setBackColor(Color.CONTROL);
statusBar1.setLocation(new Point(0, 249));
statusBar1.setSize(new Point(292, 24));
statusBar1.setTabIndex(1);
statusBar1.setText("statusBar1");
```

The method you will probably use more often than any other is the `setText()` method. This sets the text that will appear in the status bar. Of course, the `showPanels` property has to be set to `false` to use this method.

Summary

When you write Visual J++ applications, you have many controls at your disposal. These controls make it very easy to create a user interface. Adding event handling to these controls is just as easy. With the double-click of a mouse button, you can have an event handler for any of the control's events.

This ability to easily create user interfaces far surpasses the ability of a Visual C++ programmer to quickly create user interfaces. It puts Visual J++ on the same level with Visual Basic for creating user interfaces—they're both very easy.

Q&A

Q How do you add a label to your form?

A The first thing you do is create a `Label` control. You do this with the `new` operator. Normally, your `Label` control will take a single argument in its constructor. That single argument will be the text that will appear in the control. However, you don't have to worry about manually creating a `Label` control and adding it to your form. The Properties window will do everything for you.

Q What kinds of events do `Edit` controls offer?

A They offer most of the standard events, such as double-click, drag drop, drag enter, drag leave, and drag over. Some of the specific events they offer that you'll be interested in are the key down, key press, and key up events. One additional event you'll be interested in is the text changed event. This is triggered when the `text` property for this control changes.

Q What is a `RichEdit` control, what can it be used for, and why does it make your job as a Visual J++ programmer easier?

A The `RichEdit` control contains formatted text. Unlike the `Edit` control and the `TextArea` control, it supports font selection, boldface, and other type attributes. You can easily use this control to create a simple text editor or word processor as part of your application. This control takes the pain out of creating word processors because all you have to do is put up the control and respond to several events.

Exercises

1. Create a program and add a label at the top. Below that label, add an Edit field. In the Edit field, respond to the `textChanged` event by changing the text in the label to reflect what's in the Edit field.

2. Create another program with a label at the top. Below this label, create a list box. Add eight items to the list box. Then add an item event handler for the `selectIndexChanged()` method. Respond to this event by changing the text in the label after users make selections in the list box.

WEEK 2

DAY 9

Dialogs

Today you'll learn how to create, display, manipulate, and interact with dialog boxes. Next to menus, dialog boxes (referred to for the rest of the chapter as dialogs) are the most important user-interface item. Dialogs communicate with users. They notify users of things they need to know, and ask for information that the program needs.

Dialogs aren't magical or mysterious. They're just windows that are treated in a slightly different way. Mainly, dialogs are modal windows that prevent users from doing anything else in an application until the dialog has been closed.

Today you'll complete these tasks:

- Learn how to create and display a dialog.
- Learn about methods that are important when programming dialogs.
- Find out what other important methods will help you when dealing with Forms in general.

Today's lesson ends the user-interface section. After this, you'll have user-interface programming well under control.

Creating a Dialog

Creating a dialog is the same as creating a Form. Editing a dialog is the same as editing a Form. Displaying and interacting is the main difference. To start, create a new project named AboutDialog. Do that now.

When you've created the program, you'll see the default form, named Form1. Complete source code is given later, in Listings 9.1 and 9.2, but for you to learn this topic thoroughly, it's far more valuable for you to perform these steps as you read through them. Double-click on Form1 and have it in the edit window. Now, double-click on the form so that you get a Form1_click() method.

Tip

> The reason we want the Form1_click() method is so that we have a convenient place to create and display the dialog. This is the easiest way to get a program to give you a place to test something. Keep this in mind when you want to test things in your Visual J++ applications.

Now we're ready to add a dialog to the project. We really add a form, not a dialog specifically. Select Project, Add Form from the menu. Make sure that the category that's opened is Form. Make sure that the item that's selected is Form. In the Name field, type a meaningful name for your dialog. I'd suggest About.java because that's what I did. Figure 9.1 shows the Add Item dialog right before I added the About.java Form to my project.

FIGURE 9.1

Notice that the Form category is open and the Form item is selected. The name I added is About.java.

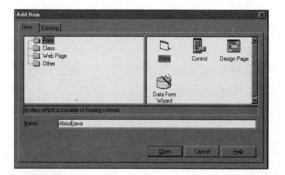

You'll see the About.java file appear in the Project Explorer Window, and the About Form appear in the edit window. You're ready to start adding controls to the Form. I added two, a label and a button, as shown in Figure 9.2.

FIGURE 9.2

This Form has two controls: a label and a button.

The rest is easy. In the `Form1_click()` method, we create the Form with the new operator and then call its `showDialog()` method. The code I added follows. If you're following along with the discussion, go ahead and add it to your program. Compile the application and then run it.

```
private void Form1_click(Object source, Event e)
{
    About dlg = new About();
    dlg.showDialog();
}
```

When the program runs, you see a blank Form. When you click in the blank Form, the About dialog comes up. There's no response when you click the OK button. You'll learn more about handling those events later. You'll have to use the window's close button in the upper-right corner.

You might have noticed that the About dialog has minimize and maximize buttons. Dialogs by protocol don't. You need to stick with the standard Windows dialog presentation and remove the minimize and maximize buttons. To do this, go to the About Form properties. Set the `minimizeBox` and `maximizeBox` properties to `false`.

Caution

Dialogs don't ordinarily have minimize and maximize buttons. Your program will look maladjusted if your dialogs have these two buttons. Be sure to remove them from all of your dialogs.

Let's review the basics of creating and displaying a dialog for a Visual J++ application. The summary steps follow:

1. Start with a Visual J++ application.
2. Add a Form and name it something meaningful. The best way to name dialogs is based on what they do.
3. To create the dialog, use the `new` operator.
4. To show a modal dialog (which 99.5% of them are), make a call to the `showDialog()` method.

I want to make absolutely sure that you're with me 100%. For that reason, I'll show you the program I have so far. The source code is given in Listings 9.1 and 9.2.

LISTING 9.1   THE SOURCE CODE FOR Form1 IN OUR DIALOG PROGRAM

```
1    import com.ms.wfc.app.*;
2    import com.ms.wfc.core.*;
3    import com.ms.wfc.ui.*;
4    import com.ms.wfc.html.*;
5
6    /**
7     * This class can take a variable number of parameters on the command
8     * line. Program execution begins with the main() method. The class
9     * constructor is not invoked unless an object of type 'Form1' is
10    * created in the main() method.
11    */
12   public class Form1 extends Form
13   {
14       public Form1()
15       {
16           // Required for Visual J++ Form Designer support
17           initForm();
18
19       }
20
21       /**
22        * Form1 overrides dispose so it can clean up the
23        * component list.
24        */
25       public void dispose()
26       {
27           super.dispose();
28           components.dispose();
29       }
30
31       private void Form1_click(Object source, Event e)
32       {
33           About dlg = new About();
34           dlg.showDialog();
35       }
36
37       /**
38        * NOTE: The following code is required by the Visual J++ form
39        * designer.  It can be modified using the form editor.  Do not
40        * modify it using the code editor.
41        */
42       Container components = new Container();
43
44       private void initForm()
```

```
45    {
46        this.setText("Form1");
47        this.setAutoScaleBaseSize(13);
48        this.setClientSize(new Point(292, 273));
49        this.addOnClick(new EventHandler(this.Form1_click));
50    }
51
52    /**
53     * The main entry point for the application.
54     *
55     * @param args Array of parameters passed to the application
56     * via the command line.
57     */
58    public static void main(String args[])
59    {
60        Application.run(new Form1());
61    }
62 }
```

LISTING 9.2 THE SOURCE CODE FOR THE ABOUT FORM

```
1    import com.ms.wfc.app.*;
2    import com.ms.wfc.core.*;
3    import com.ms.wfc.ui.*;
4    import com.ms.wfc.html.*;
5
6    /**
7     * This class can take a variable number of parameters on the command
8     * line. Program execution begins with the main() method. The class
9     * constructor is not invoked unless an object of type 'About' is
10    * created in the main() method.
11    */
12   public class About extends Form
13   {
14       public About()
15       {
16           super();
17
18           // Required for Visual J++ Form Designer support
19           initForm();
20
21   }
22
23       /**
24        * About overrides dispose so it can clean up the
25        * component list.
26        */
27       public void dispose()
28       {
```

continues

LISTING 9.2   CONTINUED

```
29              super.dispose();
30              components.dispose();
31          }
32
33          /**
34           * NOTE: The following code is required by the Visual J++ form
35           * designer.  It can be modified using the form editor.  Do not
36           * modify it using the code editor.
37           */
38          Container components = new Container();
39          Label label1 = new Label();
40          Button button1 = new Button();
41
42          private void initForm()
43          {
44              this.setText("About");
45              this.setAutoScaleBaseSize(13);
46              this.setClientSize(new Point(305, 88));
47
48              label1.setFont(new Font("MS Sans Serif", 12.0f));
49              label1.setLocation(new Point(8, 8));
50              label1.setSize(new Point(280, 24));
51              label1.setTabIndex(0);
52              label1.setTabStop(false);
53              label1.setText("Hello Dialog World!");
54              label1.setTextAlign(HorizontalAlignment.CENTER);
55
56              button1.setLocation(new Point(88, 48));
57              button1.setSize(new Point(128, 24));
58              button1.setTabIndex(1);
59              button1.setText("OK");
60
61              this.setNewControls(new Control[] {
62                                    button1,
63                                    label1});
64          }
65
66          /**
67           * The main entry point for the application.
68           *
69           * @param args Array of parameters passed to the application
70           * via the command line.
71           */
72          public static void main(String args[])
73          {
74              Application.run(new About());
75          }
76      }
```

When the program runs, you'll see the blank Form window. When you click in the Form window, the About dialog appears, as shown in Figure 9.3. (Notice that the minimize and maximize buttons have been removed.)

FIGURE 9.3

The dialog comes up when users click in the blank Form window.

 You should note a few important things in the source code of Listings 9.1 and 9.2. First and foremost, notice how similar they are. The `Form1` and `About` classes are both extended from the `Form` class.

The `Form1` class has a `Form1_click()` method. (Remember, this is a convenient way to get a place to test things in your program.) In this method, in lines 31–35 of Listing 9.1, you can see that an `About` class was created, and then a call to its `showDialog()` method was made.

Where the `About` class is different is in the controls that were added to it. Notice that at lines 39 and 40 of Listing 9.2, there are declarations for a `Label` and a `Button` class. These objects are set up in the `initForm()` method. The nondefault properties for the `label1` object are set in lines 48–54. In lines 56–59 you can see that the nondefault properties are set for the `button1` object.

Handling Dialog Button Events

So you have a program that displays a dialog. Now you need to handle the events. One event is already handled for you—the close event. When users click the close button in the upper-right corner of the dialog, it closes and returns control to your program.

Let's take the current program with the About dialog. We'll make the OK button the Accept button.

NEW TERM In Visual J++, the Accept button is the one that users click to accept the values in a dialog. These buttons are usually labeled with "OK."

NEW TERM Also in Visual J++, the Cancel button is the one that users click to cancel a dialog without changing any values. These buttons are usually labeled with "Cancel."

There are two steps to doing this. First, go to the `About` Form's properties and find the `acceptButton` property. Edit the property so that the button you want for your accept button is selected.

Next, go to the OK button's properties. Find the `dialogResult` property and select OK. Now, when you run your program and bring up the About dialog, clicking the OK button will cause the dialog to disappear.

I hope you're doing these steps as I describe them. If you are, you'll see the following code, which sets the properties for the `Button` and the `About` form in the `initForm()` method:

```
button1.setLocation(new Point(88, 48));
button1.setSize(new Point(128, 24));
button1.setTabIndex(1);
button1.setText("OK");
button1.setDialogResult(DialogResult.OK);

this.setText("About");
this.setAcceptButton(button1);
this.setAutoScaleBaseSize(13);
this.setClientSize(new Point(305, 88));
this.setMaximizeBox(false);
this.setMinimizeBox(false);
```

So how is the calling code supposed to know the difference? Did the user click the close button or the OK button? Note that the `Button`'s properties have set the `dialogResult` property to `DialogResult.OK`. Also bear in mind that the close button has its own `dialogResult` property of `DialogResult.CANCEL`.

The calling code can use the `getDialogResult()` method to obtain the result code that was generated by the user. The following code shows how to handle the two possibilities in our program:

```
About dlg = new About();
dlg.showDialog();
int nResult = dlg.getDialogResult();
if( nResult == DialogResult.OK )
{
    // We got an OK signal.
}
else if( nResult == DialogResult.CANCEL )
{
    // We got a CANCEL signal.
}
```

Table 9.1 shows the fields in the `DialogResult` class that you'll want to use as your dialog results.

TABLE 9.1 THE FIELDS IN THE DialogResult CLASS THAT ARE USED FOR YOUR DIALOG RESULTS

Constant	Description
ABORT	The user has aborted an operation.
CANCEL	The user has canceled an operation.
IGNORE	The user has chosen to ignore the information that the dialog has presented.
NO	The user has answered no to a dialog query.
NONE	The user has answered none to a dialog query.
OK	The user has accepted the values in the dialog.
RETRY	The user has chosen to retry an operation.
YES	The user has answered yes to a dialog query.

Performing Tasks When Users Click

You might want to perform certain tasks when users click a button. To handle these situations, select the button control. Go to its event list in the Properties window, and find the click event. Double-click on it. An event handler for the click event will be added, and it will open the source code to the newly added method.

In the handler, you can add any code you need for handling the click event. If you want to close the dialog after you're done, just call the close() method. Bear in mind that the close() method will return a value of DialogResult.CANCEL.

Useful Form Methods

Various methods in the Form class can be useful for programming dialogs. They're also useful at other times. In this section, I'll mention and explain some of these.

The getDisplayRect() method returns the display area used to display components on the Form. The area may be a virtual area if the Form is scrollable. The following example shows how to get the display rectangle for a Form:

```
Rectangle rect;
rect = getDisplayRect();
int nWidth = rect.width;
int nHeight = rect.height;
int nX = rect.x;
int nY = rect.y;
```

The getFormState() method returns bits associated with the specified form state. The bits that are returned are determined by the integer argument passed to the method. Table 9.2 shows the possible values.

TABLE 9.2   VALUES FOR THE `getFormState()` METHOD

Constant	Description
`FORMSTATE_AUTOSCALING`	Represents the form's `autoScale` property.
`FORMSTATE_AUTOSCROLLING`	Represents the form's `autoScroll` property.
`FORMSTATE_BORDERSTYLE`	Represents the form's `borderStyle` property.
`FORMSTATE_CONTROLBOX`	Represents the form's `controlBox` property.
`FORMSTATE_HELPBUTTON`	Represents the form's `helpButton` property.
`FORMSTATE_HSCROLLVISIBLE` or `FORMSTATE_KEYPREVIEW`	Represents the form's `keyPreview` property.
`FORMSTATE_MAXIMIZEBOX`	Represents the form's `maximizeBox` property.
`FORMSTATE_MINIMIZEBOX`	Represents the form's `minimizeBox` property.
`FORMSTATE_PALETTEDIRTY` or `FORMSTATE_PALETTEMODE`	Represents the form's `paletteMode` property.
`FORMSTATE_SETCLIENTSIZE`	Represents the form's `size` property.
`FORMSTATE_STARTPOS`	Represents the form's `startPosition` property.
`FORMSTATE_TASKBAR`	Represents the form's `taskBar` property.
`FORMSTATE_WINDOWSTATE`	Represents the form's `windowState` property.

The following example returns the value of 1 if there is a maximize button on the Form. It returns 0 if there isn't.

```
int nValue;
nValue  = getFormState( FORMSTATE_MAXIMIZEBOX );
if( nValue == 1 )
{
    // Yes maximize box.
}
else
{
    // No maximize box.
}
```

The `getWindowState()` method returns the current state of the window. The returned value equates to one of the enumeration constants defined in the `FormWindowState` class. Those values are shown in Table 9.3.

TABLE 9.3 VALUES FOR THE FormWindowState CLASS

Constant	Description
MAXIMIZED	Represents a maximized window.
MINIMIZED	Represents a minimized window.
NORMAL	Represents a normally sized window.

The following example gets the current state of the window:

```
int nState;
nState = getWindowState();
if( nState == FormWindowState.MAXIMIZED )
{
    // The Form window is maximized.
}
else if( nState == FormWindowState.MINIMIZED )
{
    // The Form window is minimized.
}
else if( nState == FormWindowState.NORMAL )
{
    // The Form window is in a normal state.
}
```

The pointToScreen() method converts a point in terms of the Form to coordinates in terms of the screen. The following example shows how it's done:

```
Point formPoint = new Point( 10, 10 ); // Form coordinate 10, 10
Point screenPoint = pointToScreen( formPoint );
// Now screenPoint has the converted coordinates.
```

The setFormState() method sets elements of the Form's state. These elements are the ones that the getFormState() method deals with. (Refer to Table 9.2 for more information.) After you call the setFormState() method, the values returned in the getFormState() method will reflect the change. Any changes that result in visible changes to the window will be seen immediately.

The following example removes the minimize box from the Form:

```
setFormState( FORMSTATE_MINIMIZEBOX, false );
```

Almost every Windows programmer has at one time or another wanted to create a window that didn't place an item in the system taskbar. You can use the setShowInTaskBar() method to either allow or prevent a Form window from appearing in the system taskbar. The following example shows how to prevent the Form from appearing in the system taskbar:

```
setShowInTaskBar( false );
```

9

The last method we're going to talk about in this chapter sets the window's visibility to either visible or invisible. The setVisible() method takes a Boolean argument. The value of true makes the window visible; the value of false makes it invisible. The following example shows how to make a window invisible:

```
setVisible( false );
```

Summary

Dialogs are a powerful tool in your user-interface arsenal. And Visual J++ makes it easy to create and use them. After you've worked your way through this chapter, you should take some time and create dialogs of your own design. This experimentation will go far toward helping you feel comfortable with dialogs in Visual J++.

Q&A

Q Why are dialogs so important in Windows programs?

A They allow you to present many types of information to users and to ask for all kinds of information that the application needs in order to function. For instance, you might need to ask for the user's name and address. You might want to ask other users to select from a list of choices.

Q What's the difference between a Form and a dialog?

A Not much in the way they're created and designed. To add a dialog, you start by adding a Form to your project. You use the same user-interface objects, such as combo boxes, buttons, and list boxes, to add functionality. Where they differ is in how they're displayed. A dialog is displayed with the showDialog() method. This method then shows the dialog as a modal window.

Q How can you get input from OK and Cancel buttons?

A You start by adding them to the Form. Then you have to set the button dialogResult properties to OK and Cancel. Finally, in the dialog's Form class, set the acceptButton property to the OK button and the cancelButton property to the Cancel button.

Q Why should dialogs be modal? Why should interaction with the main program be paused until users are finished with the dialog?

A The main purpose for a dialog is to get information from a user that's needed to continue program execution. In most cases, the program wouldn't be able to continue without the information requested by the dialog, so it's only natural to pause the program until all the information has been given.

Q What are some dialog "don'ts"?

A Don't have minimize and maximize buttons on dialogs. Don't use pull-down menus in dialogs. Make sure that users can answer all queries and enter all information without having to refer to something in the main program.

Exercises

1. Create a Visual J++ application. Add a Form named Test. Add an OK and a Cancel button to the form and a label. Set the `acceptButton` property to the OK button and the `cancelButton` property to the Cancel button. Set each button's `dialogResult` property (`OK` and `Cancel`). In the main program, make a place to create and display the dialog (remember the click event handler). Compile and run the program.

2. Create an application. Add menus that give users three choices. Create three dialogs. For each of the menu selections, create and display one of the dialogs.

3. Create an application with a dialog. Ask users for their name and address. When users have made their entries and clicked the OK button, display the information that they entered.

DAY 10

Fonts and Text

Drawing text to a Java window is different from putting text into a Java control. When you draw text to a Java window, you're actually using graphics commands instead of just inserting text into a control. Today you'll learn how to draw to a Java window, how to alter the fonts so that you can draw with different font styles and colors, and even how to change font styles and colors in controls. In this chapter, we'll cover the following:

- The Graphics class
- Graphics screen coordinates
- The Font class
- Drawing text
- The FontMetrics class
- The Color class
- Finding the available system fonts

After you're familiar with the ins and outs of Java text and fonts, you can create applets and applications that are far more useful. That's because drawing with text makes your presentation richer and allows you a greater degree of flexibility in your display.

The Graphics Class

Before we talk about drawing text to a Java window, we need to talk about the Graphics class. The reason we have to start off by talking about the Graphics class is that drawing text to a Java window is a graphics operation. The Graphics class is what you use to perform all graphics operations. The Graphics class is a descriptor of the window to which you'll be drawing. It's similar to the device context in Visual C++; for any of you who have developed with Visual C++, you know that you must have a device context with which to draw. It's the same in Java; you must have a Graphics class.

With Java's graphics capabilities, you can draw lines, shapes, characters, and images to the screen inside of your applet or application. Most of the graphics operations in Java are methods defined in the Graphics class. You don't have to create an instance of the Graphics class in order to draw something in your applet. When you override your applet's paint method, or your application's onPaint method, you're given a Graphics class. By drawing to that class, you draw to your program's window, and the results appear onscreen.

Methods to Override for Painting

You can override two different methods if you want to paint every time your window is redrawn. For an application, you will want to override the onPaint() method. For an applet, you will want to override the paint() method. After these methods are overridden, every time the window is redrawn in response to a window event or a mouse movement, or something similar, either the onPaint() method for an application or the paint() method for an applet will be called. This will give you the opportunity to draw in your window.

This is what the onPaint() method in an application looks like:

```
protected void onPaint(PaintEvent pe)
{
    pe.graphics.drawString( "Hello Visual J++ World.", 10, 10 );
}
```

Notice that the PaintEvent class, named pe in this case, has a member class called graphics. This member class is the Graphics class we mentioned in the preceding section. One of its member methods is drawString(). That's the method we use to draw text to the Graphics class.

Next, you need to learn how to draw to an applet window. The method you will override for an applet is simply named paint(). It gets, as an argument, a Graphics class.

The following example shows you what a paint() method looks like for an applet. It also uses the drawString() member method to display "Hello Visual J++ World!" in the applet window.

```
protected void onPaint(PaintEvent pe)
{
g.drawString( "Hello Visual J++ World!", 100, 100 );
}
```

The repaint() and update() Methods

The repaint() and update() methods can be overridden in Java applets. They are members of the Component class. The Java system, or your program, might call the repaint() method to request that the window be refreshed. Typically, you call it if you have new things to display.

> **Caution**
>
> *Never override this method!* It calls the update() method to clear and repaint the screen.

10

The update() method belongs to the Component class. The default implementation clears the window area and then calls the paint() method. You should not directly call the update() method. The update() method is called by the repaint() method. You might want to override the update() method to perform additional functions. I often use it when I don't want the screen cleared before the paint() method is called.

If you clear the window for every screen refresh, you get a lot of screen flicker. Two things can remedy this problem: first, override the update() method, and second, don't clear the background of the screen each time a window refresh is called for. The window refresh will be smoother and your applet might look better.

Try It Yourself!

Before we get too much further, you need to create an application or an applet in which you draw a text string. Run Visual J++. If you're writing an application, open the form source code; if you're writing an applet, open the applet source code. Listing 10.1 shows how to draw text to an application window. The results are shown in Figure 10.1.

INPUT   **LISTING 10.1**   USING THE onPaint METHOD IN AN APPLICATION

```
1    protected void onPaint(PaintEvent pe)
2    {
3        pe.graphics.drawString( "Hello Visual J++ World.", 10, 10 );
4    }
```

FIGURE 10.1

*This Visual J++
application uses the
onPaint() method to
display text to the
window.*

ANALYSIS Adding the onPaint() method overrides the superclass onPaint() method. If
you've forgotten, refer to the discussion of the terms *superclass* and *override* in
Chapter 5.

There's another alternative to adding an onPaint() method. With Form1 in the Properties
window, click on the Events button in the Properties window. Scroll down until you find
the paint event. Double-click on the event and a Form1_paint() method will be added
for you. This method gets a PaintEvent method just like the onPaint() method.

For an application, add an onPaint() method exactly as shown in Listing 10.1. Then
compile the program and run it. You should see "Hello Visual J++ World!" in the window, as shown in Figure 10.1. For an applet, add a paint() method as shown in Listing
10.2. Compile the applet and then run it. You should see "Hello Visual J++ World!" in
the applet window, as shown in Figure 10.2.

INPUT   **LISTING 10.2**   USING THE paint() METHOD IN AN APPLICATION

```
1   protected void onPaint(PaintEvent pe)
2   {
3       g.drawString( "Hello Visual J++ World!", 100, 100 );
4   }
```

OUTPUT

FIGURE 10.2

*This Visual J++ applet
uses the paint()
method to display text
to the window.*

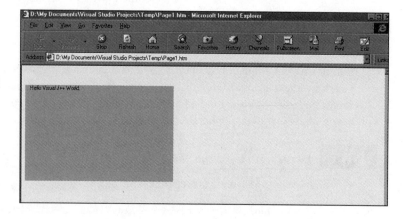

The Graphics Coordinate System

To draw an object onscreen, you call one of the drawing methods available in the Graphics class. All the drawing methods have arguments representing endpoints, corners, or starting locations of the object whose values are in the program's coordinate system. For example, a line might start at the point (10,10) and end at the point (20,20).

Java's coordinate system has the origin (0,0) in the upper-left corner. Positive x values go to the right. Positive y values go down. All pixel values are integers. There are no partial or fractional pixels. Figure 10.3 shows how you might draw a rectangle using a coordinate system.

FIGURE 10.3

The Java graphics coordinate system.

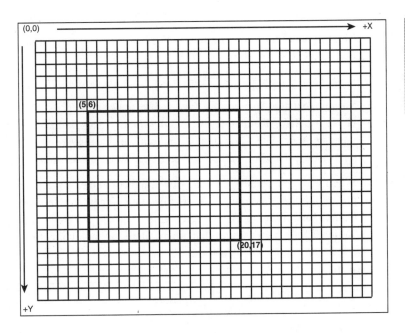

Java's coordinate system is different from many painting and layout programs that have their x and y intersection in the lower-left corner. If you're not used to working with upside-down graphics systems, this system might take a while to get used to. Let's experiment by going back to the applet or application you just wrote, in which you saw "Hello Visual J++ World!" onscreen. The second and third arguments of the drawString() method are the x and y coordinates. That's the point at which the string "Hello Visual J++ World!" will be drawn. Go ahead and change those values, recompile, and run the program. See what effect that change has on the appearance of the application or applet. Your program will look different because you're changing the points at which those strings will be drawn. Change the coordinates several times to experience the full effect.

The Font Class

There's always a font set in the Graphics class. If there wasn't, the drawString() method would not result in any text being drawn. Until now, we have drawn with the drawString() method using whatever font was currently selected in the Graphics class.

You can change the font that's currently selected in the Graphics class by first creating a font and then selecting it into the Graphics class. After a font is selected into a Graphics class, all subsequent text-drawing operations will be done using that font.

The following line creates a font with a TimesRoman font base in a plain style with a point size of 25:

```
Font font = new Font( "TimesRoman", Font.PLAIN, 25 );
```

Various fonts are standard for Java applications and applets. You can usually count on Helvetica, TimesRoman, Courier, and Symbol. Later in this chapter, we'll talk about how you can interrogate the system to find out which fonts are actually available. For now, we will assume that the standard and common fonts can be used.

When you create a new font, the first argument is the font typeface name. Some examples of this were mentioned in the preceding paragraph: Helvetica, TimesRoman, Courier, and Symbol. The second argument when you create a new font is the style. Table 10.1 shows the styles that are available when you create a font in Java.

TABLE 10.1 FONT STYLES

Name	Description
Font.BOLD	The bold style constant
Font.ITALIC	The italicized style constant
Font.PLAIN	The plain style constant

You can combine font styles. For instance, your style can be the italic style combined with the bold style, as this example shows:

```
Font font = new Font( "Courier", Font.BOLD + Font.ITALIC, 30 );
```

After you've created a font, you have to set it into a Graphics class before it can be used. The following example shows a newly created font being selected into the Graphics class:

```
Font font = new Font( "Helvetica", Font.BOLD, 50 );
g.setFont( font );
```

Note

> Many of the example applets and applications are simplified to zero in on the topic that's being covered. These applets and applications will run just fine, but much of the startup code that's created has been removed.

I've created a simple demonstration applet in the paint() method. Two fonts are created and used to draw strings to the applet window. Listing 10.3 shows this simple applet. See whether you can take this straightforward applet and enhance and embellish it to do other interesting things.

10

INPUT **LISTING 10.3** A SIMPLE APPLET FOR YOU TO TRY

```
1       import java.awt.*;
2       import java.applet.*;
3
4       public class Applet1 extends Applet
5       {
6           /**
7            * The entry point for the applet.
8            */
9           public void init()
10          {
11              initForm();
12          }
13
14          /**
15           * Initializes values for the applet and its components
16           */
17          void initForm()
18          {
19              this.setBackground(Color.lightGray);
20              this.setForeground(Color.black);
21          }
22
23          public void paint(Graphics g)
24          {
25              // Create the first font.
26              Font font1 = new Font( "TimesRoman",
```

continues

LISTING 10.3   CONTINUED

```
27                    Font.PLAIN, 35 );
28                // Select the first font into the
29                // graphics class.
30                g.setFont( font1 );
31                // Draw the text to the Graphics
32                // class.
33                g.drawString( "This is the first line.", 5, 45 );
34
35                // Create the second font.
36                Font font2 = new Font( "Courier",
37                    Font.ITALIC, 45 );
38                // Select the second font into the
39                // graphics class.
40                g.setFont( font2 );
41                // Draw the text to the Graphics
42                // class.
43                g.drawString( "This is the second line.", 5, 100 );
44
45            }
46
47        }
```

When the applet runs, you'll see two lines of text. The first line will be in a smaller font, saying, "This is the first line." The second line will be in a larger italic font, saying, "This is the second line." You can see the applet running in Figure 10.4.

OUTPUT

FIGURE 10.4

This applet creates and uses two different fonts.

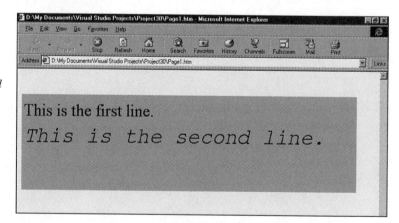

Note The default applet size that's created is 320×200. For this applet, you'll need to change the width so that these large text strings will fit in the window. I changed mine to 720×200 and the text strings could be seen completely.

Drawing Text

We've already talked about drawing text to a Graphics class using the drawString() method. This method takes three different arguments: the first argument is the string you want to draw to the Graphics class; the second argument is the x coordinate to which you'll be drawing; and the third argument is the y coordinate.

There is another method that belongs the Graphics class that allows you to draw text to the window. It is called drawChars(). This method contains five arguments: the first argument is a character buffer containing the characters you want drawn to the screen; the second argument is an integer indicating the index of the starting character you want to draw; the third argument tells it how many characters to draw; the fourth argument is the x coordinate; and the fifth argument is the y coordinate.

Note You can draw a text string with the drawChars() method and begin at any character within the string. For instance, you might have a string "This is a test" and just want "is a test" to be output. In this case, the starting character you'd specify would be 5 because the "i" character is at index 5.

Following is a short example showing how to allocate a character buffer, assign it characters, and then draw to the window using the drawChars() method:

```
char txt[] = new char [10];
txt[0] = 'H';
txt[1] = 'e';
txt[2] = 'l';
txt[3] = 'l';
txt[4] = 'o';
g.drawChars( txt, 0, 5, 50, 50 );
```

The drawChars() method is obviously not as easy to use as the drawString() method. You'll use the drawChars() method only in rare circumstances when you need extra control over what's being drawn on the screen. One example of this situation might be when you've loaded data from a file, or data from some sort of Internet URL, and you want to display only part of it. Another example of this is when you have a text string and you want more control over where each character is displayed in the window. You could display the first character at a certain coordinate, then add 15 to the x coordinate and add 5 to the y coordinate for the second character to make a more interesting display of your character string. I've written a method called drawCrazyText(). It takes that same "Hello" character buffer and draws it at random y locations, so it looks sort of crazy.

The drawCrazyText() method is used in the program shown in Listing 10.4. The result is shown in Figure 10.5.

LISTING 10.4 SOURCE CODE FOR A PROGRAM THAT USES THE drawCrazy() METHOD

```
1    import java.awt.*;
2    import java.applet.*;
3
4    public class Applet1 extends Applet
5    {
6
7        public void init()
8        {
9        }
10
11       public void paint( Graphics g )
12       {
13           drawCrazyText( g );
14       }
15
16       public void drawCrazyText(Graphics g)
17       {
18           Font font = new Font( "TimesRoman", Font.PLAIN, 20 );
19           g.setFont( font );
20
21           char txt[] = new char [10];
22           txt[0] = 'H';
23           txt[1] = 'e';
24           txt[2] = 'l';
25           txt[3] = 'l';
26           txt[4] = 'o';
27
28           g.drawChars( txt, 0, 5, 50, 50 );
29
30           for( int i=0; i<5; i++ )
31           {
32               int nRnd = (int) ( Math.random() * 10.0 );
33               g.drawChars( txt, i, 1, 50 + i * 10, 80 + nRnd );
34           }
35
36       }
37
38   }
```

FIGURE 10.5

This program calls the drawCrazy() method, which displays the string drawn normally and the string drawn haphazardly.

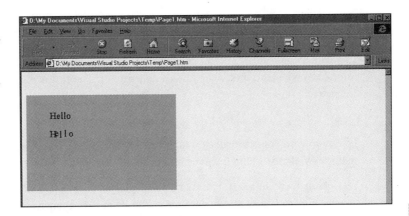

ANALYSIS The drawCrazy() method starts off by creating a new font and selecting it into the Graphics class in lines 8 and 9. A char buffer is created at line 11, and lines 12–16 assign characters to the first five array elements. Line 18 draws the character to the screen with a normal appearance. But in the for loop that starts at line 20, the characters are drawn one at a time, each with random x and y offsets so that the characters appear to be drawn haphazardly.

RANDOM NUMBERS

You might have noticed in the drawCrazyText() method that a random number was generated using the Math.random() method. The Math.random() method generates a floating-point number from 0.0 to 1.0. If you want to get a range of values from 0 to 5, as in this example, multiply by 5.0. That way you get all sorts of floating-point (decimal) values from 0.0 to 5.0. Whatever your range is, you multiply Math.random() by your highest number. Then you need to make sure that if you need an integer instead of an actual floating-point number, you cast it, as I did in the drawCrazyText() method.

Setting Colors in Java

You can set the color with which the Graphics class will draw in Java by first creating a Color class and then selecting the Color class into the Graphics class. Colors have three components: a red, a green, and a blue component. Each component is represented by a byte value that describes the color's intensity. These values range from 0 to 255. The lower the number, the less of that color is mixed in the resulting shade. For instance, if the red component has a value of 0, there will be no red in the resulting shade. If the green component has a value of 255, the resulting shade will contain the most green allowed. These three-color components are commonly referred to as the RGB model, with RGB standing for red, green, and blue.

To create a color class, all you need to do is use the new operator and supply the three-color components to the Color class's constructor. The following code illustrates how it's done:

```
Color color = new Color( r, g, b );
```

These three component values, represented here by r, g, and b, are integer values. Once again, they should contain values ranging from 0 to 255.

You can also create a Color class by specifying explicit RGB values in the color constructor. For instance, if you want the red to be at half intensity, you can specify 128, which is approximately half of 255. If you want green and blue to be somewhat less, you can specify 100. This will give you a reddish-gray tint.

The following example shows you how to create such a color:

```
Color color = new Color( 128, 100, 100 );
```

The Color class has 13 predefined colors that might be all you need. Using these is much easier than creating custom colors by using RGB values. They represent the common colors of black, blue, cyan, dark gray, and so forth. Table 10.2 shows these values and their RGB equivalents.

TABLE 10.2 STANDARD COLORS

Color Name	RGB Value
Color.white	255, 255, 255
Color.black	0, 0, 0
Color.lightGray	192, 192, 192
Color.gray	128, 128, 128
Color.darkGray	64, 64, 64,
Color.red	255, 0, 0
Color.green	0, 255, 0
Color.blue	0, 0, 255
Color.yellow	255, 255, 0
Color.magenta	255, 0, 255
Color.cyan	0, 255, 255
Color.pink	255, 175, 175
Color.orange	255, 200, 0

After a color class has been created, you must select it into the Graphics class before any draw operations can use it. To do this, you use the setColor() method. The following source-code example shows you how to use the setColor() method:

```
g.setColor( color );
```

Anytime you want to change the color you're drawing with, you must select the desired color into the Graphics class. You can also set colors into the canvas itself. The canvas is the main window of the applet. To do this, simply use the setForeground() and setBackground() methods. The following example shows how to create two colors and then set the foreground color and the background color of the canvas:

```
Color color_f = new Color( 255, 255, 0 );
Color color_b = new Color( 0, 255, 255 );
setForeground( color_f );
setBackground( color_b );
```

10

Tip

You'll have a hard time getting the exact color you want if you have to rely on your judgment (except for a handful of colors that you might have memorized). The way I find the exact color I want is to run Microsoft Paint. I then double-click on a color to bring up the Edit Colors dialog box. Then I click on the Define Custom Colors button, which brings up an addition to the dialog box that then lets me experiment with colors. I can find out what any numeric value will look like, or use a color selector to go the other direction and find the numeric values for a color.

The FontMetrics Class

You can use the FontMetrics class to compute the exact length and width of a string. This is helpful for measuring a string size in order to display it in the right position. For example, you can center strings in the viewing area using the FontMetrics class. A FontMetrics class has the following attributes:

- *Leading:* This is pronounced *ledding*. This is the amount of space between lines of text.
- *Ascent:* This is the height of a character, from the baseline to the top.
- *Descent:* This is the distance from the baseline to the bottom of a descending character, such as *j*, *y*, and *g*.
- *Height:* This is the sum of leading, ascent, and descent.

The concepts in the preceding list are illustrated in Figure 10.6.

FIGURE 10.6

Java's font terminology originated mostly in the publishing field.

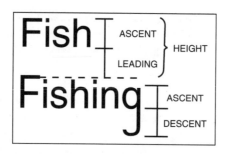

To get a `FontMetrics` object for either the selected font or a specific font, choose one of the following:

```
FontMetrics fm = g.getFontMetrics();
FontMetrics fm = g.getFontMetrics( font );
```

Notice that one line in the example gives the `getFontMetrics()` method an argument, and one does not. The version of the `getFontMetrics()` method that does not take an argument returns the `FontMetrics` class for whatever font is currently selected into the `Graphics` class. The `getFontMetrics()` method that takes an argument of a `Font` class returns a `FontMetric` class for the `Font` class that was passed into it.

After you have a `FontMetrics` class, you will frequently use five methods: `getAscent()`, `getDescent()`, `getLeading()`, `getHeight()`, and `stringWidth()`. I have written a short method that takes two arguments: a `Graphics` class and a `Fonts` class. It returns a string that contains all the information available about the font. The source code for this method follows:

```
String getFontInfo(Graphics g, Font font)
{
    String strInfo;
    FontMetrics fm;

    fm = g.getFontMetrics( font );

    strInfo = "The ascent is " + fm.getAscent() + ". ";
    strInfo += "The descent is " + fm.getDescent() + ". ";
    strInfo += "The leading is " + fm.getLeading() + ". ";
    strInfo += "The height is " + fm.getHeight() + ". ";
    strInfo += "The string width of 'Hello' is " +
        fm.getStringWidth( "Hello" ) + ".";

    return( strInfo );

}
```

Finding Out Which Fonts Are Available

If you're using Windows or a similar operating system environment, you can have many fonts installed on your system. Unfortunately, Java applets can't access your system fonts. Java applications, however, can.

For Java applets, depending on your version of the Java Virtual Machine (JVM), the fonts that are available to the JVM might differ slightly from those of another user. To help you identify the fonts you have available, you can use the getFontList() method.

Note

> **UNDERSTANDING THE Toolkit CLASS**
>
> The Toolkit class is an abstract class you can use to get information about your system, such as the available fonts, screen resolution, and screen size. To access the Toolkit object, your applet must call the getDefaultToolkit() method, using the method's return as a reference to the object. In addition to the getFontList() method used in the FontQuery1 applet, you might want to use the getScreenResolution() method, which returns the screen's resolution in dots per inch.

10

The source code for the complete FontQuery1 applet is shown in Listing 10.5. The applet is shown running in Figure 10.7.

INPUT   **LISTING 10.5**   THE FONTQUERY1 APPLET

```
1    // FontQuery1.java
2
3    import java.awt.*;
4    import java.applet.*;
5
6    public class FontQuery1 extends Applet
7    {
8        public void init()
9        {
10       }
11
12       TextArea txArea = new TextArea();
13
14       public void populateFontList()
15       {
16           Toolkit toolkit = Toolkit.getDefaultToolkit();
17           String strFontList[] = toolkit.getFontList();
18           for( int i=0; i<strFontList.length; i++ )
19               txArea.append( strFontList[i] + "\n" );
20       }
21
22}
```

Figure 10.7

*The FontQuery1
applet.*

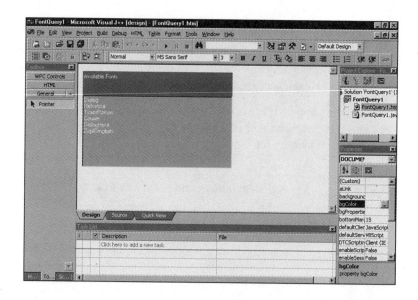

Fonts in Visual J++ Applications

If you're writing an application in Visual J++, selecting and setting fonts couldn't be easier. All you have to do to select the font for a label, or any other control for that matter, is
pull up the Font Selector Common dialog box.

Let's start by creating a new Visual J++ Windows application named ChangeFonts.
Double-click the Form1.java file in the Project Explorer window so that the form window is displayed. Place four labels on the form as shown in Figure 10.8.

Figure 10.8

*Place four labels on
the blank form.*

In the Properties window, find the font property as shown in Figure 10.9.

FIGURE 10.9

Find the font property in the Properties window.

If you click on the button that's to the right of the font property field, a font selector box will appear. It'll allow you to select the font type, style, and size as shown in Figure 10.10. Go ahead now and change the font type for all four labels. You can see my program in Figure 10.11—all four labels have a different font.

FIGURE 10.10

The font selector allows you to set the font type, style, and size.

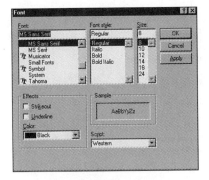

FIGURE 10.11

All four labels of the form are set in different fonts.

A Marquee Applet

And now for the question everyone who has a home page is asking: How do I create one of those marquee applets that continuously scrolls a text message?

When programmers who aren't familiar with Java find out I know Java, that's one of the first questions they ask. Well, this section is dedicated to those individuals who are dying to put such an applet on their home page. Figure 10.12 shows a simple marquee applet that's running. (It's hard to capture the motion in a book!) The source code for the applet is given in Listing 10.6.

INPUT   **LISTING 10.6**   SOURCE CODE FOR A SIMPLE MARQUEE APPLET

```
1    // Applet1.java
2
3    import java.awt.*;
4    import java.applet.*;
5
6    /**
7     * This class reads PARAM tags from its HTML host page and sets
8     * the color and label properties of the applet. Program execution
9     * begins with the init() method.
10    */
11   public class Applet1 extends Applet implements Runnable
12   {
13       private Thread      m_Applet1 = null;
14       int x = 740;
15       int y = 45;
16       String m_strMessage = "Visual J++ is really cool. AND I MEAN
         ➥COOL!!!";
17
18       /**
19        * The entry point for the applet.
20        */
21       public void init()
22       {
23           initForm();
24       }
25
26       /**
27        * Initializes values for the applet and its components
28        */
29       void initForm()
30       {
31           this.setBackground(Color.lightGray);
32           this.setForeground(Color.black);
```

```
33      }
34
35      public void destroy()
36      {
37      }
38
39      public void paint(Graphics g)
40      {
41          FontMetrics fm = g.getFontMetrics();
42          g.drawString( m_strMessage, x, y );
43          x -= 5;
44          if( x < -fm.stringWidth( m_strMessage ) )
45              x = 740;
46      }
47
48      public void start()
49      {
50          if (m_Applet1 == null)
51          {
52              m_Applet1 = new Thread(this);
53              m_Applet1.start();
54          }
55      }
56
57      public void stop()
58      {
59          if (m_Applet1 != null)
60          {
61              m_Applet1.stop();
62              m_Applet1 = null;
63          }
64      }
65
66      public void run()
67      {
68          while (true)
69          {
70              try
71              {
72                  repaint();
73                  Thread.sleep(50);
74              }
75              catch (InterruptedException e)
76              {
77                  stop();
78              }
79          }
80      }
81
82}
```

FIGURE 10.12

A simple marquee applet.

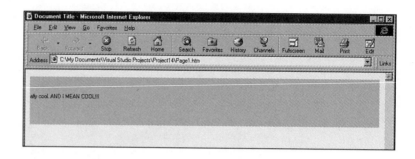

Setting the Font of a Control

At times you will want to change the font of a control in your program. Controls use a default font that can change from machine to machine. If you want complete control over what your controls look like, you'll want to explicitly set their font instead of relying on the default font, which might not be what you're expecting.

Setting the font of a control is easy: simply create a new font and then use the control's setFont() method. The following example creates a Label control, creates a new font, calls the label's setFont() method, and then adds the label to the container:

```
Label label1 = new Label( "This is a new label" );
Font font = new Font( "TimesRoman", Font.PLAIN, 25 );
label1.setFont( font );
add( label1 );
```

All the controls such as Label, TextArea, Choice, and Button have setFont() methods. This is because these controls are extended from the Container class that has a setFont() method. The following simple applet shows you a complete program in Listing 10.7 that creates and adds two labels with different fonts. The program is shown running in Figure 10.13.

INPUT   **LISTING 10.7**   SOURCE CODE FOR THE PROGRAM THAT CREATES AND ADDS TWO LABELS WITH DIFFERENT FONTS

```
1     import java.awt.*;
2     import java.applet.*;
3
4     public class Applet1 extends Applet
5     {
6
7         public void init()
8         {
9             Label label1, label2;
10
11            label1 = new Label( "This is label 1" );
```

```
12          Font font1 = new Font( "TimesRoman", Font.PLAIN, 25 );
13          label1.setFont( font1 );
14          label2 = new Label( "This is label 2" );
15          Font font2 = new Font( "Courier", Font.BOLD | Font.ITALIC, 35
);
16          label2.setFont( font2 );
17
18          add( label1 );
19          add( label2 );
20      }
21
22  }
```

OUTPUT

FIGURE 10.13

*This is what the simple
program shown in
Listing 10.7 looks like
when it runs.*

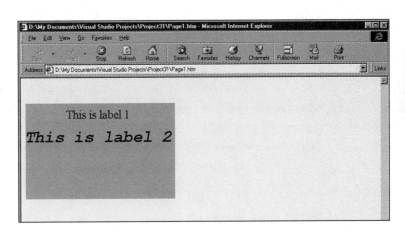

10

When you add controls such as Labels and Buttons in a Visual J++ application, you can
easily set the font by changing the control's properties.

Summary

In this chapter you've learned how to create fonts, how to select them into the Graphics
class, and how to draw to the Java window. You've also learned how to create colors and
select them for your drawing. Using text and fonts in your Visual J++ programs is an
essential part of creating professional-looking programs.

The techniques shown in this chapter are just the basics. It's up to you now to take what
you've learned and experiment with it.

Q&A

Q Why do we need to know about the `Graphics` class to draw text?

A Drawing text to a Java screen is part of Java's `Graphics` class. Anytime you draw to the Java window, you need to use the `Graphics` methods. The most notable exceptions to this rule are the Java controls. They take care of drawing text themselves. But you can be sure that somewhere within the inner workings of the Java controls, text is being drawn in a way similar to what you do when you draw text with the `Graphics` class.

Q In what methods does the Java window perform screen updates in response to window and mouse events?

A For applets, screen updates happen in the `paint()` method. For applications, screen updates happen in the `onPaint()` method. Neither of these methods is created when the startup code for a project is generated by Visual J++. You must add them yourselves. When added, they override the default methods.

Q What are the `repaint()` and `update()` methods?

A The `repaint()` method can be called from anywhere in a Java applet to force the screen to be updated. It's usually called when a display element changes and a screen redraw is necessary. The `update()` method is called in response to a request for a screen update. This can be either as a result of a window or mouse event, or the program actually calling the `repaint()` method. You should never call the `update()` method yourself.

Q How is the Java screen coordinate system laid out?

A The upper-left corner of the window starts at 0,0. As you move to the right, the x value increases. For each pixel you move, the value increments by one. As you move down, the y value increase. As with the x values, for each pixel you move, the value increments by one.

Q What is the `Font` class?

A The `Font` class is a Java object that can be created and that represents a font. When it's created, the font type name, font style, and font size must be specified. Font objects must be selected into the `Graphics` class before they're actually used.

Q Which font styles are available?

A There are three font styles: `PLAIN`, `ITALIC`, and `BOLD`. You can combine them by adding their values.

Q What methods can be used to draw text to the Java window?

A There are two: the `drawString()` and `drawChars()` methods. By far, the `drawString()` method is the easiest to use. You'll end up using it 99% of the time.

Q If the `drawChars()` method is more difficult to use than the `drawString()` method, why use it?

A Because it gives you greater control over how the string is drawn. You can draw each character separately. It also draws the contents of a `char` buffer. This means that you can load in data from a file or URL and then display it.

Q How can I change the color with which my text draws?

A You must first create a `Color` class. `Color` classes take three values: red, green, and blue. Depending on how you mix these three color channels, you can get any one of millions of colors. There are 13 predefined `Color` classes for the most common colors, including white, black, red, blue, and orange.

Q How can I find out the pixel width of a text string?

A You can use the `FontMetrics` class. For any font, you simply obtain a `FontMetrics` class, then use its `getStringWidth()` member method.

Q Why do you need to know which fonts are available?

A Some Java Virtual Machines, especially for different operating systems, might have different fonts available. Your presentation might depend on the way the text looks. For this reason, you might want to find out which fonts are available.

Q How do you set the font for a Visual J++ Windows application control?

A Make sure that the control is selected (you'll see the heavy border around it when it is). Find the font property in the Properties window, and click the button on the right side of the field. A file selector will appear. Use the file selector to determine the font that the control will use.

Q How can changing fonts enhance your programs?

A If your program uses the same font as every other program, it's boring for a user. It's also not going to necessarily communicate what you want to communicate. For instance, some programs cry out for large, bold text. Examples of this are programs that issue warnings to users—you want warnings to stand out. Color also helps you communicate with users. Red tells readers to pay special attention, whereas soft yellow tends to blend in and be less obtrusive.

Q Why not just use `Label` controls instead of drawing with text and changing the font?

A `Label` controls don't give you much control. It's hard to move them around in the window, and harder to center them in the window. All around, drawing with methods such as `drawString()` and `drawChars()` gives you far greater control than just adding a label to your program.

10

Review Exercises

1. Create a simple applet and add a `paint()` method. Inside the `paint()` method, create a new font. Select the font into the `Graphics` class with the `setFont()` method. Then draw a string to the program's window. Compile and run the program. Experiment with different fonts.

2. Create a new applet and add a `paint()` method. Inside the `paint()` method, create three fonts. Create them with different attributes. Try giving one a style of `Font.PLAIN`, one a style of `Font.ITALIC`, and one a style of `Font.BOLD`. Create all three with different sizes. Then create three `Color` classes and make sure that their colors will be clearly different. Draw three strings to the window. Before drawing the first string, select the first font and the first color. Before drawing the second string, select the second font and the second color. Before drawing the third string, select the third font and the third color.

3. Create a new application. Add three labels to the form. Change the text of the labels to something other than the default label1, label2, and label3 text. Then set the font for each label to something different. Compile and run the program.

DAY 11

Drawing

It's easy to get an application or an applet up and running with Visual J++. All you have to do is create a startup program and put some controls in the Java window, and you can have a program that performs useful functions.

But before long you'll outgrow this capability. You'll want to make your programs fancy; you'll want to make them look better; you'll want them to communicate more than what your text controls can. Today you'll learn how to use the Java drawing commands to make your programs look great.

In this chapter, you will do the following:

- Learn how to draw these items:
  Lines
  Rectangles
  Ovals
  Arcs
  Polygons
- See a demonstration program that uses these graphics techniques

- Learn how to copy areas in Java windows
- Learn how to clear your program's window

After you've mastered all these techniques, your programs will take on a new dimension. They'll start to look professional, unlike some of the amateur and shareware programs you currently see out there. With the drawing commands you'll learn today, your programs will sparkle.

The Graphics Class

In the preceding chapter, we covered drawing fonts to Java windows. We used the Graphics class and two of its member functions to perform this task. The two methods we used were drawString() and drawChars().

We got the Graphics class in an applet's paint() method or an application's onPaint() method. If you're writing an applet, it's possible, though, to get a Graphics class for a component in another method besides the paint() method. You can use the getGraphics() method to obtain a Graphics class with which you can do all of your drawing.

The following line of source code shows you how to get a Graphics class in an applet:

```
Graphics g = getGraphics();
```

Note

> When you draw in the paint() method, you'll already have a Graphics class and won't have to use the getGraphics() method. When you draw elsewhere, you'll have to get a Graphics class with the getGraphics() method.

So now, if you're in a method that doesn't have anything to do with a paint() method, you can go ahead and get a Graphics class and draw to a Java window. The only problem is that when the applet redraws or refreshes in response to some sort of a window move or window message, whatever you drew to the window that isn't in the paint() method will not be redrawn.

In what situation would you want to get a Graphics class outside of the paint() method and paint to the window? One example might be when you want to temporarily draw a small figure to a large window. You'd draw the figure to the program window, and then when you wanted it to go away, you could call repaint().

Lines

You can draw a line with the Graphics class drawLine() method. This method takes four arguments. The first and second arguments are the x and y coordinates of the starting point of your line; the third and fourth arguments are the x and y coordinates of the ending point of your line.

The following example draws a line in an applet's paint() method:

INPUT

```
public void paint(Graphics g)
    {
    // Draw from (25, 30) to (160, 170)
    g.drawLine( 25, 30, 160, 270 );
}
```

When you draw a line in an application's onPaint() method, your source code will look slightly different from that in the preceding example. That's because you don't get a Graphics class in an onPaint() method; you get a PaintEvent class. Of course, the PaintEvent class has a Graphics class as one of its member variables.

The following example shows the source code for drawing a simple line in a Visual J++ application's onPaint() method. Figure 11.1 shows what this application looks like when it runs.

INPUT

```
protected void onPaint(PaintEvent pe)
    {
    pe.graphics.drawLine( 25, 30, 160, 270 );
}
```

OUTPUT

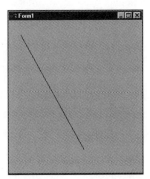

FIGURE 11.1

This simple Java application draws a line in the onPaint() *method.*

One of the problems with the drawLine() method is that it draws a line that's only a single pixel wide. Many times when you're drawing, you want wide lines—lines that have widths of three, four, five, six, and more pixels. One of the ways I've solved this dilemma is to write special functions that draw wide lines. Diagonal lines are slightly more difficult. The best way to accomplish this job is by drawing a polygon that simulates a thick line—I'll show you how after talking about polygons later. As an example, I have two methods to show you. One is called drawHorizontalLine(); the other is called drawVerticalLine(). They draw horizontal and vertical lines of any thickness. The source code is shown in Listing 11.1.

INPUT **LISTING 11.1**   METHODS TO DRAW THICK HORIZONTAL AND VERTICAL LINES

```
1    public void drawHorizontalLine( Graphics g, int x1, int y1,
2        int x2, int y2, int nThickness )
3    {
4        for( int i=0; i<nThickness; i++ )
5            g.drawLine( x1, y1 + i, x2, y2 + i );
6    }
7
8    public void drawVerticalLine( Graphics g, int x1, int y1,
9        int x2, int y2, int nThickness )
10   {
11       for( int i=0; i<nThickness; i++ )
12           g.drawLine( x1 + i, y1, x2 + i, y2 );
13   }
```

Before you draw lines, you'll also probably want to set the color. You do this the same way as you did when you drew text to the Java window. The first thing you do is either create a color object of your own or use one of the predefined Color classes, such as Color.white or Color.black. You then select your color object into the Graphics class. It's just like drawing with text: from that point on, anytime you draw to the Graphics class, the draw operation will be in that color.

You can get some really interesting effects with lines and colors. For instance, you can do a gradient fill in the background of your Java window. I've written a special function that draws a gradient fill in shades of blue in the Java window. This method, called doGradientFill(), is as follows, and its result is shown in Figure 11.2:

INPUT
```
public void doGradientFill( Graphics g, int nWinWidth, int
nWinHeight )
{
    int nStep = (int) ( (double) nWinWidth / 256.0 );

    int nX = 0;
    for( int i=255; i>=0; i— )
    {
        Color color = new Color( 0, 0, i );
        g.setColor( color );
```

```
        for( int j=0; j<nStep; j++ )
            g.drawLine( nX + j, 0, nX + j, nWinHeight );
        nX += nStep;
    }

}
```

FIGURE 11.2

A program using the
`doGradientFill()`
method.

OUTPUT

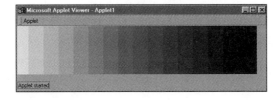

Two other methods draw lines: the `drawLines()` and `drawLineTo()` methods. The `drawLines()` method draws a series of connected lines based on an array of points. An example that uses the `drawLines()` method follows:

```
Point pt[] = new Point[5];
for( int i=0; i<5; i++ )
{
    int x = (int) ( Math.random() * 300 );
    int y = (int) ( Math.random() * 300 );
    pt[i] = new Point( x, y );
}
pe.graphics.drawLines( pt );
```

The `drawLineTo()` method draws a line from the current pen position to the specified location. The `drawLineTo()` method is available only in Visual J++ applications. The two most common forms of the `drawLineTo()` method follow:

```
Point pt( 20, 60 );
g.drawLineTo( pt );

g.drawLineTo( 50, 68 );
```

Rectangles

Java provides three types of rectangles:

- Plain rectangles
- Rounded rectangles
- Three-dimensional rectangles

For each of these rectangle types, you can choose between two methods. One draws the rectangle in outline form; the other draws the rectangle filled with a solid color.

11

Plain Rectangles

To draw a plain rectangle to the screen, you can use either the drawRect() or the fillRect() method. The drawRect() method draws a rectangle that is not filled; it's just an outline that's one pixel wide. The fillRect() method draws a rectangle that is filled with a solid color. Both methods take four arguments. The first two arguments are the x and y coordinates of the upper-left corner of the rectangle. The next two arguments are the width and height of the rectangle you want to draw.

The following example (shown in Figure 11.3) shows you how to draw two rectangles using the paint() method of an applet (note that fillRect() is available only in applets):

INPUT

```
public void paint( Graphics g )
{

    g.drawRect( 20, 40, 70, 80 );
    g.fillRect( 20, 130, 70, 80 );

}
```

OUTPUT

FIGURE 11.3

The program that uses the paint() *method just shown.*

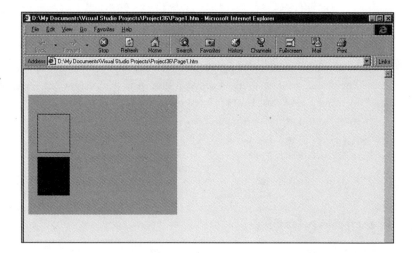

ANALYSIS The first call inside of the onPaint() method is to the graphics drawRect() method. The upper-left corner of the rectangle to be drawn is at x,y coordinate (20,40). It will draw a rectangle that is 70 pixels wide and 80 pixels high. The second call found in the onPaint() method is to the graphics fillRect() method. It will draw a solid rectangle. The upper-left corner of the rectangle that will be drawn is at the x,y coordinate (20,90). It will draw a rectangle that is 70 pixels wide and 130 pixels high.

Both of these methods will use whatever the currently selected color is. As with lines and text, you can select the color with which these methods will draw by creating a color object and selecting it into the Graphics class. Figure 11.3 clearly shows this.

Rounded Rectangles

Rounded rectangles are, as you might expect, rectangles with rounded edges. To draw them, you'll use the drawRoundRect() and fillRoundRect() methods. These methods are similar to those that draw regular rectangles except that the methods that draw rounded rectangles need two extra arguments. These arguments determine the width and height of the angle of the corners. Those two arguments determine how far along the edges of the rectangle the arc for the corner will start. The first argument is for the angle along the horizontal plane; the second argument, for the vertical. Larger values for the angle width and height make the overall rectangle more rounded. Values equal to the width and height of the rectangle itself produce a circle.

The following source code shows a paint() method that draws three rounded rectangles that appear in an applet window. Figure 11.4 shows these examples of rounded rectangles.

INPUT
```
public void paint( Graphics g )
{
    g.drawRoundRect( 10, 10, 120, 100, 30, 30 );
    g.drawRoundRect( 200, 10, 120, 100, 80, 30 );
    g.drawRoundRect( 140, 150, 50, 50, 50, 50 );

}
```

11

FIGURE 11.4

Examples of rounded rectangles.

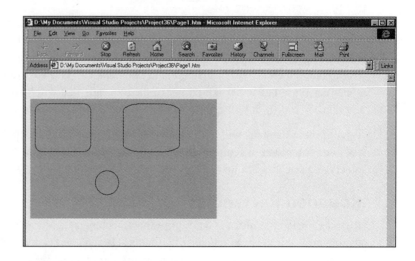

There is another method—this one available only in applications—that allows you to draw rectangles with rounded corners. It is the `drawRoundedRect()` method. It's less complicated than the `drawRoundRect()` method, but it gives you less control. Instead of letting you specify the `arcWidth` and `arcHeight` separately, the `drawRoundRect()` method simply lets you specify a radius value. This means that the rectangle will have symmetrically rounded corners and won't have a variance between the x and y extents of the corners. The following example shows how to use the `drawRoundedRect()` method:

```
int x = 50;
int y = 60;
int nWidth = 100;
int nHeight = 110;
int nRadius = 10;
g.drawRoundedRect( x, y, nWidth, nHeight, nRadius );
```

Three-Dimensional Rectangles

The last type of rectangle that's available for use in your Java programs is three-dimensional rectangles. They aren't really 3D; instead, they have a shadow effect that makes them appear either raised or indented from the surface of the window.

Three-dimensional rectangles have four arguments for the x and y of the start position and the width and height of the rectangle. The fifth argument is the Boolean value indicating whether the 3D effect is to raise the rectangle or indent it. If you want to raise the rectangle, the value will be `true`; if you want to indent the rectangle, the value will be `false`. As with other rectangles, there are also different methods for drawing and filling. The `draw3DRect()` method draws a rectangle that is not filled and is just a border. The `fill3DRect()` method draws a 3D rectangle that is filled with a solid color.

The following example shows a `paint()` method in an applet that draws two 3D rectangles:

```
public void paint( Graphics g )
{

    g.draw3DRect( 20, 20, 50, 60, true );
    g.fill3DRect( 20, 100, 50, 60, false );

}
```

The preceding source code draws two 3D rectangles. The first rectangle is not filled in; the second one is filled. Figure 11.5 shows an application with these two 3D rectangles drawn in its window.

FIGURE 11.5

This application shows two 3D rectangles that have been drawn.

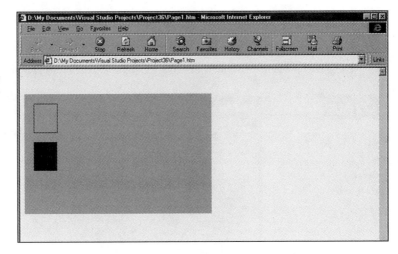

11

Polygons

Polygons are shapes with an unlimited number of sides. To draw a polygon, you need a set of x,y coordinates. The drawing method starts at the first coordinate, proceeds to the next coordinate and so forth until it has drawn all the lines in the polygon.

As with rectangles, you can draw an outline or a filled polygon. The methods you use for these tasks are `drawPolygon()` and `fillPolygon()`. You also have a choice of how you want to indicate the list of coordinates. They can be arrays of x and y coordinates, or they can be contained in an instance of the `Polygon` class. Let's start by using arrays of x and y coordinates. You can look back to Day 2, "Java Language Fundamentals," to refresh your memory about arrays.

To be specific, you need two separate arrays. One array is an integer array that contains all the x values. The other array is an integer array that contains all the y values. The `drawPolygon()` method takes three arguments. The first argument is the array of x coordinates, the second is the array of y coordinates, and the third is an integer value (either a constant or a variable) with the number of points in the polygon.

The following example draws a polygon by using two arrays—one of the x values, and the other of the y values:

INPUT
```
public void paint( Graphics g )
{
    int x[] = { 40, 90, 100, 140, 50, 60, 30 };
    int y[] = { 30, 75, 40, 70, 110, 80, 100 };
    int nPoints = x.length;

    g.drawPolygon( x, y, nPoints );

}
```

The `paint()` method in the preceding example is part of an applet shown in Figure 11.6.

OUTPUT

FIGURE 11.6

This applet shows a polygon that has been drawn in the window.

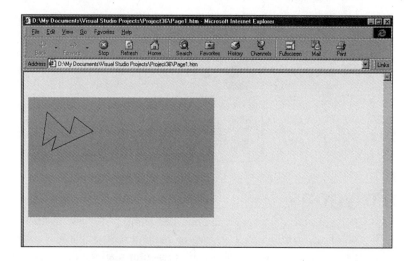

Earlier versions of Java did not necessarily close a polygon. If you wanted to draw a closed polygon, the last vertex would have to be the same as the first vertex. In current versions of Java, your polygon will automatically close, even if your last vertex is not the same as your first.

There's another way to draw a polygon. The second version of the `drawPolygon()` method takes a single argument. This single argument is an instantiation of a `Polygon` class. To use this second `drawPolygon()` method, you first create a `Polygon` class, and then you add the vertices of your polygon to the `Polygon` class. The following example shows you how to create a `Polygon` class and then use it to draw with:

```java
public void paint( Graphics g )
{

    // Instantiate the polygon class.
    Polygon polygon = new Polygon();

    // Add points to the polygon.
    polygon.addPoint( 20, 30 );
    polygon.addPoint( 50, 35 );
    polygon.addPoint( 60, 90 );
    polygon.addPoint( 35, 100 );
    polygon.addPoint( 10, 50 );

    // Draw the polygon.
    g.drawPolygon( polygon );

}
```

Drawing Thick Lines with Polygons

You can use the `drawPolygon()` method to draw thick lines. Let's say that you want to draw a line that's three pixels wide from (5,15) to (100,200). The following code in an applet will do this:

```java
Polygon polygon = new Polygon();
polygon.addPoint( 5, 15 );
polygon.addPoint( 8, 18 ); // Three pixels below line.
polygon.addPoint( 103, 203 ); // Three pixels below line.
polygon.addPoint( 100, 200 );
g.drawPolygon( polygon );
```

Ovals

You can draw an oval or an ellipse with the `drawOval()` and `fillOval()` methods. To draw an oval as an outline figure, use the `drawOval()` method. To draw a filled-in oval, use the `fillOval()` method. In Java, the oval is drawn based on its bounding rectangle. Therefore, give the parameters as if you were to draw a rectangle. The first two arguments are the upper-left corner of the rectangle. The next two arguments are the width and height of the rectangle. The following example shows you how to draw an outline oval:

```java
int x = 50;
int y = 76;
```

```
int w = 100;
int h = 110;
g.drawOval( x, y, w, h );
```

To draw a filled oval with its bounding rectangle's upper-left corner starting at x,y coordinate (100,110) with a width of 50 and a height of 60, you could use the following:

```
g.fillOval( 100, 110, 50, 60 );
```

Figure 11.7 shows the relationship between the x and y coordinates of the upper-left corner of the bounding rectangle and the width and height of what's actually drawn for the oval.

FIGURE 11.7

The drawOval() *method draws an oval based on its bounding rectangle.*

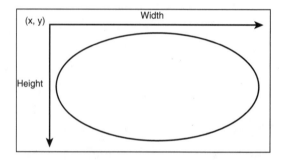

It's a lot of fun to experiment with ovals. You can create programs that produce interesting results. The following example applet, given in Listing 11.2 and shown in Figure 11.8, creates random filled and outlined ellipses in the Java window.

INPUT   **LISTING 11.2**   THE OVALS APPLET

```
1    // Applet1.java
2
3    import java.awt.*;
4    import java.applet.*;
5
6    /**
7     * This class reads PARAM tags from its HTML host page and sets
8     * the color and label properties of the applet. Program execution
9     * begins with the init() method.
10    */
11   public class Applet1 extends Applet
12   {
13       /**
14        * The entry point for the applet.
15        */
16       public void init()
17       {
```

```
18          initForm();
19
20      }
21
22      /**
23       * Initializes values for the applet and its components
24       */
25      void initForm()
26  {
27          this.setBackground(Color.lightGray);
28          this.setForeground(Color.black);
29      }
30
31      public void paint(Graphics g)
32      {
33
34          for( int i=0; i<10; i++ )
35          {
36              int x, y, w, h;
37              x = (int)( Math.random() * 300 ) + 20;
38              y = (int)( Math.random() * 200 ) + 20;
39              w = (int)( Math.random() * 150 ) + 30;
40              h = (int)( Math.random() * 100 ) + 30;
41              if( Math.random() > .5 )
42                  g.drawOval( x, y, w, h );
43              else
44                  g.fillOval( x, y, w, h );
45          }
46
47      }
48  }
```

11

OUTPUT

FIGURE 11.8

The program shown in Listing 11.1 draws random, filled, and outlined ellipses in the Java window.

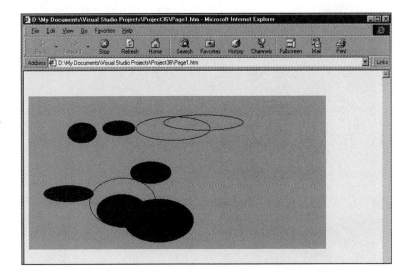

Arcs

Arcs are probably the most complex shapes to draw in Java. An arc is nothing more than part of an oval. Figure 11.9 shows an application with some arcs drawn in it.

FIGURE 11.9

Arcs drawn in a Java window.

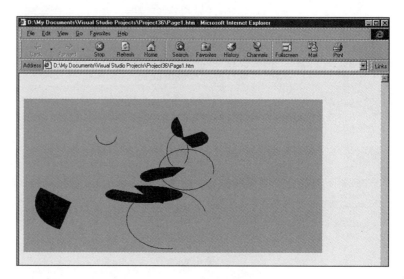

There are two ways of drawing arcs. The drawArc() method draws an arc without filling it. The fillArc() method draws an arc and fills its interior. Both take six arguments. The first two arguments are the x and y coordinates of the upper-left corner of the bounding rectangle—the same as for the oval. The next two arguments are the width and height of the bounding rectangle. Once again, the first four arguments of the arc methods are exactly the same as those of the oval methods. The fifth and sixth arguments to the arc methods specify the starting and stopping angles for the arcs. Filled arcs are drawn as if they were sections of a pie instead of being joined across the two endpoints. Both endpoints are joined to the center of the circle.

Tip

> The important thing to understand about arcs is that you're actually formulating the arc as an oval and then drawing only some of that oval. The starting corner and the width and height are *not* the starting point and width and height of the actual arc that is drawn onscreen; they're the width and height of the full ellipse of which the arc is a part.

The first two arguments determine the size and shape of the arc. The last two arguments, the starting and ending degrees, determine the starting and ending points. Let's draw a simple arc, an example that will be a U-shape. Figure 11.10 shows this arc drawn in an applet window. The source code for the paint() method of the program follows:

```
public void paint( Graphics g )
{
    g.drawArc( 10, 50, 200, 150, 180, 180 );
}
```

FIGURE 11.10

An arc in the shape of a U.

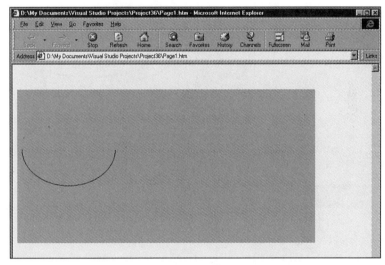

11

The U-shaped arc is actually part of a complete circle. To construct the method to draw this arc, the first thing you do is think of the arc as a complete circle. Then, you find the x and y coordinates and the height and width of the circle. Those four values are the first four arguments of the drawArc() or fillArc() methods. Figure 11.11 shows you how to get those values from the arc.

To get the last two arguments, think in degrees around the circle. You find 0 degrees at 3 o'clock; 90 degrees at 12 o'clock; 180 degrees at 9 o'clock; and 270 degrees at 6 o'clock. In this example, the starting point is to the left of the circle where the U begins at 180 degrees. That will be the fifth argument.

The sixth and final argument is another degree value indicating how far around the circle to sweep, and the direction to go in. It's not the ending degree, as you might think. In this case, because you're going halfway around the circle, you're sweeping 180 degrees. Therefore, 180 degrees is the last argument you'll give to the drawArc() method. The important part is that you're sweeping 180 degrees counterclockwise, which is in the positive direction in Java. If you're drawing an upside-down U, you're sweeping 180 degrees clockwise, which is in the negative direction, and the last argument is negative 180 degrees.

FIGURE 11.11

Constructing a circular arc.

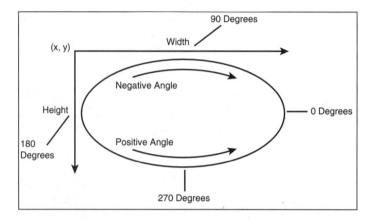

Here's the code for the example of drawing a U. A filled U is below it, as shown in Figure 11.12.

INPUT

```
public void paint( Graphics g )
{
    g.drawArc( 10, 10, 200, 150, 180, 180 );
    g.fillArc( 10, 170, 200, 150, 180, 180 );
}
```

OUTPUT

FIGURE 11.12

Two semicircular arcs.

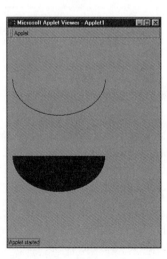

The `copyArea()` and `clearRect()` Methods

The `copyArea()` method copies an area of the component's window by a distance specified by two arguments. It also needs a coordinate for the upper-left corner of the source rectangle. This method copies downward and to the right. To copy an area of the component to the left or upward, specify a negative value for the distance value. If a portion of the source rectangle lies outside the bounds of the component or is obscured by another window or component, `copyArea()` will be unable to copy the associated pixels. The area that is omitted can be refreshed via a call to the component's `paint()` method.

The following source code shows you how to copy the rectangle at (10,25) with a width of 100 and a height of 80 to a rectangle that's 250 pixels to the right and 280 pixels down:

```
g.copyArea( 10, 25, 100, 80, 250, 280 );
```

The `clearRect()` method clears a rectangular region of your program's window. It takes four arguments: the first two are the upper-left corner of the rectangle to clear; the next two, the width and height of the rectangle to clear. The following source code shows how to use `clearRect()`:

```
int x = 50, y = 65;
int nWidth = 100, nHeight = 150;
g.clearRect( x, y, nWidth, nHeight );
```

11

Summary

Using Java's graphics capabilities will make your programs far more professional-looking than just putting some controls in the window. A program that uses graphics communicates far better than one that simply uses text. It also shows that you're willing to take the time to make your program look great.

Java provides many methods with which you can draw. Many of them were presented in this chapter. Although there are some other methods in the `Graphics` class, what you learned in this chapter will cover 99% of all of your needs. Learn these methods well!

Q&A

Q Are there other ways to obtain a `Graphics` class in an applet besides waiting for one to be passed to your `paint()` method?

A Yes. You can use the `getGraphics()` method. The problem with drawing outside of the `paint()` or `onPaint()` methods is that screen refreshes will redraw only code that's invoked from the `paint()` or `onPaint()` methods.

Q How do you draw lines?

A The easiest way is with the `drawLine()` method. It takes four arguments. The first two are the starting coordinates of the line, and the next two are the ending coordinates of the line. The line is drawn with the currently selected color.

Q Are there different methods that draw lines?

A Yes, the `drawLines()` and the `drawLineTo()` methods can be used. The `drawLines()` method draws multiple lines. The `drawLineTo()` method draws a single line from the currently set draw coordinate to another specified point.

Q What kinds of rectangles can you draw?

A There are three main types: a plain rectangle, a rounded rectangle, and a 3D rectangle. You can draw a plain rectangle with the `drawRect()` method. You can draw a rounded rectangle with the `drawRoundRect()` or `drawRoundedRect()` methods. You can draw a 3D rectangle with the `draw3DRect()` method.

Q How can you draw polygons?

A The easiest way is with the `drawPolygon()` method. It takes as an argument an array of points. These points are then used to draw a polygon.

Q Are ovals difficult to draw?

A No more difficult than other shapes. The thing to remember about an oval is that you specify a bounding rectangle for it. Imagine a rectangle into which the oval will fit. Use the x,y coordinate of the rectangle's upper-left corner for the first two arguments of the `drawOval()` method. Then get the width and height of the rectangle into which your oval fits. This gives you the third and fourth arguments for the `drawOval()` method.

Q Why do you need a `Graphics` class to draw?

A The `Graphics` class provides the draw methods with a context in which it will paint. It's important that all painting be done in light of the context in which the operations will be performed. In this way, the paint methods can be used in varying contexts, such as windows, printers, and other devices.

Q Why isn't a method to draw circles provided?

A The `drawOval()` method easily accomplishes the same thing. And there isn't a native circle-drawing function in the Windows API, so nothing would map to any API calls.

Q Why is it important to draw to a Visual J++ program's window? Why not just use text and user-interface controls?

A Drawing can communicate much more than text and user-interface controls. For instance, you can draw graphics and charts and can illustrate ideas.

Review Exercises

1. Create an applet. Using a `for` loop, draw lines across the window from top to bottom with one color. After you've done this, go back and change the color each time through the loop.

2. Draw a picture of a bus with the Java drawing commands. Try to use mostly lines, rectangles, and ovals.

3. Create an application that draws text inside of drawn rectangles. Center the text in the rectangles. Then add some ovals with text centered in them. Refer to Day 10, "Fonts and Text," to refresh yourself on using the `TextMetrics` class to center a text string.

11

DAY 12

Images

You've already learned how to draw with fonts so that you can present your program using lots of text. And you've learned how to draw to the Java window so that your presentations can be richer and more professional looking. This chapter will teach you how to use images so that your programs can display just about anything you want.

Today you will complete these tasks:

- Understand the `Image` class
- Learn about Image observers
- Load images
- Learn about GIF and JPG files
- Use the `PictureBox` control that's provided with Visual J++ for applications
- Draw images
- Use `MediaTracker` to help you wait for images to come in
- Create a clipping region before you draw

- Create borders for your images
- Invert your images

Don't underestimate the importance of images. Up until now, you've probably seen Java applets on the Web doing cute little animations, but that's not the full extent of what you'll be using images for. Images let you load photographs and complex drawings. These allow you to present information and data that would otherwise be impossible to present in your programs.

Picture File Types: GIF and JPG

It's a good idea to start off with a thorough understanding of the types of image files your Java applets and applications will usually be dealing with. Java will load two major types of image files. Java applications actually load more than two types, but applets on the Web load only two types; so we'll discuss these two types in this chapter.

The two types we'll talk about are GIF images and JPG images. GIF stands for Graphics Interchange Format. JPG (sometimes JPEG) stands for Joint Photographic Experts Group. What we'll do now is describe the two image file formats and discuss the different advantages and disadvantages of each. Deciding which image to use in which setting will be important.

GIF Image Files

The GIF format, a creation of CompuServe, is used to store multiple bitmap images in a single file for exchange between platforms and systems. In terms of number of files in existence, GIF is perhaps the most widely used format for storing multibit graphics and image data. Even a quick peek into the graphics file section of most BBSs and Internet servers seems to prove this true. Many of these are high-quality images of people, landscapes, and cars, and astrophotographs. Most GIF files contain 16- or 256-color quality images. Grayscale images such as those produced by scanners are also commonly stored using GIF, although monochromographics such as clip art and document images rarely are—instead they're usually stored as TIF documents.

GIF is not associated with any particular software application. GIF also is not created for any particular software application need, although most software applications that read and write graphical image data, such as paint programs, scanner and video software, and most image-file display and conversion programs, usually support GIF.

The biggest contrast between GIF and JPG is that GIF uses a lossless compression. The compression method GIF uses is LZW. This compression method does not degrade the picture quality at all. Every time you save and load the same GIF image, it is re-created with 100 percent integrity. For this reason, if you have an image that must be crisp and clear, and must be reproduced with the absolute highest quality, GIF would be your choice.

One limitation of GIF in certain circumstances is that it is limited to 256 simultaneous colors. The 256 colors, though, are selected from a palette of millions of colors, but GIF files can use only 256 of those colors at a time. For most Web applications, there's a commonly accepted palette known as the browser-safe palette that many GIF images now use. If you use this browser-safe palette, your GIF images are almost guaranteed to have the best reproduction on systems all over the world. However, if you use some custom palette that is not easy to match on all systems, your image might not look the same and might suffer when it is displayed on another system. One big advantage of GIF files is that one GIF file can store multiple images, and the multiple images can be displayed in sequential order within a browser. These are called animated GIFs, and they are very popular on the Web.

Note

One of the ideals in Web development are pages with sharp, clear colors for the most commonly used eight-bit color displays. Image designers are recommended to use the palette of 216 Internet-safe colors that will not change or dither when viewed cross-platform over the Internet. Almost every imaging program offers you the choice of using the Internet-safe palette.

12

JPG Images

JPG refers to a standards organization, a method of file compression, and sometimes a file format. The JPG file interchange format is designed to allow files containing JPG and coded data streams to be exchanged between otherwise incompatible systems and applications. For instance, a Macintosh and an IBM-compatible computer can share the same file. JPG files, unlike GIF files, use a compression method that degrades the image at least somewhat. This is called lossy compression; that is, there is a certain amount of loss every time the file is saved. For this reason, if you need an exact replication of the original image, JPG is not necessarily the choice you should make.

One advantage of JPG, however, is that even with the image degradation you get, for photographic images, you really can't tell much of a difference. It does a great job in images of near photographic quality as opposed to those with crisp, sharp edges. JPG images are also composed of 24-bit colors. Each pixel in a JPG image can be a different color selected from a palette of millions. This is far better than the limitation of 256 colors in a GIF palette. In this case, a JPG image can consist of millions and millions of simultaneous colors.

GIF and JPG Comparisons

Let's start by taking some examples so that we can see the difference in different types of images. First, we'll start with an image that is simple and has clearly defined edges and colors. This image was created with PC Paint and then saved as a bmp file. It was then converted to a GIF file using a conversion program. In Figure 12.1, you can see the GIF file.

Lots of conversion programs are available. I have a free one named ImageView that can be downloaded from www.infinitevision.net. This is a very simple program, but it's in the public domain and can be used free of charge.

FIGURE 12.1

The GIF file looks identical to the bmp file that was created originally. There is no loss of image integrity..

This same image saved as a JPG file with a moderate compression begins to lose its definition. It's not as clear and it's not nearly as crisp as the original. Figure 12.2 shows this image saved as a JPG with moderate compression.

FIGURE 12.2

The image saved as a JPG with moderate compression experiences degradation.

In this case, with an image that has sharp contrasts and clear colors, the GIF file saves to a smaller file than the JPG. With this image, the GIF file is 2,771 bytes and the JPG file is 8,382 bytes. Many times, we think of JPG files as saving to a smaller size than GIF files. This is not necessarily so, however, in the case of clean colors, crisp definition, and sharp edges.

The tables are turned between these file formats when you get to images that are photographic or near-photographic quality. Figure 12.3 shows the photograph of a parrot. This is the original image.

FIGURE 12.3

*The original photo-
graphic image of a
parrot.*

This photographic image of a parrot, saved as a GIF file, has near-perfect reproduction of
the original image. It saves to a GIF file as 81,640 bytes. As a JPG image, with moderate
compression, it saves to a file size of 22,518 bytes—a significant savings! JPG excels at
saving photographic and near-photographic images to small sizes without losing much
perceptible quality.

The `Image` Class

When you get right down to it, an image is nothing more than a collection of data. The
data is a set of RGB values that determine the color of each pixel. For instance, if you
have an image that's 10×10 (10 pixels across and 10 pixels high), there will be a total of
100 sets of data in that image. These sets of data will determine the color of each pixel in
the image. In Java, there are three components for each pixel: red, green, and blue. Just
as with the `Color` class that we talked about several chapters ago, these RGB values in an
image range from 0 to 255.

Other information also resides in an image. Besides the data that determines the color of
each pixel, images include parameters that determine the width and height of the image.
This additional data is usually stored in some sort of header, or some other place outside
of the actual data set.

The `Image` class is what Java uses to encapsulate all image data and image attribute data
that describe the color of each pixel, and the width, height, and other attributes of the
image.

You won't create an `Image` class with a new operator. You'll almost always get an `Image`
class from the applet or in an application from a `pictureBox` control.

An `Image` class has several methods you'll find useful. I've listed the ones I use often in
Table 12.1.

12

TABLE 12.1 IMPORTANT METHODS OF THE IMAGE CLASS

Method	Description
flush()	The flush() method flushes all resources and data used by the image object. The image object is reset to a state similar to when it was first created. The image data, therefore, must be re-created or reloaded after you've called the flush() method.
getGraphics()	This method is almost identical to the getGraphics() method we talked about several chapters ago. The Image class's getGraphics() method returns a Graphics class with which you can draw to the Image class. For instance, if you want to draw a line to your image, you simply retrieve the Graphics class by using the getGraphics() method, and then you draw a line to that Graphics class. It's simple!
getHeight()	This method returns the height of the image. It's possible that the Image class won't be able to determine the height. It can't determine the height, for instance, if the image isn't completely loaded yet. The getHeight() method will return a -1 if this is the case.
getWidth()	The getWidth() method returns the width of the image. If for some reason the width can't be determined yet, such as if the image is still being loaded, the getWidth() method will return a value of -1.
getSource()	The getSource() method is sometimes used in image processing. The getSource() method returns an ImageProducer class. The getSource() method gets the object that produces the pixels for the image. This method is called by the image filtering classes and by methods that perform image conversion and scaling.
getScaledInstance()	This method returns an Image class. The Image class is a scaled version of the original image. A new image object is returned that will render the image at the specified width and height by default. The new image object may be loaded asynchronously even if the original source image has already been loaded completely. If either the width or the height is a negative number, the value is substituted to maintain the aspect ratio of the original image dimensions. When you use the getScaledInstance() method, you can use various options to do the scaling. The first one is SCALE_AREA_AVERAGING. This option uses the area-averaging, image-scaling algorithm. The SCALE_DEFAULT option uses the default image-scaling algorithm. The SCALE_FAST option chooses an image-scaling algorithm that gives higher priority to scaling speed and smoothness of the scaled image. The SCALE_REPLICATE option uses the image-scaling algorithm embodied in the ReplicateScaleFilter class. The SCALE_SMOOTH option chooses an image-scaling algorithm that gives higher priority to image smoothness than to scaling speed.

ImageObserver

The Component class of an applet is able to know when an image arrives because it implements the ImageObserver interface. Most of Java's image manipulation routines are asynchronous, meaning they return immediately and let you know when they have finished an assignment. The notification, which flows to the ImageObserver interface, contains the following method:

```
public abstract boolean imageUpdate( Image img, int infoFlags, int x, int
y, int width, int height );
```

The Component class uses this method, but you can override it to get information about your image. The infoFlags parameter is a bit flag. Settings for the bits are shown in Table 12.2.

TABLE 12.2 BIT SETTINGS FOR THE INFOFLAGS PARAMETER

Name	Meaning
WIDTH = 1	Width is available and can be read from the width parameter.
HEIGHT = 2	Height is available and can be read from the height parameter.
PROPERTIES = 4	Image properties are now available. The getProperty() method can be used.
SOMEBITS = 8	Additional pixels for drawing a scaled image are available. The bounding box that the pixels can be read from have x and y width and height parameters.
FRAMEBITS = 16	A complete image frame has been built and can now be displayed.
ALLBITS = 32	A complete static image has been built and can now be displayed.
ERROR = 64	An error occurred. No further information will be available, and drawing will fail.
ABORT = 128	Image processing has been aborted. Set at the same time as ERROR. If ERROR is not also set, you can try to paint the object again.

12

The following routine is used to repaint the applet when the complete image arrives:

```
public boolean imageUpdate( Image which, int flags, int x, int y, int w,
int h )
{
    if( ( flags & ( ERROR ¦ FRAMEBITS ¦ ALLBITS ) ) != 0 )
    {
        repaint();
        return( false );
    }
```

```
    return( true );

}
```

The return value of the `imageUpdate()` method specifies whether you want to continue to get information on this image. Returning `false` will stop future notifications.

Loading Images

We have to talk about two topics when we go through loading images. The first topic we'll cover is loading images for Java applets; the second topic is loading images for Java applications. Although there are a lot of similarities between the two, there are enough differences that it will be wise to cover them separately.

Loading Images in Java Applets

There are two forms of loading images in Java applets. They both use the `getImage()` method. The first version of `getImage()` simply takes a fully qualified URL. If you know the entire URL path and filename, this will be easy enough to use; just give it an argument such as `http://www.myserver.com/image.gif` or something similar. The second version of the `getImage()` method takes two arguments. The first argument is a URL that represents the base URL. For instance, in the preceding example this would point to `http://www.myserver.com`. It could also point to some other directory within that server, such as `http://www.myserver.com/mystuff/images`. The second argument that this version of the `getImage()` method takes is the filename of the actual image. This filename is relative to the base. The following two examples of code show you how to use the `getImage()` method:

```
try
{
    URL url = new URL( "http://www.myserver.com/picture.gif" );
    Image im = getImage( url );
}
catch( MalFormedURLException e )
{
}

try
{
    URL url = new URL( "http://www.myserver.com" );
    Image im = getImage( url, "picture.gif" );
}
catch( MalFormedURLException e )
{
}
```

> **Note**
>
> At this moment, there's no way to add images to Visual J++ applets in the same way they're added to Visual J++ applications. For applications, you simply place an image control on the form. For applets, you must add the code to your source-code module.

The second version of the getImage() method is the most commonly used because applets can load only from the server they originated on. The methods to get either the URL of the page or the applet code's URL can then be combined with the final name of the image to construct a complete path. For instance, the following two source-code examples show you how the getDocumentBase() and the getCodeBase() methods can be used to simplify your image retrieval:

```
Image img = getImage( getDocumentBase(), "picture.gif" );
```

or

```
Image img = getImage( getCodeBase(), "picture.gif" );
```

The call you use depends on whether your image is grouped with the class files or the HTML Web pages on your server.

> **Note**
>
> You must be aware of the organization of your various data files in the server. If your images reside with your class files, use getCodeBase(). However, if your images reside with your HTML files, use getDocumentBase(). Many times, class files are grouped together with HTML files. In this case, both methods will return the same URL.

12

Remember that applets can read only from the server they originated on. Allowing applets to read from a local drive is definitely a security violation. If you try to read local files, they will cause a security exception.

Loading Images in Java Applications

Loading images in Java applications is almost a no-brainer. That's because the Visual J++ IDE offers an image control in its Toolbox window. With your Form window open, take a look at the WFC controls that are in the Toolbox window. This view is shown in Figure 12.4.

Notice in Figure 12.4 that the image icon in the WFC Controls window is selected. To put an Image control on the form, you simply press the left mouse button and pull down to create the control the size you want it. When you drag the `pictureBox` control to the form, though, it will be blank; it won't actually have a picture.

FIGURE 12.4

Make sure that you have the WFC controls selected in the Toolbox window.

Now you should notice that as long as the `pictureBox` is selected, (that is, as long as the `pictureBox` has been clicked on and you can see the thick border around it), the Properties window will reflect the properties in the `pictureBox`. Figure 12.5 shows the Properties box for this newly added `pictureBox` control.

FIGURE 12.5

The Properties box for the `pictureBox` *control.*

The `pictureBox` properties allow you a lot of control in determining how your `pictureBox` displays the image and responds to users. Table 12.3 provides an easy reference to each property name, its description, and its default.

TABLE 12.3 THE `PICTUREBOX` PROPERTIES

Property Name	Description	Default
allowDrop	Determines whether the control will receive drag/drop notifications.	False
anchor	Defines at which edges of the container a certain control is found. When a control is anchored to the edge, the distance between the control's closest edge and the specified edge will remain constant.	Top Left
backgroundColor	Displays text and graphics in a control.	Background Gray
borderStyle	Controls which type of border the `pictureBox` should have.	None
contextMenu	A pop-up menu to show when the user right-clicks the control.	None
cursor	Determines which cursor will appear when the mouse passes over the control.	Normal
dock	Determines the docking location of the control.	None
enabled	Indicates whether the control is enabled.	True
image	Determines the image that's displayed in the `pictureBox`.	None
location	Determines the position of the upper-left corner of the control with respect to its container.	0, 0
modifiers	Indicates the visibility level of the object.	None
name	Indicates the name used in code to identify the object. (See following Note box.)	None
size	Determines the width and height of the `pictureBox`.	Normal
sizeMode	Controls how the `pictureBox` will handle image placement and control sizing. Draws the image inside of the box without resizing the box in any way or scaling the image.	Normal
centerImage	Centers the image in the window.	False

continues

TABLE 12.3   CONTINUED

Property Name	Description	Default
tabIndex	Determines the index in the tab order that this control will occupy.	1
visible	Determines whether the control is visible or hidden.	True

Referring to the image property: if you click the button on the right part of the field, it brings up a Selector box with which you can select the image that will be displayed. Now, suppose I have just selected a JPG file. As you can see in Figure 12.6, when you select an image file, it shows up in your control.

FIGURE 12.6

When you select an image file, it shows up in a control.

In some of the examples, we will change the visible property to False so that we can do our own image drawing and manipulation; but for most of your uses, this will always be set to True.

 Note

In the name field, you can name your file anything you want. I recommend that you name it something that's meaningful to your program for easier reference.

FOR THE AMBITIOUS READER

In the section before this, where we talked about getting images in a Java applet, we used the getImage() method to load in an image from some URL out on the Internet. Well, in an application, you're not going to be loading images off of Internet servers, but you might want to get the same kind of access to an image that you get when you're working with Image classes. Image classes will give you a lot more flexibility because you can use the image to draw many times, you can do image processing, and you can do things the pictureBox control won't let you do. The pictureBox control has its own getImage() method. You can use this getImage() method just like you used the getImage() method in an applet. The following example shows you how to obtain the image from a pictureBox in an application:

```
// The pictureBox1 control already contains an image.
Image img = pictureBox1.getImage();
```

Displaying Images

To draw images, you'll use the Graphics class's drawImage() method. There are several variations of this, but the easiest one to use takes three arguments: the first argument as an Image class, the second argument as the x coordinate of the upper-left corner of the image, and the third argument as the y coordinate of the upper-left corner of the image. The following examples show you how to use this easiest form of drawImage() in both an application and an applet:

```
// Application
protected void onPaint( PaintEvent pe )
{
    // m_Image is an Image class that's already loaded
    int x = 10, y = 10;
    pe.graphics.drawImage( m_Image, x, y );
}

// Applet
public void paint( Graphics g )
{
    // m_Image is an Image class that's already loaded
    int x = 10, y = 10;
    g.drawImage( m_Image, x, y, this );
}
```

12

Figure 12.7 (shown after Listing 12.1) shows an application. The application used a pictureBox to load the image of the sailboats, but then the visible property of the pictureBox was set to False. Our first action, then, used the pictureBox's getImage() method to get the image. Next we used the drawImage() method and the onPaint() method to draw this image ourselves. So rather than rely on pictureBox's native drawing capabilities, we went ahead and drew the image ourselves. In this case, it was just to show you how to draw an image in an application. However, in the future at times you'll want more control than a pictureBox offers, and you'll want to draw the image yourself. The source code for an entire application is given in Listing 12.1.

INPUT

LISTING 12.1 AN APPLICATION THAT USES THE PICTUREBOX CLASS'S GETIMAGE()
METHOD

```
1   import com.ms.wfc.app.*;
2   import com.ms.wfc.core.*;
3   import com.ms.wfc.ui.*;
4   import com.ms.wfc.html.*;
5
6   public class Form1 extends Form
7   {
8       Image m_Image;
9
10      public Form1()
11      {
12          initForm();
13          m_Image = pictureBox1.getImage();
14      }
15
16      public void dispose()
17      {
18          super.dispose();
19          components.dispose();
20      }
21
22      private void Form1_click(Object source, Event e)
23      {
24
25      }
26
27      // Application
28      protected void onPaint( PaintEvent pe )
29      {
30          // m_Image is an Image class that's already loaded
31          int x = 10, y = 10;
32          pe.graphics.drawImage( m_Image, x, y );
33      }
34
35      Container components = new Container();
36      PictureBox pictureBox1 = new PictureBox();
37
38      private void initForm()
39      {
40
41          IResourceManager resources = new ResourceManager(this,
            ➥"Form1");
42          this.setText("Form1");
43          this.setAutoScaleBaseSize(13);
44          this.setClientSize(new Point(292, 273));
45          this.addOnClick(new EventHandler(this.Form1_click));
46
47          pictureBox1.setLocation(new Point(64, 40));
```

```
48              pictureBox1.setSize(new Point(192, 136));
49              pictureBox1.setTabIndex(0);
50              pictureBox1.setTabStop(false);
51              pictureBox1.setText("pictureBox1");
52              pictureBox1.setVisible(false);
53              pictureBox1.setImage((Bitmap)resources.getObject
          ➥("pictureBox1_image"));
54
55              this.setNewControls(new Control[] {
56                              pictureBox1});
57      }
58
59      public static void main(String args[])
60      {
61              Application.run(new Form1());
62      }
63  }
```

OUTPUT

FIGURE 12.7

This application displays the image, but not in the pictureBox *control.*

12

Waiting for Images: Using the `MediaTracker` Class

Waiting for images to load is the part users will dislike about any applet. But to make it worse, `getImage()` doesn't stop and wait for an image to be retrieved completely; it gets the process started and returns. The image is then retrieved incrementally in the background.

It's bad enough that users have to wait for images to come in, but applets that draw images in progressive states of completion do nothing to enhance the applet's appearance. If you let images draw while they're being loaded, users will see partial images draw to the applet window. The outcome is ugly—a situation that should be avoided.

The solution is to use a MediaTracker object that allows you to wait for the image retrieval to be completed. You use the addImage() method to add the Image object to the media list, then use the waitForID() method to wait until the image retrieval is complete. The steps in simplified form follow:

```
MediaTracker tracker = new MediaTracker( this );
pictureImage = getImage( getCodeBase(), "TEST.GIF" );
tracker.addImage( pictureImage, 0 );
try
{
    tracker.waitForID( 0 );
}
catch( InterruptedException e )
{
}
```

You could even turn the preceding code into a method that makes it easy to load and wait for an image. The method shown in Listing 12.2 does just that—it loads an image and waits for completion of the loading.

LISTING 12.2 A METHOD THAT WAITS FOR AN IMAGE TO LOAD BEFORE RETURNING

```
1    public Image waitForImage(String filename,String status)
2    {
3        Image image;
4        MediaTracker tracker = new MediaTracker( this );
5        showStatus( status );
6        image = getImage( getCodeBase(), filename );
7        tracker.addImage( image, 0 );
8        try
9        {
10           tracker.waitForID( 0 );
11       }
12       catch( InterruptedException e )
13       {
14       }
15
16       showStatus( "" );
17
18       return( image );
19
20   }
```

Drawing Part of an Image

You can draw just part of an image to the Java window if you want. You can't do it, though, with any arguments that get past the `drawImage()` method. You have to do it by setting a clipping rectangle in the `Graphics` class. For example, let's say you want to draw the image at (0,0) and the image is 300×300; but you want only the middle section of the image to show up. Set a clipping region for the `Graphics` class that might have an upper-left corner of, say, (40,40) with a width of (20,20). Figure 12.8 shows just such an applet in which an image that was 300×300 was drawn with a clipping rectangle as described.

NEW TERM *Clipping* is a technique used to limit where updates will occur in a window. If you have a window that's 100×100 and you want to update only the upper-left quadrant, you'll select a clipping area that has its upper-left corner starting at (0,0) and its lower-right corner at (49,49).

The following source code is exactly what was used to draw the applet shown in Figure 12.8.

INPUT

```
public void paint( Graphics g )
{
    g.clipRect( 100, 100, 100, 100 );
    g.drawImage( img, 0, 0, this );
}
```

OUTPUT

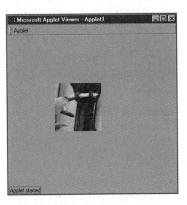

FIGURE 12.8

This window would have been completely filled by an image if the clipping rectangle hadn't been set.

12

Adding Borders to Your Images

You might want to draw borders around your images. If you draw the same image in several places, it might be easier to draw the border into the image itself. This section shows you how to draw a border around an image—not to the applet window, but to the image itself.

To draw a border that's a single pixel wide, use the example given in Listing 12.3.

INPUT   **LISTING 12.3**   THIS PROGRAM DRAWS A BORDER AROUND THE IMAGE

```
1    import java.awt.*;
2    import java.applet.*;
3
4    public class Applet1 extends Applet
5    {
6        Image m_Image;
7        boolean m_bLoaded = false;
8
9        public void init()
10       {
11       }
12
13       public void paint( Graphics g )
14       {
15           if( !m_bLoaded )
16           {
17               m_bLoaded = true;
18               Image TempImage;
19               TempImage = getImage( getCodeBase(), "Image.jpg" );
20               MediaTracker Tracker = new MediaTracker( this );
21               Tracker.addImage( TempImage, 0 );
22               try
23               {
24                   Tracker.waitForAll();
25                   int nWidth = TempImage.getWidth( this );
26                   int nHeight = TempImage.getHeight( this );
27                   m_Image = createImage( nWidth, nHeight );
28                   Graphics g1 = m_Image.getGraphics();
29                   g1.drawImage( TempImage, 0, 0, this );
30                   g1.drawRect( 0, 0, nWidth - 1, nHeight - 1 );
31               }
32               catch( InterruptedException e )
33               {
34               }
35           }
36           g.drawImage( m_Image, 0, 0, this );
37       }
38
39   }
```

When the program runs, you'll see a large image with a border around it, as shown in Figure 12.9.

OUTPUT

FIGURE 12.9

*The image with a
black border
around it.*

Caution

It's important that you wait until the entire image has been loaded before
you get a `Graphics` class from it or draw to it. The preceding example uses a
`MediaTracker` class to ensure that the image is fully loaded.

The next example, in Listing 12.4, draws a red border around an image. The border is 5
pixels wide.

INPUT   **LISTING 12.4**   THIS PROGRAM DRAWS A WIDE RED BORDER AROUND THE IMAGE

```
1    import java.awt.*;
2    import java.applet.*;
3
4    public class Applet1 extends Applet
5    {
6        Image m_Image;
7        boolean m_bLoaded = false;
8
9        public void init()
10       {
11       }
12
13       public void paint( Graphics g )
14       {
15           if( !m_bLoaded )
16           {
17               m_bLoaded = true;
18               Image TempImage;
19               TempImage = getImage( getCodeBase(), "Image.jpg" );
```

continues

12

LISTING 12.4   CONTINUED

```
20              MediaTracker Tracker = new MediaTracker( this );
21              Tracker.addImage( TempImage, 0 );
22              try
23              {
24                  Tracker.waitForAll();
25                  int nWidth = TempImage.getWidth( this );
26                  int nHeight = TempImage.getHeight( this );
27                  m_Image = createImage( nWidth, nHeight );
28                  Graphics g1 = m_Image.getGraphics();
29                  g1.drawImage( TempImage, 0, 0, this );
30                  g1.setColor( Color.red );
31                  for( int i=0; i<5; i++ )
32                      g1.drawRect( i, i, nWidth - 1 - i * 2, nHeight - 1
                        ➥- i * 2 );
33              }
34              catch( InterruptedException e )
35              {
36              }
37          }
38          g.drawImage( m_Image, 0, 0, this );
39      }
40
41  }
```

When the program runs, you'll see a large image with a wide red border around it (you'll have to visualize the color for yourself), as shown in Figure 12.10.

OUTPUT

FIGURE 12.10

The image with a wide red border around it.

The last example in this section, in Listing 12.5, draws a border that's graduated shades of gray. It looks like a 3D border.

LISTING 12.5 THIS PROGRAM DRAWS A 3D BORDER AROUND THE IMAGE

```
1   import java.awt.*;
2   import java.applet.*;
3
4   public class Applet1 extends Applet
5   {
6       Image m_Image;
7       boolean m_bLoaded = false;
8
9       public void init()
10      {
11      }
12
13      public void paint( Graphics g )
14      {
15          if( !m_bLoaded )
16          {
17              m_bLoaded = true;
18              Image TempImage;
19              TempImage = getImage( getCodeBase(), "Image.jpg" );
20              MediaTracker Tracker = new MediaTracker( this );
21              Tracker.addImage( TempImage, 0 );
22              try
23              {
24                  Tracker.waitForAll();
25                  int nWidth = TempImage.getWidth( this );
26                  int nHeight = TempImage.getHeight( this );
27                  m_Image = createImage( nWidth, nHeight );
28                  Graphics g1 = m_Image.getGraphics();
29                  g1.drawImage( TempImage, 0, 0, this );
30                  for( int i=0; i<7; i++ )
31                  {
32                      int j = 255 - ( Math.abs( 4 - i ) * 40 );
33                      Color color = new Color( j, j, j );
34                      g1.setColor( color );
35                      g1.drawRect( 0, 0, nWidth - 1 - i * 2, nHeight - 1
                          ➥ - i * 2 );
36                  }
37              }
38              catch( InterruptedException e )
39              {
40              }
41          }
42          g.drawImage( m_Image, 0, 0, this );
43      }
44
45  }
```

12

When the program runs, you'll see a large image with a 3D border around it, as shown in Figure 12.11.

OUTPUT

FIGURE 12.11

The image with a 3D border around it.

Drawing Your Images Inverted and Reversed

With clever use of the setClip() method, you can draw your images inverted and reversed. The idea is to set the clipping rectangle so that it has a width of 1 pixel. If you're inverting an image, the clipping rectangle will be 1 pixel high and will have the same width as the image. If you're reversing an image, the clipping rectangle will be 1 pixel wide, and it'll be the same height as the image.

The position of the clipping rectangle moves inside of a for loop. When you're drawing an image upside down, the clipping rectangle will move down 1 pixel at a time. When you're drawing an image that's reversed, the clipping rectangle will move over 1 pixel at a time.

You then must move the position at which you draw the image. The source code for the paint() method is shown in Listing 12.6. Figure 12.12 shows an applet in which the image in the upper-left corner is normal, the image in the upper-right corner is inverted, and the image in the lower-left corner is reversed.

INPUT

LISTING 12.6 SOURCE CODE FOR THE paint() METHOD THAT INVERTS AND REVERSES AN IMAGE

```
1    public void paint( Graphics g )
2
3        g.drawImage( m_Image1, 10, 10, this );
4
5        int nWidth = m_Image1.getWidth( this );
6        int nHeight = m_Image1.getHeight( this );
7
8        int x = 330, y = 10;
9
10       // Upside-down image.
11       for( int i=0; i<nHeight; i++ )
12       {
13           g.setClip( x, y + i, nWidth, 1 );
14           g.drawImage( m_Image1, x, y - nHeight + 1 + i * 2, this );
15       }
16
17       x = 10;
18       y = 250;
19       // Reversed image.
20       for( int i=0; i<nWidth; i++ )
21       {
22           g.setClip( x + i, y, 1, nHeight );
23           g.drawImage( m_Image1, x - nWidth + 1 + i * 2, y, this );
24       }
25
26   }
```

12

OUTPUT

FIGURE 12.12

Two of these images are altered.

Summary

Images are one of the things that make Java cool. The ability to load any picture or illustration for your applet or application gives you enormous power and flexibility. Before going live with an applet or application that loads images, test to make sure that the waiting time for the images to come over the phone line doesn't turn users off. Even the prettiest images might not be worth waiting for. Surf the Web to find more examples of effective use of images. You'll get good ideas you can use for your own applets and applications.

Q&A

Q What are the two types of images common to Visual J++ programs?

A They are GIF and JPG files. Both have advantages and disadvantages. GIFs are better for images that need a clear definition. JPGs are better for photographic images.

Q What's the difference between loading images in applets and loading them in applications?

A In applets, you load images into an Image class using the getImage() method. In applications, you load images into the PictureBox class—it's normally done automatically for you.

Q What's wrong with loading an image into an applet and immediately displaying it?

A Chances are that the image will take some time to come in. That's because phone lines can be slow and there might be a lot of network congestion. You'll want to use a MediaTracker class to make sure that the image has been completely loaded before you display it.

Q Why might you want to do your own displaying on images in PictureBox controls?

A Because you'll have more control. You can do much more with an Image class than with a pictureBox class.

Q What considerations should you give when you create images for your Web site?

A First and foremost, GIF images should use the Internet-safe palette. Then, consider the size of the images. Users don't want to wait long before the entire page is completely loaded.

Review Exercises

1. Create an applet that loads an image and displays it in the paint() method. Test it locally; then upload it to your Web site and note the difference in performance between loading a local image and loading an image that must come in over the phone line.

2. Create an application that loads an image into a PictureBox class. Allow the PictureBox class to do all the displaying.

3. Create an application that loads an image into a PictureBox class. Then use the PictureBox getImage() method to copy the image into an Image class. Use the newly created Image class to display the image.

12

DAY 13

Image Processing

If you work with images in your program, you'll quickly notice how much disk space they consume. Even a CD gets full rather quickly when the graphics get intensive. Most people (and if you're talking about Web development, most Web servers) are constantly trying to keep disk space usage to a minimum. For my Web site, I pay extra money for extra storage space. So keeping the sizes of my images smaller, or keeping the number of images I'm using smaller, saves me money.

You can create variations of images by using image processing techniques. This saves you from having to store all the individual processed images on the Web server or on the application hard drive. Instead, when the application or applet is loaded, you can do the image processing right then and there.

Today we'll cover the following:

- Getting data from an applet or application image
- Creating an image from data in an applet or application
- Working with pixel data in applets and applications
- How to perform image point processing

Today you'll learn to produce your own processed versions of original images. You'll learn techniques such as colorization, grayscale conversion, and blurring (median filtering).

Getting Pixel Data from Applet Images

Before you can process an image, you need to get the actual image pixel data from it. In Java, you don't have access to pointers and the actual data of these objects, so you have to go through several steps to get the pixel data. The first thing you want to do before you get the data from an image is to make sure that the image has been completely loaded. To do that, use a MediaTracker class just as you learned on Day 12, "Images." After all the image data has been loaded, you can get the data out of the image.

The first thing you'll need to do is take the original image and get the width and height. To do this, simply use the getWidth() and getHeight() methods of the Image class.

After you have the width and height, you'll have to create an array of integers that will contain pixel data from this image. To calculate how large to allocate the array, you simply multiply the width of the image by the height of the image. This gives you the total number of pixels in the image.

Now, you must create a PixelGrabber class. The PixelGrabber's constructor takes several arguments. The first argument is the image from which you'll retrieve the pixels. The second argument is the x coordinate of the upper-left corner of the rectangle of pixels to retrieve from the image. This is relative to the default size of the image. The third argument is the y coordinate of the upper-left corner of the rectangle of pixels to retrieve from the image. The fourth argument is the width of the rectangle of pixels to retrieve. The fifth argument is the height of the rectangle of pixels to retrieve. The sixth argument is the array of integers that are to be used to hold the RGB pixels retrieved from the image. The seventh argument is the offset into the array in which you'll store the first pixel. The eighth and final argument is the distance from one row of pixels to the next in the array.

The PixelGrabber has a method called grabPixels(). The grabPixels() method takes no arguments, but it uses the information you supply to the PixelGrabber constructor to do its job. It takes the pixel data from the image and places it into an array. It throws an exception, though. To use the grabPixels() method, you'll have to catch InterruptedException objects. When you've successfully completed the grabPixels() method, that's all there is to getting the pixel data out of the image.

The source-code example in Listing 13.1 shows the entire process for loading an image: using the MediaTracker to wait for the image, then creating a PixelGrabber class and using it to obtain the pixel data.

INPUT **LISTING 13.1** SOURCE CODE TO LOAD AN IMAGE AND GET THE PIXEL DATA

```
1     MediaTracker Tracker = new MediaTracker( this );
2     m_Original = getImage( getCodeBase(), "Image1.gif" );
3     Tracker.addImage( m_Original, 0 );
4     try
5     {
6         Tracker.waitForID( 0 );
7     }
8     catch( InterruptedException e )
9     {
10    }
11
12
13    int nWidth = m_Original.getWidth( this );
14    int nHeight = m_Original.getHeight( this );
15
16
17    int nNumPixels = nWidth * nHeight;
18
19
20    int nRawPixels[] = new in[nNumPixels];
21
22    PixelGrabber Grabber =
23        new PixelGrabber( m_Original, 0, 0, nWidth, nHeight,
          ➥nRawPixels, 0, nWidth );
24
25    try
26    {
27
28        Grabber.grabPixels();
29    }
30    catch( InterruptedException e )
31    {
32    }
```

ANALYSIS At lines 1–10 we use a MediaTracker class to make sure that the entire image is loaded before proceeding. Look back to Day 12 for review on using a MediaTracker class. At lines 13 and 14 we get the width and height of the image. We then calculate the number of pixels by multiplying nWidth * nHeight at line 17. An array of integers into which the pixel data will be stored is created at line 20. At lines 22 and 23 you can see how the PixelGrabber class is created.

Now to grab the pixels. To use the grabPixels() method, you must catch InterruptedException objects as is done in the try block beginning at line 25. Finally, we grab the pixels from the image into the integer array at line 28.

13

Getting Pixel Data from Application Images

The process for getting pixel data from application images is completely different from that for getting pixel data from applets.

> This method of obtaining pixel data from application images works only when the original image was a BMP file with 24 bits of color depth.
>
> If you're using images other than 24-bit BMP files, I suggest getting a conversion program so that you can put your files in the correct format. You can download ImageView from www.infinitevision.net. It can be freely used without cost.

The first thing you must do when you obtain image data from an application's `Image` class is load the original image. That's easy enough to do, especially if you use the `PictureBox` class's `getImage()` method. The nice thing about this as opposed to loading applet images is you don't have to wait for the data to come in. It will load and return from the `PictureBox`'s `getImage()` method only after the data is in.

After the image is loaded, you must calculate the number of pixels in the image. You do this the same way you do it for the applet's image: you multiply the width by the height.

The next thing you must do in the process is create a buffer large enough to hold the entire image data. This is different than what we did in the applet image. The first difference is that it will be an array of bytes rather than an array of integers. The second difference is that the data that will be stored in the byte array will be an exact duplicate of the image's disk file. BMP images, when they're stored on disk, have two headers before the actual image data. Those two headers will be stored in the first part of this byte array.

The total size of both of the BMP headers is 54 bytes. We just have to keep that in mind after we've gotten the data from the image. We also have to keep it in mind when we allocate enough space in this byte buffer from the image data.

There's also one more consideration: this is a byte buffer, and the pixel data that's contained in BMP image files has three bytes per pixel describing the red, blue, and green components of the pixel.

And there's yet one more twist in the form of the BMP files. Every scan of a BMP file must be an even multiple of 4 bytes. Let's say you had a scan line of 2 pixels. Each pixel is 3 bytes. That gives you a total of 6 bytes for the scan line—but that's not an even multiple of 4. The file will actually contain 8 bytes for the scan line. The last 2 bytes will be completely ignored, but you still need to allocate enough space so that the entire scan line of data will be stored. In the source-code example that comes later, you'll see a small amount of calculation to ensure that the byte width for each scan line is an even multiple of 4 bytes.

Now to create the buffer into which the image data will go. You simply use the new operator to create a byte array, making sure that you multiply the byte width by the height and then add the extra 54 bytes for the BMP file headers.

After the buffer has been created, you need to create a `MemoryStream` object. To do that, you simply give the `MemoryStream` constructor a single argument. That will be the byte buffer you just allocated.

Okay, now the easy part. You simply use the `Image` class's `save()` method and pass the `MemoryStream` object into it as its only argument. The `save()` method will then go ahead and save to this `MemoryStream` object just as if it were a disk file. That's why the memory buffer will contain information exactly as a disk file will.

After you've saved to the `MemoryStream` object, its position will be at the very end of the file because that's the position at which it just performed its last operation. Before you read in any of that data, or use it to create a new image, you'll have to set the position pointer back to the beginning of the `MemoryStream` object. To do this, you'll have to use the `MemoryStream`'s `setPosition()` method with an argument of `0`. The source code in Listing 13.2 and the following analysis guide you step-by-step through all the instructions I have given you regarding getting pixel data from application images.

LISTING 13.2 SOURCE CODE TO LOAD AN IMAGE AND GET THE PIXEL DATA IN A VISUAL J++ APPLICATION

```
1       m_Original = pictureBox1.getImage();
2
3       int nWidth = m_Original.getSize().x;
4       int nHeight = m_Original.getSize().y;
5
6       int nNumPixels = nWidth * nHeight;
7
8       int nByteWidth = nWidth * 3;
9       while( ( nByteWidth & 3 ) != 0 )
10          nByteWidth++;
11
12      byte SrcBuffer[] =
13          new byte[nByteWidth*nHeight+54];
14      if( SrcBuffer == null )
15          return;
16      MemoryStream MemStream = new MemoryStream( SrcBuffer );
```

13

continues

LISTING **13.2**   CONTINUED

```
17        if( MemStream == null )
18            return;
19
20        m_Original.save( MemStream );
21        MemStream.setPosition( 0 );
```

ANALYSIS   We begin the process by loading the image, as you can see in line 1. Then, at lines 3 and 4 we get the width and height of the image. At line 6 we calculate the number of pixels in the image by multiplying the width by the height.

Each pixel in a 24-bit BMP file has 3 bytes. There's a quirk for BMP files. The number of bytes in each scan line must be evenly divisible by 4. In line 8 we multiply the number of pixels by 3 to find the number of bytes per scan line. We then make sure at lines 9 and 10 that the number of bytes is evenly divisible by 4.

At lines 12 and 13 we create the byte buffer that will contain the pixel data. At line 16 we create the MemoryStream object that will send the data into our buffer.

At line 20 you can see where we've called the MemoryStream's save() method, and at line 21 we reset the position to the beginning of the buffer.

Creating an Image from Pixel Data in an Applet

To create an image for pixel data in an applet, you have just a few steps to go through. You first must get a color model. This is easy; you simply use the color model's static getRGBdefault() method. After you have the color model, you need to create a MemoryImageSource object.

There is more than one version of the MemoryImageSource constructor. I've always used the one I'll describe here. It takes six arguments. The first argument is the width of the image you'll be creating. The second argument is the height. The third argument is the color model you'll be using. For this, we're going to use the default RGB model we obtained with the getRGBdefault() method described in the preceding paragraph. The fourth argument is an array of integers that contains all the pixel data. The fifth argument is the offset into the pixel array from which the pixel data for this image will be contained. The sixth and final argument is the width of each scan line.

The next step is to use the createImage() method. This method is a member method of the Component class. The createImage() method returns an image object. In this case, we'll be passing it a single argument, and it will be our MemoryImageSource that we created.

Here again, it's possible that after you make the call to createImage(), the image won't be fully created before the program execution continues. For this reason, it's recommended that you use a MediaTracker class so that you don't go forward with your program until the image is fully created. The source code in Listing 13.3 shows you how to take an array of pixel data and create an image from it.

INPUT

LISTING 13.3   SOURCE CODE TO LOAD AN IMAGE AND GET THE PIXEL DATA IN A VISUAL J++ APPLICATION

```
1    ColorModel cm = ColorModel.getRGBdefault();
2
3    MemoryImageSource ImageSource =
4        new MemoryImageSource( nWidth, nHeight, cm, nRawPixels, 0,
         ➥nWidth );
5
6    m_Processed = createImage( ImageSource );
7
8    MediaTracker Tracker = new MediaTracker( this );
9    Tracker.addImage( m_Processed, 1 );
10   try
11   {
12       Tracker.waitForID( 0 );
13   }
14   catch( InterruptedException e )
15   {
16   }
```

ANALYSIS   We begin the code example by getting the default color model at line 1 with the getRGBdefault() method. The MemoryImageSource object is created at lines 3 and 4—this will be used to get the pixels. At line 6 we create an Image object into which we'll place the processed image.

Lines 8–16 do the standard waiting while the image creation is complete. The interesting thing here is that the image is being created from an array of integers instead of being loaded from a disk file or over an Internet connection.

Creating an Image from Pixel Data in an Application

It takes only a single line of code to create an image in an application from pixel data, as long as you already have the MemoryStream object created. You use the Image class's

13

static method `loadImage()`. One thing you have to make sure about, though, is that you catch any WFC exceptions that are thrown. The following source-code example shows you how to create a new image from a `MemoryStream` object:

```
try
    {
        m_Processed = Image.loadImage( MemStream );
    }
    catch( WFCException e )
    {
        // Handle the error.
    }
```

Working with Pixel Data in Applets

In applets, the data for each pixel is represented by a single integer. These integers, while they're in an array of many integers, should be treated singly for each pixel. The `ColorModel` class gives you three methods that return the red, green, and blue components for a single integer of pixel data. The following source-code example shows you how to obtain those values:

```
ColorModel cm = getRGBdefault();
int r = cm.getRed( nRawPixels[x] );
int g = cm.getGreen( nRawPixels[x] );
int b = cm.getBlue( nRawPixels[x] );
```

After you've obtained the red, green, and blue component values, you can work with these to transform your image pixel data in any way you choose.

Putting the RGB value back into the pixel data array is not quite as simple, because the `Color Model` class does not offer you a method that combines all three of the color components into a single integer. The blue component occupies the lower 8 bits of the final integer. The green component is the next higher 8 bits, and the red component occupies bits 17–24 of the integer. One very important point is that all the top 8 bits of the integer must be set. The following source code shows you how to take the red, green, and blue components and combine them into a single integer, which can then be put back into the array of pixel data:

```
// Make sure r, g, and b are all in the range from 0-255.
int nNewPixelData;
// The hex format of the pixel data is ffrrggbb where ff is all
// bits set, rr is red, gg is green, and bb is blue.
nNewPixelData = 0xff000000 ¦ ( r << 16 ) ¦ ( g << 8 ) ¦ b;
```

Working with Pixel Data in Applications

The pixel data in applications is byte oriented. Each scan line of the image data that was extracted has a triplet of bytes for each pixel. The triplets of bytes specify the red, green, and blue components for the pixel. The strange thing, though, is that red and blue are in reverse order of what you'd think. Actually, the bytes go in the order of the blue byte, the green byte, then the red byte.

> **Note**
>
> One thing you need to make sure about when you're working with pixel data in applications is that you remember that the width and byte of each scan line must be an even multiple of 4.

I've written four methods that are shown in Listing 13.4. The first method, called the setPixel() method, sets a pixel in an array of bytes. You can either utilize this method or use it as a reference to further understand how to work with pixel data. The second, third, and fourth methods I've created pull out individual color components from pixel data. The getRed() method pulls out the red component of the pixel data, the getGreen() method pulls out the green component, and (oddly enough) the getBlue() method pulls out the blue component.

INPUT **LISTING 13.4** FOUR METHODS FOR WORKING WITH PIXELS IN AN APPLICATION

```
1     public void setPixel( int x, int y, int r, int g, int b, int
      ➥nImageWidth, int nImageHeight,
2         byte PixelData[] )
3     {
4
5         int nByteWidth = nImageWidth * 3;
6         while( ( nByteWidth & 3 ) != 0 )
7             nByteWidth++;
8
9         y = nImageHeight - y - 1;
10
11        int nOffset;
12        nOffset = y * nByteWidth + x * 3;
13
14        PixelData[nOffset] = (byte) b;
15        PixelData[nOffset+1] = (byte) g;
16        PixelData[nOffset+2] = (byte) r;
17
18    }
```

13

continues

LISTING 13.4   CONTINUED

```
19
20      public int getRed( int x, int y, int nImageWidth, int
        ➥nImageHeight, byte PixelData[] )
21      {
22
23          return( getPixelComponent( 2, x, y, nImageWidth, nImageHeight,
            ➥PixelData ) );
24
25      }
26
27      public int getGreen( int x, int y, int nImageWidth, int
        ➥nImageHeight, byte PixelData[] )
28      {
29
30          return( getPixelComponent( 1, x, y, nImageWidth, nImageHeight,
            ➥PixelData ) );
31
32      }
33
34      public int getBlue( int x, int y, int nImageWidth, int
        ➥nImageHeight, byte PixelData[] )
35      {
36
37          return( getPixelComponent( 0, x, y, nImageWidth, nImageHeight,
            ➥PixelData ) );
38
39      }
40
41      public int getPixelComponent( int nColorOffset, int x, int y, int
        ➥nImageWidth,
42          int nImageHeight,
43          byte PixelData[] )
44      {
45
46          int nByteWidth = nImageWidth * 3;
47          while( ( nByteWidth & 3 ) != 0 )
48              nByteWidth++;
49
50          y = nImageHeight - y - 1;
51
52          int nOffset;
53          nOffset = y * nByteWidth + x * 3;
54
55          return( (int) PixelData[nOffset+nColorOffset] );
56
57      }
```

ANALYSIS The first method we'll be talking about is the `setPixel()` method that spans lines 1–18. At lines 5–7 we calculate the byte width for each scan line and store it in the `nByteWidth` variable. In line 9 we take into account the fact that BMP file data is stored upside down—we simply transform the y coordinate. At lines 11 and 12 we declare and calculate the `nOffset` variable. This is the offset into the `PixelData` buffer. Finally, we set the three color components in the `PixelData` buffer at lines 14–16.

The `getRed()`, `getGreen()`, and `getBlue()` methods all call the `getPixelComponent()` method to get the data for the appropriate color component at a specified pixel. These three methods can be seen in lines 20–39.

The method that does the work in retrieving color component values is the `getPixelComponent()` method found at lines 41–57. At lines 46–48 we calculate the width in bytes for each scan line. At lines 52 and 53 we calculate the offset into the `PixelData` array based on the x coordinate, the y coordinate, and the scan line width. Lastly, at line 55 we return the color component value.

Image Point Processing

Point processes are techniques that are performed on single pixels. Because single pixels are all considered points of an image, the term "point processes" is used to describe operations to single pixels.

Point processes are fundamental image processing operations. They are the simplest and probably the most frequently used of the image processing algorithms. Because they are less complex than other image processing algorithms, they are a natural starting place for this chapter's image processing discussion.

Point processes are algorithms that modify a pixel's value in an image based solely on the pixel's value and sometimes its location. No other pixel values are involved in the transformation. Individual pixels are replaced with new values that are algorithmically related to the pixel's original value. As a result of the algorithmic relationship between the original and the new pixel value, point processes can generally be reversed.

13

Converting Images to Grayscale

Many times you'll have images that are in the full range of RGB colors, but for whatever reason you want to convert them to grayscale. The algorithm is extremely simple. What you're actually going to be doing when you perform this operation is to recalculate the red, green, and blue components so that they are equal for each pixel. Gray pixels always have an equal value of red, green, and blue, but the lightness of the gray pixel will depend on the original values of the red, green, and blue components. The following single line of source code calculates the relative gray level given a red, a green, and a blue color component:

```
int nGrayLevel = ( r * 30 + g * 59 + b * 11 ) / 100;
```

We're now going to create a simple program that loads an image, creates a second image, converts the second image to gray, and displays both images side by side in a window.

Listing 13.5 gives you the entire source code for the ImagePr1 applet. This applet loads in an image (which is mountain scenery), converts it into grayscale as a second image, and then displays both images side by side. You can see the program running in Figure 13.1.

INPUT   **LISTING 13.5**   THE IMAGEPR1 APPLET SOURCE CODE

```
import java.awt.*;
1    import java.awt.*;
2    import java.applet.*;
3    import java.awt.image.*;
4
5    public class ImagePr1 extends Applet
6    {
7        Image m_Original, m_Processed;
8
9        public void init()
10       {
11
12           MediaTracker Tracker = new MediaTracker( this );
13           m_Original = getImage( getCodeBase(), "Image6.jpg" );
14           Tracker.addImage( m_Original, 0 );
15           try
16           {
17               Tracker.waitForID( 0 );
18               m_Processed = processImage();
19           }
20           catch( InterruptedException e )
21           {
22           }
23
24       }
25
26       public void paint( Graphics g )
27       {
28           g.drawImage( m_Original, 10, 10, this );
29
30           g.drawImage( m_P1, 10 + m_Original.getWidth( this ) + 10,
31               10, this );
32
33       }
```

```
34
35      public Image processImage()
36      {
37          Image img = null;
38
39          int nWidth = m_Original.getWidth( this );
40          int nHeight = m_Original.getHeight( this );
41          int nNumPixels = nWidth * nHeight;
42
43          int nRawPixels[] = new int[nNumPixels];
44
45          PixelGrabber Grabber =
46              new PixelGrabber( m_Original, 0, 0, nWidth, nHeight,
                ➥nRawPixels, 0, nWidth );
47
48          try
49          {
50              Grabber.grabPixels();
51
52              ColorModel cm = ColorModel.getRGBdefault();
53
54              MemoryImageSource ImageSource =
55                  new MemoryImageSource( nWidth, nHeight, cm,
                    ➥nRawPixels, 0, nWidth );
56
57              for( int nPixel=0; nPixel<nNumPixels; nPixel++ )
58              {
59                  int r = cm.getRed( nRawPixels[nPixel] );
60                  int g = cm.getGreen( nRawPixels[nPixel] );
61                  int b = cm.getBlue( nRawPixels[nPixel] );
62
63          int nNewGray = ( ( r * 30 ) + ( g * 69 ) + ( b * 11 ) ) / 100;
64
65                  r = nNewGray;
66                  g = nNewGray;
67                  b = nNewGray;
68
69                  nRawPixels[nPixel] = 0xff000000 ¦
70                      ( r << 16 ) ¦ ( g << 8 ) ¦ b;
71
72              }
73
74              img = createImage( ImageSource );
75
76              MediaTracker Tracker = new MediaTracker( this );
77              Tracker.addImage( img, 1 );
78              Tracker.waitForID( 1 );
79          }
80          catch( InterruptedException e )
```

continues

13

LISTING 13.5   CONTINUED

```
81              {
82              }
83
84              return( img );
85
86        }
87
88   }
```

OUTPUT

FIGURE 13.1

*The ImagePr1
applet. The image on
the left is the original
image, and the image
on the right has been
changed to shades of
gray.*

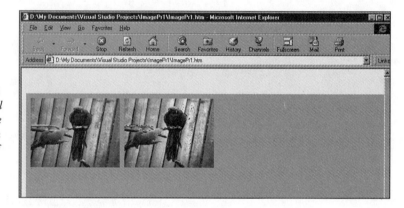

ANALYSIS   The first thing you should notice about this program is that at line 7 two `Image`
classes are declared. The first will contain the original image, and the second will
contain the processed images. The `init()` method occupies lines 9–24. It does two
things: load the original image and wait for its completion (lines 12–17), and call the
`processImage()` method so that the processed `Image` object is created (line 18).

The `paint()` method can be seen at lines 26–33. It simply draws both images. Refer to
Figure 13.1 for the output of the program.

The `processImage()` method is the workhorse of the program—it does most of the work.
Lines 39–41 get the width and height of the original image and calculate the number of
pixels that are in it. Line 43 allocates the integer array that will contain the pixel data.
Lines 45 and 46 is where the `PixelGrabber` object is created. And line 50 is where the
pixels are actually extracted with the `grabPixels()` method. Notice that we catch the
`InterruptedException` exception—this is required!

Next we need to get the color model, and we do this at line 52 with the
`getRGBdefault()` method. Then, a `MemoryImageSource` object is created at lines 54 and
55—this will be used to create the new image after the data has been processed.

Now to the image processing. We enter a loop that's going to iterate through all the image pixels. At lines 59–61 we get the red, green, and blue color components for the current pixel. At line 63 we calculate the grayscale value. Red is factored in by 30 percent, green by 69 percent, and blue by 11 percent. At lines 69 and 70 we store the color components for this pixel in the pixel data array.

At line 74 we create the new image. We use a `MediaTracker` object to wait for the image to be completely created before we proceed (lines 76–78).

Finally, at line 84 we return the newly created image.

Changing the Brightness of an Image

One of the things everyone does with his or her television set is to change the brightness. Individual tastes vary, and the brightness of the television picture will change accordingly.

Some computer images need a brightness change because they've been acquired through maladjusted hardware, or during less than optimal circumstances. By changing the brightness of the RGB values in an image, you can adjust the brightness of an image.

Note

> You'll have to be careful when adjusting the brightness. If you start with an image that's fairly bright, increasing the brightness by very much will cause many of the colors to oversaturate. You'll also have to be careful that you don't exceed the value of 255 for any of the color components.

The algorithm for changing the brightness of an image is to simply change each color component (red, green, and blue) by the same percentage. For instance, if you want to double the brightness, you double the red, green, and blue component values. The following short source-code example shows you how to increase the brightness by 20 percent:

```
// Get the red, green, and blue components.
int r = cm.getRed( nRawPixels[nPixel]);
int g = cm.getGreen( nRawPixels[nPixel]);
int b = cm.getBlue( nRawPixels[nPixel]);

// Adjust them so that they're 20 percent brighter.
r = ( r * 120 ) / 100;
g = ( g * 120 ) / 100;
b = ( b * 120 ) / 100;

// Make sure they're not greater than 255.
if( r > 255 )
```

13

```
    r = 255;
if( g > 255 )
    g = 255;
if( b > 255 )
    b = 255;

// Store the value back in the pixel array.
nRawPixels[nPixel] = 0xff000000 ¦ ( r << 16 ) ¦ ( g << 8 ) ¦ b;
```

I've taken the last applet we wrote, ImagePr1, and simply altered the processImage()
method so that it makes the image 40 percent brighter. I've also loaded a different image
in; so instead of showing you the entire listing for the applet, I'm showing you only the
processImage() method. Listing 13.6 shows you the entire processImage() method that
brightens the image by 40 percent.

LISTING 13.6   THE PROCESSIMAGE() METHOD THAT BRIGHTENS THE IMAGE BY 40
INPUT   PERCENT

```
1        public void processImage()
2        {
3                int nWidth = m_Original.getWidth( this );
4                int nHeight = m_Original.getHeight( this );
5                int nNumPixels = nWidth * nHeight;
6
7                int nRawPixels[] = new int[nNumPixels];
8
9                PixelGrabber Grabber =
10                   new PixelGrabber( m_Original, 0, 0, nWidth, nHeight,
                     ➡nRawPixels, 0, nWidth );
11
12               try
13               {
14                   Grabber.grabPixels();
15
16                   ColorModel cm = ColorModel.getRGBdefault();
17                   MemoryImageSource ImageSource =
18                       new MemoryImageSource( nWidth, nHeight, cm,
                         ➡nRawPixels, 0, nWidth );
19
20                   for( int nPixel=0; nPixel<nNumPixels; nPixel++ )
21                   {
22                       int r = cm.getRed( nRawPixels[nPixel] );
23                       int g = cm.getGreen( nRawPixels[nPixel] );
24                       int b = cm.getBlue( nRawPixels[nPixel] );
25
26                       r = ( r * 140 ) / 100;
27                       g = ( g * 140 ) / 100;
28                       b = ( b * 140 ) / 100;
29
```

```
30                    if( r > 255 )
31                        r = 255;
32                    if( g > 255 )
33                        g = 255;
34                    if( b > 255 )
35                        b = 255;
36                    nRawPixels[nPixel] = 0xff000000 ¦
37                        ( r << 16 ) ¦ ( g << 8 ) ¦ b;
38
39                }
40
41            m_Processed = createImage( ImageSource );
42
43            MediaTracker Tracker = new MediaTracker( this );
44            Tracker.addImage( m_Processed, 1 );
45            Tracker.waitForID( 1 );
46        }
47        catch( InterruptedException e )
48        {
49        }
50
51    }
```

You can see the applet running in Figure 13.2. On the left is the original image with two sailboats. On the right is the brightened image of the same sailboats.

FIGURE 13.2

The altered applet ImagePr1 has brightened the image by 40 percent.

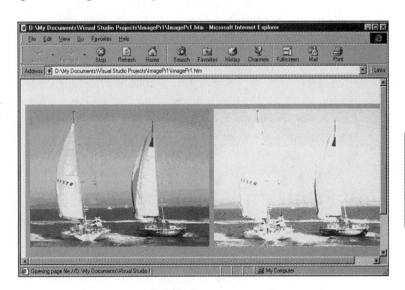

13

Colorizing Images

When you have the RGB values of a pixel, you can also colorize them. For instance, you might want to make them all shades of red so that your image, instead of being a full spectrum of red, green, and blue shades, would be only shades of red. Or you might simply want the image to be all shades of green.

I've found many uses for this technique. Although it sounds somewhat farfetched, it's a great way to highlight an area of an image when the user makes a selection or moves the mouse into a region. The source code in Listing 13.7 shows you how to colorize an image. This example changes the pixel into shades of red.

INPUT   **LISTING 13.7**   COLORIZING IMAGE DATA

```
1       int r = cm.getRed( nRawPixels[nPixel] );
2       int g = cm.getGreen( nRawPixels[nPixel] );
3       int b = cm.getBlue( nRawPixels[nPixel] );
4
5       int nSaturationLevel = ( r * 30 + g * 59 + b * 11 ) / 100;
6
7       r = nSaturationLevel;
8       g = 0;
9     b = 0;
10
11      nRawPixels[nPixel] = 0xff000000 ¦ ( r << 16 ) ¦ ( g << 8 ) ¦ b;
```

If your colorized values tend to be a little dark, you might want to bump up the green and blue values (the ones that aren't actually being used) to something brighter than zero. If you keep them low, yet give them a value, the resulting shade of red will be brighter, but you won't see any blue and green components showing through. Figure 13.3 shows four images. The image in the upper-left corner is the original image. The image in the upper-right has been colorized red. The image in the lower-left has been colorized blue, and the image in the lower-right has been colorized green.

One Program, Many Processes

In this section, you'll learn three image processing techniques. We're going to start off by creating one program that's generic. In fact, it's named Generic. This program can then be used to easily add each of the three image processing techniques as they're discussed. Most programmers know this as minimum redundancy coding. It's a technique we all learn to love because it saves everyone time. Although the program that consists of the code in Listing 13.8 through Listing 13.15 is not shown here in its entirety, the complete listing is available online. We'll start with the init() method, as shown in Listing 13.8.

OUTPUT

FIGURE 13.3

Colorized images in shades of red, blue, and green.

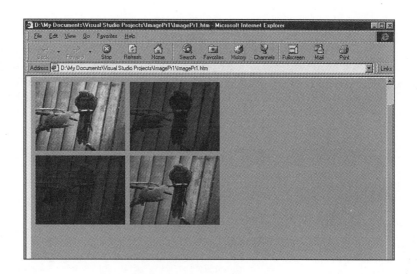

INPUT   LISTING 13.8   THE init() METHOD WE'LL USE

```
 1   public void init()
 2   {
 3
 4       // Call the method to load the images.
 5       loadImages();
 6       // Call the method to pull the pixels from the
 7       // image and place them in an integer array.
 8       pullPixels();
 9
10       // Process the image.
11
12       // Call the method that creates a new image from
13       // the array of pixels.
14       pushPixels();
15
16   }
```

13

ANALYSIS   Here's how the program works. The init() method calls the methods that do all
the work. First, the loadImages() method is called. This method loads two
images from the current directory. The reason we load two images is that one is
processed and one remains unchanged. That way we can see them both in the applet
window and compare them.

The next thing that's called is the pullPixels() method. This method creates an integer array into which it places the pixel data.

In the init() method, after the pullPixels() method, is where you perform your image processing. This will be one of the six image processing methods we'll talk about later.

The last thing that's called from the init() method is the pushPixels() method. This creates a new Image class from the pixel data that's been processed.

Next, the source code for the paint() method is shown in Listing 13.9.

INPUT   **LISTING 13.9**   THE paint() METHOD WE'LL USE

```
1   public void paint( Graphics g )
2   {
3       g.drawImage( m_NormalImage, 10, 10, this );
4       g.drawImage( m_ProcessedImage,
5           10 + m_NormalImage.getWidth( this ) + 10, 10, this );
6   }
```

ANALYSIS   The paint() method simply paints both images side by side in the applet window.

The source code for the loadImages() method is shown in Listing 13.10.

INPUT   **LISTING 13.10**   LOADING THE IMAGES

```
1   // Declare the Image classes.
2   Image m_NormalImage;
3   Image m_ProcessedImage;
4
5   public void loadImages()
6   {
7
8       // Load the image into both Image classes
9       m_NormalImage = getImage( getCodeBase(), "Picture.jpg" );
10      m_ProcessedImage = getImage( getCodeBase(), "Picture.jpg" );
11
12      // Create a MediaTracker class so we can wait for
13      // the images to be completely loaded.
14      MediaTracker Tracker = new MediaTracker( this );
15      // Add the images to the MediaTracker class.
16      Tracker.addImage( m_NormalImage, 0 );
17      Tracker.addImage( m_ProcessedImage, 1 );
18      try
19      {
20          // Wait for the images to completely arrive.
```

```
21          Tracker.waitForAll();
22      }
23      catch( InterruptedException e )
24      {
25      }
26
27  }
```

ANALYSIS The loadImages() method is a collection of techniques you've already learned about. Above the method, the two Image classes are declared. The m_NormalImage object will contain the unaltered image. The m_ProcessedImage will load the normal image but will later change to reflect the image processing technique that's being used.

First, the loadImages() method uses the getImage() method to load the Picture.jpg images into the Image classes. The file name is hard-coded here to Picture.jpg. You could easily get this from an HTML parameter.

After the getImage() method is called for both Image classes, a MediaTracker class is created. Both Image classes are added to the MediaTracker class. The MediaTracker's waitForAll() method is then used to make sure that the images have arrived completely before returning to the calling code.

The code that gets the pixel data from the image is shown in Listing 13.11.

INPUT   **LISTING 13.11**   GETTING THE PIXEL DATA

```
1   // Declare the pixel array.
2   int m_nProcessedPixels[];
3
4   public void pullPixels()
5   {
6
7       // Call the method that creates the pixel array.
8       m_nProcessedPixels = getPixels( m_ProcessedImage );
9
10  }
11
12  public int[] getPixels( Image img )
13  {
14
15      // Get the width and height of the image.
16      int nWidth = img.getWidth( this );
17      int nHeight = img.getHeight( this );
18      // Calculate the number of pixels.
```

13

continues

LISTING **13.11**   CONTINUED

```
19      int nNumPixels = nWidth * nHeight;
20
21      // Create the array of integers for the pixel data.
22      int nRawPixels[] = new int[nNumPixels];
23      if( nRawPixels == null )
24          return( null );
25
26      // Create a PixelGrabber class.
27      PixelGrabber Grabber =
28          new PixelGrabber( img, 0, 0, nWidth, nHeight, nRawPixels, 0,
            ➥nWidth );
29
30      try
31      {
32          // Get the pixels into the integer array.
33          Grabber.grabPixels();
34      }
35      catch( InterruptedException e )
36      {
37      }
38
39      // Return the array.
40      return( nRawPixels );
41
42  }
```

ANALYSIS   The pullPixels() method contains code similar to what we developed earlier in this chapter. Above it, an integer array named m_nProcessedPixels is declared. This array will contain the pixel data form the m_ProcessedImage and then the data after it's been processed.

The pullPixels() method actually just calls the getPixels() method. But it passes the m_ProcessedImage to the getPixels() method and is returned an integer array.

The getPixels() array finds the width and height of the image. It then calculates the number of pixels in the image by multiplying the width by the height.

A local variable named nRawPixels is allocated so that it has enough space to hold the image pixel data. A PixelGrabber class is created. Then the PixelGrabber's grabPixels() method is called. This method copies all the Image class pixel data into the array. The integer array is then returned to the pullPixels() method.

Putting the pixels back is the next chunk of code we'll tackle. The pushPixels() and storePixels() methods make it all work. They are shown in Listing 13.12.

```
1    public void pushPixels()
2    {
3
4        // Call the method that creates the new Image class.
5        m_ProcessedImage = storePixels( m_ProcessedImage,
         ➥m_nProcessedPixels );
6
7    }
8
9    public Image storePixels( Image img, int nRawPixels[] )
10   {
11
12       // Get the width and height of the image.
13       int nWidth = img.getWidth( this );
14       int nHeight = img.getHeight( this );
15       // Calculate the number of pixels.
16       int nNumPixels = nWidth * nHeight;
17
18       // Get the ColorModel object.
19       ColorModel cm = ColorModel.getRGBdefault();
20
21       // Create the MemoryImageSource object.
22       MemoryImageSource ImageSource =
23           new MemoryImageSource( nWidth, nHeight, cm, nRawPixels, 0,
             ➥nWidth );
24
25       // Create the image.
26       img = createImage( ImageSource );
27
28       // Wait for the image to be created.
29       MediaTracker Tracker = new MediaTracker( this );
30       // Add the image to the MediaTracker.
31       Tracker.addImage( img, 0 );
32       try
33       {
34           // Wait for the completion of the image.
35           Tracker.waitForID( 0 );
36       }
37       catch( InterruptedException e )
38       {
39       }
40
41       return( img );
42
43   }
```

13

ANALYSIS   The pushPixels() and storePixels() methods are the last of the generic code shown in Listing 13.12. The pushPixels() method simply calls the storePixels() method with two arguments: an Image class and an array of integers. The storePixels() method returns an Image class.

The storePixels() array finds the width and height of the image. It then calculates the number of pixels in the image by multiplying the width by the height.

A ColorModel class is obtained via a call to the getRGBdefault() method. A MemoryImageSource class is created. This class is needed to create the new Image class. Finally, the createImage() class creates the new image from the MemoryImageSource class. One last detail, though, is to use a MediaTracker class to make sure that the image is completely created before returning to the calling code.

Horizontal and Waves

Now that our generic applet is created, all we have to do is add one method to perform an image processing function. The following methods and variables show you what was used:

- The horzWave() method is very simple, yet extremely effective when it comes to animation.

- The dNumWaves variable contains the number of waves you want in the image.

- The dPercent variable contains the amplitude of the wave, given in percent of the image's width.

- The dOffset variable describes the wave's position.

NEW TERM   *Amplitude* is the strength, or height, of the wave. It's similar to waves at the beach. The higher the wave, the greater the amplitude.

To add this method to the Generic applet, simply place it below the line in the init() method that says // Process the image. The source code for horzWave() is shown in Listing 13.13.

INPUT   **LISTING 13.13**   THE METHOD THAT CREATES A HORIZONTAL WAVE

```
1    public void horzWave()
2    {
3
4        // Get the width and height of the image.
5        int nWidth = m_ProcessedImage.getWidth( this );
6        int nHeight = m_ProcessedImage.getHeight( this );
7
8        // Point nPixels to the pixel data and
```

```
9      // create a new array.
10     int nPixels[] = m_nProcessedPixels;
11     m_nProcessedPixels = new int[nWidth*nHeight];
12
13     // These values are our constants. Change them
14     // for different effects.
15     double dNumWaves = 3.0;
16     double dOffset = 15.0;
17     double dPercent = 5.0;
18
19     // Calculate the wave frequency, wave offset,
20     // and radius.
21     double dWaveFreq = ( dNumWaves * Math.PI * 2.0 ) / nHeight;
22     double dWaveOffset = ( dOffset * dNumWaves * Math.PI * 2.0 ) /
       ➥100.0;
23     double dRadius = ( nWidth * dPercent ) / 100.0;
24
25     int nIndex = 0;
26     for( int y=0; y<nHeight; y++ )
27     {
28         // Calculate the adjusted x position.
29         int xOffset = (int) Math.round( Math.sin( y * dWaveFreq +
           ➥dWaveOffset ) *dRadius );
30         for( int x=0; x<nWidth; x++ )
31         {
32             // If the adjusted x position is in range, store
33             // the pixel value in the adjusted location.
34             if( xOffset >= 0 && xOffset < nWidth )
35                 m_nProcessedPixels[nIndex++] =
                   ➥nPixels[xOffset+nWidth*y];
36             // Otherwise make the pixel gray.
37             else
38                 m_nProcessedPixels[nIndex++] = 0xff808080;
39             xOffset++;
40         }
41     }
42
43 }
```

When the applet runs, you'll see the original image in the left side of the applet window, and the processed image in the right side of the window. Figure 13.4 shows the applet running inside of Internet Explorer.

Creating Line Art from Images

This filter turns color images into line drawings. The technique is done like this. First, you scan each line from left to right. The only thing you have to care about is how much each color component changes in intensity from pixel to pixel. If a color changes from black to white, this difference is big and therefore the contrast is sharp; so a line is detected and plotted. In essence, what you have is a contrast detector. High contrasts will cause the corresponding pixel in the filtered image to appear bright, and low contrasts will hardly show at all.

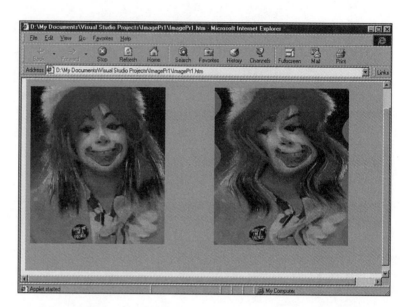

OUTPUT

FIGURE 13.4

The wave effect is shown in the image in the right half of the applet window.

The method that was created to perform the conversion from image to line art is called makeLines(). It starts off by doing some routine stuff such as getting the image width and height, and creating a new array into which the processed data will be placed. A variable named nIntensity can be changed. The greater the value, the more lines you'll have in your final image. The lower the value, the fewer lines. If your image has a low contrast, keep the nIntensity variable to a low value (1–4). If your image has a high contrast, you might go as high as 8.

For each scan line of the image (except the very first scan line), go from left to right. Look at the pixel above and to the left of the pixel you're currently on. If the contrast is great, make the final value high so that a line will be plotted.

Add with the last process, to add this method to the Generic applet, simply place it below the line in the init() method that says // Process the image. The source code for makeLines() is shown in Listing 13.14.

INPUT   LISTING 13.14   THE METHOD THAT MAKES LINE ART OF AN IMAGE

```
1    public void makeLines()
2    {
3
4        // Get the width and height of the image.
5        int nWidth = m_ProcessedImage.getWidth( this );
6        int nHeight = m_ProcessedImage.getHeight( this );
7
8        // Point nPixels to the pixel data and
9        // create a new array.
10       int nPixels[] = m_nProcessedPixels;
11       m_nProcessedPixels = new int[nWidth*nHeight];
12
13       // The intensity variable can be changed.
14       int nIntensity = 2;
15
16       // The first line is undefined; make it gray.
17       for( int nIndex=0; nIndex<nWidth; nIndex++ )
18           m_nProcessedPixels[nIndex] = 0xff808080;
19
20       for( int nIndex=nWidth; nIndex<nWidth*nHeight; nIndex++ )
21       {
22           // Get the pixel to the left of this pixel.
23           int c = nPixels[nIndex-1];
24           int r1 = ( c & 0x00ff0000 ) >> 16;
25           int g1 = ( c & 0x0000ff00 ) >> 8;
26           int b1 = ( c & 0x000000ff );
27
28           // Get the pixel above this pixel.
29           c = nPixels[nIndex-nWidth];
30           int r2 = ( c & 0x00ff0000 ) >> 16;
31           int g2 = ( c & 0x0000ff00 ) >> 8;
32           int b2 = ( c & 0x000000ff );
33
34           // Get this pixel.
35           c = nPixels[nIndex];
36           int r = ( c & 0x00ff0000 ) >> 16;
37           int g = ( c & 0x0000ff00 ) >> 8;
38           int b = ( c & 0x000000ff );
39
40           r = Math.min( ( Math.abs( r2 - r ) + Math.abs( r1 - r ) ) *
                 ➥nIntensity, 255 );
41           g = Math.min( ( Math.abs( g2 - g ) + Math.abs( g1 - g ) ) *
                 ➥nIntensity, 255 );
42           b = Math.min( ( Math.abs( g2 - b ) + Math.abs( b1 - b ) ) *
                 ➥nIntensity, 255 );
43
44           m_nProcessedPixels[nIndex] = 0xff000000 |
```

13

continues

LISTING **13.14**   CONTINUED

```
45                    ( r << 16 ) ¦ ( g << 8 ) ¦ b;
46        }
47
48    }
```

When the program runs, you'll see a mountainside photo in an image in the left side of the applet window. The right side of the applet window will contain the processed version of this mountainside. It will be reduced to line art. Figure 13.5 shows the applet running.

OUTPUT

FIGURE **13.5**

The mountainside has been converted to line art in the image in the right side of the applet window.

Blurring Images

Background images are fine if you want to spice up your Java applet or application, but they have a tendency to take center stage. One of the most effective ways to make your images less conspicuous is to use a blur filter on them.

You smooth a pixel by finding the average color of all pixels surrounding it within a given distance. The larger the distance, the more blurred the pixel will seem. You find the average color of an area by adding all intensities for each red, green, and blue color component. Then, you divide these sums by the number-of-components counter. The resulting values are your average colors.

And once again, to add this method to the Generic applet, simply place it below the line in the init() method that says // Process the image. The source code for makeBlurry() is shown in Listing 13.15.

INPUT **LISTING 13.15** THE METHOD THAT MAKES IMAGES BLURRY

```
1    public void makeBlurry()
2    {
3
4        // Get the width and height of the image.
5        int nWidth = m_ProcessedImage.getWidth( this );
6        int nHeight = m_ProcessedImage.getHeight( this );
7
8        // Point nPixels to the pixel data and
9        // create a new array.
10       int nPixels[] = m_nProcessedPixels;
11       m_nProcessedPixels = new int[nWidth*nHeight];
12
13       // This variable can be changed.
14       int nPower = 5;
15
16       int nIndex = 0;
17       for( int y=0; y<nHeight; y++ )
18       {
19           for( int x=0; x<nWidth; x++ )
20           {
21               int r = 0, g = 0, b = 0, nColors = 0;
22               for( int dy=-nPower+y; dy<=nPower+y; dy++ )
23               {
24                   for( int dx=-nPower+x; dx<=nPower+x; dx++ )
25                   {
26                       if( dx >= 0 && dx < nWidth && dy >= 0 && dy <
                            ➥nHeight )
27                       {
28                           int c = nPixels[dx+dy*nWidth];
29                           r += ( ( c & 0x00ff0000 ) >> 16 );
30                           g += ( ( c & 0x0000ff00 ) >> 8 );
31                           b += ( c & 0x000000ff );
32                           nColors++;
33                       }
34                   }
35               }
36               r /= nColors;
37               g /= nColors;
38               b /= nColors;
39               m_nProcessedPixels[nIndex++] = 0xff000000 |
40                   ( r << 16 ) | ( g << 8 ) | b;
41           }
42       }
43
44   }
```

13

When the applet runs, you'll see the unprocessed image to the left and the processed image to the right. The blur factor can be increased by an increase of the value of nPower. Making nPower have a lower value will make the blur factor decrease. You can see the applet in Figure 13.6.

FIGURE 13.6

The image on the right is blurred. Note that the image is still discernible even though it's been blurred.

Summary

Image processing is a useful technique for your Visual J++ programs. Not only will it save disk space, but it's a lot of fun. And you can even do image processing in real time in response to user input.

You must master several underlying concepts before actually processing images. The first thing you must know is how to pull the pixel data from an Image class. The second is how the pixel data is organized after it's been extracted. The final thing is how to create an image from the raw pixel data.

This chapter showed you several image processing techniques such as colorization and blurring. There are many others you can implement on your own.

Q&A

Q Can you use the pixel data in an `Image` class directly?

A No. You must extract the pixel data into an array of integers (for applets) or bytes (for applications). In an applet you'll create and use a `PixelGrabber` class. In an application you can save a BMP image to a `MemoryStream` object.

Q Can you just put the pixels back after you've extracted and processed them?

A No, it's not that easy. For an applet, you have to create a `MemoryImageSource` object and then use the `createImage()` method with the `MemoryImageSource` object. For an application, you can use the `loadImage()` method (as long as the data is in BMP format).

Q How is pixel data arranged after it's extracted from an `Image` class in an applet?

A It's in an array of integers. For each pixel, there's an integer. So to find the number of pixels (and the number of integers), multiply the image width by the image height. For each row of *n* pixels, there are *n* integers. If the image is 10 pixels wide, each row of pixels will be 10 integers. To calculate the position of pixel data in the integer array given x and y coordinates, multiply the y value by the image width (giving you the offset to the start of the scan line), and then add the x value (giving you the offset to the specified pixel in the scan line). Each integer contains the color data for the red, green, and blue components.

Q How is pixel data arranged after it's extracted from an `Image` class in an application?

A For all of our example source code, it's arranged exactly as a 24-bit BMP file is. First are the two headers—occupying a total of 54 bytes for both. Then comes the color data. One quirky thing you should know is that the scan lines are upside down. Each pixel occupies 3 bytes—one each for the red, green, and blue color components. Another oddity, though, is that each scan line is an even multiple of 4 bytes—sometimes there are unused bytes at the end of each scan line that simply pad the scan line so that it's an even multiple of 4 bytes.

Q Why would you want to use image processing techniques? Can't you use an image processing program and save the different images to the server?

A Sure. But this consumes storage space. It might be better to load a single image and then process it in many ways. This method cuts down on the amount of storage space you'll need on the server.

13

Q Are there any drawbacks to processing images when Visual J++ programs run?

A Yes, it can be slow. You must weigh the benefits of real-time image processing and see whether they outweigh the slowness.

Review Exercises

1. Create a program that loads a single image. Use a `PixelGrabber` class to get the pixel data from the image. Now create a new image from the pixel data.

2. Create a program that loads a single image. Obtain the pixel data. Now darken each pixel of the image. Create a second image from the darkened pixel data. Now display both images in the program's window.

WEEK 2

DAY 14

Animation

Today we'll cover something that Java is famous for—animation. There are many ways to create and implement animation in Java programs, and you'll get a representative sampling.

You can't browse the Web without seeing animated ad banners. They find their way to practically every commercial Web page there is. These ad banners are perfect examples of using Java's animation capabilities.

The techniques aren't too hard to master. If you follow the material in this chapter, you'll be ready for just about any animation you'll need to add to your Visual J++ programs.

Today we'll cover these items:

- Using threads and timers
- Line animation
- Using multiple line animation
- Bouncing ball animation
- Double buffering to prevent flicker
- Using multiframe image animation
- Creating animated ad banners

This chapter is jam-packed with techniques you can use directly in your program development. If you want, you can cut and paste some of the methods developed into your code. This chapter is also full of techniques you'll want to expand on to achieve leading-edge programs. For these, cut and paste the methods into your code, then go to town with modifications.

Threads and Timers

This chapter is not about threads and timers. As a matter of fact, we'll spend all of Day 17's chapter, "Threads," learning about threads. But we can't wait that long to use them. This short section will show you enough about threads and timers that you can use them in these animation programs. Then, when you get to Day 17, you'll be able to learn all about them and master that subject too.

The thing about animation is that it needs to be maintained at regular intervals. For instance, your ad banner might need to update itself every half second as it's moving from one ad to another. You might also have a spinning globe that needs to be updated every quarter of a second.

The way to maintain the animations is from threads and timers. We'll use threads for applets, and timers for applications. Each one has the capability to maintain an animation at a regular time interval.

Threads in Visual J++ Applets

A thread can be thought of as a single path of execution in your program. No matter how small or how simple a program is, it always has at least one thread.

At times an application will need to take advantage of having multiple threads. One of the primary reasons for Java's acceptance as the language for World Wide Web development is its capability to easily allow the developer to create a multithreaded application to support animation. The problem with animation is that to emulate motion, you need to render the next image in your sequence of images every n milliseconds. This is very processor intensive and prevents the rest of your program from running normally. For example, your program could never respond to the stop() request because it is spending so much time trying to display images. Actually, you would never see any images because you would be in such a "tight loop" that the paint() method could never be called.

Without further ado, I'll show you a simple applet that implements a thread. We can model our applets that have animation after it. This applet calls repaint every 50 milliseconds. In the `paint()` method, the `m_nValue` variable is displayed. Each time the applet window is repainted, the `m_nValue` variable is incremented. This way, you can watch the applet running and know that the thread is doing its job. The source code for the applet is given in Listing 14.1.

LISTING 14.1 A SIMPLE APPLET WHICH IMPLEMENTS A THREAD THAT CAN BE USED FOR ANIMATION

```
1   import java.awt.*;
2   import java.applet.*;
3
4   public class AppletThread extends Applet implements Runnable
5   {
6
7       Thread m_AppletThread = null;
8       int m_nValue = 0;
9
10      public void init()
11      {
12
13      }
14
15      public void start()
16      {
17          if( m_AppletThread == null )
18          {
19              m_AppletThread = new Thread( this );
20              m_AppletThread.start();
21          }
22      }
23
24      public void stop()
25      {
26          if( m_AppletThread != null )
27          {
28              m_AppletThread.stop();
29              m_AppletThread = null;
30          }
31      }
32
33      public void run()
34      {
35          while( true )
36          {
37              try
38              {
39                  repaint();
```

14

continues

LISTING 14.1   CONTINUED

```
40                    Thread.sleep(50);
41               }
42               catch (InterruptedException e)
43               {
44                   stop();
45               }
46          }
47     }
48
49     public void paint( Graphics g )
50     {
51          g.drawString( "m_nValue=" + m_nValue, 10, 10 );
52          m_nValue++;
53     }
54
55 }
```

You can see the effect of the applet's thread in Figure 14.1. The applet window displays the value of the m_nValue variable.

FIGURE 14.1

You can see that the thread is doing its job because the m_nValue *variable continually increments.*

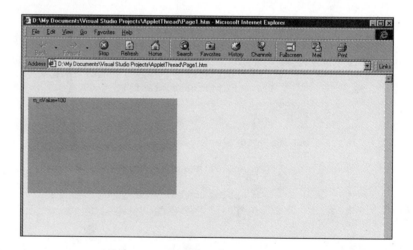

ANALYSIS   The first thing you should notice is that the applet implements the Runnable interface at line 4. Then, as with most applets that implement the Runnable interface, a Thread class is declared as shown at line 7. The declaration at line 8 is simply an integer that will be constantly incremented so that we'll know that the thread is actually doing something.

Lines 15–22 contain a boilerplate `start()` method. When this method is called, the thread is instantiated and started with its `start()` method.

Lines 24–31 contain a boilerplate `stop()` method. When this method is called, the thread is stopped with its `stop()` method, and the thread is set to `null`.

You can see the `run()` method at lines 33–47. Note that our program stays stuck in the `while` loop because it's testing `true` to be true. Then, a `try` block is where the work is done. Note that it calls `repaint()` at line 39 and then employs the `sleep()` method for 50 milliseconds at line 40. The last thing in the `run()` method is where an `InterruptedException` is caught. This is the only way the `run()` method will be exited because it calls the `stop()` method at line 44.

The `paint()` method at lines 49–53 is simple. It shows the value of the `m_nValue` variable and then increments the variable.

Okay, that's great. But say you have an applet already started and want to add a thread. Or you just want to make sure that you know how to add a thread to a new applet. Here's a step-by-step list of what to do:

1. Find the top of your applet class (in this example, the applet is named MyApplet). It's the line that starts like this:

   ```
   public class MyApplet extends Applet
   ```

2. Add information to this line so that your applet implements the `Runnable` interface. The new line will be as follows:

   ```
   public class MyApplet extends Applet implements Runnable.
   ```

3. Add a declaration for a `Thread` class at the top of the applet. (The top of the applet is just the traditional place for it; it really can be anywhere.) The source code will look like the following:

   ```
   Thread m_MyApplet = null;
   ```

4. Add a `start()` method somewhere in the body of the applet. The source code for the `start()` method will look like this:

   ```
   public void start()
   {
       if( m_MyApplet == null )
       {
           m_MyApplet = new Thread( this );
           m_MyApplet.start();
       }
   }
   ```

5. Add a `stop()` method somewhere in the body of the applet. The source code for the `stop()` method will look like the following:

14

```
public void stop()
{
    if( m_AppletThread != null )
    {
        m_AppletThread.stop();
        m_AppletThread = null;
    }
}
```

6. Finally, add a run() method somewhere in the body of the applet. The value you give to the Thread.sleep() method is the number of milliseconds that the program will wait before proceeding waking up and executing more code. The source code for the run() method will look like the following:

```
public void run()
{
    while( true )
    {
        try
        {
            // Do stuff here...
            Thread.sleep(50);
        }
        catch( InterruptedException e )
        {
            stop();
        }
    }
}
```

Caution

If the duration that your thread sleeps is too small (less than 10 or 20 milliseconds), your applet might not perform very well. This is because the run() method chews up too much CPU time. It's a good idea to use sleep() for at least 50 milliseconds and yield to other tasks in your program.

Timers in Visual J++ Applications

A timer is completely different from a thread. The only thing it has in common with a thread is that it lets you do things at specified intervals.

Three things happen in a timer's life. The first is that the timer is created. When this happens, the Windows operating system is notified that a timer is being created. All the information necessary for the timer's operation is given, including the method that the timer message will invoke and the timer duration. The second thing in a timer's career is the timer notifications. The operating system sends a timer message (WM_TIMER for you

Visual C++ programmers) to your program's window, and your program decides which method to invoke. The last thing in a timer's life is its death. A timer can be killed during the execution of a program, or at the termination of a program when everything is being cleaned up.

It's easy to tell your Visual J++ application that you want a timer. Start by opening the Form Design window. Make sure that the WFC controls are selected in the Toolbox window. Find the timer control (it looks like a clock) and drag it onto your form. You can see in Figure 14.2 the timer that's been placed on the form.

FIGURE 14.2

Select the timer in the WFC controls and drag it to the form to add a timer to your application.

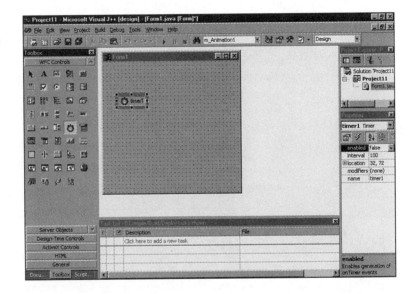

Make sure that the timer control is selected on your form. You'll notice that the properties window now allows you to specify information about your timer's operation. The first property lets you determine whether the control is enabled. Assuming that you put the timer on the form for a reason, this will usually be true. The next property lets you specify the duration between timer events. This value is in milliseconds, so the default value of 100 translates to one-tenth of a second. The location property can be ignored. The modifiers property will not be changed for most applications. And you're free to change the name of the timer as you see fit.

You have a timer control on your form, but no event handler. Click on the Events button. Then when the timer event appears in the list (the only thing that will be in the list), double-click on it to add an event handler to your form.

14

After you have your timer event handler, you can maintain your animation. The following source code shows you what a simple timer event method will look like:

```
private void timer1_timer(Object source, Event e)
{

}
```

Timer notifications are never allowed to stack up in the message queue, which is a very good thing. Think about what could happen if a timer was set to fire every 250 milliseconds but the code executing as a result of the timer message took longer to run. If the messages were allowed to stack up in the queue, a race condition would result. Messages would queue up faster than your application could service them. Your code would never empty the queue and so would continue to run all the time.

Instead, because Windows doesn't allow messages to stack up, this potential problem is solved. In this example, after the loop of code finishes executing, it will receive another message at the end of the next 250 millisecond cycle.

Still, a Windows application should never spend an excessive amount of time processing a message unless processing has been delegated to a secondary thread. Responsiveness will suffer if the primary thread goes too long without checking the message queue.

Double Buffering

In the "Images" chapter on Day 12, we talked about reducing screen flicker by overriding an applet's update() method. The reason this works, in many cases, is that it prevents the entire applet window from being cleared before it's redrawn. That works well in many situations, but there's one more step you can take if that's not enough.

With double-buffering, you can create a second surface, do all your painting to that surface, and then draw the whole surface at once onto the visible applet window—instead of drawing to the applet's actual visible graphics surface. Because all the work actually goes on behind the scenes, there's no opportunity for interim parts of the drawing process to appear accidentally and disrupt the smoothness of the animation.

Double-buffering isn't always the best solution. If your applet is suffering from flicker, try overriding the update() method and drawing only portions of the screen as your first line of defense—that might solve your problem. Double-buffering is less efficient than regular buffering and takes up more memory and space, so if you can avoid it, make an effort to do so. In terms of nearly eliminating animation flicker, however, double-buffering works exceptionally well.

To implement double-buffering, you need two things: an image to draw into and a graphics context (`Graphics` class) for that image. Those two together mimic the effect of the applet's drawing surface: the graphics context to provide the drawing methods, such as `drawImage()` and `drawString()`, and the `Image` class to hold the image data that gets drawn.

There are four major steps to adding double-buffering to your applet:

1. Your offscreen image and graphics context need to be stored in instance variables so that you can pass them to the `paint()` method. We're going to add double-buffering to the BouncingBalls applet. The following source-code lines are what we'll add to the top of the applet to declare the variables we'll need:

   ```
   Image m_OffscreenImage;
   Graphics m_og;
   ```

2. During the initialization of the applet, you'll instantiate an `Image` and a `Graphics` class and assign them to these variables. The `createImage()` method gives you the instance of the `Image` class. After you have the `Image` class created, you can use its `getGraphics()` method to obtain the `Graphics` class for the `Image`. The following source code shows you what we'll add to the `init()` method of our BouncingBalls applet:

   ```
   m_OffscreenImage = createImage( 680, 340 );
   m_og = m_OffscreenImage.getGraphics();
   ```

3. Whenever you have to draw to the screen (usually in the `paint()` method), rather than drawing to the `paint()` method's `Graphics` class, you draw to the offscreen graphics. For example, to draw an image called `img` at position 10, 10, use the following line:

   ```
   m_og.drawImage( img, 10, 10, this );
   ```

4. At the end of your `paint()` method, after all the drawing to the offscreen image is done, add the following line to display the offscreen buffer to the visible window:

   ```
   g.drawImage( m_OffscreenImage, 0, 0, this );
   ```

We'll definitely override the `update()` method so that the window won't be cleared each time the window is redrawn. This would cause a large amount of flicker. The source code in Listing 14.2 shows the new `paint()` method and the overridden `update()` method.

14

INPUT **LISTING 14.2** THE NEW paint() AND THE ADDITIONAL update() METHODS TO IMPLEMENT DOUBLE-BUFFERING IN THE BOUNCINGBALLS APPLET

```
1    public void paint( Graphics g )
2    {
3
4        m_og.setColor( getBackground() );
5        m_og.fillRect( 0, 0, 680, 340 );
6
7        // Set to red.
8        m_og.setColor( Color.red );
9        // Draw the red ball.
10       m_og.fillOval( xPos[0], yPos[0], 15, 15 );
11
12       // If the count is greater than 60,
13       // we'll draw the green ball.
14       if( count > 60 )
15       {
16           // Set to green.
17           m_og.setColor( Color.green );
18           // Draw the green ball.
19           m_og.fillOval( xPos[1], yPos[1], 15, 15 );
20       }
21
22       // If the count is greater than 120,
23       // we'll draw the blue ball.
24       if( count > 120 )
25       {
26           // Set to blue.
27           m_og.setColor( Color.blue );
28           // Draw the blue ball.
29           m_og.fillOval( xPos[2], yPos[2], 15, 15 );
30       }
31
32       g.drawImage( m_OffscreenImage, 0, 0, this );
33    }
34
35    public void update( Graphics g )
36    {
37        paint( g );
38    }
```

ANALYSIS Here are the main steps for adding double-buffering to your applet:

1. Create an image as large as the visible window (or another size if you desire).

2. Obtain a Graphics class for the image you created.

3. Update the update() method so that the window won't be cleared for each redraw.

4. In the `paint()` method, draw to the offscreen `Graphics` class.

5. At the end of the `paint()` method, draw the offscreen `Image` class to the visible window (use the `paint()` method's `Graphics` class).

Line Animation

We'll start off with some simple programs and work our way up to the more difficult ones later in the chapter. In this section we're going to create programs that perform animation by simply drawing lines. Every time the animation is maintained by the thread or timer, the position of the lines will change.

The SimpleLineAnimation Applet

In the applet example, when we draw our lines, we won't have to worry about erasing the old lines. That's because we'll be calling the `repaint()` method to cause the window to update. The `repaint()` method clears the window before getting to the `paint()` method, thus erasing the old lines for us.

To keep things simple, we'll draw two lines: one horizontal and one vertical. The vertical line will move back and forth across the window, and the horizontal line will move up and down on the window.

The applet's source code is simple. It has the additions necessary for support of a thread. In the `run()` method, two variables are updated: `m_nHorizontal` and `m_nVertical`. These determine where the horizontal and vertical lines are drawn when the applet window is updated. After these variables are updated to reflect new values, they're checked to make sure that the lines haven't gone off the screen. If the lines moved off the screen, the direction for the lines' movement reverses.

The `paint()` method simply draws two lines. It uses the `Graphics` class `drawLine()` method to draw the lines. The source code for the SimpleLineAnimation applet is given in Listing 14.3.

| INPUT | **LISTING 14.3** SOURCE CODE FOR THE SIMPLELINEANIMATION APPLET |

```
1    import java.awt.*;
2    import java.applet.*;
3
4    public class SimpleLineAnimation extends Applet implements Runnable
5    {
6        Thread m_Thread = null;
7
```

14

continues

LISTING 14.3   CONTINUED

```
8        int m_nHorizontal = 0;
9        int m_nHDir = 5;
10       int m_nVertical = 0;
11       int m_nVDir = 5;
12
13       public void init()
14       {
15       }
16
17       public void start()
18       {
19           if( m_Thread == null )
20           {
21               m_Thread = new Thread( this );
22               m_Thread.start();
23           }
24       }
25
26       public void stop()
27       {
28           if( m_Thread != null )
29           {
30               m_Thread.stop();
31               m_Thread = null;
32           }
33       }
34
35       public void run()
36       {
37           while( true )
38           {
39               try
40               {
41                   Thread.sleep(50);
42
43                   m_nHorizontal += m_nHDir;
44                   if( m_nHorizontal > 199 || m_nHorizontal < 0 )
45                   {
46                       m_nHDir = -m_nHDir;
47                       m_nHorizontal += ( 2 * m_nHDir );
48                   }
49
50                   m_nVertical += m_nVDir;
51                   if( m_nVertical > 319 || m_nVertical < 0 )
52                   {
53                       m_nVDir = -m_nVDir;
54                       m_nVertical += ( 2 * m_nVDir );
55                   }
56                   repaint();
```

```
57                          }
58                      catch( InterruptedException e )
59                      {
60                          stop();
61                      }
62                  }
63          }
64
65      public void paint( Graphics g )
66      {
67          g.drawLine( 0, m_nHorizontal, 319, m_nHorizontal );
68          g.drawLine( m_nVertical, 0, m_nVertical, 199 );
69      }
70
71  }
```

When the program runs, you'll see a horizontal and a vertical line move around on the screen. Figure 14.3 shows the applet running inside of Internet Explorer.

OUTPUT

FIGURE 14.3

The SimpleLineAnimation applet moves two lines around on the screen.

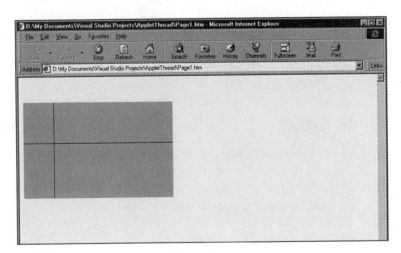

ANALYSIS Important to note in the program is that we use sleep() for 50 milliseconds in line 41 to give the system a chance to perform its other duties. At line 43 we move the horizontal line and check at line 44 to see whether it's out of range. If the horizontal position has gone out of range, we reverse directions at line 46 and get the value back in range at line 47.

At line 50 we move the vertical line. Of course, we must check to see whether the vertical line has gone out of range. We do this at line 51. If it has gone out of range, we reverse the direction of the vertical line at line 53 and adjust its value at line 54 so that it's back inside the window.

14

Finally, at line 56 we call `repaint()` to update the applet's window. The `paint()` method, at lines 65–69, is very simple. It just draws both the horizontal and the vertical lines.

The RandomLine Application

The next thing we'll do is create some simple animation from a Visual J++ application. This is somewhat different from the applet we created in the preceding example. For starters, it's an application and we'll use a timer rather than a thread.

Another big difference is the absence of the `repaint()` method that applets have. Instead, we use a combination of the `invalidate()` and `update()` methods. The `invalidate()` method causes the entire form window to become invalid. In the next `paint` message, the entire form will be redrawn. The problem with that is that the `paint` message is queued and might not happen immediately. The `update()` method causes the form window to be redrawn immediately without any delay.

The program source code is fairly simple. An array of integers stores the 32 coordinates for the eight lines. Each line requires four coordinates: an x,y pair for one end and an x,y pair for the other end.

During the `Form1()` constructor, all 32 integers are randomly generated. Their values will range from `0` to `400`. This gives a different starting look to the program every time it runs.

The `Form1_paint()` method simply draws all eight lines from within a `for` loop.

The real action takes place in the `timer1_timer()` method. All 32 array elements are randomly updated. The first thing that happens is that for each of the 32 array elements, a value from `-16` to `16` is generated. This value is added to the array element. The value is checked to make sure that it's not out of range—for instance, if it becomes negative. Then, the `timer1_timer()` method simply calls the `invalidate()` and `update()` methods.

The source code for the RandomLine application is given in Listing 14.4.

INPUT **LISTING 14.4** SOURCE CODE FOR THE RANDOMLINE APPLICATION

```
1    import com.ms.wfc.app.*;
2    import com.ms.wfc.core.*;
3    import com.ms.wfc.ui.*;
4    import com.ms.wfc.html.*;
5
6    /**
7     * This class can take a variable number of parameters on the command
```

```
8    * line. Program execution begins with the main() method. The class
9    * constructor is not invoked unless an object of type 'Form1' is
10   * created in the main() method.
11   */
12  public class Form1 extends Form
13  {
14
15      // We'll need 32 integers, 4 for each of the 8 lines.
16      int m_nLineCoords[] = new int[32];
17
18      public Form1()
19      {
20          // Randomize the values of the line coordinates
21          // with values ranging from 0 to 400.
22          for( int i=0; i<32; i++ )
23              m_nLineCoords[i] = (int) ( Math.random() * 400 );
24
25          // Required for Visual J++ Form Designer support
26          initForm();
27
28      }
29
30      /**
31       * Form1 overrides dispose so it can clean up the
32       * component list.
33       */
34      public void dispose()
35      {
36          super.dispose();
37          components.dispose();
38      }
39
40      private void Form1_click(Object source, Event e)
41      {
42
43      }
44
45      private void Form1_paint(Object source, PaintEvent e)
46      {
47          // Draw all 8 lines.
48          for( int i=0; i<8; i++ )
49              e.graphics.drawLine( m_nLineCoords[i*4],
              ➥m_nLineCoords[i*4+1],
50                  m_nLineCoords[i*4+2], m_nLineCoords[i*4+3] );
51      }
52
53      private void timer1_timer(Object source, Event e)
54      {
55          // Go through and move each of the 32
```

14

continues

LISTING 14.4 CONTINUED

```
56         // line coordinate values. Use random
57         // numbers to move them around.
58         for( int i=0; i<32; i++ )
59         {
60             // Get a direction value from -16 to 16.
61             int nDirection = 16 - (int) ( Math.random() * 33 );
62             // Add the value.
63             m_nLineCoords[i] += nDirection;
64             // Make sure the coordinate is in range.
65             if( m_nLineCoords[i] < 0 )
66                 m_nLineCoords[i] = 0;
67             else if( m_nLineCoords[i] > 400 )
68                 m_nLineCoords[i] = 400;
69         }
70         // Invalidate the window rectangle and
71         // cause a window update.
72         invalidate();
73         update();
74     }
75
76     /**
77      * NOTE: The following code is required by the Visual J++ form
78      * designer.  It can be modified using the form editor.  Do not
79      * modify it using the code editor.
80      */
81     Container components = new Container();
82     Timer timer1 = new Timer(components);
83
84     private void initForm()
85     {
86         this.setText("RandomLine");
87         this.setAutoScaleBaseSize(13);
88         this.setClientSize(new Point(292, 273));
89         this.addOnClick(new EventHandler(this.Form1_click));
90         this.addOnPaint(new PaintEventHandler(this.Form1_paint));
91
92         timer1.setEnabled(true);
93         timer1.addOnTimer(new EventHandler(this.timer1_timer));
94         /* @designTimeOnly timer1.setLocation(new Point(24, 88)); */
95     }
96
97     /**
98      * The main entry point for the application.
99      *
100      * @param args Array of parameters passed to the application
101      * via the command line.
102      */
103     public static void main(String args[])
104     {
```

```
105        Application.run(new Form1());
106    }
107 }
```

You can see the program running in Figure 14.4. Eight lines are drawn in the form window. Their coordinates are generated randomly, so where they appear when the program first starts is anyone's guess. Then, they're updated randomly. They move around the screen in haphazard ways with no real continuous direction.

OUTPUT

FIGURE 14.4

This application has eight random lines that move around in the form window.

Bouncing Balls

On to something more interesting than lines. We're still going to draw with Graphics class methods, but the bouncing balls you'll see in this applet will be far more interesting than the lines you saw in the previous two programs.

The source code for the BouncingBalls applet is fairly simple. It's shown in Listing 14.5. In the paint() method, the three balls are drawn. The method doesn't draw the green and blue balls until the count has exceeded a threshold so that the green and blue balls don't start immediately.

In the run() method, the ball coordinates are updated. The x direction is simply added to the x position. If the x position goes off of the right or left side of the window, the direction is reversed. The y direction is added to the y position. The y direction value changes so that it seems as though gravity is acting on the ball.

INPUT   **LISTING 14.5** SOURCE CODE FOR THE BOUNCINGBALLS APPLET

```
1    import java.awt.*;
2    import java.applet.*;
3
4    public class BouncingBalls extends Applet implements Runnable
```

continues

14

LISTING 14.5 CONTINUED

```
5    {
6         Thread m_Thread = null;
7
8         int xPos[] = { 20, 20, 20 };
9         int yPos[] = { 40, 40, 40 };
10        int xDir[] = { 10, 10, 10 };
11        int yDir[] = { 1, 1, 1 };
12        int count = 0;
13
14        public void init()
15        {
16        }
17
18        public void paint( Graphics g )
19        {
20            g.setColor( Color.red );
21            g.fillOval( xPos[0], yPos[0], 15, 15 );
22
23            if( count > 60 )
24            {
25                g.setColor( Color.green );
26                g.fillOval( xPos[1], yPos[1], 15, 15 );
27            }
28
29            if( count > 120 )
30            {
31                g.setColor( Color.blue );
32                g.fillOval( xPos[2], yPos[2], 15, 15 );
33            }
34        }
35
36        public void start()
37        {
38            if( m_Thread == null )
39            {
40                m_Thread = new Thread( this );
41                m_Thread.start();
42            }
43        }
44
45        public void stop()
46        {
47            if( m_Thread != null )
48            {
49                m_Thread.stop();
50                m_Thread = null;
51            }
52        }
53
```

```
54      public void run()
55      {
56          while( true )
57          {
58              try
59              {
60                  count++;
61
62                  int i, j = 1;
63                  if( count >= 60 )
64                      j++;
65                  if( count >= 120 )
66                      j++;
67
68                  for( i=0; i<j; i++ )
69                  {
70                      xPos[i] += xDir[i];
71
72                      if( xPos[i] > 640 )
73                      {
74                          xDir[i] = -xDir[i];
75                          xPos[i] = 640;
76                      }
77                      else if( xPos[i] < 20 )
78                      {
79                          xDir[i] = -xDir[i];
80                          xPos[i] = 20;
81                      }
82
83                      yPos[i] += yDir[i];
84                      yDir[i]++;
85
86                      if( yPos[i] > 340 )
87                      {
88                          yPos[i] = 680 - yPos[i];
89                          yDir[i] = -yDir[i] + 3;
90                      }
91                  }
92                  repaint();
93                  Thread.sleep(50);
94              }
95              catch (InterruptedException e)
96              {
97                  stop();
98              }
99          }
100     }
101
102 }
```

14

You can see the applet running inside of Internet Explorer in Figure 14.5. Three balls go back and forth and appear to fall and bounce according to the laws of gravity.

FIGURE 14.5

The bouncing balls, all out of phase, make for an interesting display.

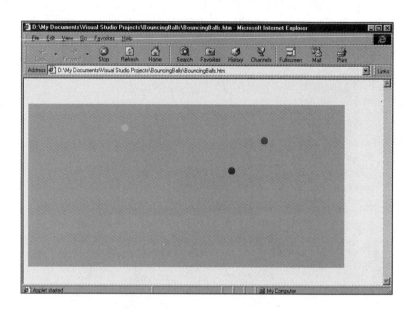

ANALYSIS At lines 8–11 you can see where we declare several arrays in which we'll keep track of positions and directions. The count variable at line 12 is just to keep track of when to start the second and third ball.

At lines 20 and 21 we set the draw color to red and then draw the red ball at its proper position. At line 23 we check to see whether the count has gone past 60 so that we can begin drawing the green ball. If so, we set the draw color to green and draw the green ball at its proper position. At line 29 we see whether the count has gone past 120 and we can begin drawing the blue ball. If so, we set the draw color to blue and draw the blue ball at its proper position.

At line 36 you can see the beginning of a basic start() method, and at line 45 you can see the beginning of a basic stop() method.

The run() method is where the ball positions are updated. It spans lines 54–100. At line 60 we increment the counter. At line 62 we declare a variable named j. It starts with a value of 1 but is increased to 2 if the count is greater than 60 (meaning that the green ball is now in motion), and it's increased to 3 if the count is greater than 120 (meaning that the blue ball is now in motion).

Having the variable j contain a number that reflects the number of balls in motion allows us to create a loop in which we can update the balls in an efficient manner. Without the loop, we'd need redundant code for each ball to update its position and direction.

The update loop is in lines 68–91. At line 70 the x position is changed according to the x direction. At line 72 we check to see whether the ball has gone off the right side of the applet window—if it has, we adjust the position and reverse the x direction. At line 77 we check to see whether the ball has gone off the left side of the applet window—if it has, we adjust the position and reverse the x direction.

At line 83 we change the y position according to the y direction. Notice that at line 84 we make a change to the y direction. This is so that the change in the y velocity changes and resembles the force of gravity as it speeds up when it gets close to the bottom and slows down at the top. At lines 86–90 we make sure that the y position doesn't go out of range.

After the ball positions have been updated, we call the `repaint()` method at line 92 and call `sleep()` in line 93 to let the system perform other tasks.

Multiframe Images

Do you remember getting those little pads in Cracker Jacks boxes? When you flipped through the pad at a steady speed, you saw what looked like a cartoon figure moving around. Real cartoons are created in the same way. Animators draw one frame at a time. Each frame has the characters in the scene in a slightly different position. When you watch the frames in sequence at a steady speed, you see smooth motion.

That's the same idea used for multiframe animation computer graphics. You have a list of image frames. Going from the first frame to the end frame, the figures in the animation frames move. Watching the frame images draw in sequence at a steady speed gives you smooth animation.

In this section, I'm going to show you how to write a program, load in a list of animation frames, and then play them back in the Java window.

The first thing you need is a set of images. I'm using something from a previous project I worked on. I wrote Championship Chess, which has an animated set. The animated set has attack and defend sequences. For instance, when the queen kills the knight, you first see the queen attack. Then, the knight dies before your very eyes in an animation sequence.

Because most of the chapter so far has used applets for the demonstration programs, I decided to write an application. This might be a good thing because applications give

14

you an `ImageList` control that makes it extremely easy to load a list of animation images.

In Visual J++, I started by dragging an `ImageList` control to my form. The `images` property lets you select an entire sequence of images. It worries about loading all the images at runtime. To add images, you simply click the Add button and, with a file selector, add an image to the list. Figure 14.6 illustrates this.

FIGURE 14.6

The `ImageList` *control lets you add an entire set of images to a single control. This makes it easy to manage a sequence of animations.*

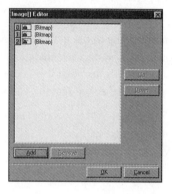

With the images in the `ImageList`, the next thing was to add a timer control. The timer control, as we've seen in previous animation programs, lets us maintain our animations at regular time intervals. I added a paint event handler at the same time named `Form1_paint()`.

By adding seven lines of code to this program, I got the animation working. The complete source code is given in Listing 14.6.

INPUT **LISTING 14.6** SOURCE CODE FOR THE FRAMEANIMATION APPLICATION

```
1 import com.ms.wfc.app.*;
2 import com.ms.wfc.core.*;
3 import com.ms.wfc.ui.*;
4 import com.ms.wfc.html.*;
5
6 /**
7  * This class can take a variable number of parameters on the command
8  * line. Program execution begins with the main() method. The class
9  * constructor is not invoked unless an object of type 'Form1' is
10  * created in the main() method.
11  */
12 public class Form1 extends Form
13 {
14     // Keeps track of the image that's currently displayed.
```

```
15      int m_nCurrentIndex = 0;
16
17      public Form1()
18      {
19          // Required for Visual J++ Form Designer support
20          initForm();
21
22          // TODO: Add any constructor code after initForm call
23      }
24
25      /**
26       * Form1 overrides dispose so it can clean up the
27       * component list.
28       */
29      public void dispose()
30      {
31          super.dispose();
32          components.dispose();
33      }
34      private void timer1_timer(Object source, Event e)
35      {
36          // Force a window refresh.
37          invalidate();
38          update();
39
40          // Cause the index counter to increment.
41          m_nCurrentIndex++;
42          // Keep it a value from 0 to 31.
43          if( m_nCurrentIndex > 31 )
44              m_nCurrentIndex = 0;
45      }
46
47      private void Form1_paint(Object source, PaintEvent e)
48      {
49          // Draw the current image.
50          e.graphics.drawImage( imageList2.getImage( m_nCurrentIndex ),
            ➥ 10, 10 );
51      }
52
53      private void Form1_click(Object source, Event e)
54      {
55
56      }
57
58      /**
59       * NOTE: The following code is required by the Visual J++ form
60       * designer.  It can be modified using the form editor.  Do not
61       * modify it using the code editor.
62       */
```

14

continues

LISTING 14.6   CONTINUED

```
63      Container components = new Container();
64      Timer timer1 = new Timer(components);
65      ImageList imageList2 = new ImageList();
66
67      private void initForm()
68      {
69          // NOTE:  This form is storing resource information in an
70          // external file.  Do not modify the string parameter to any
71          // resources.getObject() function call.  For example, do not
72          // modify "foo1_location" in the following line of code
73          // even if the name of the Foo object changes:
74          //     foo1.setLocation((Point)resources.getObject
75                      ➥("foo1_location"));
76          IResourceManager resources = new ResourceManager(this,
                ➥"Form1");
77          this.setText("Form1");
78          this.setAutoScaleBaseSize(13);
79          this.setClientSize(new Point(292, 273));
80          this.addOnClick(new EventHandler(this.Form1_click));
81          this.addOnPaint(new PaintEventHandler(this.Form1_paint));
82
83          timer1.setInterval(200);
84          timer1.setEnabled(true);
85          timer1.addOnTimer(new EventHandler(this.timer1_timer));
86          /* @designTimeOnly timer1.setLocation(new Point(56, 152)); */
87
88          imageList2.setImageSize(new Point(60, 130));
89          imageList2.setImageStream((ImageListStreamer)
                ➥resources.getObject("imageList2_imageStream"));
90          /* @designTimeOnly imageList2.setLocation(new Point(48, 80));
                ➥*/
91      }
92
93      /**
94       * The main entry point for the application.
95       *
96       * @param args Array of parameters passed to the application
97       * via the command line.
98       */
99      public static void main(String args[])
100     {
101         Application.run(new Form1());
102     }
103 }
```

When the program runs, you'll see the chess queen go through its attack sequence. The program is shown in Figure 14.7.

FIGURE 14.7

This program shows you a chess queen on the attack.

ANALYSIS The `timer1_timer()` method does most of the work. First, it causes the window to refresh by calling the `invalidate()` and `update()` methods. Then, the `m_nCurrentIndex` variable is incremented. Because there are 32 images, we have to keep the value of `m_nCurrentIndex` to a range from 0 to 31. If it exceeds 31, we reset it to 0 and start the animation all over again.

Ad Banners

Just about every Web page has a Java banner that displays ads. The banner usually alternates between different ad banners. By now, this will be an easy animation technique for you to master.

This section shows you how to create a simplified version of the ad banner applets you see on the Web. You can easily modify it so that it does much more.

The way the program works is simple. First, load two images. One of the images will be the background of the applet while the other moves across the window from right to left. When the moving image reaches the far left, it becomes stationary and the stationary image begins to move from right to left.

In the `paint()` method, the code decides which image is stationary and executes one of two chunks of code. The x position for the moving image is decremented so that it moves to the left. If it hits the far-left side of the applet window, it's time to switch the roles of each image. The complete source code is given in Listing 14.7.

14

```
1    import java.awt.*;
2    import java.applet.*;
3
4    public class AdBanner extends Applet implements Runnable
5    {
6
7        Thread m_Thread = null;
8
9        // This is the offscreen image and the Graphics class
10       // we'll use to reference it.
11       Image m_OffscreenImage;
12       Graphics m_og;
13
14       // The file names for the image files.
15       String m_strImage1File;
16       String m_strImage2File;
17
18       // The two ad banner images.
19       Image m_Image1;
20       Image m_Image2;
21
22       // The movement variables.
23       int m_nWhichImage = 0;
24       int m_nImageX;
25
26       /**
27        * The entry point for the applet.
28        */
29       public void init()
30       {
31           usePageParams();
32
33           // Set our initial x position.
34           m_nImageX = this.getSize().width - 10;
35           // Create the offscreen image for double buffering.
36           m_OffscreenImage = createImage( this.getSize().width,
              ➥this.getSize().height );
37           // Get the offscreen image's Graphics class.
38           m_og = m_OffscreenImage.getGraphics();
39           // Create a new MediaTracker class so that we'll wait for
40           // the images to come in before we go on.
41           MediaTracker Tracker = new MediaTracker( this );
42           // Load the two images.
43           m_Image1 = getImage( getCodeBase(), m_strImage1File );
44           m_Image2 = getImage( getCodeBase(), m_strImage2File );
45           // Tell the MediaTracker class which image to wait for.
46           Tracker.addImage( m_Image1, 0 );
47           Tracker.addImage( m_Image2, 1 );
```

```
48              // Wait for all of the images to come in.
49              try
50              {
51                  Tracker.waitForAll();
52              }
53              catch( InterruptedException e )
54              {
55              }
56          }
57
58          /**
59           * Reads parameters from the applet's HTML host and sets applet
60           * properties.
61           */
62          private void usePageParams()
63          {
64              // Get the image file names.
65              m_strImage1File = getParameter( "Image1" );
66              m_strImage2File = getParameter( "Image2" );
67          }
68
69          public void start()
70          {
71              if( m_Thread == null )
72              {
73                  m_Thread = new Thread( this );
74                  m_Thread.start();
75              }
76          }
77
78          public void stop()
79          {
80              if( m_Thread != null )
81              {
82                  m_Thread.stop();
83                  m_Thread = null;
84              }
85          }
86
87          public void run()
88          {
89              while( true )
90              {
91                  try
92                  {
93                      repaint();
94                      Thread.sleep(50);
95                  }
96                  catch (InterruptedException e)
```

14

continues

LISTING 14.7 CONTINUED

```
97                  {
98                      stop();
99                  }
100             }
101         }
102
103         public void update( Graphics g )
104         {
105             paint( g );
106         }
107
108         public void paint( Graphics g )
109         {
110             // In this case, draw Image1, then draw Image2
111             // on top at the correct x position.
112             if( m_nWhichImage == 0 )
113             {
114                 m_og.drawImage( m_Image1, 0, 0, this );
115                 m_og.drawImage( m_Image2, m_nImageX, 0, this );
116             }
117             // The same thing here, except that Image2
118             // is drawn before Image1.
119             else
120             {
121                 m_og.drawImage( m_Image2, 0, 0, this );
122                 m_og.drawImage( m_Image1, m_nImageX, 0, this );
123             }
124
125             // Now draw the offscreen image to the visible window.
126             g.drawImage( m_OffscreenImage, 0, 0, this );
127
128             // Decrement the x position and check to see
129             // if it went too far to the left (value is negative).
130             m_nImageX -= 10;
131             if( m_nImageX < 0 )
132             {
133                 m_nImageX = this.getSize().width - 10;
134                 m_nWhichImage ^= 1;
135             }
136         }
137
138 }
```

Figure 14.8 shows the ad banner applet in action.

OUTPUT

FIGURE 14.8

This simple ad banner applet will give you a good start on your own version. And if you don't want to make any changes, you can use this one just as it is.

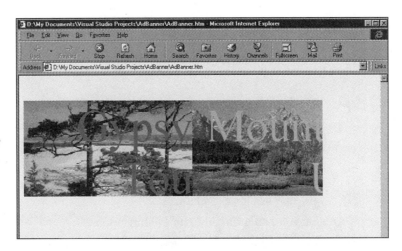

ANALYSIS There are many variables in this applet. But you should notice the `m_OffscreenImage` and `m_og` variables. They're going to allow us to double-buffer the images. Without double buffering, we'd have a lot of screen flicker.

In an applet like this, you must make sure that the images are fully loaded before you get started. Be sure to use a `MediaTracker` class to wait for the images to load.

The `paint()` method is pretty simple. Decide which is stationary, `Image1` or `Image2`. There are two chunks of code—only one of which you'll use. The one that gets executed depends on the value of the `m_nWhichImage` variable.

Caution

If you type this program or get the source code online, be sure to create the images it needs.

Summary

Animation is one of the things that has made Java famous. It's also a lot of fun to program.

Animation is your best bet for activating your page. An active page can be very attractive to users. With several well-planned animations, your Web page will come alive and be very popular.

Animation can also be used to illustrate things such as molecular rotation or airport flight patterns. It's not only attractive, but also very useful.

14

In this chapter, you learned the basics of animation. Two main techniques were used: one technique uses the Java draw API to animate; the other cycles through frames of images to achieve animation.

Q&A

Q Why do you need threads and timers?

A Because animation requires maintenance at regular intervals. For instance, you might have a spinning globe animation and you want it to move from frame to frame every half second. You need some way of calling a method at periodic intervals, such as threads and timers.

Q Can you add a thread to an existing applet?

A Yes, but you need to take several steps. First, you must have your applet class implement the `Runnable` interface. Next, you must declare a `Thread` class. And then you have to add `start()`, `stop()`, and `run()` methods. You can check the early part of this chapter for the contents of generic `start()`, `stop()`, and `run()` methods.

Q What's the difference between a thread and a timer?

A A thread is a separate path of execution, whereas a timer is a Windows message that your application's window gets at regular intervals.

Q Can you animate with the Java draw API?

A Yes, you can get many animation effects by simply using the Java draw API. In this chapter we worked with two programs that used the `drawLine()` method to create animation. Other draw methods can be used just as easily to get animation effects.

Q What is double buffering?

A Double buffering is a method in which an `Image` object is created for the sole purpose of drawing to it. When you draw to an `Image`, users of your programs can't see anything while the drawing is occurring. After all the drawing is finished, the entire `Image` object can be drawn to the visible screen. This reduces screen redraw flicker to almost nothing.

Q How does overriding the `update()` method help reduce screen flicker?

A If you override the `update()` method, you can prevent the Java window from clearing itself in response to a `repaint()` call or a redraw message. When the screen is cleared and then redrawn, there is a very noticeable amount of screen flicker.

Q **How can you use a list of images to create animation?**

A You simply draw one image at a time at a steady speed. As a result, the animation is smooth and continuous.

Q **Why are there timers *and* threads? Isn't one enough?**

A Applets don't have timers and therefore must use threads for animation. Applications have both, but timers are usually easier to add and use.

Q **How much delay time should you use for applications and timers?**

A It depends on how fast your animation should update. On a practical level, your delay shouldn't be less than 50 milliseconds. For most animations, 500 milliseconds is good, giving an update every half second.

Q **What's better, animation with images or animation that's drawn?**

A It depends on what you're doing. Animation that uses the draw commands is better because you don't have to load images. The drawback is that it's not always very realistic and detailed. Animation with images can be far more realistic.

Review Exercises

1. Create an applet and implement a thread. Draw text that goes across the screen as you've seen in banners on Web pages.

2. Create a sequence of eight images. Load them into a Visual J++ application. Add a timer to your application and cycle through the images, displaying one each time the timer is fired.

14

WEEK 3

At a Glance

- Exceptions
- Mouse Input
- Threads
- Strings
- Stream I/O
- ActiveX
- J/Direct

15

16

17

18

19

20

21

DAY 15

Exceptions

Today you'll learn about exceptions. As implied by the name, exceptions are unexpected events that make a program unable to perform its duties in a logical manner. Exception handling empowers you to handle these little surprises rationally.

In this lesson, you will do the following:

- Learn about exceptions
- Understand how Java and J++ support exception handling
- Throw exceptions from your methods
- Define your own exceptions
- Learn the exception classes supported by Java
- Learn the Java keywords needed to handle exceptions
- Handle file I/O exceptions
- Implement user-defined exceptions

What Are Exceptions?

Let's suppose you want to use the DataInputStream class and you try to call its read() method. The DataInputStream.read() method reports an int that has the number of bytes read from the underlying source of data. If an abnormal condition occurs, such as the data being inaccessible due to a hardware failure, this method will throw an exception of the type IOException.

Exception handling should not be used to handle usual or normal errors from which the program can easily recover. In the preceding example, the caller of the DataInputStream.read() method expected to receive the number of bytes read. This number might be less than the number of bytes requested if end-of-file had been reached, but the caller would be expected to handle this condition. However, the caller would not be expected to handle an abnormal condition such as the data source not being present when the read is attempted or some type of hardware failure when an attempt is made to read from the data source.

After a serious error, the calling method would then "catch" an exception of type IOException and could make a decision to "throw" it back to another level (its caller) or handle the exception itself. Later, we will discuss the different ways you can go after you catch an exception.

Returning an error code to the calling method and allowing the caller to figure out a solution based on the returned value has always been the basic approach to handling an error. However, several problems with this approach come to mind:

- There is no guarantee that the caller will check the error code, because the error handling happens outside the scope of the called method.

- The method does not have enough data to handle the error. That is, the error might be out of the realm of the method that receives the error.

- The error-handling code needs to be every place that the method is called, so error handling cannot be localized.

- The error can occur under several layers of the code path. This creates a problem in that you must know which method handles which errors, and how much information each layer of code should have regarding the next layer.

- Without the use of exceptions, error conditions are checked and handled within the logic of the calling code. The capability to read, and subsequently maintain, the code is hampered. The reason it's hampered is because error detection and recovery code is mixed with the logic of the calling code itself.

- Maintenance is virtually impossible. Each time a new error is detected that might occur in the called method, the calling code must be updated to handle this new kind of error.

Because of these problems, the best error-handling subsystem would have to be outside the normal flow of execution—a system that could discover an error and return the program to its last known good state. A good state is an area in the code where you can return and continue working while keeping the integrity of the system after receiving an unexpected error condition. In addition, the error-handling subsystem would allow the programmer to localize the error-handling code so that all errors of the same type could be pinpointed in one place in the system to avoid handling them over and over again. Consequently, the code would be easier to maintain.

NEW TERM In programming, a *good state* is an area in the code where you can return and continue working while keeping the integrity of the system after receiving an unexpected error condition.

Exception handling is built on all the premises listed previously. As the developer, you only must tell the system which kinds of errors you are able to handle in the context of the code you are writing. This code should be bracketed in a `try` statement. For instance, let's say you write a method to create a bitmap image from a disk file. You (the developer of this method) call that method and pass the name of the file used. If that file is corrupted or nonexistent, the method you called might decide that the error is outside the realm of its capability. It would catch the error and throw it back to the calling method. You, the caller, could then choose at that layer what to do with the error. You might choose to throw the exception back up to another layer, or you might decide that you have enough data to suitably process the error. The idea is to have each layer of code continuing to throw the exception back up to yet another layer of code until it's handled properly. In this way, exception handling gives a flexible and productive means of error handing.

Exception Handling the Java Way

Exception handling is not new to Java. It has been around a while in various forms, whether directly supported by the language (such as Borland C++, Microsoft Visual C++, and Borland Delphi) or home-grown by the programmer (for example, with ANSI C). Luckily for us, the designers of Java chose to incorporate a very easy-to-use, flexible, yet powerful implementation of exception handling. If you wanted to program in C, you would call `setjmp()` to bookmark a place in your code and, if needed, call `longjmp()` to return to that place if an unexpected error happened. Then, all local variables previously created on the stack would be automatically cleaned up by the stack pointer simply being moved to the site marked with the `setjmp()` call. That's okay for simple data types, but when you have complex data types like Java objects, cleaning up becomes much more complicated. Java's implementation of exception handling makes the chore of cleaning up and returning the objects created obsolete, because it is automatically handled for you.

15

NEW TERM The `Throwable` class is the superclass of all errors and exceptions in the Java language. Only objects that are instances of this class (or of one of its subclasses) are thrown by the Java Virtual Machine or can be thrown by the Java `throw` statement. Similarly, only this class or one of its subclasses can be the argument type in a `catch` clause.

A `Throwable` class contains a snapshot of the execution stack of its thread at the time it was created. It can also contain a message string that gives more information about the error.

As previously mentioned, Java equips you with a smooth, direct way of dealing with exceptions. Java's `Exception` class extends the `Throwable` class. The system will simply throw only an instance of the `Throwable` class (or one of its subclasses). When you are writing your Java applet, use the keyword `try` to communicate to the system everything you are going to attempt to get done as a group of related methods. That group of methods is labeled the `try` block. You in turn use the keyword `catch` to alert the system as to which kinds of exceptions you are going to handle. That group of methods is labeled the `catch` block. In the `catch` block, you designate the type of exception you are trying to catch and what you want to do if an exception of that type is thrown. You can designate only a class of type `Throwable` (or a subclass of `Throwable`). Of course, situations will arise in which you will want certain code executed regardless of whether an exception was caught. This code is put in a `finally` block. Here's an example of these keywords in action:

```
try
{
    // try some things here
    // try some more things…
}
catch( SomeKindOfExceptionClass exceptionVariable )
{
    // do what you want to do here upon catching the
    // exception
}
finally
{
    // this code will execute whether or not an exception is
    // thrown from the code in the try block
}
```

Java also allows you to easily throw your own exceptions from your own methods. As you define a method, you state that the method can throw a certain class of exception. Here's an example:

```
public void yourMethod( int i ) throws IOException
{
    // your code
}
```

This statement tells the Java compiler that your method can throw an IOException, as well as any of its subclasses. If you try to throw a class that is not a subclass of IOException, you will get an error when you try to compile your applet—a handy thing when you are writing a generic method and meet up with an error that you think the caller will want to handle. You can simply catch the exception and throw it back to the caller. If you desire to throw more than one type of exception, you must separate them with commas:

```
public void yourMethod2( int i )  throws IOException,
     NullPointerException
{
    // your code
}
```

Lastly, the thing I want to touch on here is the ability you have to easily create your own exception classes. You declare the exception class as you would any other class and, as mentioned previously, tell the compiler which methods are allowed to throw these exceptions. One of the greatest things about exception handling in Java is that the compiler forces you to at least catch the exception. For instance, let's say the DataInputStream.readLine() method throws an IOException. So if you try to call this method outside of a try/catch block, you will get an error when you try to compile your program. Java is making you honor the fact that the method might throw an exception. If the process of how to create your own exceptions is still clear as mud, don't worry. We will look at using and defining your own exception classes in the second demo program in this chapter.

Java's Exception Classes

As you will see in the following table, Java uses quite a few exception classes to deal with everything from file exceptions to security exceptions. Table 15.1 lists the exception classes shipped with Microsoft Visual J++. You can see the package name in the left column.

TABLE 15.1   JAVA EXCEPTION CLASSES FOR VISUAL J++

Package	Exception Class
java.awt	AWTException
java.awt	IllegalComponentStateException
java.awt.datatransfer	UnsupportedFlavorException
java.beans	IntrospectionException
java.beans	PropertyVetoException
java.io	CharConversionException

continues

TABLE 15.1 CONTINUED

Package	Exception Class
java.io	EOFException
java.io	FileNotFoundException
java.io	InterruptedIOException
java.io	InvalidClassException
java.io	InvalidObjectException
java.io	NotActiveException
java.io	NotSerializableException
java.io	ObjectStreamException
java.io	OptionalDataException
java.io	StreamCorruptedException
java.io	UTFDataFormatException
java.io	UnsupportedEncodingException
java.lang.reflect	InvocationTargetException
java.net	BindException
java.net	ConnectException
java.net	MalformedURLException
java.net	NoRouteToHostException
java.net	ProtocolException
java.net	SocketException
java.net	UnknownHostException
java.net	UnknownServiceException
java.security	DigestException
java.security	InvalidKeyException
java.security	InvalidParameterException
java.security	KeyException
java.security	KeyManagementException
java.security	NoSuchAlgorithmException
java.security	NoSuchProviderException
java.security	ProviderException
java.security	SignatureException
java.security.acl	AclNotFoundException
java.security.acl	LastOwnerException

Package	Exception Class
java.security.acl	NotOwnerException
java.sql	DataTruncation
java.sql	SQLException
java.sql	SQLWarning
java.text	ParseException
java.util	EmptyStackException
java.util	MissingResourceException
java.util	NoSuchElementException
java.util	TooManyListenersException
java.util.zip	DataFormatException

Demo: An Applet That Handles File I/O Exceptions

Let the fun begin! The demo applet given in Listing 15.2 shows the use of exception handling when file I/O is being performed. After you have typed or read this demo, you will see just how simple it is to take advantage of Java's way of exception handling. This straightforward demo shows you how to utilize the IOException class to catch exceptions while doing file I/O. The demo uses parameters set in the HTML file (see Listing 15.1) to determine the file to be designed and written to and the data to be output to that file.

All you need to do to try this program is change the param outputFileName below to an invalid entry. For instance, change the drive letter to M (if you do not have a drive M on your system). That will make an exception when you try to write to the file. If the filename is valid, a file will be written and you will get a message that appears in the applet window. If the filename is not valid, you will get a message in the status bar saying your applet caught the exception and the file was not successfully written.

INPUT   **LISTING 15.1**   write.html

```
1    <HTML>
2    <HEAD>
3    <META NAME="GENERATOR" Content="Microsoft Visual Studio 98">
4    <META HTTP-EQUIV="Content-Type" content="text/html">
5    <TITLE>Document Title</TITLE>
6    </HEAD>
```

continues

LISTING 15.1   CONTINUED

```
7    <BODY>
8
9
10   <!-- Insert HTML here -->
11       <applet
12           code=Write.class
13           name=Write
14           width=320
15           height=200 >
16           <param name=file value="c:\test.txt">
17           <param name=data value="This is a test">
18           <param name=background value="008080">
19           <param name=foreground value="FFFFFF">
20       </applet>
21
22   </BODY>
23   </HTML>
```

INPUT   **LISTING 15.2**   write.java

```
1    // Write.java
2
3    import java.awt.*;
4    import java.applet.*;
5    import java.io.*;
6
7    /**
8     * This class reads PARAM tags from its HTML host page and sets
9     * the color and label properties of the applet. Program execution
10    * begins with the init() method.
11    */
12   public class Write extends Applet
13   {
14       String m_strFileValue;
15       String m_strDataValue;
16
17       /**
18        * The entry point for the applet.
19        */
20       public void init()
21       {
22           initForm();
23
24           usePageParams();
25
26           doWrite();
27       }
```

```
28
29      private    final String fileParam = "file";
30      private final String dataParam = "data";
31      private    final String backgroundParam = "background";
32      private    final String foregroundParam = "foreground";
33
34      /**
35       * Reads parameters from the applet's HTML host and sets applet
36       * properties.
37       */
38      private void usePageParams()
39      {
40          final String defaultFile = "c:\temp.txt";
41          final String defaultData = "Test";
42          final String defaultBackground = "C0C0C0";
43          final String defaultForeground = "000000";
44          String backgroundValue;
45          String foregroundValue;
46
47          /**
48           * Read the <PARAM NAME="label" VALUE="some string">,
49           * <PARAM NAME="background" VALUE="rrggbb">,
50           * and <PARAM NAME="foreground" VALUE="rrggbb"> tags from
51           * the applet's HTML host.
52           */
53          m_strFileValue = getParameter(fileParam);
54          m_strDataValue = getParameter(dataParam);
55          backgroundValue = getParameter(backgroundParam);
56          foregroundValue = getParameter(foregroundParam);
57
58          if ((m_strDataValue == null) || (m_strFileValue == null) ||
59              (backgroundValue == null) || (foregroundValue == null))
60          {
61              /**
62               * There was something wrong with the HTML host tags.
63               * Generate default values.
64               */
65              m_strFileValue = defaultFile;
66              m_strDataValue = defaultData;
67              backgroundValue = defaultBackground;
68              foregroundValue = defaultForeground;
69          }
70
71          /**
72           * Set the applet's string label, background color, and
73           * foreground colors.
74           */
75          label1.setBackground(stringToColor(backgroundValue));
76          label1.setForeground(stringToColor(foregroundValue));
```

continues

LISTING 15.2 CONTINUED

```
77              this.setBackground(stringToColor(backgroundValue));
78              this.setForeground(stringToColor(foregroundValue));
79          }
80
81          /**
82           * Converts a string formatted as "rrggbb" to an awt.Color object
83           */
84          private Color stringToColor(String paramValue)
85          {
86              int red;
87              int green;
88              int blue;
89
90              red = (Integer.decode("0x" +
                 ➥paramValue.substring(0,2))).intValue();
91              green = (Integer.decode("0x" +
                 ➥paramValue.substring(2,4))).intValue();
92              blue = (Integer.decode("0x" +
                 ➥paramValue.substring(4,6))).intValue();
93
94              return new Color(red,green,blue);
95          }
96
97          /**
98           * External interface used by design tools to show properties
                 ➥of an applet.
99           */
100         public String[][] getParameterInfo()
101         {
102             String[][] info =
103             {
104                 { fileParam, "String", "File to be opened" },
105                 { dataParam, "String", "Data to be written" },
106                 { backgroundParam, "String", "Background color, format
                     ➥\"rrggbb\"" },
107                 { foregroundParam, "String", "Foreground color, format
                     ➥\"rrggbb\"" },
108             };
109             return info;
110         }
111
112     Label label1 = new Label();
113
```

```
114     /**
115      * Initializes values for the applet and its components
116      */
117     void initForm()
118     {
119         this.setBackground(Color.lightGray);
120         this.setForeground(Color.black);
121         this.setLayout(new BorderLayout());
122         this.add("North",label1);
123     }
124
125     public void doWrite()
126     {
127         FileOutputStream outputFile = null;
128         DataOutputStream outputData = null;
129
130         String s = "";
131         try
132         {
133             outputFile = new FileOutputStream( m_strFileValue );
134             outputData = new DataOutputStream( outputFile );
135
136             outputData.writeChars( m_strDataValue );
137
138             outputData.close();
139
140             s = "File written!!!";
141         }
142         catch( IOException e )
143         {
144             s = e.getMessage();
145         }
146         catch( Exception e )
147         {
148             s = e.getMessage();
149         }
150         finally
151         {
152             label1.setText( s );
153         }
154
155     }
156
157}
```

OUTPUT

FIGURE 15.1

In this example, no exception was thrown and the file was successfully written. Observe the message in the applet window reporting success.

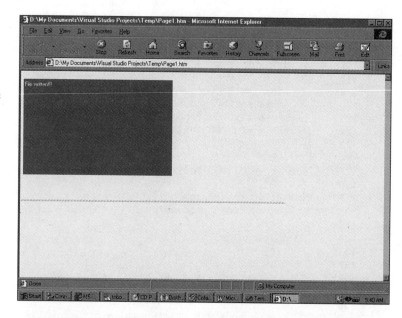

FIGURE 15.2

In this instance, an exception of type IOException was caught and the file was not written successfully. Observe the error message in the applet window.

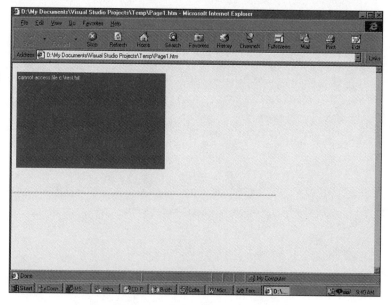

These are the highlights of the demo program. All you do is declare and initialize a `FileOutputStream` object that allows you to write to a disk file. Then, you declare and initialize a `DataOutputStream` object. This allows you to write data out to somewhere (here, in the `FileOutputStream` object). At that point, you have a `try` block. Within that block, tell the system everything you want to attempt as a block of code for which you have exception handling. After you "new" the `DataOutputStream` object and the `FileOutputStream` object, try to write data to the `DataOutputStream` object. The `writeChars()` method can throw an exception of type `IOException`. When you make it this far, call the `DataOutputStream` object's `close()` method and set the status bar string to show your success.

If an exception is thrown while the `try` block executes the methods, call the method `Throwable.toString()`. This action returns a string pinpointing exactly what type of exception was thrown and any other text that might aid you in eradicating the problem. Let me stress the importance of the `finally` keyword. It lets you experience your program's great success (or its untimely demise) by printing a string on the status bar. Figure 15.1 and Figure 15.2 show you the applet in action. Notice that the status bar in Figure 15.1 shows that the program ran correctly, and the status bar in Figure 15.2 shows that an exception was caught and handled.

Demo: Implementing User-Defined Exceptions

In this example, we design an exception class (`ATMRequestException`) that is a subclass of the `Exception` class. A method is set (`ATMRequest()`) that throws an exception of this type. Another method is also written that will call the `ATMRequest()` method and catch an exception if it is thrown. One large difference between this demo and the preceding one is that data will come in via a `TextField` (explained later) versus coming from the HTML parameters. This allows the applet to be tested in a more dynamic manner. Listing 15.3 shows the HTML; Listing 15.4 shows the source.

INPUT **LISTING 15.3** NewExceptionApplet.html

```
1    <html>
2    <head>
3    <title>NewExceptionApplet</title>
4    </head>
5    <body>
6    <hr>
7    <applet
8      code=NewExceptionApplet.class
```

continues

LISTING 15.3   CONTINUED

```
9         id=NewExceptionApplet
10        width=150
11        height=240
12        align=LEFT>
13       </applet>
14       This is an example of how to create your own Exception
15            subclass. If you
16       enter an amount of less than $10 or more than $500, the method
17         that processes
18       the request will throw an ATMRequestException. The caller
19            should catch
20       this exception and print a message in the status bar of the
21            browser.
22       <BR CLEAR=ALL>
23       <hr>
24       <a href="NewExceptioinApplet.java">The source.</a>
25       </body>
26       </html>
```

INPUT   **LISTING 15.4** NewExceptionApplet.java

```java
1   // NewExceptionApplet.java
2
3   import java.awt.*;
4   import java.applet.*;
5   import java.awt.event.*;
6
7   /**
8    * This class reads PARAM tags from its HTML host page and sets
9    * the color and label properties of the applet. Program execution
10   * begins with the init() method.
11   */
12  public class NewExceptionApplet extends Applet
13  {
14      protected Label m_lblPin = new Label( "Enter your PIN:" );
15      protected TextField m_txtPin = new TextField(10);
16
17      protected Label m_lblAmount = new Label( "Withdrawal amount:" );
18      protected TextField m_txtAmount = new TextField(10);
19
20      protected Button m_btnWithdraw = new Button( "Withdraw money" );
21
22      protected long m_lCurrentAmount;
23
24      Thread    m_thread = null;
25
26      MyListener Listener = new MyListener();
27
```

```
28      /**
29       * The entry point for the applet.
30       */
31      public void init()
32      {
33          add( m_lblPin );
34          add( m_txtPin );
35          add( m_lblAmount );
36          add( m_txtAmount );
37          add( m_btnWithdraw );
38
39          m_lCurrentAmount = 0;
40          m_btnWithdraw.addActionListener( Listener );
41      }
42      void makeWithdrawal()
43      {
44          try
45          {
46              ATMRequest atmRequest = new ATMRequest( m_lCurrentAmount
                ➥);
47              showStatus( "Withdraw completed." );
48          }
49          catch( ATMRequestException e )
50          {
51              showStatus( e.getMessage() );
52          }
53      }
54
55      public class MyListener implements ActionListener
56      {
57
58          public void actionPerformed( ActionEvent ae )
59          {
60              String strPIN = m_txtPin.getText();
61              if( strPIN.length() == 0 )
62              {
63                  showStatus( "You must enter a PIN number." );
64                  return;
65              }
66              String strAmount = m_txtAmount.getText();
67              if( strAmount.length() == 0 )
68              {
69                  showStatus( "You must enter an amount." );
70                  return;
71              }
72              try
73              {
74                  m_lCurrentAmount = Long.parseLong( strAmount );
75                  makeWithdrawal();
76              }
```

continues

LISTING **15.4**   CONTINUED

```
77                   catch( NumberFormatException nfe )
78                   {
79                       showStatus( "There was an error parsing your
                         ➥withdrawal." );
80                   }
81
82               }
83
84           }
85       class ATMRequest extends Object
86       {
87           long m_lAmount;
88
89           ATMRequest( long lAmount ) throws ATMRequestException
90           {
91               if( lAmount < 10 ¦¦ lAmount > 500 )
92               {
93                   throw new ATMRequestException( "Amount is out of the
                     ➥value range of 10-500" );
94               }
95           }
96       }
97       class ATMRequestException extends Exception
98       {
99
100          ATMRequestException()
101          {
102              super();
103          }
104
105          ATMRequestException( String str )
106          {
107              super( str );
108          }
109
110      }
111
112 }
```

Lines 14–20 declare the user interface controls.

Lines 33–37 add the components to the container via the Container.add() method and initialize the amount variable.

Line 40 adds an ActionListener so that we'll get notification when the user presses the Withdraw button.

OUTPUT

FIGURE 15.3

Defining and implementing an exception class of your own.

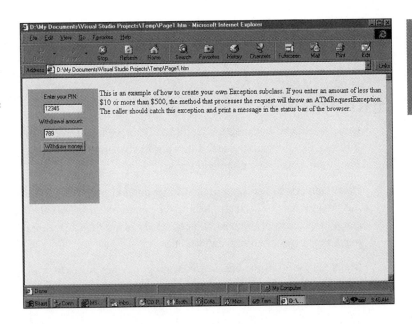

The makeWithdrawal() (lines 42–53) method gets called when the user clicks the Withdraw button, as long as there's some text in the PIN and Amount fields. It simply creates an ATMRequest object and catches an exception if one is thrown.

Lines 60–65 get the text that's in the PIN field. If there's no text there, put a warning text in the status bar and return.

Lines 66–71 get the text in the Amount field. If there's no text there, put a warning in the status bar and return.

Lines 72–80 parse the Amount field into a long. You must make sure that the NumberFormatException will be caught if it's thrown.

In lines 85–96 is the ATMRequest class. The constructor will check the amount passed to it versus the valid range of 10 to 500 and throw an ATMRequestException if the amount is not within that range. Note how you construct an exception by passing it a string value. This string value is what is returned when the caller who catches the exception calls the toString() or getMessage() methods. It is this string value that the makeWithdrawal() method uses when it is printing the error message on the status bar.

Lines 97–110 is the definition for the ATMRequestException class. All you really need to do is implement the two constructors that are necessary anytime you subclass the Exception class. You don't need to do anything within the Exception class itself. The two constructors call the superclass's implementation.

An `ATMRequestException` will be thrown and caught when you run the applet and enter a number that is either less than 10 or greater than 500. On the status bar, you will see an error message printed, as shown in Figure 15.3.

Summary

Benefits abound in exception handling. Because Java forces you to write `try/catch` blocks when you call a method that has the capability to throw an exception, your programs are considered more bulletproof.

Error handling is executed in the proper context because it is done only by a method that has enough data to correctly handle the error condition. All alternative methods that catch the exception in question keep on throwing the exception until the method that can handle the error condition catches it.

Maintenance is simple because your programs are easier to read, due to the fact that error-handling code for each particular type of exception can be pinpointed to one area of the system.

Checking for errors and recovery from errors is more extensive than maintenance because it handles not only expected error conditions, but the occasional abnormal conditions as well.

Q&A

Q Should I always use exceptions to handle errors?

A Not necessarily. Normal errors that are easy to handle by checking return values probably don't need exceptions. Difficult errors, especially those that are many layers deep, should use exceptions.

Q What are some limitations when you're not using exceptions?

A Callers might not check return codes and therefore not handle the error. Exceptions enforce error handling. Methods might not have enough information to handle errors. The error-handling code will be in many different places.

Q What is a good state?

A A good state is an area in the code where you can return and continue working while keeping the integrity of the system after receiving an unexpected error condition.

Q **What is a try block?**

A When you are writing your Java program, a `try` block contains everything you are going to attempt to get done as a group of related methods.

Q **When does a catch block become active?**

A If your program is in a `try` block and a method that has been called throws an exception, program execution will immediately proceed to the `catch` block that catches the exception type that was thrown.

Q **What about classes that you write for distribution? How will programmers know about the exceptions that your classes throw?**

A You need to document them thoroughly. Give enough details about the exceptions and the conditions in which they're thrown that developers can intelligently use your classes.

Q **Does the compiler always force you to catch exceptions that are thrown?**

A I used to think I was safe if the compiler didn't complain. I thought that if the code compiled, I'd caught every exception that would be thrown. This, painfully, isn't so. A good example is the `Integer` class. The `Integer.parseInt()` method throws a `NumberFormatException`, but your code will compile, even if you don't catch it. This creates havoc with applets because your applet will probably hang up when this exception is thrown and you don't catch it. Always check the online help for every method you use if you're not sure about the exceptions it throws.

Review Exercises

1. Create an applet. Declare a string and assign the text "This is a test" to it. In the `init()` method, use the `Integer.parseInt()` method to get an integer evaluation of the string. When you run the applet, it'll hang up because `Integer.parseInt()` will throw a `NumberFormatException` exception. Then catch the `NumberFormatException` exception and your applet should not hang up.

2. Create a program and add your own class. Then create a class that extends the `Exception` class. From your new class, create two methods. Have these methods take integer arguments. Then throw your newly created exception if certain integers are given to your class methods.

DAY 16

Mouse Input

In today's lesson, you'll learn how to receive mouse input from users. Mouse input includes when users click the mouse buttons, when they move the mouse, when they enter your window with a mouse, and when they leave your window with a mouse.

Handling these events, though, is different in applets and applications. First, we'll cover how you handle mouse events in applets; then we'll tackle handling mouse events in applications.

Today, you'll

- Learn about the `MouseListener` interface.
- Learn about the `MouseMotionListener` interface.
- Understand a demo applet that handles mouse button, enter, and leave events.
- Understand a demo applet that handles mouse motion events.
- See and understand a demo applet that handles mouse events and displays the results graphically in the window.
- Learn how to add mouse event handlers in applications.
- Learn how to create an application that uses mouse events.

All of these topics together will give you a solid foundation for using mouse events in your programs. This all-important user input device will probably be used in most of your programs.

Using the `MouseListener` Interface

For any applet component that needs to receive mouse button, enter, and leave events, you need to create a class that implements the `MouseListener` interface. Then you need to instantiate your newly declared class and use the component's `addMouseListener()` method so that the component knows where to send `MouseListener` event notifications.

The `MouseListener` interface handles almost every mouse event that you'll want to know about in an applet except for mouse movement, which is discussed later when we talk about the `MouseMotionListener` interface. For now, we'll be handling all mouse events except for mouse movements.

In your applet, you have to create a new class that implements the `MouseListener` interface. In my applets, I create a class called `MyMouseListener`. Here's how to start the framework for the class.

```
public class MyMouseListener implements MouseListener
{
}
```

The problem with this is that if you compile, you get five errors. The compiler expects you to also add the following methods: `mousePressed()`, `mouseReleased()`, `mouseEntered()`, `mouseExited()`, and `mouseClicked()`. These methods handle the specific events that you'll be handling.

The bare-bones class that you'll need to declare will have the five methods included. The following example shows how to create a minimal class that implements the `MouseListener` interface. It has the five methods it needs and will compile.

```
public class MyMouseListener implements MouseListener
{

    public void mousePressed( MouseEvent me )
    {
    }

    public void mouseReleased( MouseEvent me )
    {
    }
```

```
        public void mouseEntered( MouseEvent me )
        {
        }

        public void mouseExited( MouseEvent me )
        {
        }

        public void mouseClicked( MouseEvent me )
        {
        }

    }
```

Notice that each of the methods in our class gets a mouse event class as a parameter. The two methods you'll use most often are the getX() method and the getY() method. The getX() method returns the x position for the mouse when the event was triggered. The getY() method returns the y position to the mouse when the event was triggered. Note that these x and y coordinates are not the x and y coordinates of the entire screen, but they are the x and y coordinates relative to the component. The following example shows you how to retrieve the x and y coordinates of the mouse when the mouse has been pressed.

```
    public void mousePressed( MouseEvent me )
    {
        int nX = me.getX();
        int nY = me.getY();
    }
```

The MouseListener actually has two somewhat redundant methods. The mousePressed() method is triggered when a mouse button has been pressed on a control. The mouseClicked() method is triggered when you click on a control and then release the mouse. So, in a sense they both serve the same purpose: they can notify you when a control has been clicked. I almost always use the mousePressed() method and rarely use the mouseClicked() method.

INPUT   The program in Listing 16.1 declares a class that implements the MouseListener interface. It displays the events that the MouseListener interface handles in the window.

LISTING 16.1   THIS PROGRAM SHOWS A SIMPLE APPLET THAT DECLARES A CLASS THAT
IMPLEMENTS THE MouseListener INTERFACE

```
1    import java.awt.*;
2    import java.applet.*;
3    import java.awt.event.*;
4
5    public class Applet1 extends Applet
6    {
7
8        boolean m_bButtonPressed = false;
9        boolean m_bEntered = false;
10       int m_nMouseX = 0, m_nMouseY = 0;
11
12       public void init()
13       {
14           addMouseListener( new MyMouseListener() );
15       }
16
17       public void paint( Graphics g )
18       {
19           String strMouseState = "Mouse button not pressed.";
20           if( m_bButtonPressed )
21           strMouseState = "Mouse button pressed.";
22
23           strMouseState += " Mouse X:" + m_nMouseX;
24           strMouseState += ", Mouse Y:" + m_nMouseY + ".";
25
26           if( m_bEntered )
27               strMouseState += " Mouse is entered.";
28           else
29               strMouseState += " Mouse is not entered.";
30
31           g.setFont( new Font( "TimesRoman", Font.PLAIN, 20 ) );
32           g.drawString( strMouseState, 30, 30 );
33
34       }
35
36       public class MyMouseListener implements MouseListener
37       {
38
39           public void mousePressed( MouseEvent me )
40           {
41               m_bButtonPressed = true;
42               m_nMouseX = me.getX();
43               m_nMouseY = me.getY();
44               repaint();
```

```
45              }
46
47              public void mouseReleased( MouseEvent me )
48              {
49                  m_bButtonPressed = false;
50                  m_nMouseX = me.getX();
51                  m_nMouseY = me.getY();
52                  repaint();
53              }
54
55              public void mouseEntered( MouseEvent me )
56              {
57                  m_bEntered = true;
58                  m_nMouseX = me.getX();
59                  m_nMouseY = me.getY();
60                  repaint();
61              }
62
63              public void mouseExited( MouseEvent me )
64              {
65                  m_bEntered = false;
66                  m_nMouseX = me.getX();
67                  m_nMouseY = me.getY();
68                  repaint();
69              }
70
71              public void mouseClicked( MouseEvent me )
72              {
73                  m_nMouseX = me.getX();
74                  m_nMouseY = me.getY();
75                  repaint();
76              }
77
78          }
79
80  }
```

OUTPUT   When the program runs, you'll see a text string drawn in the applet window that shows you the state of the mouse. When the button is clicked, you see that. When the mouse enters the window you see that, also. The mouse coordinates for each event are shown. You can see the program running in Internet Explorer in Figure 16.1.

16

FIGURE 16.1

This simple program shows you the results of mouse events that are handled by a class that implements the MouseListener *interface.*

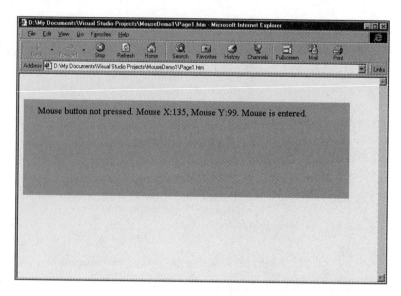

ANALYSIS Lines 8, 9, and 10 declare some global variables that keep track of the mouse state. Line 14 adds the class that implements MouseListener to the applet component. Line 17 is where the paint() method starts. At lines 19, 20, and 21 contain the information in the string about whether the mouse button is currently being pressed. In lines 23 and 24 the mouse x and y position to the information display string is added. Lines 26 through 29 show whether the applet window has been entered by the mouse. At line 31, the font is set larger than the default font so the information string is easier to read. Line 32 displays the string. Line 36 is where the class that implements the MouseListener interface begins. The class is called MyMouseListener. Line 39 is the mousePressed() method. In that method, the button flag is set to true to indicate that the button has been pressed. We also store the mouse x and y coordinates and repaint the applet window so the new information is reflected. The mouseReleased() method does virtually the same thing, except that instead of the button flag being set to true, it is set to false. Line 55 is where the mouseEntered() method begins. In this method, we set our enter flag to true, record the x and y coordinates of the mouse position, and repaint the applet. Line 63 is where the mouseExited() method begins. It does virtually the same thing as the mouseEntered() method, except it sets the entered flag to false. The last method is the mouseClicked() method, which starts at line 71 and simply stores the x and y coordinates and then repaints the applet window.

Using the `MouseMotionListener` Interface

The `MouseMotionListener` interface is the complement of a `MouseListener` interface. It adds that one extra mouse event that you'll probably need to handle the mouse motion event. Anytime the mouse is moved within your window, you'll receive notification that this event has happened. This is true whether users are dragging, by holding a button down, or by moving the mouse without a button pressed. When you declare a class that implements the `MouseMotionListener` interface, only two methods must be included. The first method is the `mouseMoved()` method; the second is the `mouseDragged()` method. The `mouseMoved()` method handles the event where the mouse is moved and the user is not holding a button down. The `mouseDragged()` method handles the cases where the user is moving the mouse while holding a button down. The following example shows you a basic class called the `MyMouseMotionListener` class that implements the `MouseMotionListener` interface.

```
public class MyMouseMotionListener implements MouseMotionListener
{

    public void mouseMoved( MouseEvent me )
    {
    }

    public void mouseDragged( MouseEvent me )
    {
    }

}
```

Notice that both the methods in the newly declared class take `MouseEvent` objects as parameters. These objects are the same as the ones discussed for the `MouseListener` methods.

INPUT Here is another simple program that shows you how to use a class that implements the `MouseMotionListener` class. It displays the mouse coordinates in the applet window. The source code for this applet can be seen in Listing 16.2.

LISTING 16.2 THIS SIMPLE DEMONSTRATION APPLET SHOWS HOW TO USE A CLASS THAT IMPLEMENTS THE `MouseMotionListener` INTERFACE

```
1    import java.awt.*;
2    import java.applet.*;
3    import java.awt.event.*;
```

continues

LISTING 16.2   CONTINUED

```
4
5    public class Applet1 extends Applet
6    {
7
8        int m_nMouseX = 0, m_nMouseY = 0;
9
10       public void init()
11       {
12           addMouseMotionListener( new MyMouseMotionListener() );
13       }
14
15       public void paint( Graphics g )
16       {
17           String strMouseState = ""Mouse X:" + m_nMouseX +
             ➥", Mouse Y:" + m_nMouseY + ì.î;
18
19           g.setFont( new Font( "TimesRoman", Font.PLAIN, 20 ) );
20           g.drawString( strMouseState, 30, 30 );
21
22       }
23
24       public class MyMouseMotionListener implements
          ➥MouseMotionListener
25       {
26
27           public void mouseMoved( MouseEvent me )
28           {
29               m_nMouseX = me.getX();
30               m_nMouseY = me.getY();
31               repaint();
32           }
33
34           public void mouseDragged( MouseEvent me )
35           {
36               m_nMouseX = me.getX();
37               m_nMouseY = me.getY();
38               repaint();
39           }
40
41       }
42
43   }
```

OUTPUT   When the program first runs, you'll see a small window inside of Internet Explorer that displays two pieces of information: the mouse x coordinate, and the mouse y coordinate. As you move the mouse around inside of the applet window, these values will change. The program can be seen running within Internet Explorer in Figure 16.2.

FIGURE 16.2

This program displays the mouse's x coordinate and the mouse's y coordinate.

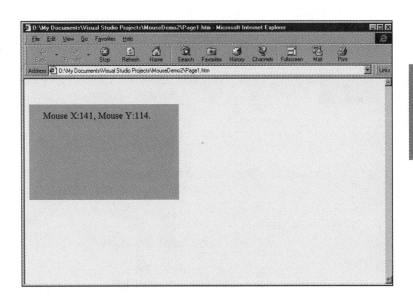

FIGURE 16.2

This program displays the mouse's x coordinate and the mouse's y coordinate.

16

ANALYSIS This simple program is only 43 lines long. There isn't much to it, so it will be easy to understand. At line 8, the mouse x and y coordinate variables are declared. These variables will contain the mouse x and y position. At line 12, MouseMotionListener is added to the applet component. Without doing this, the class which we declare that implements the MouseMotionListener class will never catch any events. At line 15, the paint() method begins. In the paint() method, a string that shows the mouse x and y values is created. The font is set to something slightly bigger than the default font, and the information string in the applet window is drawn. Line 24 is where our class, MyMouseMotionListener, is declared. This class implements the MouseMotionListener interface. Line 27 holds mouseMoved() method, which stores the x and y coordinates for the mouse, and then calls repaint(). At line 34, the mouseDragged() method begins, simply stores the mouse x and y coordinates, and calls repaint().

Handling Mouse Events

Almost every program that you write will require mouse events. For this reason, your programs need a MouseListener and a MouseMotionListener. Listing 16.3 shows the source code for a program that handles both events as users move the mouse around in the applet window and click in the applet window. As users move around in the applet window, a rectangular region underneath the mouse turns black. If users click, the rectangular region turns red. This is more like the kind of application you'll be writing than the two demo applets shown previously in this chapter, which simply displayed the mouse coordinates.

INPUT

LISTING 16.3 THIS PROGRAM SHOWS AN APPLET THAT HANDLES ALL MOUSE EVENTS AND DISPLAYS THE RESULTS GRAPHICALLY

```
1    import java.awt.*;
2    import java.applet.*;
3    import java.awt.event.*;
4
5    public class Applet1 extends Applet
6    {
7
8        boolean m_bButtonPressed = false;
9        boolean m_bEntered = false;
10       int m_nMouseX = 0, m_nMouseY = 0;
11       int m_nRow = -1, m_nCol = -1;
12       Color m_Color = Color.black;
13
14       public void init()
15       {
16           addMouseListener( new MyMouseListener() );
17           addMouseMotionListener( new MyMouseMotionListener() );
18       }
19
20       public void handleMouseEvents()
21       {
22           int nCol = m_nMouseX / 40;
23           int nRow = m_nMouseY / 40;
24
25           if( !m_bEntered )
26               nCol = nRow = -1;
27
28           Color color = Color.black;
29           if( m_bButtonPressed )
30               color = Color.red;
31
32           if( nCol != m_nCol ||
33               nRow != m_nRow ||
34               color != m_Color )
35           {
36               m_Color = color;
37               m_nRow = nRow;
38               m_nCol = nCol;
39               repaint();
```

```
40              }
41
42      }
43
44      public void paint( Graphics g )
45      {
46          if( m_nRow != -1 && m_nCol != -1 )
47          {
48              g.setColor( m_Color );
49              g.fillRect( m_nCol * 40, m_nRow * 40, 40, 40 );
50          }
51      }
52
53      public class MyMouseListener implements MouseListener
54      {
55
56          public void mousePressed( MouseEvent me )
57          {
58              m_bButtonPressed = true;
59              m_nMouseX = me.getX();
60              m_nMouseY = me.getY();
61              handleMouseEvents();
62          }
63
64          public void mouseReleased( MouseEvent me )
65          {
66              m_bButtonPressed = false;
67              m_nMouseX = me.getX();
68              m_nMouseY = me.getY();
69              handleMouseEvents();
70          }
71
72          public void mouseEntered( MouseEvent me )
73          {
74              m_bEntered = true;
75              m_nMouseX = me.getX();
76              m_nMouseY = me.getY();
77              handleMouseEvents();
78          }
79
80          public void mouseExited( MouseEvent me )
81          {
82              m_bEntered = false;
83              m_nMouseX = me.getX();
84              m_nMouseY = me.getY();
85              handleMouseEvents();
86          }
87
88          public void mouseClicked( MouseEvent me )
```

16

continues

LISTING 16.3 CONTINUED

```
89              {
90              }
91
92      }
93
94      public class MyMouseMotionListener implements MouseMotionListener
95      {
96
97          public void mouseMoved( MouseEvent me )
98          {
99              m_nMouseX = me.getX();
100             m_nMouseY = me.getY();
101             handleMouseEvents();
102         }
103
104         public void mouseDragged( MouseEvent me )
105         {
106             m_nMouseX = me.getX();
107             m_nMouseY = me.getY();
108             handleMouseEvents();
109         }
110
111     }
112
113 }
```

OUTPUT You won't see anything when the program runs if the mouse is not in the applet window. However, as you move the mouse around inside the applet window, a black rectangular region will follow your mouse around. If you click the mouse button, the region will turn red as shown in Figure 16.3.

ANALYSIS In lines 8 through 12, the global variables are declared. These variables keep track of the current mouse state, including whether the mouse button is pressed, whether the mouse is entered into the applet window, and the location of the mouse x and y coordinates. At line 16 the MouseListener class is added, and at line 17 the MouseMotionListener class is added. Both classes in order to handle both mouse events. At line 20, handleMouseEvents() method begins. This method is called after every single mouse event that is triggered. What this method does is first calculate the row and column at which the mouse is pointing. There are eight columns across and four rows down. You can change the number of rows and columns by changing their size or by changing the size of the applet window. If no button is pressed, the color drawn with is black. Otherwise, the button is red. Set a Color class to the corresponding color. If the row and column or the color have changes, store global variables with new values; then call repaint(). Don't call repaint() every single time because you don't want to cause the entire applet window to have to be redrawn. This would cause a lot of unnecessary screen flicker. Line 44 contains the paint() method. The paint() method is simple; it sets the color, and then it draws the filled rectangle. Line 53 holds the class that implements the MouseListener interface. In it, the mousePressed(), mouseReleased(), mouseEntered(), and mouseExited() methods are used to set the button and entered flags, and record the mouse x and y position. Notice that at line 88, the mouseClicked() method is ignored. At line 94 the declared class that implements the MouseMotionListener interface begins. The two methods in this class are the mouseMoved() and the mouseDragged() methods, which set the mouse x and y coordinates.

FIGURE 16.3

This applet graphically shows you the results of mouse events.

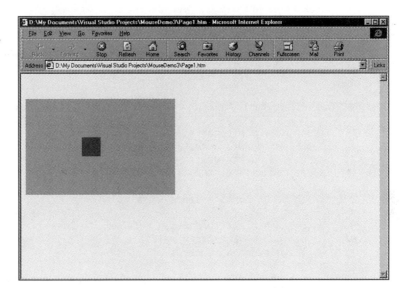

Adding Mouse Events in Visual J++ Applications

It's a snap to add mouse event handlers to Visual J++ Applications. All you have to do is make sure that your form is listed in the Properties window and that the events button is clicked. Notice in the Properties window, with the events button selected, that there are many interesting events. The mouseDown event, the mouseEnter event, the mouseLeave event, the mouseMove event, and mouseUp event are all events that you'll use. To add the event handlers to your form, double-click the event that you want to add. When you do this, the event will be added and you will be taken in the editor to the method that was added. The mouseEnter and mouseLeave handlers will not give you MouseEvent objects as parameters; they will give you Event objects. Therefore, these event handlers are used as a reminder of whether the mouse has entered or left your form's window. The mouseDown, mouseMove, and mouseUp event handlers, however, give you a MouseEvent object as a parameter. This makes it very convenient to give the coordinates of the mouse when these events are triggered.

The MouseEvent class is different for Visual J++ applications than for Visual J++ applets. The two fields that you'll be most interested in are the x and y fields. The x field specifies the x coordinate of the mouse, and the y field specifies the y coordinate of the mouse. In applications, the MouseEvent class does not have a getX() and a getY() method as it does in an applet's MouseEvent class.

INPUT   Listing 16.4 contains the source code for a simple application that displays information about mouse events. The mouse event handlers are mouseDown, mouseEnter, mouseLeave, mouseMove, and mouseUp.

LISTING 16.4 THIS SIMPLE VISUAL J++ APPLICATION SHOWS INFORMATION ABOUT THE MOUSE

```
1    import com.ms.wfc.app.*;
2    import com.ms.wfc.core.*;
3    import com.ms.wfc.ui.*;
4    import com.ms.wfc.html.*;
5
6    public class Form1 extends Form
7    {
8        boolean m_bButtonPressed = false;
9        boolean m_bEntered = false;
10       int m_nMouseX, m_nMouseY;
11
12       public Form1()
13       {
14           initForm();
15       }
16
17       public void dispose()
18       {
19           super.dispose();
20           components.dispose();
21       }
22
23       private void Form1_click(Object source, Event e)
24       {
25       }
```

```
26
27      private void Form1_doubleClick(Object source, Event e)
28      {
29      }
30
31      public void showMouseInfo()
32      {
33          String strMouseState = "Mouse button not pressed.";
34          if( m_bButtonPressed )
35              strMouseState = "Mouse button pressed.";
36
37          strMouseState += " Mouse X:" + m_nMouseX;
38          strMouseState += ", Mouse Y:" + m_nMouseY + ".";
39
40          if( m_bEntered )
41              strMouseState += " Mouse is entered.";
42          else
43              strMouseState += " Mouse is not entered.";
44
45          label1.setText( strMouseState );
46      }
47
48      private void Form1_mouseDown(Object source, MouseEvent e)
49      {
50          m_bButtonPressed = true;
51          m_nMouseX = e.x;
52          m_nMouseY = e.y;
53          showMouseInfo();
54      }
55
56      private void Form1_mouseEnter(Object source, Event e)
57      {
58          m_bEntered = true;
59          showMouseInfo();
60      }
61
62      private void Form1_mouseLeave(Object source, Event e)
63      {
64          m_bEntered = false;
65          showMouseInfo();
66      }
67
68      private void Form1_mouseMove(Object source, MouseEvent e)
69      {
70          m_nMouseX = e.x;
71          m_nMouseY = e.y;
72          showMouseInfo();
73      }
74
```

16

continues

LISTING **16.4** CONTINUED

```
75      private void Form1_mouseUp(Object source, MouseEvent e)
76      {
77          m_bButtonPressed = false;
78          m_nMouseX = e.x;
79          m_nMouseY = e.y;
80          showMouseInfo();
81      }
82
83      Container components = new Container();
84      Label label1 = new Label();
85
86      private void initForm()
87      {
88          this.setText("Form1");
89          this.setAutoScaleBaseSize(13);
90          this.setClientSize(new Point(292, 273));
91          this.addOnClick(new EventHandler(this.Form1_click));
92          this.addOnDoubleClick(new EventHandler
            ➥(this.Form1_doubleClick));
93          this.addOnMouseDown(new MouseEventHandler
            ➥(this.Form1_mouseDown));
94          this.addOnMouseEnter(new EventHandler
            ➥(this.Form1_mouseEnter));
95          this.addOnMouseLeave(new EventHandler
            ➥(this.Form1_mouseLeave));
96          this.addOnMouseMove(new MouseEventHandler
            ➥(this.Form1_mouseMove));
97          this.addOnMouseUp(new MouseEventHandler
            ➥(this.Form1_mouseUp));
98
99          label1.setFont(new Font("MS Sans Serif", 10.0f));
100         label1.setLocation(new Point(8, 8));
101         label1.setSize(new Point(272, 32));
102         label1.setTabIndex(0);
103         label1.setTabStop(false);
104         label1.setText("Mouse Info");
105         label1.setTextAlign(HorizontalAlignment.CENTER);
106
107         this.setNewControls(new Control[] {
108                             label1});
109     }
110
111     public static void main(String args[])
112     {
113         Application.run(new Form1());
114     }
115 }
```

OUTPUT When the program runs, you'll see a label that shows information about the mouse at the top of the window. You can see this in Figure 16.4.

FIGURE 16.4

This simple application shows you information about the mouse in a label.

ANALYSIS At lines 8, 9, and 10, global variables that contain information about the mouse are declared. The showMouseInfo() method is at line 31. In this method, a string is created that tells whether the mouse button was pressed, the position of the mouse, and whether the mouse has entered the window. At line 45 the label text is set so the users will see the state of the mouse. Line 48 is the mouseDown event handler, which sets the button flag to true, records the mouse position, and calls the showMouseInfo() method. The mouseEnter() method is at line 56. This method records that form window was entered and then calls the showMouseInfo() method. Line 62 is where the mouseLeave() method begins, which is almost identical to the mouseEnter() method except that mouseLeave() sets the entered flag to false. At line 68, the mouseMove() method begins. It records the mouse x and y positions and calls the showMouseInfo() method. The last method for handling mouse events begins at line 75. This is the mouseUp() method, which does the same thing as the mouseDown() method except it sets the button flag to false instead of true.

Using Mouse Events in an Application

The following demonstration program was previously used to show you how to handle all mouse events. Here it has been translated to a Visual J++ application. This demonstration applet drew a rectangular region underneath the mouse as the user moved it around in the applet window(refer to Figure 16.3).

INPUT The source code is similar to the source code in the applet demo; that is, the part that calculates the row, the column, and performs the drawing. It can be seen in its entirety in Listing 16.5.

Listing 16.5 This Program Handles Mouse Events in a Visual J++ Application and Graphically Shows You the Results

```
1    import com.ms.wfc.app.*;
2    import com.ms.wfc.core.*;
3    import com.ms.wfc.ui.*;
4    import com.ms.wfc.html.*;
5
6    public class Form1 extends Form
7    {
8        boolean m_bButtonPressed = false;
9        boolean m_bEntered = false;
10       int m_nMouseX = 0, m_nMouseY = 0;
11       int m_nRow = -1, m_nCol = -1;
12       Color m_Color = Color.BLACK;
13
14       public Form1()
15       {
16           initForm();
17       }
18
19       public void dispose()
20       {
21           super.dispose();
22           components.dispose();
23       }
24
25       public void handleMouseEvent()
26       {
27           Rectangle rect = getDisplayRect();
28           int nColWidth = rect.getRight() / 8;
29           int nRowHeight = rect.getBottom() / 8;
30
31           int nCol = m_nMouseX / nColWidth;
32           int nRow = m_nMouseY / nRowHeight;
33
34           if( !m_bEntered )
35               nCol = nRow = -1;
36
37           Color color = Color.BLACK;
38           if( m_bButtonPressed )
39               color = Color.RED;
40
41           if( nCol != m_nCol ||
42               nRow != m_nRow ||
43               color != m_Color )
44           {
45               m_Color = color;
46               m_nRow = nRow;
47               m_nCol = nCol;
```

```
48                      invalidate();
49                      update();
50              }
51
52      }
53
54      private void Form1_mouseDown(Object source, MouseEvent e)
55      {
56              m_bButtonPressed = true;
57              m_nMouseX = e.x;
58              m_nMouseY = e.y;
59              handleMouseEvent();
60      }
61
62      private void Form1_mouseEnter(Object source, Event e)
63      {
64              m_bEntered = true;
65              handleMouseEvent();
66      }
67
68      private void Form1_mouseLeave(Object source, Event e)
69      {
70              m_bEntered = false;
71              handleMouseEvent();
72      }
73
74      private void Form1_mouseMove(Object source, MouseEvent e)
75      {
76              m_nMouseX = e.x;
77              m_nMouseY = e.y;
78              handleMouseEvent();
79      }
80
81      private void Form1_mouseUp(Object source, MouseEvent e)
82      {
83              m_bButtonPressed = false;
84              m_nMouseX = e.x;
85              m_nMouseY = e.y;
86              handleMouseEvent();
87      }
88
89      private void Form1_paint(Object source, PaintEvent e)
90      {
91              if( m_nRow != -1 && m_nCol != -1 )
92              {
93                      Rectangle rect = getDisplayRect();
94                      int nColWidth = rect.getRight() / 8;
95                      int nRowHeight = rect.getBottom() / 8;
```

16

continues

LISTING 16.5   CONTINUED

```
96
97                        e.graphics.fill( m_nCol * nColWidth, m_nRow
                        ➥* nRowHeight, nColWidth,
98                          nRowHeight, new Brush( m_Color, BrushStyle.SOLID ) ) );
99            }
100      }
101
102      private void Form1_click(Object source, Event e)
103      {
104
105      }
106
107      Container components = new Container();
108
109      private void initForm()
110      {
111          this.setText(ìForm1î);
112          this.setAutoScaleBaseSize(13);
113          this.setClientSize(new Point(365, 273));
114          this.addOnMouseDown(new MouseEventHandler
                ➥(this.Form1_mouseDown));
115          this.addOnMouseEnter(new EventHandler
                ➥(this.Form1_mouseEnter));
116          this.addOnMouseLeave(new EventHandler
                ➥(this.Form1_mouseLeave));
117          this.addOnMouseMove(new MouseEventHandler
                ➥(this.Form1_mouseMove));
118          this.addOnMouseUp(new MouseEventHandler
                ➥(this.Form1_mouseUp));
119          this.addOnPaint(new PaintEventHandler(this.Form1_paint));
120      }
121
122      public static void main(String args[])
123      {
124          Application.run(new Form1());
125      }
126 }
```

OUTPUT   When the program runs, if the mouse isn't in the form window, you won't see
anything. However, as you drag the mouse around inside the form window, a
black rectangle will follow the mouse. If you hold the mouse down, the rectangle is red
instead of black (see Figure 16.5).

FIGURE 16.5

This application, similar to the demo applet that you've seen, graphically displays the results of mouse events that have been handled.

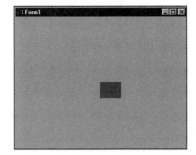

ANALYSIS Lines 8 through 12 store the global variables that keep track of the mouse state. Line 25 is the `handleMouseEvent()` method. This method is called after every mouse event has been handled providing a common method for dealing with changes in the mouse state. In this method column width and the row height must be calculated because the form window can change size. Unlike an applet window, which can be fixed, the form window can be resized by users. This value will be in pixels.

At lines 31 and 32, the column number and the row number are calculated. To perform the calculation, divide the mouse x coordinate by the column width and the mouse y coordinate by the row height. If the mouse is not in the form window, however, no matter what the row and column are calculated to be, set it to − 1, as shown in lines 34 and 35 because if the mouse is not in the form window, you don't want to draw the rectangular region. Lines 37, 38, and 39 show where color is set to black by default unless a button is pressed, in which case, it will be red.

Also, in this method, if the column, row, or color was changed, we store all three values in the global variables (lines 45–47). At lines 48 and 49, the window is invalidated and then updated.

Lines 54–87 are the mouse event handlers: `mouseDown()`, `mouseEnter()`, `mouseLeave()`, `mouseMove()`, and `mouseUp()`. At line 89 is a `paint()` handler. Here, the rectangular region is drawn if the row and column are not -1. The row and column will be -1 if the mouse is outside of the window. Otherwise, the row and column will have a valid value with which you can draw the rectangular region.

Summary

Visual J++ makes it easy to respond to mouse events. When you're writing applets, add classes that implement the `MouseListener` and `MouseMotionListener` interfaces. In applications, you add the mouse event handlers. In either case, it's simple to handle mouse events with Visual J++.

16

Q&A

Q **In an applet, how do I handle an event when a mouse button is pressed?**

A The first thing you have to do is declare a class that implements the MouseListener interface. In this class, you must have the five methods that have to be in any class that implements the MouseListener interface: mousePressed(), mouseReleased(), mouseEntered(), mouseExited(), and mouseClicked(). Then, you'll add any code to these methods that you need to handle the events. The last thing you'll have to do is use the component's addMouseListener() method to add an instantiation of your class in your applet code.

Q **How do I handle mouse movement events?**

A It's similar to the way you handle mouse button events. You declare a class that implements the MouseMotionListener interface. In this class, you must have mouseMoved() and mouseDragged() methods. In these two methods, you add the code that handles these events properly. Then input the addMouseMotionListener() method to add an instantiation of your class. Without using the addMouseMotionListener() method, no events will be sent to your class.

Q **How do I handle mouse events in an application?**

A It's easy! You begin by selecting your form in the Properties window, and clicking the events button. You then double-click on any mouse event that you want to handle. The code for this event will be added automatically. You can add any code that lets you properly handle the mouse event inside of the newly added method.

Exercises

1. Create an applet. Then create a class that implements the MouseListener interface. Make sure you add all five methods to your newly declared class. Instantiate the class; then use the addMouseListener() method to let your applet know where to send mouse messages. Now add code to any or all of the methods in your class to handle mouse events.

2. Create an applet. Declare a class that implements the MouseMotionListener interface. Make sure you add both methods that you need for the MouseMotionListener interface. Instantiate your newly declared class, and use the addMouseMotionListener() method from your component so that it knows where to send the mouse motion events. Lastly, add code inside of the methods of your class to handle these mouse events.

3. Create an application. Add a mouse moved handler. Add a label to the top of the application window. Every time the mouse is moved, update the text in the label to reflect the x and y position of the mouse.

16

DAY 17

Threads

A thread can be thought of as a single path of execution in your program. No matter how small or how simple a program is, it always has at least one thread. Today, you'll learn about those times when one thread is not enough.

Today you'll learn the following:

- About threads
- How threads can benefit you
- When to use multiple threads within a single program
- How to implement a multithreaded program
- About the `Thread` class and the `Runnable` interface
- When to use the synchronized method modifier
- About daemon threads
- How to debug threads
- About writing a single-threaded program with a tight loop in initialization
- About writing a multithreaded program with a tight loop in initialization
- How to write Conway's Game of Life to illustrate the use of multiple threads

Threads in Brief

We've already talked a little, in Day 14's chapter, "Animation," about how threads are essential for animation. In this chapter we'll continue with a more in-depth look at threads.

In a preemptive multitasking operating system such as Microsoft's Windows NT or IBM's Warp OS/2, the other processes' threads would continue to run because the operating system guarantees you that they will get their timeslice. However, because your program (in this example) is single threaded, your only thread is effectively tied up and cannot do anything else—even handle a request to stop or paint itself! In fact, if you were to write your application like that and then attempt to terminate it, you would likely get a message from the operating system stating that the process had "stopped responding." This is because Windows attempted to send a message to the process to shut down, and the process never answered.

The workaround to this situation obviously involves designing your program a little differently. By using multiple threads, you allow your program to handle the processing of the images in one thread while communicating with the system in another thread. That way, the animation plays and the program can still respond to other system requests. Using multiple threads in your programs can greatly increase their robustness. If you are new to multithreaded programming, this technique will require a slight change in the way you design your programs. You will probably also need some guidelines for deciding when to use multiple threads. There are certainly many times when using multiple threads is not needed. The following are some examples of when you should consider using multiple threads:

- If your drawing or painting code takes a long time to complete. You could place your drawing code in a separate thread and still allow the user to interact with the program without having to wait. You see this every time you use your browser. When you transfer to a Web page, it might take several seconds for the page to be fully drawn, but you can always stop the process. This is an example of the browser itself being multithreaded. Imagine what it would be like if you could never stop this process and every time you went to a Web page you were forced to wait until the entire page had been drawn!

- If you have to read data from a file that you know the user will eventually need in your program. In a single-threaded program you could read this data when the user needs it ("on demand"), or you could read the data when the program initializes. Either way, users are forced to wait until you have read the data before they can continue using your program. Needless to say, this does not make for happy users. A better way of designing this program would be to spawn a thread during initialization to read the data while continuing to process the rest of the program. That way, when users need to access the data, the program could check a variable that indicates whether the thread has completed its work. At the worst, users have to wait a fraction of the time they would have needed to wait without a second thread. At best, users would not have to wait at all.

- If users do not need immediate feedback from a process (such as page formatting, printing, file I/O, or intensive calculations), that process can be relegated to the background via a spawned thread. These are tasks that, when initiated, can be done in a separate thread from the thread that is handling user interaction. This keeps the interaction with the user immediate and responsive.

- If you want to provide an asynchronous service, you might want to accept the incoming request, spawn a thread to do the actual work, and then return. That way, the caller continues to work. Of course, when you finish, you would need some way of communicating that fact back to the caller, such as a callback function. This requires a bit more work on your part, but at least the caller is not blocked on the call to your method.

- If you have multiple tasks that your program needs to perform and they can be done concurrently, you might want to consider splitting them into separate threads instead of processing each task synchronously in the same thread.

Implementing Multiple Threads

Now that you've been introduced to threads and understand their benefits, you can learn how to implement multiple threads in a Java program. Threads are implemented in Java via one of two techniques, the Thread class or the Runnable interface.

Using the Thread Class

If you choose to implement multiple threads using the Thread class, you simply derive your class from the Thread superclass and implement the run() method. This technique is shown in the following example:

```
class MyThread extends Thread
{
    public void run()
    {
    }

    // any other methods and data that you want MyThread to
    // declare
}
```

17

To actually instantiate your new thread and start it, simply do the following:

```
MyThread myThread = new MyThread();
myThread.start();
```

After you call the thread's `start()` method, the Java Virtual Machine (JVM) will invoke the thread's `run()` method. I usually use this method sparingly, when I want to start a process that can run with little or no interaction with the main program.

Using an Interface

The other technique involves using an interface. By now you know what a class is; you haven't, however, been introduced to interfaces.

NEW TERM　　An *interface* in Java defines a set of function definitions. An interface can inherit from any base interface.

Java, unlike C++, does not support multiple inheritance. That is, you cannot derive a class from more than one class at the same time. For example, suppose you're writing a C++ application and you have two base classes: `CBase1` and `CBase2`. Suppose you want to include the functionality of these two classes into your new class. In C++ you simply use multiple inheritance and derive your new class from both classes at the same time, like this:

```
class CDerived : public CBase1, public CBase2
{
};
```

ABOUT INTERFACES

Java's designers at Sun decided to not go with multiple inheritance for various reasons. Using multiple inheritance can produce more problems than it solves. For example, you need to know the rules that your specific compiler implements regarding resolving ambiguity when both base classes have member functions (methods in C++ are typically referred to as member functions) with the same name. Java's designers decided to eliminate this problem by providing only single inheritance, which you have used throughout this book. Enter the concept of interfaces. Remember, an interface is a collection of method declarations (not their definitions) that can be included and defined by other classes.

An example is in order here. Java provides an interface called `Runnable` (via the `java.lang` package). This interface can be implemented (remember this term) by any class that wants to take advantage of multiple threads. Because `Runnable` is an interface and not a class, you would not derive your class from it. In fact, you can't. It is simply a collection of undefined methods that you are saying, as the author of your particular class, that you want to implement. The way you do this is simple. You use the keyword `implements` and then define any methods that are appropriate for that interface. Remember that the interface only declares these methods. It is up to you to actually define, or code, them.

With the `Runnable` interface, the only method you need to define is the `run()` method. Therefore, one of the most common ways to write a Java program that is multithreaded is to derive your class from Program and implement the `Runnable` interface, as in the following example:

```
public class TestApplet extends Applet implements Runnable
```

If you declare a class as implementing an interface and neglect to define the appropriate methods, you will receive an error similar to the following when you attempt to compile your Java code:

```
Declare the class abstract, or implement abstract member 'void
Runnable.run()' (J0063)
```

In this example, I neglected to implement the `run()` method, and I received an error during compilation. As you can see, if the class was an abstract class, there would have been no problem. However, I am indeed attempting to instantiate an instance of the `TestApplet` class; therefore, my code is in error.

An important thing to remember here is that although Java allows only one superclass (hence, single inheritance), you can implement any number of interfaces for that class.

Coding a Multithreaded Program

Now that you understand what an interface is, you need to learn how to code a multi-threaded program using the `Runnable` interface. It's much simpler than you might imagine. All you have to do when you derive your class is also specify that it implements the `Runnable` interface. That tells the JVM that your class is going to act as a proxy for the thread. In other words, your class is going to implement the `run()` method. In your class you would declare an object of type `Thread`, create the thread, and call the thread's `start()` method. That's it. The JVM then (because your object is acting as the proxy) calls your `run()` method to do the actual work.

Here is an example of this technique:

```
public class MyApplet extends Applet implements Runnable
{
    Thread myThread = null;

    public void start()
```

17

```
    {
        myThread = new Thread;
        myThread.start();
    }

    public void run()
    {
        // this is where the real work gets done!
    }

}
```

The preceding example is incomplete, but it is meant to show the syntax and basic flow of creating a thread with the Runnable interface. You will see how to actually write a complete program when you get to the demos and the hands-on part of the chapter.

Using the Synchronized Method Modifier

A very important method modifier that pertains to threads is the synchronized modifier. Let's say you have multiple threads in your program, but you want to make sure that only one thread at a time can enter a specific method that you write. You would declare that method as being synchronized:

```
public synchronized void myMethod()
```

This guarantees that only one thread at a time can enter into this method. When a thread enters this method, no other thread will be allowed to enter it. You can also define a block of code within a method as being synchronized:

```
public void mySecondMethod()
{
    synchronized( x )
    {
        // once we get to this point, no other thread
        // can enter ANY synchronized code block
        // within this object!!!
    }
}
```

Note that Java implements this lock on an object basis as opposed to a method basis. That means that if you declare a method or section of code as being synchronized (as in the previous examples) and your thread enters that code, no other thread can enter any synchronized block of code. This limitation holds true even if the methods involved have no logical correlation to one another.

Learning About Daemon Threads

In Java, you have the ability to specify that a thread is a "daemon" thread. A daemon is something that runs in the background and does not require any user interaction. Let's say you have an email package that gives you the option of checking for incoming mail every so often. The package has probably started a daemon process that is running in the background. This daemon process "sleeps" for the amount of time you indicated somewhere within the application. When it "awakens," it checks the mail server to see whether any mail has arrived for you.

The difference between nondaemon threads and daemon threads is that when all nondaemon threads have exited, the program stops. By failing to make a thread a daemon, you are specifying that you want the program to continue as long as the thread is alive. By making it a daemon, you are specifying that the program should exit whether or not this thread has terminated if all the other nondaemon threads have terminated. In the latter case, the daemon thread is responsible for its own termination.

17

Debugging Threads

The final thing you need to know before reading through the demo program is how to debug threads. With the help of Visual Studio 6, debugging Visual J++ programs that contain multiple threads is easy and straightforward. When you want to view the different threads in your program, simply set a breakpoint in your source code and run the program by pressing F5. When you reach the breakpoint, choose the Debug|Thread menu option. You'll see a list of all the threads running within the current process. Figure 17.1 shows the MDS Threads dialog as displayed on a very simple program. As you can see, there can be times when a class you are using might create its own threads. In this example, the AWT (Abstract Windowing Toolkit) has its own thread as well as "my" two threads.

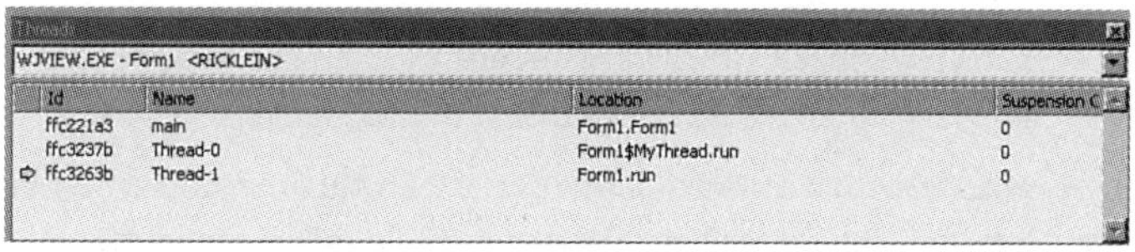

FIGURE 17.1

The Thread dialog is displayed while you debug a simple applet. Notice the options available to aid in debugging different threads.

Thread Class Definition

As you can see from the following list, the people who developed Java did quite a bit to make your life easier when attempting to implement multiple threads. Here is the list of methods and their descriptions for the Thread class:

- `public Thread();`   This is one of the many constructors for the Thread class. It takes no arguments and is the same as specifying no group and no target.

- `public Thread( Runnable target );`   This is the constructor you would normally use if you use the Runnable interface. When you construct the Thread object, you pass the object that implemented the Runnable interface. The JVM will then call that object's `run()` method after the Thread object's `start()` method has been called.

- `public Thread( Runnable target, String name );`   This constructor has the same effect as the `public Thread(Runnable target)` constructor except that you explicitly name the thread as opposed to allowing the JVM to create one on your behalf.

- `public Thread( String name );`   This has almost the same effect as the default constructor (the constructor with no arguments) except that here you explicitly name the thread instead of accepting a generated name.

- `public Thread( ThreadGroup group, Runnable target );`   This constructor specifies the thread group for the thread and the target whose `run()` method is called after the thread has been started.

- `public Thread( ThreadGroup group, Runnable target, String name );`   This constructor specifies the thread group for the thread and the target whose `run()` method is called after the thread has been started, and the name of the thread.

- `public Thread( ThreadGroup group, String name );`   This constructor specifies the thread group for the thread and the name of the thread.

- `public static int activeCount();`   Call this method to find out the current number of active threads in this thread's group.

- `public void checkAccess();`   Call this method when you want to determine whether the current thread can modify this thread. If it cannot, a SecurityException will be thrown.

- `public int countStackFrames();`   This method is called to count the number of stack frames in the current thread. For this method to be called, the thread must be suspended.

- `public static Thread currentThread();` This method returns the currently executing thread.

- `public void destroy();` This method destroys the current thread. Be careful when using this method because no cleanup is performed.

- `public static void dumpStack();` When debugging, you can call this method to print the stack of this thread.

- `public static int enumerate( Thread tarray[] );` This method returns an array of all threads in this thread's group.

- `public final String getName();` This method returns the name of the thread. If the name was not specified when the thread was created or later via a call to the `setName(String strName)` method, the name will be in the form "Thread-" + n, where n is an integer supplied by the JVM.

- `public final int getPriority();` This method returns the thread's current priority. See also the `setPriority()` method.

- `public final ThreadGroup getThreadGroup();` This method returns a `ThreadGroup` object that represents this thread's group.

- `public void interrupt();` This is used to interrupt a thread's execution. If a thread is waiting or sleeping and it is interrupted, an `InterruptedException` will be thrown.

- `public static boolean interrupted();` This is used to test whether a thread has been interrupted.

- `public final boolean isAlive();` This is used to test whether a thread is alive.

- `public final boolean isDaemon();` Call this to test an assumption that a thread is a daemon thread.

- `public boolean isInterrupted();` Call this to verify that the thread has been interrupted.

- `public final void join();` Call this when you want to wait for this thread to die.

- `public final void join( long millis );` Call this when you want current processing to halt and wait for this thread to die. The parameters tell the JVM the maximum time you will wait in milliseconds.

- `public final void join( long millis, int nanos )` Call this when you want to wait for this thread to die. The parameters tell the JVM the maximum time you will wait in milliseconds and nanoseconds.

17

- `public final void resume();`   Call this function to resume a suspended thread.
- `public void run();`   If this thread was created by an object that was defined as extending `Runnable`, its `run()` method will be called. Otherwise, this method returns without doing anything.
- `public final void setDaemon( boolean on );`   This is how you specify whether the thread is a user thread or a daemon thread.
- `public final void setName( String name );`   This is used to set or change the name of a thread.
- `public final void setPriority( int newPriority );`   This is used to set the priority of the thread. The priority must be in the range `MIN_PRIORITY` to `MAX_PRIORITY`.
- `public static void sleep( long millis );`   Call this method to temporarily pause the execution of the thread.
- `public static void sleep( long millis, int nanos )`   Call this method to temporarily pause the execution of the thread.
- `public void start();`   This method starts a thread's execution.
- `public final void stop();`   This method stops the execution of the thread.
- `public final void stop( Throwable obj );`   This is the same as `stop()` except that you can pass an exception that is a subclass of `Throwable`.
- `public final void suspend();`   This temporarily suspends the execution of a thread. To restart the thread, the `resume()` method must be called.
- `public String toString();`   This returns the name of the thread in a `String` object.
- `public static void yield();`   Call this method to allow other threads to execute.

Demo: A Single-Threaded Applet with a Tight Loop in Initialization

Now you get the chance to put what you've learned into practice. The first demo applet illustrates the problems encountered with a single-threaded applet when initialization takes too long. In this demo you simply put a `for` loop in the `start()` method to count to 100,000. This could be your applet reading n records upon initialization. For this demo, you increment the counter and call `repaint()`, which in turn displays the current value of the counter. The source code is shown in Listing 17.1.

INPUT   **LISTING 17.1**   SingleThreadedTightLoop.java

```
1    import java.applet.*;
2    import java.awt.*;
3
4    public class SingleThreadedTightLoop extends Applet
5    {
6        long m_lCounter;
7
8        public SingleThreadedTightLoop()
9        {
10       }
11
12       public void init()
13       {
14       }
15
16       public void paint(Graphics g)
17       {
18       g.drawString( "Current Count = " + m_lCounter, 10, 20 );
19       }
20
21       public void start()
22       {
23           for( m_lCounter=0; m_lCounter<100000; m_lCounter++ )
24               repaint();
25       }
26   }
```

Note   You'll want to edit your HTML file to have a width of at least 640 so that all the text is in view.

ANALYSIS   At line 6 we declare a variable to use to hold the current value of the counter. The paint() method starts at line 16 and doesn't do anything except display the string that shows the counter value.

In the start() method (lines 21–25), a for loop that counts to 100,000 is included. This could just as well be your applet reading in database records for display, connecting to a remote host, or doing anything that requires the user to wait. Notice how the repaint() method is used to show the current value of the counter.

As a test, try to predict what will happen with the preceding demo before you enter the last section of code. If you said the user will not be able to interact with the applet until the for loop completes, you're partly correct. If, however, you said that the counter's value will never be shown until the `for` loop completes (despite the calls to `repaint()`), you're entirely correct (and can move to the head of the class). The code is in such a tight loop that it cannot even paint.

So how do you solve this problem? By using another thread, of course. The following demo shows the same applet written slightly differently and using multiple threads.

Demo: A Multithreaded Applet with a Tight Loop in Initialization

The following demo applet will resolve the problems encountered with the first demo. It will do so by implementing a second thread to do the work of the applet while the primary thread is left free to respond to other events such as handling paint messages. That way, we can actually see the applet print the current counter value this time! The source code is given in Listing 17.2, with comments.

INPUT   **LISTING 17.2**   MULTITHREADEDTIGHTLOOP.JAVA

```
1    import java.applet.*;
2    import java.awt.*;
3
4    public class MultiThreadedTightLoop extends Applet
5        implements Runnable
6    {
7        Thread m_MultiThreadedTightLoop = null;
8        long m_lCounter;
9
10       public MultiThreadedTightLoop()
11       {
12       }
13
14       public void init()
15       {
16       }
17
18       public void paint(Graphics g)
19       {
20           g.drawString( "Current Count = " + m_lCounter, 10, 20 );
21       }
22
23       public void start()
24       {
25           if( m_MultiThreadedTightLoop == null )
26           {
27               m_MultiThreadedTightLoop = new Thread(this);
```

```
28                      m_MultiThreadedTightLoop.start();
29          }
30      }
31
32      public void stop()
33      {
34          if( m_MultiThreadedTightLoop != null )
35          {
36              m_MultiThreadedTightLoop.stop();
37              m_MultiThreadedTightLoop = null;
38          }
39      }
40
41      public void run()
42      {
43          showStatus( "Reading database records..." );
44          for( m_lCounter=0; m_lCounter<100000; m_lCounter++ )
45              repaint();
46      }
47  }
```

17

If you type the demo, you will see that with a few minor changes the applet now works as you would expect it to. You actually see the counter run up to the number you asked for, and the user could still interact with the applet had you defined any controls for them to do so. Figure 17.2 shows the multithreaded applet running using Microsoft Explorer. In this simple multithreaded demo, a `for` loop is used to count to 100,000. Because you placed your code in another thread, the applet maintains the capability to respond to other events (such as paint messages), even though you are in a very tight loop.

OUTPUT

FIGURE 17.2

A simple multithreaded applet.

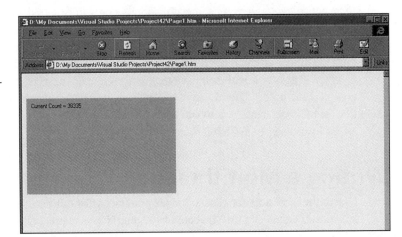

ANALYSIS At the beginning of the class definition, you need to do two important things. First, tell the compiler that the class will be derived from Applet and will extend Runnable. Second, instantiate a Thread object and set its value to null. You also need to declare a counter variable.

The paint() method, shown here in lines 18–21, doesn't change from the preceding demo.

In the start() method at lines 23–30, you begin to see a couple of differences between this program and the preceding one. However, they are minor changes and are simple. All you did was change the start() method to create the new thread and start it. The Applet.start() method is called every time your Web page is entered by the user. First, check the thread object's value. If the thread object has not been created yet (it will have a value of null), create it using the new keyword. Then call its start() method. Remember that the JVM will then call the Applet-derived class's run() implementation.

The stop() method at lines 32–39 is called when the user exits the page. To keep this demo simple, the thread is shut down each time the user exits the page and then restarted when the user returns. Obviously, this is a decision that you as the developer must make. In the preceding stop() method, the demo first checks to make sure that a Thread object exists. If there is one, the Thread.stop() method is called and the object's value is set to null so that the start() method works properly.

The run() method (lines 41–46) is called by the JVM after the thread's start() method is called. The code is exactly the same as the code in the start() method in the first demo.

In an actual applet, if you had been reading records in from a database, you probably would need to declare a global variable that would tell you whether the records had all been read. That way, if the user attempted to do something that could not be accomplished without all the records being read, you could display a message box explaining that fact. The user would then have to wait for the balance of records to be read. Of course, if the user did not do anything that required the use of these records until after they had all been read, you would have successfully removed a needless delay in your applet by moving this file I/O to another thread.

Writing a Multithreaded Program

One of the most popular games that programmers like to use to learn a new language is "Conway's Game of Life." Invented by Cambridge mathematician John Conway, the game is different from most computer games. It centers around a grid of life forms, or cells, that can either live or die depending on how many other life forms are around it.

What you are going to do here is implement a simple form of the game to show a multi-threaded applet at work. You'll remember from earlier in the chapter that one of the benefits of making your applet multithreaded is overcoming the problem of having a series of instructions that are repeated until the user leaves the page. This is a perfect example of that situation. After the grid is set up, the thread sleeps for a short period, wakes up, decides on who lives or dies (the rules are listed shortly), and repaints the screen. If you did not do this in another thread, the user would not be able to stop the applet in a normal fashion.

Because it is not the goal of this chapter to teach a lot of graphics or dialog controls, that part of the game is kept as simple as possible in this applet. Instead, you should concentrate on what multiple threads can do for you and how the game itself works.

Here is a listing of the rules for Conway's Game of Life:

- If a cell is alive and there are fewer than two surrounding cells, the cell dies.
- If a cell is alive and there are two surrounding cells, the cell remains alive.
- If a cell is alive and there are three surrounding cells, the cell remains alive.
- If a cell is alive and there are more than three surrounding cells, the cell dies.
- If a cell is dead and there are three surrounding cells, the cell comes to life.

The source code for Conway's Game of Life is given in Listing 17.3, and the output is shown in Figure 17.3.

INPUT   **LISTING 17.3**   SOURCE CODE FOR CONWAY'S GAME OF LIFE

```
1    // Life.java
2
3    import java.awt.*;
4    import java.applet.*;
5
6    public class Life extends Applet implements Runnable
7    {
8        public static final int COLUMNS = 50;
9        public static final int ROWS = 15;
10       boolean m_lifeBoard[][] = new boolean[COLUMNS][ROWS];
11       FontMetrics m_fm;
12       Thread m_Life = null;
13
14       /**
15        * The entry point for the applet.
16        */
17       public void init()
```

continues

LISTING 17.3 CONTINUED

```
18      {
19          Graphics g = getGraphics();
20          m_fm = g.getFontMetrics();
21
22      }
23
24      public synchronized void paint(Graphics g)
25      {
26          char chr[] = new char[1];
27          chr[0] = 'X';
28
29          for( int x=0; x<COLUMNS; x++ )
30          {
31              for( int y=0; y<ROWS; y++ )
32              {
33                  if( m_lifeBoard[x][y] == true )
34                  {
35                      g.drawChars( chr, 0, 1, x * m_fm.charWidth( chr[0]
                    ➥),
36                          y * m_fm.getHeight() );
37                  }
38                  else
39                  {
40                      g.setColor( getBackground() );
41                      g.drawChars( chr, 0, 1, x * m_fm.charWidth( chr[0]
                    ➥),
42                          y * m_fm.getHeight() );
43                      g.setColor( getForeground() );
44                  }
45              }
46          }
47      }
48
49      public void start()
50      {
51          if( m_Life == null )
52          {
53              m_Life = new Thread( this );
54
55              for( int x=0; x<COLUMNS; x++ )
56              {
57                  for( int y=0; y<ROWS; y++ )
58                  {
59                      m_lifeBoard[x][y] = false;
60                      if( Math.random() > .76 )
61                          m_lifeBoard[x][y] = true;
62                  }
63              }
64
```

```
65                    m_Life.start();
66             }
67      }
68
69      protected synchronized void updateBoard()
70      {
71          int i;
72          Point p = new Point( 0, 0 );
73
74          for( int x=0; x<COLUMNS; x++ )
75          {
76              for( int y=0; y<ROWS; y++ )
77              {
78                  boolean bCurrentIsCellAlive =
79                      ( m_lifeBoard[x][y] == true );
80                  int iSurroundingLives = 0;
81                  // row above current cell
82                  if( y > 0 )
83                  {
84                      p.y = y - 1;
85                      for( i=-1; i<=1; i++ )
86                      {
87                          if( ( x + i ) < 0 ) continue;
88                          if( ( x + i ) == COLUMNS ) continue;
89
90                          p.x = x + i;
91
92                          if( m_lifeBoard[p.x][p.y] == true )
93                              iSurroundingLives++;
94                      }
95                  }
96
97                  // row below current cell
98                  if( y < ( ROWS - 1 ) )
99                  {
100                     p.y = y + 1;
101                     for( i=-1; i<=1; i++ )
102                     {
103                         if( ( x + i ) < 0 ) continue;
104                         if( ( x + i ) == COLUMNS ) continue;
105
106                         p.x = x + i;
107
108                         if( m_lifeBoard[p.x][p.y] == true )
109                             iSurroundingLives++;
110                     }
111                 }
112
113                 // left and right columns relative to current cell
```

17

continues

LISTING 17.3   CONTINUED

```
114                    for( i=-1; i<=1; i+= 2 )
115                    {
116                        if( ( x + i ) < 0 ) continue;
117                        if( ( x + i ) == COLUMNS ) continue;
118
119                        p.x = x + i;
120                        p.y = y;
121
122                        if( m_lifeBoard[p.x][p.y] == true )
123                            iSurroundingLives++;
124                    }
125                if( bCurrentIsCellAlive )
126                {
127                    if( iSurroundingLives < 2 ) m_lifeBoard[x][y] =
                       ➥false;
128                    if( iSurroundingLives == 2 );
129                    if( iSurroundingLives == 3 );
130                    if( iSurroundingLives > 3 ) m_lifeBoard[x][y] =
                       ➥false;
131                }
132                else
133                {
134                    if( iSurroundingLives == 3 ) m_lifeBoard[x][y] =
                       ➥true;
135                }
136            }
137        }
138    }
139
140    public void run()
141    {
142        while( true )
143        {
144            try
145            {
146                Thread.sleep( 1000 );
147                updateBoard();
148                repaint();
149            }
150            catch( InterruptedException e )
151            {
152                stop();
153            }
154        }
155    }
156
157 }
```

OUTPUT

FIGURE 17.3

Conway's Game of Life.

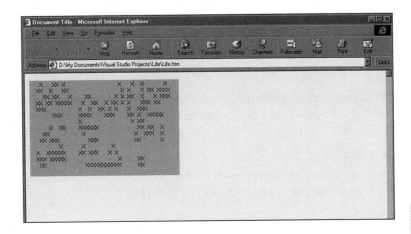

ANALYSIS Notice that we changed the default class definition of

```
public class Applet1 extends Applet
```

to this:

```
public class Life extends Applet implements Runnable
```

In lines 8 and 9, we add constant declarations. These variables state the number of rows and columns you want in your game. You are, of course, free to change these values. To make your own game a little nicer, you might want to dynamically size your grid based on the size of the applet.

Next in line 10, we add the declaration of the grid, or board, on which you will see Life. As you can see, it is a two-dimensional array of boolean values that represents whether the cell in question is alive. The paint() method looks at this value when painting the grid. There are also two other declarations shown later that you'll need.

The FontMetrics object in line 11 is used later to display the life forms correctly. When this is placed in the init() method (rather than the start() method), the FontMetrics object is initialized only once rather than each time the user refreshes the page.

In the paint() method (lines 24–47), a nested for loop is used to paint the cells of the grid. As you can see, an ✕ is printed if the cell contains a living cell. If, however, the cell does not contain a living cell, the code changes the color to the background color and draws the same ✕. This has the effect of "erasing" the previous ✕ if one has previously been drawn. Notice the use of the FontMetrics object that was declared earlier. You need it to know the size characteristics of the letters with the current font so that the grid prints correctly.

The start() method comes next, in lines 49–67. Before starting the thread, we randomly set a few of the cells to living so that you can see the program run a little. One thing you might want to try is to allow the user to "set up" the grid, by allowing mouse clicks in different regions to toggle the cells' living state on and off.

The updateBoard() method spans lines 69–138 and is the meat of the program. This is where you actually implement the rules of the game and update the grid accordingly. After you have counted the number of living cells surrounding the current cell, you can apply the rules of the game.

In the run() method we just want to update the board and repaint the result every 1 second. The time is arbitrarily set at 1 second so that you can see the cells coming to life and dying.

Summary

The use of multiple threads in your application can indeed make your application more robust in various ways. However, one common mistake many programmers make when first learning multithreading is to overuse it. Therefore, it is important to keep in mind that threads have their place and should not be abused. As you have seen in this chapter, a bit more planning goes into designing a multithreaded applet. There can also be problems with synchronizing threads and communicating between them. Keep in mind that as with any other tool in your repertoire, you need to be cognizant of when to use threads. That means knowing their benefits and drawbacks. The guidelines presented at the beginning of this chapter should give you a good feel for when you might want to consider using multiple threads.

Q&A

Q What is a thread?

A A thread is a single path of execution in your program. All programs have at least one thread.

Q When would an application need multiple threads?

A When it needs to perform more than one simultaneous task. An example of this is animation that's maintained while other things are going on.

Q What are some advantages to using multiple threads?

A If your drawing or painting code takes a long time to complete, you can place your drawing code in a separate thread and still allow the user to interact with the program without having to wait. Multiple threads are also handy if you have to read data from a file that you know the user will eventually need in your program. In a single-threaded program you could read this data when the user needs it ("on demand"), or you could read the data when the program initializes.

Q **What are the three main thread methods?**

A The run() method is the method in which the thread executes. The start() method is the method in which the thread is kicked off. The stop() method terminates the thread's execution.

Q **What is the Runnable interface?**

A Because Runnable is an interface and not a class, you would not derive your class from it. In fact, you can't. It is simply a collection of undefined methods that you are saying, as the author of your particular class, that you want to implement. The way you do this is simple. You use the keyword implement and then define any methods that are appropriate for that interface. Remember that the interface only declares these methods. It is up to you to actually define, or code, them.

Q **How will you know when your thread isn't sleeping long enough to give other tasks on your system enough time to perform their functions?**

A When the system performance becomes noticeably slower. The mouse might be jerky, menus might pull down slowly, and overall performance will suffer. I'd suggest a minimum value of 30 when you call the sleep() method.

Q **When should you avoid using threads?**

A A certain amount of overhead is added when you use threads. You add extra code and more Java classes are loaded. Because of this, if you can think of an easy way to carry out the task you need to carry out without using threads, try it.

Review Exercises

1. Create an applet that implements the Runnable interface. Add start(), stop(), and run() methods as shown earlier in the chapter. Create an integer variable that counts by tens and displays in the applet window every time it's updated.

2. Create an applet which has a class that extends the Thread class. Instantiate this newly declared class and have it do some calculations. When it's done, have it stop.

DAY 18

Strings

Strings are arguably the most important data type in any high-level language (HLL). They represent the way in which most applications communicate with the user. Go to any Web page, and even though the page might contain many graphics, the written word will always be the predominant way of getting the message across. For that reason, this entire chapter is devoted to dealing with strings in Java. The developers at Sun Microsystems must have also realized the importance of strings, because unlike with other primitive data types, such as `short`, `long`, and `char`, there is an entire class specifically for the manipulation of strings.

Today you will do the following:

- Learn the difference between character arrays, the `String` class, and the `StringBuffer` class
- Understand the demo programs for working with strings
- Write your own `String` subclass that adds functionality to the `String` class

Strings and Character Arrays in Java

If you are familiar with a language such as C or C++, you are accustomed to dealing with strings as an array of characters. In fact, C/C++ strings are actually nothing more than character arrays and as a result are saddled with all the inherent problems of dealing with arrays in C/C++ (pointer arithmetic, reference indexes that are out of bounds, and so on). In Java, you can still create a character array, but it is usually more convenient to use the String class when you're dealing with text. Let's look at how a character array is declared and initialized in Java.

You can assign values to an array when you declare it. Simply declare a char array as follows:

```
char[] myCharArray = {'H', 'e', 'l', 'l', 'o'};
```

As with any array, you can declare the variable first, then populate it as shown here:

```
char[] myCharArray = new char[5];
myCharArray[0] = 'H';
myCharArray[1] = 'e';
myCharArray[2] = 'l';
myCharArray[3] = 'l';
myCharArray[4] = 'o';
```

Arrays work great for certain types of data, but they come up short in too many areas when dealing with text.

The first problem with character arrays is that each element is 1 byte in length. Strings use 2 bytes for each character in the string to support Unicode. (See the sidebar if you are unfamiliar with Unicode.) To enjoy the benefits of Unicode, you will need to use the String class as opposed to character arrays.

UNICODE: A BRIEF DESCRIPTION

Over the past 10 years there has been a marked increase in attention to the international software market. The term used for providing software that is specific to a country (language, time and data format, and other items) is *localization*. To deal with the problems encountered in developing software for the international market, a standard was founded in 1988 by Apple and Xerox, called Unicode. In 1991, a group of large influential companies joined forces to fully define the Unicode standard. This group included Adobe, Aldus, Apple, Borland, Digital, Go, IBM, Lotus, Metaphor, Microsoft, NeXT, Novell, the Research Libraries Group, Sun, Taligent, Unisys, WordPerfect, and Xerox.

All characters in a Unicode string are represented by 2 bytes. A little math (2^{16}) shows you that this system allows Unicode to represent more than 65,000 characters. That makes it possible to represent all the characters that make up all the written languages in the world. Quite an improvement from the previous standards in which each character was represented with a single byte ($2^8 = 256$ different characters).

The second problem with using character arrays is that you simply do not have as much flexibility and power with a primitive data type as you have when you use a class. For example, if you want to search the array for a character or sequence of characters, you must do this manually. Likewise, formatting the characters in any way would result in a ton of manual work on the developer's part. The String class resolves these issues by implementing methods to provide these and more services.

Strings come in two flavors with Java: String and StringBuffer. The String class represents a string that is read-only. In other words, the only time you can assign a value to it is when you create it. Actually, to be more precise, you can reassign it a different value and append more characters to it, but you cannot do things such as changing specific characters within the string after you have assigned it. If you have needs of that nature, you must use the StringBuffer class. The StringBuffer class supports methods such as setCharAt(index, chr) and insert(offset, x). The StringBuffer.insert(offset, x) method is an overloaded method in which x represents different types of data that will be converted into their string representations and then inserted into the string at offset. (For a review of method overloading, refer to Day 5's chapter, "Frame Windows.")

The String class is the only place in the Java language where operator overloading is allowed. As you have seen in the demo programs and hands-on examples throughout the previous chapters, you can use the + and += operators to concatenate one string to another:

```
String str = new String("Hello");
str += ", world";
```

One drawback to the String class is that you cannot use the switch statement with it (for more information about the switch control statement, refer to Day 2's chapter, "Java Language Fundamentals"). That is because the switch statement can be used only on primitive data types, such as char, short, and int. To compare strings in a manner similar to the switch statement, you would have to use nested if statements and call any one of several String methods used for comparing string values. These methods and more are covered in the Demo sections of the chapter.

Demo: Retrieving and Manipulating Strings

In the first demo, you will see methods that deal with string retrieval and manipulation. For example, you will see a method to convert every other character from lower- to uppercase. You will see how to strip the ending filename from a URL. The source code is given in Listing 18.1.

INPUT LISTING 18.1 SOURCE CODE FOR THE STRINGRETRIEVALMETHODS PROGRAM

```
1    import java.applet.*;
2    import java.awt.*;
3
4    public class StringRetrievalMethods extends Applet
5    {
6        FontMetrics m_fm;
7
8    public void init()
9        {
10
11           Graphics g = getGraphics();
12           m_fm = g.getFontMetrics();
13
14       }
15
16       protected boolean numberIsEven(int i)
17       {
18           return( ( i & 1 ) != 0 );
19       }
20
21       protected String everyOtherCharToUpper( String strOriginal )
22       {
23           // This will change every other letter to upper case
24           String strNew = new String();
25           char ch;
26           for( int i=0; i<strOriginal.length(); i++ )
27           {
28               ch = strOriginal.charAt( i );
29               if (numberIsEven( i ) )
30               {
31                   strNew += Character.toUpperCase( ch );
32               }
33               else strNew += ch;
34           }
35           return( strNew );
36       }
37
38       protected String getFileNameFromURL(String strUrl)
39       {
40           String strFile = new String();
41
42           char ch;
43           int i = ( strUrl.length() - 1 );
44           boolean bFileNotFound = true;
```

```
45
46          while( bFileNotFound && i >= 0 )
47          {
48              if( ( ch = strUrl.charAt(i)) == '/' )
49                  bFileNotFound = false;
50              else i—;
51          }
52          if( !bFileNotFound )
53              strFile = strUrl.substring( i + 1 );
54
55          return( strFile );
56      }
57
58      public void paint(Graphics g)
59      {
60          int i;
61
62          String strLowerCase = new String( "this is my old string
            ➥before conversion" );
63          g.setColor( Color.black );
64          g.drawString( strLowerCase, 0, m_fm.getHeight() );
65
66          String strMixedCase = everyOtherCharToUpper( strLowerCase );
67          g.setColor( Color.red );
68          g.drawString( strMixedCase, 0, m_fm.getHeight() * 2 );
69
70          String strUrl = new String( "http://www.acme.com/index.html"
            );
71          g.setColor( Color.black );
72          g.drawString( "URL = " + strUrl, 0, m_fm.getHeight() * 4 );
73
74          String strFile = getFileNameFromURL( strUrl );
75          g.setColor( Color.red );
76          g.drawString( "File = " + strFile, 0, m_fm.getHeight() * 5 );
77      }
78  }
```

OUTPUT Figure 18.1 shows the result of running this demo.

ANALYSIS In the numberIsEven()method that starts at line 16, a common technique is used for ascertaining whether a number is odd or even. This method works on the premise that for a number to be odd, the first bit must be one. Therefore, all the method has to do is to verify that fact with the bitwise and operator to know whether a number is even or odd.

As you can see in the everyOtherCharToUpper() method at line 21, every other character is converted to uppercase in a string that is passed to it. The converted string is then returned. Three String methods are in use here. First, the length() method at line 26 is used to control how you are indexing the string itself. Then as you iterate through the string one character at a time at line 28, you use the charAt() method to get the character at the current index. After you have that character, you either convert that character to uppercase (using the Character.toUpperCase() method) and append it to the new string at line 31 (if the index is an even number), or simply append it to the new string without changing it, as shown at line 33.

FIGURE 18.1

This applet uses String methods to retrieve and extract characters from a string.

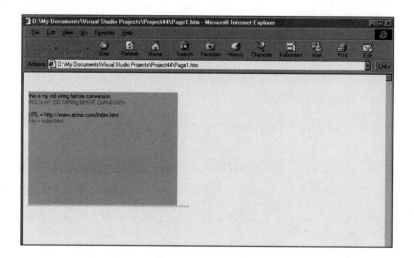

The getFileNameFromURL() method at lines 38–56 takes a URL in the form of a string and (starting from the end of the string) iterates through the string one character at a time looking for a delimiter (/). After that character is found, the method uses the substring() method at line 53 to strip the filename from the end and returns that string to the calling method.

In the paint() method (lines 58–78), the string is shown before and after conversion. The URL http://www.acme.com/index.html used in the code is an example; you can substitute any URL you desire. Also, note the use of the font metrics so that the text displays nicely.

Demo: Searching and Comparing Strings

The second demo demonstrates searching and comparing strings. This shows you how to search through a string for specific characters or strings. It enables you to enter a URL in a TextField and then, by pressing Enter or clicking the Convert button, instantiate a simple URL class. The class constructor accepts a string that defines the fully qualified URL. The URL class then takes that string and, using various String methods, searches it for several tokens that define a URL.

Note that a URL class is included in the `java.net` package. For that reason, this demo implements only a fraction of what a URL class would actually need to be truly usable. The reasoning behind using a URL class in this demo is that parsing a URL is a great way of showing you some of the `String` methods you can use when searching and comparing strings. After you have worked through the code in Listing 18.2, you will have a good grasp of some of the ways you can search and compare strings.

INPUT   **LISTING 18.2**   SOURCE CODE FOR THE SEARCHSTRINGMETHODS PROGRAM

```
1    import java.applet.*;
2    import java.awt.*;
3    import java.awt.event.*;
4    import java.net.MalformedURLException;
5
6    public class SearchStringMethods extends Applet
7    {
8
9        MyListener Listener = new MyListener();
10
11       private Label m_label = new Label( "URL:" );
12       private TextField m_textField = new TextField( 50 );
13       private Button m_button = new Button( "Convert" );
14       private Label m_status;
15
16       FontMetrics m_fm;
17
18       public void init()
19       {
20
21           add( m_label );
22           add( m_textField );
23           add( m_button );
24           String strTemp = new String( "Status:waiting" );
25           for( int i=0; i<120; i++ )
26               strTemp += " ";
27           m_status = new Label( strTemp );
28           add( m_status );
29
30           Graphics g = getGraphics();
31           m_fm = g.getFontMetrics();
32
33           m_button.addActionListener( Listener );
34
35       }
36
37       public class MyListener implements ActionListener
38       {
39
```

continues

LISTING 18.2 CONTINUED

```
40          public void actionPerformed( ActionEvent ae )
41          {
42
43              showStatus( "" );
44              if( ae.getActionCommand().equals( "Convert" ) )
45              {
46                  try
47                  {
48                      URL url = new URL( m_textField.getText() );
49                      m_status.setText( "url.getServerType = " +
                            ➥url.getServerType() +
50                                      ", url.getObject = " +
                                        ➥url.getObject() );
51                  }
52                  catch( MalformedURLException e )
53                  {
54                      m_status.setText( "Status:URL exception: " +
                            ➥e.getMessage() );
55                  }
56              }
57          }
58      }
59
60      class URL extends Object
61      {
62          protected final int HTTP = 0;
63          protected final int FTP = 1;
64          protected final int GOPHER = 2;
65          protected final int MAILTO = 3;
66          protected final int NEWS = 4;
67          protected final int WAIS = 5;
68
69          protected int m_iServerType;
70          protected String m_strAddress;
71          protected String m_strObject;
72
73          protected String m_strFullUrl;
74
75          URL( String strFullUrl ) throws MalformedURLException
76          {
77              m_strFullUrl = strFullUrl;
78
79              // get scheme (or server type)
80              if( strFullUrl.startsWith( "http" ) )
81                  m_iServerType = HTTP;
82              else if( strFullUrl.startsWith( "ftp" ) )
83                  m_iServerType = FTP;
84              else if( strFullUrl.startsWith( "gopher" ) )
```

```
85              m_iServerType = GOPHER;
86          else if( strFullUrl.startsWith( "mailto" ) )
87              m_iServerType = MAILTO;
88          else if( strFullUrl.startsWith( "news" ) )
89              m_iServerType = NEWS;
90          else if( strFullUrl.startsWith( "wais" ) )
91              m_iServerType = WAIS;
92          else
93          {
94              throw new MalformedURLException( "Server type is
                ➥invalid" );
95          }
96
97          switch( m_iServerType )
98          {
99              case HTTP:
100                 if( strFullUrl.regionMatches( 4, "://", 0, 3) )
101                 {
102                     if( strFullUrl.endsWith( ".html" ) )
103                     {
104                         int iIndex;
105                         if( ( iIndex = strFullUrl.lastIndexOf( '/'
                            ➥) ) != -1 )
106                         {
107                             m_strObject =
                                ➥strFullUrl.substring(iIndex + 1);
108                         }
109                         else throw new MalformedURLException(
110                             "html file specified without preceding
                                ➥/" );
111                     }
112                 }
113                 else throw new MalformedURLException(
114                     "://" missing after specifying server type of
                        ➥http" );
115                 break;
116
117             case FTP:
118                     break;
119
120             case GOPHER:
121                     break;
122
123             case MAILTO:
124                     break;
125
126             case NEWS:
127                     break;
128
129             case WAIS:
```

continues

LISTING 18.2 CONTINUED

```
130                              break;
131                  }
132              }
133
134      public String toString()
135      {
136          return( m_strFullUrl );
137      }
138
139      public String getServerType()
140      {
141          String strServerType = "";
142
143          switch( m_iServerType )
144          {
145              case HTTP:
146                  strServerType = "http";
147                  break;
148
149              case FTP:
150                  strServerType = "ftp";
151                  break;
152
153              case GOPHER:
154                  strServerType = "gopher";
155                  break;
156
157              case MAILTO:
158                  strServerType = "mailto";
159                  break;
160
161              case NEWS:
162                  strServerType = "news";
163                  break;
164
165              case WAIS:
166                  strServerType = "wais";
167                  break;
168          }
169
170          return( strServerType );
171
172      }
173
174      public String getObject()
175      {
176          return( m_strObject );
177      }
```

```
178
179     }
180
181 }
```

Figure 18.2 shows the result of running this demo. To run the demo, enter the URL in the `TextField` and click the Convert button.

FIGURE 18.2

This demo illustrates searching and comparing strings.

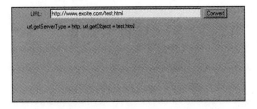

At lines 11–14 we declare the user interface items you'll use to get the URL from the user. You'll also need to declare the `MyListener` and `FontMetrics` classes.

The `actionPerformed()` method at lines 40–57 enables you to monitor, or respond to, events that occur regarding the user interface controls. When the user clicks the button, the code processes that URL and displays the results in the user's browser status label.

In the code at lines 79–91, the `startsWith()` method is used to determine whether one of the defined string sequences begins the string that the user entered for a URL.

The code found at lines 97–115 only implements one of the server types (HTTP). The `switch` statement also includes other possible server types (lines 117–132) just to show you some others you might want to implement. If the server type is HTTP, use the `regionMatches()` method (as is done at line 100) to search a specific section of a string for the characters (`://`) that should always follow the `http` server type literal. After you have ascertained that the user has entered a "valid" HTTP URL, you use the `endsWith()` method to try to determine whether the user has ended the URL with an HTML filename. If so, use the `lastIndexOf()` and `substring()` methods to extract the HTML filename and assign its value to `m_strObject`.

Writing Your Own `String` Subclass

Now it's your turn to write something that should help you solve real-life programming issues. This time, after you understand the example (Listing 18.3), you should have something you can actually plug into your existing or new applets and use right away.

18

You are going to write your own `SmartString` class to extend the functionality of the `String` class.

The first problem you encounter when attempting to derive a class from a class such as `String` or `StringBuffer` is that you can't do it. This is because `String` and `StringBuffer` are both defined as `final`. Recall from earlier in this book that the `final` class modifier dictates that the class cannot be extended. Therefore, to get around this serious obstacle, you have to declare a `String` object within your class. It's certainly a kludge workaround, but unfortunately, you can't do anything about it. The unfortunate result of this is that you cannot truly take advantage of inheritance and polymorphism. To use any method that is not implemented by `SmartString`, you have to explicitly call the embedded string's method. Normally with inheritance, you would simply call `SmartString`'s method, and if `SmartString` didn't implement the method, `String`'s implementation would be called automatically. This certainly places restrictions on how you can use the `SmartString` class, but after you start adding the methods shown in the hands-on example, the advantages of `SmartString` will outweigh the disadvantages caused by its definition as `final`.

INPUT   **LISTING 18.3**   A PROGRAM THAT BUILDS A SmartString CLASS

```
1    import java.awt.*;
2    import java.applet.*;
3
4    public class SmartStringApplet extends Applet
5    {
6        FontMetrics m_fm;
7        public void init()
8        {
9            Graphics g = getGraphics();
10           m_fm = g.getFontMetrics();
11       }
12
13       public void paint( Graphics g )
14       {
15           SmartString str;
16           String strTrimmed;
17
18           str = new SmartString( "   Test String   " );
19           g.drawString( "Before lTrim: '" + str.toString() + "'", 0,
             ➥m_fm.getHeight() );
20           g.drawString( "After lTrim: '" + str.lTrim() +  "'", 0,
             ➥m_fm.getHeight() * 2 );
21
22           str = new SmartString( "   Test String   " );
23           g.drawString( "Before rTrim: '" + str.toString() + "'", 0,
             ➥m_fm.getHeight() * 4 );
```

```
24          g.drawString( "After rTrim: '" + str.rTrim() + "'", 0,
         ➥m_fm.getHeight() * 5 );
25
26          str = new SmartString( "   Test String    " );
27          char x[] = new char[30];
28          x = str.toPaddedCharArray( x.length );
29          g.drawString( "After toPaddedCharArray(" + x.length + " ): '"
         ➥+ x + "'",
30              0, m_fm.getHeight() * 7);
31
32          str = new SmartString( "all of these words should be
         ➥capitalized" );
33          g.drawString("Before capitalizeWords: '" + str.toString() +
         ➥"'", 0, m_fm.getHeight() * 9);
34          g.drawString( "After capitalizeWords: '" +
         ➥str.capitalizeWords() + "'",
35              0, m_fm.getHeight() * 10 );
36      }
37
38  class SmartString
39  {
40      String string;
41
42      private char value[];
43      private int offset;
44      private int count;
45
46      public SmartString( String value )
47      {
48          string = new String( value );
49
50          count = value.length();
51          this.value = new char[count];
52          value.getChars( 0, count, this.value, 0 );
53      }
54
55      public String toString()
56      {
57          return( string.toString() );
58      }
59
60      public String lTrim()
61      {
62          int i = 0;
63          boolean bNonSpaceFound = false;
64          char ch;
65
66          while( !bNonSpaceFound && i < string.length() )
67          {
```

continues

18

LISTING **18.3**   CONTINUED

```
68                  if( ( ch = string.charAt( i ) ) != ' ' )
69                      bNonSpaceFound = true;
70                  else i++;
71              }
72
73              return( string.substring( i ) );
74
75          }
76
77          public String rTrim()
78          {
79              int i = string.length() - 1;
80              boolean bNonSpaceFound = false;
81              char ch;
82
83              while( !bNonSpaceFound && i >= 0 )
84              {
85                  if( ( ch = string.charAt( i )) != ' ' )
86                      bNonSpaceFound = true;
87                  else i--;
88              }
89
90              return( string.substring( 0, i + 1 ) );
91
92          }
93
94          public char[] toPaddedCharArray(int iLength)
95          {
96              char result[] = new char[iLength];
97              string.getChars( 0, string.length(), result, 0 );
98
99              int len = string.length() - 1;
100             for( int i=len; i<iLength; i++ ) result[i] = ' ';
101
102             return( result );
103
104          }
105
106         public String capitalizeWords()
107         {
108             String strNew = new String();
109             boolean bNewWord = true;
110             char ch;
111
112             for( int i=0; i<string.length(); i++ )
113             {
114                 ch = string.charAt( i );
115                 if( ch == ' ' )
116                 {
```

```
117                    bNewWord = true;
118                }
119                else if( Character.isLetter( ch ) )
120                {
121                    if( bNewWord )
122                    {
123                        ch = Character.toUpperCase( ch );
124                        bNewWord = false;
125                    }
126                }
127                strNew += ch;
128            }
129
130            return( strNew );
131
132        }
133    }
134
135 }
```

OUTPUT Figure 18.3 shows the result of running the applet with the new formatting methods in place.

18

FIGURE 18.3

The SmartString *class adds formatting methods.*

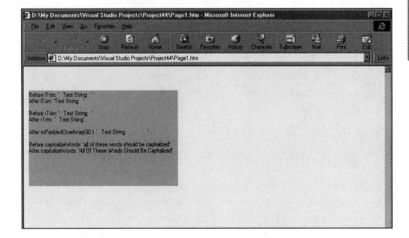

ANALYSIS Line 10 creates a FontMetrics object so that you'll know how big the characters are in the current font. That way, you can tell where you need to draw the strings in your paint() method.

In the paint() method at lines 13–36, you declare a test string and then call your new methods (which are discussed in the next step). After you call each of the new methods, you display the results below the original string.

Toward the end of the source code at lines 38–133, you can see the definition for the SmartString class. This is the SmartString class that implements all of your new methods.

Because you cannot extend from the String class and therefore inherit the String's constructors, you must cut-and-paste one. An example of this is shown in the code at lines 53–58.

The String class implements a trim() method that trims whitespace from both ends of the string and returns the resulting string. However, at many times you will want to trim only one side or the other. Hence, the first methods are lTrim() (line 60) and rTrim() (line 77). These methods return a string with the whitespace trimmed from the left and right sides.

Another important formatting method that is needed is a method to pad a character array with blanks, or spaces. The String class has a method called toCharArray() at lines 94–104, which allocates an array the same size as the string and sets its value to that of the string. This method, however, does not allow you to decide the array's size. Therefore, you must implement an enhancement to the toCharArray() method. This method, called toPaddedCharArray(), takes as its only parameter the size of the array you want allocated. You then call String.getChars() to copy the contents into the new array and pad it out with spaces. When completed, this is another new method to put into your toolkit.

The last formatting method you add is a method for converting all words to uppercase. Both the String class and the Character class have an upperCase() method, but these methods convert the entire string or character, respectively, to uppercase. There are certainly times when you want to capitalize all the words in a string. The preceding capitalizeWords() method does just that.

Extracting Fields from a String

If you have worked with strings in any language, you have no doubt run into the problem of the language not providing support for extracting fields from a string. For example, if you read in a file that is comma-delimited, such as files exported by Microsoft Excel, you always have to manually parse each line to get the fields you want. The first variation of your SmartString applet will include writing the method to support this functionality. Actually, you are going to overload the method so that the caller can pass any delimiter. If a delimiter is not passed, the method assumes that a comma is to be used. The following getFields() methods provide this functionality:

```
public Vector getFields(String s, char chDelimiter)
    {
        Vector v = new Vector();
```

```
        char c;
        String s2 = new String();
        for( int i=0; i<s.length(); i++ )
        {
            if( ( c = s.charAt( i )) == ',' )
            {
                v.addElement( s2 );
                s2 = "";
            }
            else
            {
                s2 += c;
            }
        }

    if( s2 != "" ) v.addElement( s2 );

    return( v );
    }

    public Vector getFields( String s )
    {
        return( getFields( s, ',' ) );
    }
```

This method basically walks through the passed string; then when it finds a comma, it
adds the string it has accumulated since the last comma to a Vector object as a new element. That way, the caller has an easy way of retrieving the comma-delimited fields. Just
plug this method into your SmartString class and you never have to worry about
comma-delimited strings again.

When this method returns the Vector object, it can be enumerated and used as shown
here:

```
str = new SmartString( "one,two,three" );
Vector v = m.getFields(str);
for( Enumeration e=v.elements(); e.hasMoreElements(); )
{
    String s = e.nextElement();
    // use the string s
}
```

Formatting Currency

Another problem every programmer has probably faced is formatting currency. No one,
especially in a GUI environment, wants to see an amount displayed as 352768373.
Therefore, at every job, you wind up writing a conversion method or function to display
currency. The following variation shows you how to write a conversion function for currency that you'll always have available for your Java applets:

```
public static String toCurrency( long lAmount )
{
    String strBefore = String.valueOf( lAmount );
    String strCurrency = new String();

    int iIndex = 0;
    for( int i=strBefore.length(); i>0; i-- )
    {
        if( 3 == iIndex )
        {
            strCurrency = "," + strCurrency;
            iIndex = 0;
        }
        strCurrency = strBefore.charAt( i - 1 ) + strCurrency;
        iIndex++;
    }

    return( strCurrency );

}

public static String toCurrency( long lAmount, boolean
bIncludeCurrencySymbol )
{

    return( ( SmartString.toCurrency( lAmount, true, '$' ) ) );

}

public static String toCurrency( long lAmount, boolean
bIncludeCurrencySymbol, char hCurrencySymbol )
{

    return( chCurrencySymbol + SmartString.toCurrency( lAmount ) ) ;

}
```

As you can see, these methods take a variable of type `long` and, after converting it to a `String` object, iterate through the string's value from right to left one character at a time. For every character in the unformatted string, the method sets the new formatted string to that character plus what the new formatted string has accumulated thus far. Every time it passes three characters, it prepends a comma to the new string. There are a couple of overloaded methods here for prepending a currency symbol to the final result. You can even specify a different currency symbol in one of the method implementations.

Retrieving Pairs of Values from a String

The last variation demonstrates a twist on the first variation. This time, however, instead of retrieving comma-delimited fields, you do something just a little more complex. This time, you have a list of comma-delimited points (x and y coordinates) passed to you:

```java
public Vector getPoints( String s )
{
    Vector v = new Vector();

    char c;
    String s2 = new String();
    String sx = new String();
    String sy = new String();
    boolean bHaveX = false;
    boolean bHaveY = false;

    for( int i=0; i<s.length(); i++ )
    {
        if( ( c = s.charAt( i ) ) == ',' )
        {
            if( !bHaveX )
            {
                sx = s2;
                s2 = "";
                bHaveX = true;
            }
            else // y coordinate
            {
                sy = s2;
                s2 = "";
                bHaveY = true;

                Integer Ix = Integer.valueOf( sx );
                int ix = Ix.intValue();

                Integer Iy = Integer.valueOf( sy );
                int iy = Iy.intValue();

                Point p = new Point( ix, iy );
                v.addElement( p );

                sx = "";
                sy = "";
                bHaveX = false;
                bHaveY = false;
            }
```

18

```
        }
        else
        {
            s2 += c;
        }
    }

    if( bHaveX && ( s2 != "" ) )
    {
        Integer Ix = Integer.valueOf( sx );
        int ix = Ix.intValue();

        Integer Iy = Integer.valueOf( s2 );
        int iy = Iy.intValue();

        Point p = new Point( ix, iy );
        v.addElement( p );
    }

    return( v );

}
```

In the preceding method, the technique used iterates through the string one character at a time looking for a comma. Until a comma is found, a string (s2) is formed. When a comma is found, the method checks a boolean flag to see whether an x coordinate exists. If it doesn't, the method sets the string representation of the x coordinate (sx) equal to the string so far (s2) and sets the flag on to indicate that you now have an x coordinate. Also, it empties the string that holds the current coordinate value (s2) and continues walking the string until it finds another comma. Then, when the method finds the second comma, it knows that an x coordinate has already been found by examining the boolean flag. Therefore, the method creates the y coordinate from the string (s2) that has been building during the search for the second comma. The method calls the Integer.valueOf() and Integer.intValue() methods to get the integer representation of the string coordinates (sx and sy). After the method has those integers, it creates a Point object and adds the element to the vector via the Vector.addElement() method.

To use these Point objects, the caller has only to do the following. Note the casting of the Vector element to a Point object:

```
SmartString sPoints = new SmartString( "5,5,10,10,15,15,20,20" );
Vector v = m.getPoints( sPoints );
for( Enumeration e=v.elements();  e.hasMoreElements(); )
{
    Point p = (Point)e.nextElement();
    // Use Point p
}
```

Summary

As you have seen, the String class is an important part of the Java language. However, there certainly is room for enhancement in terms of adding more functionality. One of the biggest benefits of any object-oriented language is extending and enhancing existing code to address your specific needs. By creating your own SmartString class in this chapter, you have taken a big step toward building your own library of reusable classes. You now have your own string class you can use in just about any Java applet or application.

Q&A

Q Why would you want to add functionality to the String class? Doesn't it already do everything?

A As with most classes that are part of programming languages, the String class is a generic class that does a lot. But if have specific needs for your own programming, adding to the String class will be a good idea. That way, you can take advantage of the additional functionality in programs you write later.

Q Can the String class be extended?

A No, it's declared as final and can't be extended. You can, however, create a class that contains an instance of the String class. Methods in your new class must match methods in the String class. In this way, you can get a lot of the same results you would if you extended the String class.

Q My applet has an HTML parameter that's a string which specifies a number the applet needs. I've made the applet available to others who are using it on their Web site. Several of them have told me that when they forget to include the HTML parameter, the applet crashes. Why is this?

A If the applet is looking for an HTML parameter and one hasn't been given, the getParameter() method will return a null string. Then, when you use the Integer.parseInt() method on a null string, the applet will throw an exception. There are two suggestions for avoiding this situation: (1) set a default value in your strings in case there is no HTML parameter, and (2) catch exceptions when you use methods such as Integer.parseInt().

Q I need some string manipulation methods that aren't part of the String class. Should I create a new class?

18

A Possibly. Here's how you decide: If this code is specialized and won't be reused in other programs or other places in the program, don't create a new class—just add the methods you need and use them. If the methods you're going to need can be used in many instances in this program and other programs in the future, then by all means create a new and reusable class.

Review Exercises

1. Create an applet and then instantiate three different `String` classes with different text in each one. Create a fourth `String` object and add all three `Strings` together to get the fourth.

2. Create a program that takes as input from users a text string (use a `TextField` control). Add a `TextArea` control that's large enough to display 200–300 characters. Keep a global `String` object that starts off empty. Every time users enter another string, append it to the global string and then reset the `TextArea` so that it shows the entire string.

3. Write a class that contains a `String` class within as a member variable. Add two methods that add additional functionality to your class. I'd suggest a method that removes all blank spaces and replaces them with a "." character as one of the methods.

DAY 19

Stream I/O

Today you'll learn about stream input/output. When data comes into your application from an outside source or is sent out from your application, that sequence of data is referred to as a data stream. The java.io package contains over 15 classes to support the processing of streams in your applet or application, not to mention three interfaces. The data-stream processing classes are broken into two main categories: input and output. Each of these categories is based in an abstract class (`InputStream` or `OutputStream`) from which the other more specialized classes are extended.

You'll be introduced to the input and output stream classes and subclasses, and the Java interfaces used for I/O processing. The demo programs walk you through reading a file and displaying its contents, as well as copying files.

Today you'll learn

- About input data streams.
- About output data streams.
- About the different stream interfaces.
- How to retrieve and display a file from the Web.

Input Stream Classes

The InputStream class is the base class (or superclass) for all classes that handle input streams. This class is an abstract class and therefore cannot be instantiated. It implements all of the most basic methods that input streams need, such as close(), mark(), and skip().To extend your class from this class, you have to implement the read() method. Because there are several classes that are already extended from this base class, it is highly unlikely that you would ever need to extend directly from this class. In fact, you could use one of the extended classes that are already in place.

Within the InputStream hierarchy are two categories of subclasses. The different classes that are extended from the InputStream class are usually differentiated by the source of the data or by the manner in which the data is presented.

The two main sources of a data stream are files and communications. The classes that support these two types of input streams are as follows:

- FileInputStream   Represents a data stream that is read from a File or from a FileDescriptor.

- PipedInputStream   Represents a data stream that is read from the receiving end of a communications connection.

The java.io package implements the following input stream classes, differentiated by how the data is processed or the manner in which it appears:

- ByteArrayInputStream   Represents data that is supplied in an array of bytes.

- StringBufferInputStream   Represents data that is supplied in a string. Its constructor enables you to pass it a String object from which the data will be read.

Two other major classes are extended from InputStream. One is the SequenceInputStream class, which enables you to specify that you are accepting input from multiple input sources at the same time. It works by calling its constructor with an enumeration of the streams that you want processed. Each stream is read serially until the data streams have been exhausted. The benefit of this class is that it enables you to treat the group of streams as though you were reading from a single input stream. When you finish reading from one stream, the next stream is read automatically.

The second additional class is the class you probably will use the most in your applets: FilterInputStream. Actually, this class is a superclass of all the filter input streams. You use this class, or one of its subclasses, on top of one of the input streams described previously. By adding more functionality, these classes usually make it much easier to work with input streams.

For example, suppose you want to read data from a file. You could instantiate a `FileInputStream` object and attempt to read the data that way. But the problem is that the `FileInputStream.read()` methods read a stream of data without any knowledge of the type of data that they are reading. Therefore, after you have read the data in, it is up to you to parse this data and understand exactly what type of data you have.

One of the subclasses of the `FilterInputStream` is the `DataInputStream` class. It has methods specifically for reading data and then converting it into certain types of data. The `DataInputStream` class implements methods such as `readLong()`, `readByte()`, and `readDouble()`, so that you don't have to manually convert the data after it is read into a generic byte buffer by calling the appropriate conversion methods for the specific data type. For example, all you have to do for this power and flexibility is

1. Create a `FileInputStream` object specifying the name of the file to be used.

2. Create a `DataInputStream` object specifying the underlying data stream (in this case our newly created `FileInputStream` object).

3. Call the appropriate `DataInputStream.read()` methods to read in the data.

That's it: a perfect example of how the Java stream classes make your life (programming life, anyway) easier. Later, when you see the demo programs, you'll see this knowledge put to use and see real results.

The following four classes are extended from the `FilterInputStream` class:

- `BufferedInputStream`   This class enables you to read data from an underlying stream without having to incur the overhead of causing I/O from the underlying data source. This is because the data is read by blocks into a buffer and your subsequent `read()` calls the data from the buffer.

- `DataInputStream`   As mentioned earlier, this class is handy for reading primitive data types from an underlying input source in a manner that is more convenient for your applet.

- `LineNumberInputStream`   This class enables you to read data in with an associated line number. The class keeps track of the line number so you don't have to write code to do so. When you need to have the line number, you simply call the `getLineNumber()` method. You also can set the line number with the `setLineNumber()` method. A line is defined as a sequence of characters that ends with a carriage return character; the newline character; or a carriage return *and* newline character. If you do not call the `setLineNumber()` method, the numbering automatically starts at zero.

19

- `PushbackInputStream`   This class enables you to push back a character that you have already read. This is useful when, for example, you are reading a delimited sequence of characters and after you reach the delimiter you want to go back, or push back one character.

Output Stream Classes

You now need to take a look at the classes and methods that support data output streams. The `OutputStream` class is the base class (or superclass) for all classes that handle output streams. This class is an abstract class and, therefore, cannot be instantiated. It implements all of the most basic methods that output streams would need, such as `close()` and `flush()`. To extend your class from this class, you would have to implement the `write()` method. Because there are several classes that are already extended from this base class, it's unlikely that you would need to extend directly from this class. In fact, you could use one of the extended classes that are already in place.

Within the `OutputStream` hierarchy there are two categories of subclasses. The different classes that are extended from `OutputStream` are usually differentiated by the physical destination of the data (file or communications pipe) or by the manner in which the data is formatted.

The two main destinations of an output data stream are files and communications pipes. The classes that support these two types of output streams are as follows:

- `FileOutputStream`   Represents a data stream that is written to a File or to a `FileDescriptor`.
- `PipedOutputStream`   Represents a data stream that is written to the sending end of a communications connection.

The java.io package implements only the following output stream class. Although the input stream classes included a class called `StringBufferInputStream`, unfortunately, the output stream classes do not have an equivalent class, but instead only support `ByteArrayInputStream`, which represents data that is supplied in a array of bytes.

As is the case with the `FilterInputStream` class, the class you probably will use most often in your applets that output data is the `FilterOutputStream` class. Actually, this class is a superclass of all the filter output streams. You use this class or one of its subclasses on top of one of the output streams described earlier. By adding more functionality, these classes usually make it much easier to work with output streams. For example, suppose you want to write data to a file. You could instantiate a `FileOutputStream` object and attempt to write the data using its `write()` method. However, the problem with that is the `FileOutputStream.write()` methods take an array of bytes as a parameter. Typically, in your applet you are not going to be processing data in such an anonymous, generic manner. You will probably have numbers or strings that you want to write to a file or some other destination. This requires that you massage, or convert your data from its format into a byte array. With some of the `FilterOutputStream` subclasses, you do not have to go through this step and can instead write the data out in the format in which it exists in your applet.

The following list describes the three classes that are extended from the `FilterInputStream` class:

- `BufferedOutputStream` This class enables you to write data to an underlying output stream without having to incur the overhead of causing I/O with the underlying data destination on every write because the data is written by blocks into a buffer. It is not written directly to the destination. The buffer is îflushedî or written out when the buffer is full, when you call the `flush()` method, or when you close the stream.

- `DataOutputStream` This is the class mentioned earlier that makes it easier to write data out to the output data stream without having to convert it into a byte array.

- `PrintStream` This class enables you to print types other than bytes or byte arrays. In fact, the `System.in` and `System.out` objects that enable you to print out information are actually `PrintStream` objects.

Stream Interfaces

In addition to the stream I/O classes described in the preceding two sections, java.io declares three interfaces to help you implement streams in your Java applets.

Recall the discussion earlier about the tremendous benefits that the `DataInputStream` and `DataOutputStream` classes afford you because they can respectively read and write primitive data types without forcing you to use bytes or byte arrays. They accomplish this by implementing the `DataInput` and `DataOutput` interfaces. Also recall that an interface is a collection of declared (but undefined) methods that enable a class to extend its functionality. It is actually the `DataInput` and `DataOutput` interfaces that declare the methods such as `readLong()`, `readChar()`, `writeLong()`, and `writeChar()`.

19

The only part of the java.io package that hasn't been discussed here is the FilenameFilter interface. This interface is implemented by classes that want to filter filenames. For example, the File.list() method uses this interface to filter valid filenames. The only method that the FilenameFilter interface declares is accept(), which returns a Boolean value that indicates whether the filename is valid.

The following programs teach you how to use the input and output stream classes in your applets to facilitate receiving and sending data.

Reading a File and Displaying the File's Contents

INPUT   The first program involves reading a local file in from disk (using the FileInputStream and DataInputStream classes) and displaying that file's contents on a Web page within a browser. This gives you a chance to see how to use some of the InputStream subclasses and their methods to process file input. The source code is shown in Listing 19.1.

LISTING 19.1   THIS PROGRAM LOADS AND DISPLAYS A FILE

```
1   import java.awt.*;
2   import java.applet.*;
3   import java.awt.event.*;
4   import java.io.IOException;
5   import java.io.FileInputStream;
6   import java.io.DataInputStream;
7
8    public class DisplayFile extends Applet implements Runnable
9    {
10
11      protected Label m_lblFileName =
12          new Label( "File to open:" );
13      protected TextField m_txtFileName =
14          new TextField( 50 );
15      protected Button m_btnDisplayFile =
16          new Button( "Display File" );
17      protected TextArea m_taFileContents =
18          new TextArea( 30, 50 );
19
20      Thread m_thread = null;
21      DisplayFile m_this = this;
22
23      public void init()
24      {
25          MyListener Listener = new MyListener();
26          m_txtFileName.addActionListener( Listener );
```

```
27          m_btnDisplayFile.addActionListener( Listener );
28          add( m_lblFileName );
29          add( m_txtFileName );
30          add( m_btnDisplayFile );
31          add( m_taFileContents );
32       }
33
34       public void threadComplete(boolean bSuccess)
35       {
36          // Don't erase an error msg if thread failed
37          if( bSuccess == true )
38             showStatus( "" );
39          m_thread = null;
40       }
41
42       public void start()
43       {
44       }
45
46       public void stop()
47       {
48       }
49
50       public void run()
51       {
52          try
53          {
54             String strFileContents =
55                readFile( m_thread.getName() );
56             m_taFileContents.setText( strFileContents.toString() );
57             threadComplete( true );
58          }
59          catch( IOException e )
60          {
61             showStatus( e.toString() );
62             stop();
63             threadComplete( false );
64          }
65
66       }
67
68       public String readFile( String strFileName )
69          throws IOException
70       {
71          String strBuffer = new String();
72
73          try
74          {:
75             FileInputStream inputFile =
76                new FileInputStream( strFileName );
```

continues

19

LISTING 19.1 CONTINUED

```
77                    DataInputStream inputData =
78                        new DataInputStream(inputFile);
79
80                    byte data[] = new byte[500];
81                    int nBytesRead;
82
83                    while( ( nBytesRead = inputData.read( data ) ) != -1 )
84                    {
85                        strBuffer = strBuffer + new String
                         ➥( data, 0, nBytesRead );
86                    }
87
88                    inputData.close();
89                }
90            catch( IOException e )
91            {
92                throw( e );
93            }
94
95            return( strBuffer );
96        }
97
98        public class MyListener implements ActionListener
99        {
100            public void actionPerformed( ActionEvent ae )
101            {
102                if( ae.getSource() == m_btnDisplayFile ¦¦
103                    ae.getSource() == m_txtFileName )
104                {
105                    showStatus( "" );
106                    m_taFileContents.setText( "" );
107
108                    if( m_thread == null )
109                    {
110                        String strFileName = m_txtFileName.getText();
111                        if( strFileName.length() > 0 )
112                        {
113                            m_thread = new Thread( m_this, strFileName );
114
115                            m_txtFileName.setText( "" );
116                            showStatus( "Request '" + strFileName +
                             ➥ "' submitted." );
117
118                            m_thread.start();
119                        }
120                        else
121                        {
122                            showStatus( "You must enter a
                             ➥file name before you "
```

```
123                              + "can attempt to display its contents.");
124                          }
125
126                      }
127                      else
128                      {
129                          showStatus( "Sorry - only one request
      ➥at a time allowed!!!");
130                      }
131
132                  }
133              }
134          }
135
136 }
```

OUTPUT   Figure 19.1 shows you one possible result of running this applet. A local copy of
c:\autoexec.bat is used in the example.

FIGURE 19.1

*Results of the
DisplayFile program.
The file
c:\autoexec.bat was
used in the example.*

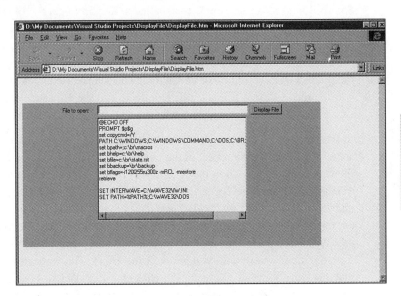

19

ANALYSIS   Lines 1–6 declare the imports for the stream classes that the program uses. The
user interface controls are declared in lines 11–18. Notice that in line 20, a thread
object is declared and initialized. When the thread is null, we know that it isn't running.
Several things happen in the init() method. A listener is instantiated and then added to
the TextField and Button controls in lines 25–27. The components are added to the
container with the add() method at lines 28–31.

A class is declared at line 98 that implements the ActionListener interface. Its actionPerformed() method is called when an action occurs within one of your applet's controls. At the beginning of your applet, a TextField control and a Button control were created. If the user presses Enter while in that TextField control or clicks on that Button control, you want to take the value that is in the TextField (at line 110) and create a thread using that value as the thread's name at line 113. The Thread.start() method is then called at line 118. The calling of the Thread.start() method results in the Applet.run() method being called. The Applet.run() method can be seen at lines 50–66.

The threadComplete() method, which begins at line 34, is called by the run() method at line 63 when the thread completes. The method checks a Boolean flag so that it won't change the status bar in case the function that handled the error displayed the error text in the status bar.

Take a look at the run() method (lines 50–66). Because the filename used is the thread's name, the filename can be acquired with the Thread.getName() method as seen in line 55. The readFile() method is then called at line 55 to get the file's contents. Notice the try block at lines 52–58. A try block is needed because the readFile() method was defined as being capable of throwing an I/O exception. Therefore, any code that calls this method must reside in a try block. The readFile() method will return the contents of the file in a String object. In line 56, you can see the TextArea is set to the string that was returned. All that is left at this point is to call the threadComplete() method to indicate a successful completion to the thread.

In this first stream program, you can see a couple of classes at work. First, you instantiate a FileInputStream object in the readFile() method at lines 75 and 76 using the filename that was passed in the form of String object. After you have your FileInputStream object, you instantiate a DataInputStream object as seen in lines 77 and 78 to sit on top of that underlying data stream. As was discussed earlier in the chapter, this enables you to call some of the methods that are specific to dealing with known data types. You then enter a while loop and use the read() method to read all of the data from the input stream until you get the value of -1. This indicates that the file is done or that there was some sort of error. For each chunk of data you read, you append it as shown in line 85 to your buffer that you will return to the caller. If, for some reason, you encounter an IO exception, such as at lines 90–93, you catch it and throw it back to the caller who, because you want to keep this method as generic as possible, will be in a better position to handle an exception than you are.

Copying Files

In the second program, you are shown how to allow the user to specify a file to copy. You will use the original filename and copy the file to a file called output.dat. This program demonstrates the use of both the input stream and output stream classes and methods in a realistic manner. You will use buffered I/O just as you would in a real applet, and when you finish, you will have a method that copies any type of local file (binary or text). The source code is shown in Listing 19.2.

INPUT **LISTING 19.2** THIS PROGRAM COPIES FILES TO A FILE NAMED output.dat

```
1    import java.applet.*;
2    import java.awt.*;
3    import java.awt.event.*;
4    import java.io.IOException;
5    import java.io.FileInputStream;
6    import java.io.BufferedInputStream;
7    import java.io.FileOutputStream;
8    import java.io.BufferedOutputStream;
9
10   public class CopyFile extends Applet implements Runnable
11   {
12       protected Label m_lblInputFileName =
13           new Label( "File to copy:" );
14       protected TextField m_txtInputFileName =
15           new TextField( 50 );
16       protected Button m_btnCopyFile =
17           new Button( "Start File" );
18
19       Thread m_thread = null;
20       CopyFile m_this = this;
21
22       public void init()
23       {
24           MyListener Listener = new MyListener();
25           m_txtInputFileName.addActionListener( Listener );
26           m_btnCopyFile.addActionListener( Listener );
27           add( m_lblInputFileName );
28           add( m_txtInputFileName );
29           add( m_btnCopyFile );
30       }
31
32       public class MyListener implements ActionListener
33       {
34           public void actionPerformed( ActionEvent ae )
35           {
36               if( ae.getSource() == m_btnCopyFile ||
37                   ae.getSource() == m_txtInputFileName )
```

continues

19

LISTING 19.2 CONTINUED

```
38                 {
39                     showStatus("");
40
41                     if( m_thread == null )
42                     {
43                         String strInputFileName =
44                             m_txtInputFileName.getText();
45                         if( strInputFileName.length() > 0 )
46                         {
47                             m_thread = new Thread( m_this,
                               ➡strInputFileName );
48                             m_txtInputFileName.setText( "" );
49                             showStatus( "Request '" +
                               ➡strInputFileName + "' submitted." );
50                             m_thread.start();
51                         }
52                         else
53                         {
54                             showStatus( "You must enter a
                               ➡file name before you "
55                                 + "can attempt to copy it." );
56                         }
57                     }
58                     else
59                     {
60                         showStatus( "Sorry - only one request
                           ➡at a time allowed!!!" );
61                     }
62                 }
63             }
64         }
65
66     public void start()
67     {
68     }
69
70     public void stop()
71     {
72     }
73
74     public void threadComplete( boolean bSuccess )
75     {
76         if( bSuccess == true )
77             showStatus( m_thread.getName() + " successfully copied" );
78         m_thread = null;
79     }
80
81     public void run()
82     {
```

```
83          try
84          {
85              copyFile( m_thread.getName() );
86              threadComplete( true );
87          }
88          catch( IOException e )
89          {
90              showStatus( e.toString() );
91              stop();
92              threadComplete( false );
93          }
94      }
95
96      public void copyFile( String strInputFile )
97          throws IOException
98      {
99          try
100         {
101             FileInputStream inputFile =
102                 new FileInputStream( strInputFile );
103             BufferedInputStream is =
104                 new BufferedInputStream( inputFile );
105
106             String strOutputFile = new String( "c:\\output.dat" );
107             FileOutputStream outputFile =
108                 new FileOutputStream( strOutputFile );
109             BufferedOutputStream os =
110                 new BufferedOutputStream( outputFile );
111
112             int i;
113             while( ( i = is.read() ) != -1 )
114             {
115                 os.write( i );
116             }
117
118             is.close();
119             os.close();
120         }
121         catch( IOException e )
122         {
123             throw( e );
124         }
125     }
126 }
```

OUTPUT   Figure 19.2 shows you one possible result of running this applet. The file named
c:\testfile.dat was used in the example.

FIGURE 19.2

This program copies a file.

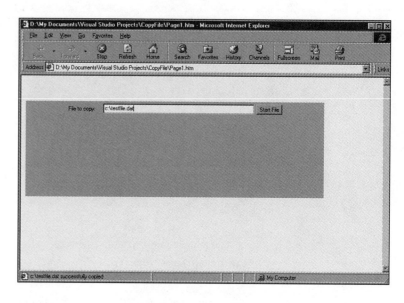

ANALYSIS Lines 1–8 declare the imports for the stream classes that are used. In lines 12–17 you can see the user-interface controls declared and initialized. A Thread class is declared and set to null in line 19. Interestingly, we store a copy of the applet's this pointer in line 20, which is used later when the Thread is created.

The init() method does several things. First, it instantiates the class that extends the ActionListener interface. This object is then added to the Button and TextField objects so that they'll know where to send event messages. The last thing the init() method does is to add the components to the container using the add() method.

The declared class that implements the ActionListener interface begins at line 32. In it, you'll see the actionPerformed() method. This is called when an action occurs within one of your applet's controls. At the beginning of your applet, you declared a TextField control and a Button control. As in the first program, if the user presses Enter while in that TextField control or clicks that Button control, you want to take the value that is in the TextField and create a thread using that value as the thread's name (Lines 43–47). The Thread.start() method is then called at line 50. The calling of the Thread.start() method results in the Applet.run() method being called.

The threadComplete() method can be found at lines 74–79 and is called by the run() method when the thread completes. The threadComplete() method checks a Boolean flag to make sure that the run() method completed successfully. If run() completes successfully, the flag is set to true and a success message is displayed in the status bar by threadComplete(). If run() is not successful, the flag is set to false and threadComplete() does nothing. This prevents threadComplete() from overwriting any error message that was displayed in the status bar by the run() method.

You can see the thread's run() method from lines 81–94. Because the filename was used as the thread's name, the filename can be acquired with the Thread.getName() method as seen at line 85. The copyFile() method is then called to copy the file's contents from the specified input file to a file named output.dat. Notice the try block at lines 83–87. A try block is needed because the copyFile() method was defined as being capable of throwing an I/O exception. Therefore, any code that calls this method must reside in a try block. When the copyFile() method returns, all that is left at that point is to call the threadComplete() method to indicate a successful completion to the thread.

As you can see, the copyFile() method instantiates a FileInputStream based on the string that the user entered as the input filename. A BufferedInputStream object is then created to use with the underlying data stream. After the declaration of the necessary objects for the input of the data, objects for the output of your data are then created. You first create an object of type FileOutputStream. The output filename is hard-coded here for simplicity, but obviously you can get this name from anywhere you like. For example, you can add controls to the dialog box to allow the user to enter the output filename or you could use the input filename as the basis for the output filename. An example of the latter would be to create the output filename by adding the extension .BAK to the input filename. After creating the FileOutputStream, a BufferedOutputStream object is created.

When all of the stream objects are in place, a While loop is used to read all of the data from the BufferedOutputStream object and write it to the BufferedInputStream object until there is no more data left to read from the input stream. After the data has been copied, the close() methods for the BufferedInputStream and the BufferedOutputStream objects are called. When you call the FilterInputStream.close() method or FilterOutputStream.close() method (or for any of their subclasses), they will automatically call the close() method of the underlying data stream's class. Another thing to realize is that when using the BufferedOutputStream, the data is being cached in a buffer. The data is written automatically to the underlying data stream's destination when one of the following occurs: the buffer is full, the stream is closed, or the flush() method is explicitly called.

19

Summary

As you have seen, the stream I/O classes make reading and writing data in Java applets and applications extremely easy. The developers at Sun obviously spent a lot of time creating many classes to satisfy a multitude of needs that developers would encounter when dealing with data streams. The only problem with that foresight is that sometimes there are so many options that you are not sure of which one is best for your specific purpose. This chapter should have helped you learn not only how to use the different stream classes, but when to use them.

Q&A

Q What are the two categories of input and output?

A There are two categories of input and output and they're based on the `InputStream` and `OutputStream` classes. Other higher level classes are extended from these, and those are the ones you'll want to use.

Q How does Visual J++ help me implement streams in my programs?

A The benefits that the `DataInputStream` and `DataOutputStream` classes afford is that they can respectively read and write primitive data types without forcing you to use bytes or byte arrays. They accomplish this by implementing the `DataInput` and `DataOutput` interfaces. Also recall that an interface is a collection of declared (but undefined) methods that enable a class to extend its functionality. It is actually the `DataInput` and `DataOutput` interfaces that declare the methods such as `readLong()`, `readChar()`, `writeLong()`, and `writeChar()`.

Exercises

1. Create an applet. Write a method that loads a file and puts it into a `TextArea` object that's been added to the applet component. After it's working successfully, try to load a file that doesn't exist. Does your program handle the error? If not, make sure it does.

2. Load a file and save a copy of it to another file. Make sure you're handling all errors.

DAY 20

ActiveX

Today you'll learn about ActiveX controls—how to use them in your Visual J++ program and how to write them for other programs to use. Although the ActiveX technology is complex, Visual J++ makes it a breeze to use. You won't have to worry about all of the nitty-gritty technical stuff; just drag a control onto your form and use it!

Today, you'll learn

- The basics of the ActiveX technology.
- How to use the ActiveX controls that are supplied with Visual J++.
- How to create wrappers for other controls.
- How to find other controls to use.

When you're done with today's lesson, you'll know enough about ActiveX to get started.

What is ActiveX?

If you ever cracked open an ActiveX programming manual and started to read, you probably had a humbling experience. ActiveX and the Component Object

Model (COM) system upon which it's built is a complex beast—downright mind boggling. Expert programmers take a year or more to wade through all the documentation and figure out how to put the concepts to work, but Visual J++ makes this unnecessary.

Object Linking and Embedding

Object Linking and Embedding (OLE) is a system that enables applications to more easily share data in two ways: data linking and data embedding. The application that holds the linked or embedded data is called a *container* application, whereas the application that supplies editing services for the linked or embedded data is called the *server* application. (There's nothing to stop an application from being both a container and a server.) When a data set is linked into a document, the document maintains a connection to the data set as part of the document. However, the linked data stays in its own file as a discrete object. Because the document maintains only a link to the data set, the document stays up-to-date as the data set changes.

When a data set is embedded into a document, the document no longer maintains a connection with the data set's file. Instead, the data set is actually copied into the document. Because there is no longer a connection between the containing document and the original data set, when the data set changes, the document doesn't reflect the changes. To update the embedded data, the user would have to load the document and change the data manually.

Whether a document links or embeds a data set, the data can be edited easily by the application that created the data. Usually, the user double-clicks the linked or embedded item, which causes the editing application to appear in its own window, or if it supports in-place editing, the editor can actually merge its toolbars and menus with the application that contains the linked or embedded data.

Version 1.0 of OLE was a step in the right direction, but lacked many features that would enable applications to take a second seat to documents. OLE 2.0 extends OLE's abilities to include not only data sharing between applications, but also functionality sharing between applications. By creating an application as a set of programmable objects (also called OLE components), applications can call upon each other for the capabilities they need, further generalizing the concept of an application.

For example, if a text-editing application needs to spell-check a document, it doesn't necessarily need to have its own spell checker. Instead, it can call upon a spell-checker object that some other application has already registered with the system.

The process of controlling another application's programmable objects is called OLE automation. So, you could also call the word processor an automation server and the text editor an automation client. Whatever terminology you want to use, programmable objects blur the boundaries between one application and another, making all the applications in the system seem to work together.

As you can see, OLE automation provides advantages to application users and developers. Users can take full advantage of the capabilities represented by all applications installed in the system, without having to know where those capabilities originate. The user can concentrate on the document and let the applications take care of themselves.

Developers, on the other hand, must face a double-edged sword. Although they no longer need to reinvent software that's been developed and installed on the user's system, they must now support OLE, which adds another layer of complexity to the development process. Luckily, as you'll see, Visual C++ developers can let Microsoft Foundation Classes (MFC) handle most of the intricacies of developing OLE applications.

OLE 2.0 also introduced the concept of OLE *controls*, programmable objects that can be embedded into an application and become an integral part of the application in much the same way an embedded document becomes a part of the containing document. Originally, OLE controls were conceived as a way to create buttons, sliders, progress indicators, and other types of custom controls. (They are called OLE controls, after all.) However, the idea soon grew to include mini-applications that offer complex services to host applications. As you can imagine, this goes way beyond a custom button or slider, being more akin to a complete application than a lowly button.

Component Object Model

Component Object Model (COM) is the technology that provides the underpinnings of OLE. Put simply, COM is a specification for creating binary objects. These binary objects can communicate with each other, controlling functions and setting properties. In a nutshell, a binary object is like a program that loads into the system but is not necessarily visible on the screen. Dynamically Linked Libraries (DLLs) are a similar type of object, in that they contain functions that other modules in the system can call.

The COM specification is a set of rules that dictate how binary objects are created and managed. These rules define a method through which applications can query a binary object to discover the types of interfaces the object supports. Some of these interfaces are standard, whereas others are proprietary. In any case, by adhering to the specifications, objects can be accessed and manipulated by any OLE-capable application.

Luckily, if you're programming with Visual J++, you don't have to know much about COM, although it's always a good idea to have a little background on the technology you're using.

20

ActiveX

Several years ago, COM and OLE were the big programming buzzwords. Now, the word ActiveX is thrown around by programmers like celebrity names at a Hollywood party. When Microsoft recently turned its attention to the Internet, it occurred to the powers-that-be at the big "M" that there was no reason the Internet should not be treated as just another peripheral like a disk drive or CD-ROM drive. Why not make the Internet so accessible from the user's computer that it seemed to become part of the operating system? With this idea came the necessity of extending OLE 2.0 so that it encompassed not just the user's local system, but also any network to which the local system was connected. ActiveX was born.

ActiveX could have been called OLE 3.0, but the capabilities of OLE had gone so far beyond object linking and embedding that the original moniker was more confusing than descriptive. So Microsoft named this newly expanded technology ActiveX. Now, virtually everywhere the word OLE is used, the word ActiveX is substituted. For example, OLE components are now ActiveX components; OLE controls are now ActiveX controls, and OLE documents are now ActiveX documents.

All of these objects that share the word ActiveX in their names are more powerful than their old OLE counterparts, however. They are now objects that expand the original OLE concepts to the Web. ActiveX controls, for example, can be placed in Web pages and transmitted automatically to the browser that's viewing the Web page. ActiveX documents, too, are much more powerful than OLE documents. Not only can these objects be transmitted over the Web, ActiveX documents also tell the receiving browser how the document should be displayed. You can think of an ActiveX document as being a storage object for information that can be interpreted, displayed, and manipulated by a receiving application.

ActiveX Applications and Components

An ActiveX container is an application that contains linked or embedded data. Such an application must be able to display the linked or embedded data as well as enable the user to select, move, delete, and edit the data.

When Microsoft Word contains linked or embedded data, it's acting as an ActiveX container. Many Windows applications support ActiveX in this way.

Suppose we use Microsoft Word as a container application. The graphic embedded in the Word document could have been created with Microsoft Paint, which makes Paint the server application. To edit the embedded graphic, the user can double-click the item. The server then should respond in one of two ways: by opening the graphic in a separate editing window or by merging its user interface with Word's.

The server response depends on how the client and server were programmed. If the applications support in-place editing (recommended), ActiveX merges the server's toolbars and menus with the container application's. This enables the user to edit the item without switching windows or applications.

The user can edit the graphic as if the graphic were loaded into Paint. Because ActiveX makes all of Paint's tools available in the toolbar, adding the ellipses takes only seconds.

Just as you have containers and servers with object linking and embedding, so you have automation clients and automation servers with ActiveX automation. An automation-client application reaches out in the system to control a component of another application, called the automation server. Of course, the process isn't quite that simple. Both applications must be specially programmed to take advantage of ActiveX automation.

For example, an application that hasn't been programmed to be an automation client cannot access programmable objects made available by an automation server. Conversely, an application that hasn't been programmed as an automation server cannot share its functionality with other applications in the system, even if the other applications support ActiveX automation.

Creating automation servers means defining interfaces that provide access to properties and methods of the programmable objects supplied by the server. On the client side, when an application wants to access a programmable object, it must know how to obtain a reference to the object's interface, as well as how to manage the object's properties and call the object's methods. For example, reusing the spell-checker example, an application that wanted to take advantage of another application's spell checker (assuming that the spell checker is a programmable object) would acquire a reference to the spell checker's interface and call the spell checker's functions through that interface.

ActiveX controls are like mini-applications that you can embed into other applications. They take the idea of programmable components and separate those components from the server. That is, ActiveX components are complete entities unto themselves and do not need to be managed by a server application.

One of the biggest advantages of ActiveX controls is their capability to provide computing power to Web pages on the Internet. In this way, ActiveX controls can act much like Java applets. Virtually any type of program you can conceive of can be programmed as an ActiveX control and included in a Web page.

20

Using ActiveX Controls with Visual J++

We're going to get our hands dirty by using one of the controls that Visual J++ supplies. Visual J++ came with 15 ActiveX controls including a `Calendar` control, a `TreeView` control, and a `Sprite` control.

Let's start by creating a Visual J++ application named `UseActiveX1`. When the project is created, select the ActiveX Controls tab in the Toolbox window. The ActiveX controls that come with Visual J++ will appear as shown in Figure 20.1.

FIGURE 20.1

The Toolbox has an ActiveX Controls tab that contains controls that come with Visual J++.

Select the `Calendar` control in the Toolbox window. Place the control on your Form window so that it occupies the entire Form window as shown in Figure 20.2.

FIGURE 20.2

Here, we've placed a Calendar control in the Form window so that it occupies almost the entire window.

You should notice in Figure 20.2 that the Properties window contains the properties for the `Calendar` control. Of course, if you select any other control or item and the `Calendar` control isn't selected, the Properties window will no longer contain the properties for the `Calendar` control.

The properties that you'll most often modify are the showDateSelector, showDays, showHorizontalGrid, showTitle, and showVerticalGrid properties. They all default to a value of true, but you can change the appearance of the control by changing any of them to false. The odd thing about this control is that when you try to change these properties, a button with an ellipsis appears. This button then brings up a dialog box in which you can edit these properties as shown in Figure 20.3.

FIGURE 20.3

A dialog box appears in which you can set important Calendar *control properties.*

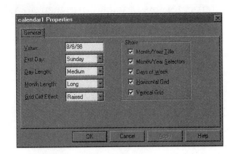

You'll also be interested in the events for ActiveX controls. Select the control so that its properties appear in the Properties window. You can then click the Events button (the one with the lightening icon) and the controlis events will appear in the Properties window.

To use the Calendar control, there are two approaches that you can take. You can use the Calendar control's methods to get the date information from somewhere in your program. The following example shows you how to get the day, month, and year from a Calendar control:

```
int nDay = calendar1.getDay();
int nMonth = calendar1.getMonth();
int nYear = calendar1.getYear();
```

You can also add an event handler for a Calendar control. The following event handler is the one I use most often:

```
private void calendar1_afterUpdate(Object source, Event e)
{
    // Handle the calendar event.
}
```

Installing the Controls

What if your friend just gave you an ActiveX control that does exactly what your program needs? How are you going to use it in your program? That's easy; all you have to do is create a COM wrapper for the control.

20

First things first. I'm going to be using two controls in this section. One was written in Visual Basic and the other in Visual C++. To use the Visual Basic control, you'll need to have the Visual Basic runtime support installed. To get these two controls, you can go to my Web site at www.infinitevision.net, go to the book section, and find the *Learn Visual J++ 6 in 21 Days* page. You'll see at the bottom of the page a link that lets you download the controls for Chapter 20.

After you download the controls for this chapter, unzip them to a directory on your hard drive.

Note

To unzip files, you'll need a copy of WinZip. It's a shareware program that manages .zip files. To obtain a copy, go to www.winzip.com and download it. If you use it regularly, you should register it because it's shareware.

With the two controls unzipped, you'll have to register them. The easiest way to do this is from a command prompt. Run a command prompt and log on to the directory into which the controls have been placed. For Windows 95 and Windows 98 systems type the following lines from the command prompt to register the controls.

 INPUT
```
c:\windows\system\regsvr32 RegistryControl.dll
c:\windows\system\regsvr32 OhmsCalculator.ocx
```

After you register each control, the regsvr32 program will display whether the registration was successful or whether an error was encountered as shown in Figure 20.4.

FIGURE 20.4

When you try to register an ActiveX control, the regsvr32 *program will show you the results.*

When you want to unregister a control, you can use the regsvr32 program. All you need to do is add the /u command line switch as follows:

INPUT   `c:\windows\system\regsvr32 /s RegistryControl.dll`

For Windows NT systems type the following lines from the command prompt to register the controls.

INPUT   `c:\winnt\system32\regsvr32 RegistryControl.dll`
`c:\winπystem32\regsvr32 OhmsCalculator.ocx`

A summary of the steps to get and register the controls follows:

1. Go to www.infinitevision.net.
2. Follow the Books page to the *Learn Visual J++ 6 in 21 Days* page.
3. Look at the bottom of the page and click on the `Download the controls for chapter 20` link.
4. Save the `Chap20Controls.zip` file (that downloads as a result of clicking on the link) to a directory on your hard drive.
5. Open a command prompt.
6. Use the regsvr32 program with each control as a command line parameter.

Now that the controls are on your hard drive and have been registered, you can create a COM wrapper for them and use them in your program. For this discussion, I created a new Visual J++ application named UseActiveX2. I suggest you do the same.

Select Add COM Wrapper from the Project menu. A dialog box will appear in which all of the ActiveX controls that are registered on the system are listed. Find the `OhmsCalculator` control and check it as shown in Figure 20.5.

FIGURE 20.5

Select the
`OhmsCalculator`
control from the list.

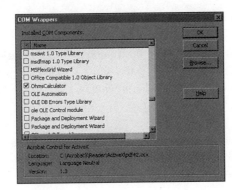

20

Using Other Controls

There are other controls that you can use in your Visual J++ programs. Many ActiveX controls either come with Visual J++ and aren't in the ActiveX control list, or they come with other packages and can be used by Visual J++.

To find other ActiveX controls that you can use in Visual J++ programs, select Customize Toolbox from the Tools menu. Click on the ActiveX Controls tab and a large list of available controls will appear. To add these to the Toolbox Window under the ActiveX tab, click on them.

Let's add a new control then use it in a program. Create a new Visual J++ application named UseActiveX3. Select Customize Toolbox from the Tools menu. Click on the ActiveX Controls tab. Check the Microsoft Web Browser control as shown in Figure 20.6.

FIGURE 20.6

Add the Microsoft Web Browser to the list of ActiveX controls.

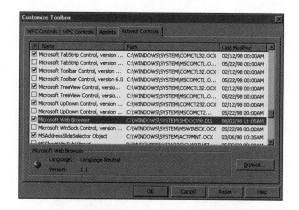

Now, select the ActiveX Controls tab in the Toolbox Window. Click on the Microsoft Web Browser control (labeled Explorer in the ActiveX tools) and place it on the Form window so that it occupies most of the Form window as shown in Figure 20.7.

Note

The process of adding the control to your form for the first time might take as much as a minute. Be patient.

Now all you need to do to get the control working is make a call to the Navigate() method. (Listing 20.1 shows the source code for the UseActiveX3 program.) This method takes five arguments.

FIGURE 20.7

The Microsoft Web Browser control should take up most of the Form window.

The first is a string designating the URL to which you'll navigate. The second is a value indicating any flags you want to use; this will always be zero for your use. The third argument is the name of the frame in which you'll display this control; we'll use a null value. The fourth argument is a value that specifies the HTTP headers to send to the server; we'll use a null value. The fifth argument is the data to send for an HTTP POST; we'll use a null value.

In almost every case, when you use the `Navigate()` method, the only argument that won't be zero or null will be the first argument.

> **Caution**
>
> The data that you pass to arguments two through five must be a variant.

The following example shows how we created Variant classes with the value of zero and passed them to the `Navigate()` method:

```
webBrowser1.Navigate( "http://www.infinitevision.net",
    new Variant( 0 ), new Variant( 0 ), new Variant( 0 ), new Variant( 0 ) );
```

INPUT The source code for the UseActiveX3 program will be helpful for you. It's shown in Listing 20.1.

20

LISTING 20.1 THIS IS THE SOURCE CODE FOR THE USEACTIVEX3 PROGRAM

```
1    import com.ms.wfc.app.*;
2    import com.ms.wfc.core.*;
3    import com.ms.wfc.ui.*;
4    import com.ms.wfc.html.*;
5    import com.ms.com.*;
6
```

continues

LISTING 20.1   CONTINUED

```
 7   /**
 8    * This class can take a variable number of parameters on the command
 9    * line. Program execution begins with the main() method. The class
10    * constructor is not invoked unless an object of type 'Form1' is
11    * created in the main() method.
12    */
13   public class Form1 extends Form
14   {
15       public Form1()
16       {
17           // Required for Visual J++ Form Designer support
18           initForm();
19
20           webBrowser1.Navigate( "http://www.infinitevision.net",
21               new Variant( 0 ), new Variant( 0 ), new Variant
                 ➥( 0 ), new Variant( 0 ) );
22
23       }
24
25       /**
26        * Form1 overrides dispose so it can clean up the
27        * component list.
28        */
29       public void dispose()
30       {
31           super.dispose();
32           components.dispose();
33       }
34
35       /**
36        * NOTE: The following code is required by the Visual J++ form
37        * designer.  It can be modified using the form editor.  Do not
38        * modify it using the code editor.
39        */
40       Container components = new Container();
41       shdocvw.WebBrowser.WebBrowser webBrowser1 = new
         ➥shdocvw.WebBrowser.WebBrowser();
42
43       private void initForm()
44       {
45           // NOTE:  This form is storing resource information in an
46           // external file.  Do not modify the string parameter to any
47           // resources.getObject() function call.  For example, do not
48           // modify "foo1_location" in the following line of code
49           // even if the name of the Foo object changes:
50           //    foo1.setLocation((Point)resources.getObject
                 ➥("foo1_location"));
51
52           IResourceManager resources = new ResourceManager
             ➥(this, "Form1");
```

```
53              this.setText("Form1");
54              this.setAutoScaleBaseSize(13);
55              this.setClientSize(new Point(691, 397));
56
57              components.add(webBrowser1, "webBrowser1");
58              webBrowser1.setLocation(new Point(8, 8));
59              webBrowser1.setSize(new Point(672, 376));
60              webBrowser1.setTabIndex(0);
61              webBrowser1.setOcxState((AxHost.State)resources.getObject
           ➡("webBrowser1_ocxState"));
62
63              this.setNewControls(new Control[] {
64                                  webBrowser1});
65
66              webBrowser1.begin();
67          }
68
69      /**
70       * The main entry point for the application.
71       *
72       * @param args Array of parameters passed to the application
73       * via the command line.
74       */
75      public static void main(String args[])
76      {
77              Application.run(new Form1());
78      }
79  }
```

OUTPUT When the program runs, you'll see it go to the Infinite Vision site at www.infinitevision.net as shown in Figure 20.8.

FIGURE 20.8

This program uses Microsoft's Web Browser *control to navigate on the Internet.*

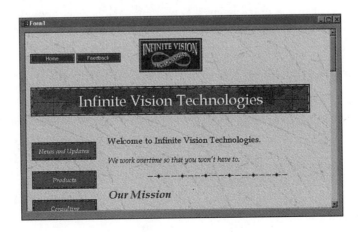

20

Summary

ActiveX controls are powerful and flexible. They let you use code that was written by other programmers and possibly in another language. Visual J++ makes it easy to use ActiveX controls, and there's no shortage of them in programming tools catalogs and on the Internet.

Take some time and get comfortable with the technology. Microsoft says, "COM is the glue that holds it all together." After seeing the developments in COM and ActiveX for the last two years, you can believe it.

Q&A

Q Are there any of ActiveX controls that you can immediately use from Visual J++?

A Yes, there are many. Among them are `Animation`, `Calendar`, and `Sprite` controls. To find them, select the ActiveX Controls tab in the Visual J++ Toolbox. Then to use them, click on them and place them on the Form window.

Q How do you add additional ActiveX controls that don't show up in the Toolbox?

A Select Customize Toolbox from the Tools menu. Click on the ActiveX Controls tab. All of the ActiveX controls that are registered on your system will show up in a list. Add a control by setting the check box to On.

Q Why ActiveX controls? Why not just link in libraries?

A ActiveX controls let many programs use the same code. This is efficient because there needs to be only one copy of the code on your hard drive. It's also convenient when you're fixing bugs. You simply send out any ActiveX controls with the fixed bugs and you don't have to send out the entire application.

Exercises

1. Create an application and use the `Calendar` ActiveX control. Set the control's properties so that it doesn't look exactly like the default control.

2. Create an application and add in an ActiveX control that's not listed in the Toolbox such as the `MonthView` control. Now place it on your form. Compile the program and run it. See if you can use the control's properties.

DAY 21

J/Direct

Today you'll learn how to access the Windows API through the Visual J++ J/Direct tool. It's easy to use and fills in the gaps where Visual J++ leaves out functionality that's in the Windows API. We're going to stick with using J/Direct for Visual J++ applications.

Today you'll learn

- About J/Direct.
- How to create a class for Windows API methods.
- About simple examples such as using a MessageBox.
- How to use the multimedia functionality.
- About how J/Direct handles data marshalling.
- Examples of using methods created with J/Direct.

The Windows API is huge, too huge to cover in this chapter. So you'll learn the basics of using J/Direct and then you can venture off on your own to take advantage of the Windows API from Visual J++ programs.

A Quick Look at J/Direct

As a language, Visual J++ is powerful. It gives you the tools you need to do serious object-oriented programming without all of the complication of C++'s object-oriented approach.

Many programmers like Visual J++ as a language—with good reason. In addition to being simpler than C++, Visual J++ also has helpful features such as garbage collection. Not having to worry about when to free memory is a big relief to most C++ programmers, so garbage collection makes them more efficient.

If you're programming for Win32, Visual J++ can still be a great choice, especially for programs where performance isn't critical.

Although the Visual J++ language is good, it is lacking in some respects. What if your Visual J++ program needs to get access to Windows functionality not supported by Visual J++?

As you well know, any language needs to be able to use the native capabilities provided by the operating system. With Visual J++, this need is especially acute because the built-in functionality is so incomplete in some areas.

Don't forget that as soon as you make any calls to the Windows API, you kiss whatever cross-platform aspirations you had goodbye. If you isolate your native calls into a small set of classes, you might be able to port most of your classes, but native anything is never a cross-platform solution. Native methods are, however, a great way to get the speed and functionality your programs may demand.

Thankfully, there are methods of accessing native code that are easy: COM integration and J/Direct.

J/Direct enables you to call most any DLL directly, without having to write an RNI or COM wrapper DLL. The VM takes care of thorny issues such as mapping of data types for you. J/Direct is best for calling APIs (in Windows or your own DLLs) that are not wrapped in COM objects. This gives you access to almost the entire Windows API, for instance, and enables a new class of Java programs: Windows programs written in Java.

Creating Classes with J/Direct

Using the J/Direct Call Builder, you can quickly create J/Direct calls to the Windows API. The J/Direct Call Builder automatically inserts Java definitions for the Windows API elements into your code, along with the appropriate @dll.import tags.

To use J/Direct Call Builder, do the following:

1. To open the J/Direct Call Builder, select Other Windows on the View menu and choose J/Direct Call Builder as shown in Figure 21.1.

FIGURE 21.1

You can show the J/Direct window by selecting Other Windows from the View menu and then choosing J/Direct Call Builder.

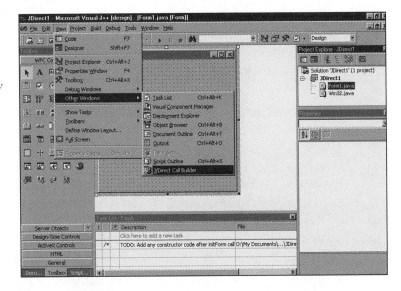

2. The J/Direct Call Builder displays elements defined in the following Windows DLLs: `advapi32.DLL`, `gdi32. DLL`, `kernel32. DLL`, `shell32. DLL`, `spoolss. DLL`, `user32. DLL`, and `winmm. DLL`.

3. The Target box identifies the class to contain the J/Direct calls. By default, the class name that will be added to your project is named Win32. It's into this class that the Windows API methods will be added. You can see the list of available Windows API items in Figure 21.2. The following steps show you how to add a class for the Windows API methods.

FIGURE 21.2

You can see the Windows API methods, structures, and constants in the J/Direct Call Builder window.

21

a. To specify a different target class, click the ellipsis button (…).

b. In the Select Class dialog box, select whether you want to view your classes in Project view or Class view. Project view displays a hierarchical list of the java files in your solution, where each file node lists the names of the classes contained in that file. Class view displays a hierarchical list of class names.

c. After you have chosen a view, select the name of the class to contain the J/Direct calls. (To copy the calls to the Windows Clipboard instead of to a class, select Clipboard.)

d. Click OK.

4. To filter the display of Win32 methods, structs, and constants, select or clear the Methods, Structs, and Constants options.

5. Now select the method, struct, or constant that you want to insert. (You can select multiple items using the SHIFT and CTRL keys.) Note that a Win32 struct will be added as a nested class inside your class. To search for an item by its initial characters, type the characters into the Find text box. The first item that matches these characters is automatically selected.

6. To insert the associated Java definition into your class, click Copy To Target. (You can also double-click the method, struct, or constant to insert it into your class.)

When a Windows API element is selected in the J/Direct Call Builder, the lower preview pane displays the associated Java definition. You can copy and paste this text into any file. To find the online reference information for a Windows API element, right-click the item and click Display API Help on the shortcut menu.

Displaying a MessageBox Through a Windows API Call

We're going to create a simple example so that you can see how easy it is to use J/Direct to create calls to the Windows API.

Start by creating a Visual J++ application named UseJDirect. Select Other Windows from the View menu and choose J/Direct Call Builder. The J/Direct Call Builder window will appear. Scroll down until you see MessageBox in the list. Double-click on MessageBox. Youill be informed that the target class doesnit exist. Click the Yes button so that itis created and a class will be added to your project named Win32. The Win32 class will contain a method named MessageBox(). After the Win32 class has been added, the Win32 classis source code will be opened in the edit window as shown in Figure 21.3.

FIGURE 21.3

You can see that the Win32 *class has been added. After this happens, the Win32 source code will be opened in the edit window.*

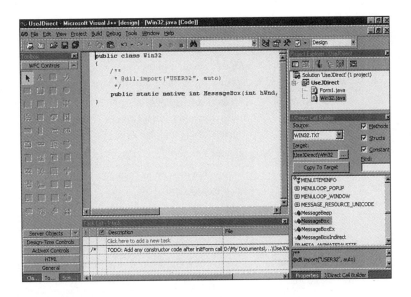

With the Win32 class in your project, it's a snap to use it. Simply create a Win32 class and call the MessageBox() method. Before you do that though, you need to know that the fourth argument to the MessageBox() method determines the type of message box that's displayed. For example, you can display a message box with a single OK button, or one with Retry, Cancel, or Abort buttons. Table 21.1 shows you what values are allowed for the fourth MessageBox() argument.

TABLE 21.1 MessageBox ARGUMENT TYPES

Constant	Description
MB_ABORTRETRYIGNORE	The message box contains three pushbuttons: Abort, Retry, and Ignore.
MB_OK	The message box contains one pushbutton: OK. This is the default.
MB_OKCANCEL	The message box contains two pushbuttons: OK and Cancel.
MB_RETRYCANCEL	The message box contains two pushbuttons: Retry and Cancel.
MB_YESNO	The message box contains two pushbuttons: Yes and No.
MB_YESNOCANCEL	The message box contains three pushbuttons: Yes, No, and Cancel.

There are additional constants that you can combine with the type flags to specify an icon type. Table 21.2 shows you these constants.

21

TABLE 21.2 CONSTANTS THAT DETERMINE MESSAGEBOX ICONS

Constant	Description
MB_ICONEXCLAMATION or MB_ICONWARNING	An exclamation-point icon appears in the message box.
MB_ICONINFORMATION or MB_ICONASTERISK	An icon consisting of a lowercase letter i in a circle appears in the message box.
MB_ICONQUESTION	A question-mark icon appears in the message box.
MB_ICONSTOP or MB_ICONERROR or MB_ICONHAND	A stop-sign icon appears in the message box.

To add these constants to the Win32 class, find them in the list in the J/Direct Call Builder window and double-click on them. Letis go ahead and find and add the MB_OK and MB_ICONEXCLAMATION constants.

Your Win32 class will look like the following:

```
public class Win32
{
    /**
     * @dll.import("USER32", auto)
     */
    public static native int MessageBox(int hWnd, String lpText,
    ➥String lpCaption, int uType);
    public static final int MB_OK = 0x00000000;
    public static final int MB_ICONEXCLAMATION = 0x00000030;
}
```

Now you can use the new class to display a message box. Find your form's constructor; it should be named Form1(). After the call to the initForm() method, add the following code:

```
Win32 WinAPI = new Win32();
WinAPI.MessageBox( 0, "Hello J/Direct World!", "Test",
➥WinAPI.MB_OK ¦ WinAPI.MB_ICONEXCLAMATION );
```

Compile the program and run it. When the program first runs, before the Form window appears, you'll see a message box as shown in Figure 21.4.

FIGURE 21.4

A message box will appear before the Form window does.

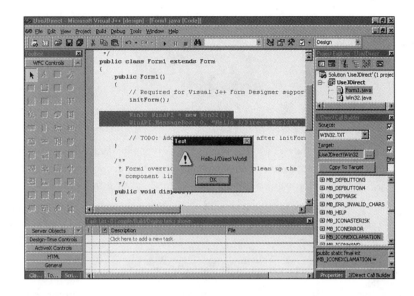

J/Direct Options

Visual J++ enables you to set two options to customize the functionality of the J/Direct Call Builder. To set J/Direct Call Builder options start by going to the Tools menu and selecting J/Direct Call Builder Options.

In the J/Direct Call Builder Options dialog box, you have several options as shown in Table 21.3 and pictured in Figure 21.5.

TABLE 21.3 J/DIRECT CALL BUILDER OPTIONS

Option	Description
Show Target Window When Copy to Target	Selected by default. When you insert a J/Direct call into your class, the builder automatically opens the .java file in the Text editor, if it is not already opened.
Disable Stack Crawl security check	Cleared by default. The Virtual Machine will initiate a stack-based for each J/Direct call. If any of the callers on the stack are not fully trusted, a security exception is thrown and the J/Direct call will not be invoked. This mainly affects Java code deployed on Web pages. When you select this option to disable the security checks, the @security(checkDllCalls=off) tag is automatically added to your class the next time you insert a J/Direct call. (If you later clear this option, any existing occurrences of the @security tag remain in your files, but no new instances will be added.)

21

FIGURE 21.5

*The J/Direct Call
Builder options are
shown in the dialog
box.*

Data Marshalling

Although they're often close, the data types in Java don't map exactly to C/C++. Built-in data types map in a natural manner, but there are some differences depending on whether the data element is a parameter to a function or a field embedded in a structure.

Strings, structures, and pointers all require special handling. Table 21.4 shows the data mappings for parameters and return values.

TABLE 21.4   DATA MAPPINGS FOR JAVA AND C/C++

Java	C/C++
byte	BYTE or CHAR
short	SHORT or WORD
int	INT, UINT, LONG, ULONG, or DWORD
char	TCHAR
long	_int64
float	float
double	double
boolean	BOOL
String	LPCTSTR
StringBuffer	LPTSTR
byte[]	BYTE * or CHAR *
short[]	SHORT * or WORD *
char[]	TCHAR *
int[]	INT *, UINT *, LONG *, ULONG *, or DWORD *
float[]	float *
double[]	double *
long[]	_int64 *
boolean[]	BOOL *

Most of the data type mappings are what you'd expect: `byte` to `char`, `int` to `int`, `long` to `_int64`, `boolean` to `BOOL`, and so on. But a few are surprising and some are different depending on whether the data is a parameter or a member of a structure (declared with `@dll.struct`).

There are no unsigned data types (except `char`) in Java, so be careful when operating on unsigned values. Don't forget that `long` is 64 bits in Java, not 32 as in C/C++.

When passed as parameters, arrays map to pointers to the element type. For instance, `byte[]` in Java maps to `char *` in C/C++. There are restrictions on return values, especially `Strings` and `StringBuffers`.

Using J/Direct: Getting System Colors

In this section, we're going to build a complete program that uses J/Direct to access a Windows API function. The program you'll learn about is one that gets some system colors and then displays them in the Form window. The first step in creating the program is to build a Win32 class with a `GetSysColor()` method. This method takes a single argument that determines which of the system colors will be returned. Table 21.5 lists the possible values. For our `Win32` class, we added the three constants (`COLOR_3DSHADOW`, `COLOR_3DFACE`, `COLOR_3DHILIGHT`) that we used for the program.

TABLE 21.5 POSSIBLE COLOR VALUES THAT CAN BE RETURNED

Constant	Description
`COLOR_3DDKSHADOW`	Dark shadow for three-dimensional display elements.
`COLOR_3DFACE` and `COLOR_BTNFACE`	Face color for three-dimensional display elements.
`COLOR_3DHILIGHT`, `COLOR_3DHIGHLIGHT`, `COLOR_BTNHILIGHT`, and `COLOR_BTNHIGHLIGHT`	Highlight color for three-dimensional display elements (for edges facing the light source).
`COLOR_3DLIGHT`	Light color for three-dimensional display elements (for edges facing the light source).
`COLOR_3DSHADOW` and `COLOR_BTNSHADOW`	Shadow color for three-dimensional display elements (for edges facing away from the light source).
`COLOR_ACTIVEBORDER`	Active window border.
`COLOR_ACTIVECAPTION`	Active window title bar.

21

TABLE 21.5   CONTINUED

Constant	Description
COLOR_APPWORKSPACE	Background color of multiple document interface (MDI) applications.
COLOR_BACKGROUND and COLOR_DESKTOP	Desktop.
COLOR_BTNTEXT	Text on pushbuttons.
COLOR_CAPTIONTEXT	Text in caption, size box, and scroll bar arrow box.
COLOR_GRADIENTACTIVECAPTION	Windows NT 5.0 and Windows 98: Right side color in the color gradient of an active window's title bar.
COLOR_ACTIVECAPTION	Specifies the left side color.
COLOR_GRADIENTINACTIVECAPTION	Windows NT 5.0 and Windows 98: Right side color in the color gradient of an inactive window's title bar.
COLOR_INACTIVECAPTION	Specifies the left side color.
COLOR_GRAYTEXT	Grayed (disabled) text. This color is set to 0 if the current display driver does not support a solid gray color.
COLOR_HIGHLIGHT	Item(s) selected in a control.
COLOR_HIGHLIGHTTEXT	Text of item(s) selected in a control.
COLOR_HOTLIGHT	Windows NT 5.0 and Windows 98: Color for a hot-tracked item. Single-clicking a hot-tracked item executes the item.
COLOR_INACTIVEBORDER	Inactive window border.
COLOR_INACTIVECAPTION	Inactive window caption.
COLOR_INACTIVECAPTIONTEXT	Color of text in an inactive caption.
COLOR_INFOBK	Background color for ToolTip controls.
COLOR_INFOTEXT	Text color for ToolTip controls.
COLOR_MENU	Menu background.
COLOR_MENUTEXT	Text in menus.
COLOR_SCROLLBAR	Scrollbar gray area.
COLOR_WINDOW	Window background.
COLOR_WINDOWFRAME	Window frame.
COLOR_WINDOWTEXT	Text in windows.

INPUT The entire source code for the application is short. It's shown in Listings 21.1 and 21.2 followed by a screen shot and explanation.

LISTING 21.1 THIS PROGRAM DISPLAYS THREE SYSTEM COLORS

```
1    import com.ms.wfc.app.*;
2    import com.ms.wfc.core.*;
3    import com.ms.wfc.ui.*;
4    import com.ms.wfc.html.*;
5
6    public class Form1 extends Form
7    {
8        public Form1()
9        {
10           initForm();
11       }
12
13       /**
14        * Form1 overrides dispose so it can clean up the
15        * component list.
16        */
17       public void dispose()
18       {
19           super.dispose();
20           components.dispose();
21       }
22
23       private void Form1_paint(Object source, PaintEvent e)
24       {
25           Win32 WinAPI = new Win32();
26
27           int nColor = WinAPI.GetSysColor( Win32.COLOR_3DSHADOW );
28           Color color = new Color( ( nColor & 0x00ff0000 ) >>
                16, ( nColor & 0x0000ff00 ) >> 8,
29               ( nColor & 0x000000ff ) );
30           e.graphics.drawRect( 149, 9, 122, 27 );
31           e.graphics.fill( 150, 10, 120, 25, new Brush( color,
                BrushStyle.SOLID ) );
32
33           nColor = WinAPI.GetSysColor( Win32.COLOR_3DFACE );
34           color = new Color( ( nColor & 0x00ff0000 ) >> 16,
                ( nColor & 0x0000ff00 ) >> 8,
35               ( nColor & 0x000000ff ) );
36           e.graphics.drawRect( 149, 59, 122, 27 );
37           e.graphics.fill( 150, 60, 120, 25, new Brush( color,
                BrushStyle.SOLID ) );
38
39           nColor = WinAPI.GetSysColor( Win32.COLOR_3DHILIGHT );
```

21

continues

LISTING **21.1**   CONTINUED

```
40          color = new Color( ( nColor & 0x00ff0000 ) >> 16,
         ➥( nColor & 0x0000ff00 ) >> 8,
41            ( nColor & 0x000000ff ) );
42          e.graphics.drawRect( 149, 109, 122, 27 );
43          e.graphics.fill( 150, 110, 120, 25, new Brush( color,
         ➥BrushStyle.SOLID ) );
44      }
45
46      /**
47       * NOTE: The following code is required by the Visual J++ form
48       * designer.  It can be modified using the form editor.  Do not
49       * modify it using the code editor.
50       */
51      Container components = new Container();
52      Label label1 = new Label();
53      Label label2 = new Label();
54      Label label3 = new Label();
55
56      private void initForm()
57      {
58          this.setText("Form1");
59          this.setAutoScaleBaseSize(13);
60          this.setClientSize(new Point(290, 155));
61           this.addOnPaint(new PaintEventHandler(this.Form1_paint));
62
63          label1.setLocation(new Point(8, 16));
64          label1.setSize(new Point(120, 16));
65          label1.setTabIndex(0);
66          label1.setTabStop(false);
67          label1.setText("COLOR_3DSHADOW");
68          label1.setTextAlign(HorizontalAlignment.RIGHT);
69
70          label2.setLocation(new Point(8, 64));
71          label2.setSize(new Point(120, 16));
72          label2.setTabIndex(1);
73          label2.setTabStop(false);
74          label2.setText("COLOR_3DFACE");
75          label2.setTextAlign(HorizontalAlignment.RIGHT);
76
77          label3.setLocation(new Point(8, 112));
78          label3.setSize(new Point(120, 16));
79          label3.setTabIndex(2);
80          label3.setTabStop(false);
81          label3.setText("COLOR_3DHILIGHT");
82          label3.setTextAlign(HorizontalAlignment.RIGHT);
83
84          this.setNewControls(new Control[] {
85                          label3,
```

```
86                              label2,
87                              label1});
88          }
89
90          /**
91           * The main entry point for the application.
92           *
93           * @param args Array of parameters passed to the application
94           * via the command line.
95           */
96          public static void main(String args[])
97          {
98              Application.run(new Form1());
99          }
100 }
```

LISTING 21.2   THE Win32 CLASS CONTAINING THE GetSysColor() METHOD

```
1   public class Win32
2   {
3        /**
4         * @dll.import("USER32",auto)
5         */
6        public static native int GetSysColor(int nIndex);
7        public static final int COLOR_3DSHADOW = 16;
8        public static final int COLOR_3DFACE = 15;
9        public static final int COLOR_3DHILIGHT = 20;
10  }
```

OUTPUT   When the program runs youill see three labels in the Form window:
COLOR_3DSHADOW, COLOR_3DFACE, COLOR_3DHILIGHT. To the right of each label,
youill see the color that was obtained when the constant for each of the system color values was passed to the GetSysColor() method. The program can be seen running in
Figure 21.6.

FIGURE 21.6

*This program retrieves
three system colors
and draws rectangles
to show the colors.*

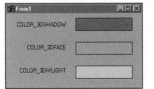

21

ANALYSIS   The code you're interested in can be seen in two sections. lines 23–44 in Listing
21.1 and all of Listing 21.2.

The `Form1_paint()` method is contained in lines 23–44 of Listing 21.1. In this method, a
`Win32` class is instantiated at line 25. At line 27, the 3D shadow color is obtained by
making a call to the `GetSysColor()` with the `COLOR_3DSHADOW` constant as an argument.
At lines 28 and 29 a `Color` object is created based on the color integer that was returned
from the `GetSysColor()` method. Note that the integer value has all three of the color
components as integral parts of its value. The lower eight bits are the blue component;
the next eight bits are the green component, and the next eight bits are the red component. To extract these color components, mask the 8 bits that you want, and shift the
value over enough bits to normalize the value so that it ranges from `0` to `255`.

At line 30, a rectangle with a black border is drawn, which makes it easier to see the colors because they are outlined. At line 31, a filled rectangle with the system color is
drawn.

Lines 33–37 and lines 39–43 repeat the process for the 3D face color and the 3D highlight color.

Listing 21.2 contains a declaration for the `GetSysColor()` method, and the three constants (`COLOR_3DSHADOW`, `COLOR_3DFACE`, and `COLOR_3DHILIGHT`).

Summary

Visual J++ is a powerful language that makes it easy to develop applications. However,
at times you'll want to go directly to the Windows API. For this reason, you should
always keep J/Direct as one of your alternatives when Visual J++ just doesn't seem to
give you what you need.

Using J/Direct is easy. While the examples in this chapter are simple, you can build on
them and create your own powerful layers to the Windows API.

Q&A

**Q How do you create a wrapper class and add methods that directly access the
Windows API?**

A You start by displaying the J/Direct Call Builder window. Then, you find the
Windows API function that you want to add in the list box and double-click on it.
Youill be asked if you want to add the class; then when you reply yes, the method
on which you double-clicked will be added to a new class.

Q **How do you pass a character string to a Windows API function that expects a pointer to a character buffer?**

A J/Direct takes care of all data marshalling. For Windows API functions that take character buffers as arguments, you pass a Java `String` object. J/Direct will take care of the conversion details.

Q **Why would anyone want to go to the trouble to access the Windows API directly? Isn't Visual J++ enough?**

A Every language from Visual C++ to Visual Basic to Visual J++ has occasion to need direct calls to the Windows API. There are so many things that programmers may require with regards to language functionality that languages can't cover every single thing that may arise. For this reason, going directly to the Windows API can give you the method to solving your programming problems.

Q **Where can I go for help when it comes to the Windows API?**

A For starters, the Visual J++ online help is excellent. Try to find "Windows API" in the help index. Next to that, a good Windows API reference book would be helpful. Usually the books geared toward C and C++ programmers are best.

Exercises

1. Create a Visual J++ application. Add a Windows API class named `Win32` and add `_lcreat()`, `_lwrite()`, and `_lclose()` methods. Use `_lcreat()` to create a file, `_lwrite()` to write "Hello world!" to the file, and `_lclose()` to close the file.

2. Create a new Visual J++ application. Add a Windows API class named `Win32` and a `GetSystemMetrics()` method. Next, add constants such as `SM_CXFULLSCREEN` and `SM_CYFULLSCREEN`. Use these constants as arguments to the `GetSystemMetrics()` method and find out information about the system.

21

APPENDIX A

Installing Visual J++ 6

This appendix will guide you through the process of installing Visual J++ 6, as well as the help system associated with the Visual Studio 6 product suite, the Microsoft Developer Network Library. To start the installation process, insert Disc 1 of the Visual Studio 6 Package, or Visual J++ 6, into your CD-ROM drive. The Installation Wizard will automatically begin, displaying a screen similar to Figure A.1.

FIGURE A.1

Insert Disc 1 of the Visual Studio 6 Enterprise Edition to start the Installation Wizard.

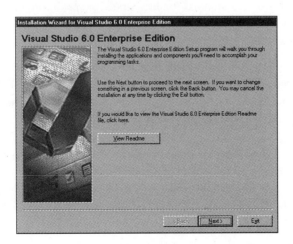

Click the View Readme button to view documentation on the products contained on the CD within your default browser. Click Next on the Installation Wizard dialog to proceed to the License Agreement dialog. Read through the license agreement and select the I Accept the Agreement radio button when you are finished. Note that the Next button on the License Agreement dialog will not be enabled until you accept the license agreement.

Once you have accepted the license agreement and chosen the Next button, the Product Number and User ID dialog of the Installation Wizard will appear, as shown in Figure A.2. Enter the product ID number from your CD case, your name, and your company in the appropriate entry fields before clicking the Next button.

FIGURE A.2

The Product Number and User ID dialog information will be validated before the installation process continues.

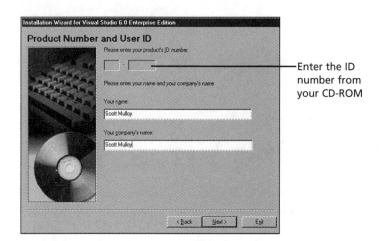

Enter the ID number from your CD-ROM

Provided you've entered the correct product ID number, the Installation Wizard will next evaluate whether or not you need to upgrade the Internet Explorer software before continuing. For the Visual Studio 6 Product Suite, Internet Explorer version 4.01 is required and is used within the MSDN help system. If you do need to upgrade Internet Explorer (IE), a dialog similar to Figure A.3 will appear.

If you already have version 4.01 of IE installed, proceed to Figure A.8 for further installation instructions. Otherwise, click the Next button on the Install Internet Explorer 4.01 dialog to proceed to the Internet Explorer 4.0 Setup dialog, as shown in Figure A.4. Before clicking the Next button, be sure to record your product ID number in case you need technical assistance for this product at a later date. As the dialog indicates, any previous versions of IE that you have installed will be automatically upgraded. However, any configuration options you have saved within IE, as well as the bookmarks you have created, will not be lost in this process.

FIGURE A.3

IE 4.01 is required before the installation of Visual J++ 6 will begin.

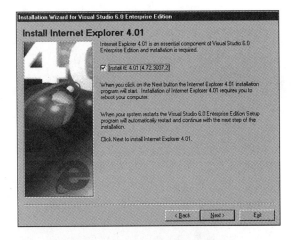

FIGURE A.4

Record your IE 4.01 product ID number before continuing with the installation process.

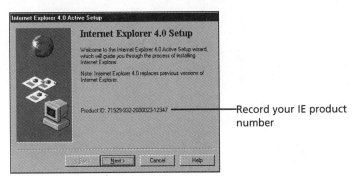

Record your IE product number

Read through and accept the license agreement with IE 4.01 and the IE Installation Option dialog will appear, as shown in Figure A.5. There are two options associated with installing IE 4.01, Standard Installation and Full Installation. A Standard Installation will install IE 4.01 and Microsoft Outlook Express, while the Full Installation also includes the NetMeeting, Microsoft FrontPage Express, NetShow, Web Publishing Wizard, and Microsoft Chat 2.0 products. Either selection is sufficient for your Visual J++ 6 development efforts, so this option is entirely a matter of personal preference.

The next dialog that will appear is the Windows Desktop Update dialog, as shown in Figure A.6. The default selection of this dialog is to install the Windows Update Desktop as part of IE 4.01. This update changes the look and feel of your desktop, offering true Web integration through changes to the taskbar, start menu, and all desktop folders. Leave the Yes radio button checked only if you are sure you would like this upgrade installed. Conversely, if you are comfortable or pleased with the current Windows environment, be sure to select the No radio button before clicking the Next button.

FIGURE A.5

Click Standard Installation or Full Installation based on your needs and preferences for the included Microsoft products.

FIGURE A.6

The Windows Desktop Update dialog results in several changes to your desktop, and should only be selected if you want the new environment.

The Installation Wizard will prompt you for the country you reside in and the directory to install IE 4.01 in before continuing with the installation. Once you have provided this information or selected the defaults, IE 4.01 will install on your PC. During this installation, a dialog similar to Figure A.7 will appear, informing you of the status.

FIGURE A.7

The IE 4 Active Setup dialog informs you of the status of the installation process.

After the IE 4.01 installation, you will have to reboot your PC for the changes to take effect. Once the PC is restarted, Windows will automatically configure the IE 4.01 software and display a dialog, similar to Figure A.8 to begin the Visual J++ 6 installation.

FIGURE A.8

Click Next on the Visual Studio dialog to continue with the Visual J++ 6 installation.

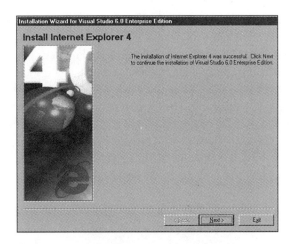

The first dialog included with any of the Visual Studio 6 products lists the Visual Studio 97 products that are already installed on your PC. With this dialog, shown in Figure A.9, you can choose whether or not to have the Installation Wizard remove the older applications from your PC. The older Visual Studio 97 and new Visual Studio 6 applications can coexist on your PC, but you may have to remove them in order to free disk or Windows Registry space. If you do want to uninstall a prior version of one of the Visual Studio 97 products, select the appropriate check box before clicking the Next button. As the dialog indicates, you can choose to leave the previous versions of development products on your PC initially, and then remove them at a later time with the Add/Remove selection in your Control Panel.

FIGURE A.9

Unless you are out of disk or registry space, you may want to leave the prior versions of your development platforms until after you are familiar with the new versions.

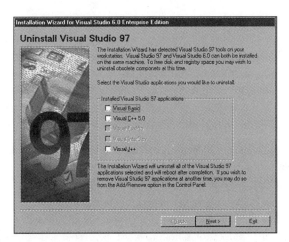

If you have purchased the entire Visual Studio 6 Enterprise Edition, the next dialog of the Installation Wizard will allow you to choose which software products you want to install based on three different categories: Custom, Products, and Server Applications. Although the different configurations associated with this installation are nearly endless, for the purposes of this book you should click either the Custom or Products radio button before clicking the Next button. The Custom option will allow you to create an integrated setup of products and server applications on your PC, while the simpler Products option will allow you to choose which high-level development products you want to install. This is not to imply that the products included with the Server Applications install are not valuable, but they are outside the scope of this book.

FIGURE A.10

For the simplest installation, click the Products radio button to install the entire Visual J++ 6 Software Product in one easy step.

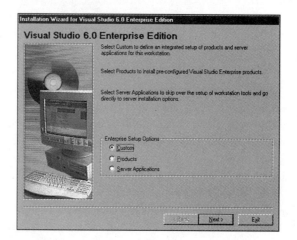

If you have chosen the Products radio button, the next step of the Installation Wizard allows you to select which particular products of the Visual Studio 6 Suite you want to install. Conversely, if you have chosen a Custom install, proceed directly to Figure A.11. The Products options include the 6 versions of Visual Basic, Visual C++, Visual J++, Visual FoxPro, and Visual InterDev, as shown in Figure A.11. At a bare minimum, click the Visual J++ 6 check box before clicking the Next button to install the software required for all of the material presented in this text.

The Installation Wizard will begin your installation by displaying your product ID number, which you should record in case you need technical assistance in the future. Then, the Visual Studio 6 Enterprise - Custom dialog will appear, as shown in Figure A.12. The Options selected in this dialog are based on the products you selected to install back in Figure A.11. Conversely, if you chose a Custom install back in Figure A.10 instead of a Product install, all application categories will be deselected, allowing you to choose exactly which items to install.

FIGURE A.11

Choose to Install Visual J++ 6 and you are on your way to accelerated Java development.

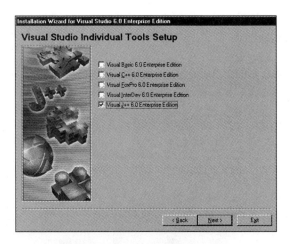

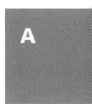

FIGURE A.12

The Custom dialog allows you to view and change the items that will be installed.

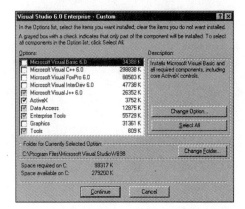

If you are interested in viewing the individual components that make up each of the items in the custom dialog, highlight the item in the listbox and click the Change Option button. For example, you can view the components that make up the Enterprise Tools option, as shown in Figure A.13.

Before clicking Continue on the Visual Studio 6 Enterprise - Custom dialog, make sure that, at a bare minimum, the Microsoft Visual J++ 6 item is selected. After clicking Continue, the products you have selected will be installed on your PC and the required Windows Registry changes will be executed. At the conclusion of this installation, you will once again have to restart Windows.

Once Windows has been restarted, the final phase of the installation will automatically begin. The Install MSDN dialog, similar to Figure A.14, will appear. Insert the MSDN

Library CD 1 into your CD-ROM drive and click the Next button to proceed to the
MSDN Visual Studio 6 Setup dialogs.

FIGURE A.13

*The Enterprise Tools
items contain useful
components such as
Visual Source Safe,
which provides some
basic Change Control
features to a team pro-
gramming environ-
ment.*

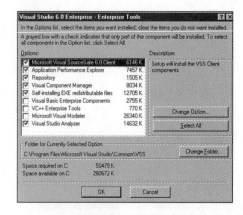

FIGURE A.14

*The installation of the
MSDN Library for
Visual Studio 6 will
automatically start
after you have restart-
ed Windows.*

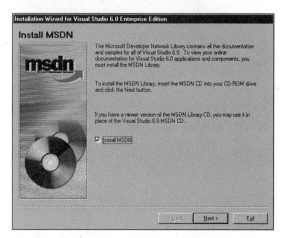

Once again, your product ID number for the MSDN library will be displayed. Write it
down. Additionally, you will again have to approve a license agreement, this one associated with the MSDN Library for Visual Studio 6. After you accept the agreement, the
MDSN VS 6 Setup dialog will appear, as shown in Figure A.15.

For most programmers, a Typical MSDN Library install will be sufficient. This will copy
the required elements of the MSDN Library, mostly index information, to your hard
drive without using too much disk space. Going forward, you will have to keep the
MSDN Library CD in your CD-ROM drive whenever you need help from the Visual
Studio 6 platform. If you don't mind leaving the MSDN CD loaded when you are using

A

Visual J++ 6, this installation option will probably make the most efficient use of your resources.

FIGURE A.15

The MSDN VS 6 Setup dialog allows you to choose which portions of the MSDN Library CDs you want to copy to your hard drive.

Choosing a Custom install will present the MSDN VS 6 - Custom dialog, as shown in Figure A.16. From this dialog, you can choose to copy additional documentation from the MSDN Library CD(s) to your hard drive, which may be beneficial if you have the free disk space or do not want to have to keep the MSDN CD loaded. You can get a brief description of each item by highlighting the item in the Options list box, which may assist you in deciding whether or not to consume disk space with each one.

FIGURE A.16

The MSDN VS 6 - Custom dialog allows you to copy additional components of the MSDN Library to your hard drive.

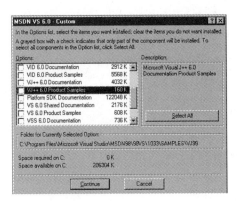

The Full installation will copy all of the help files from the MSDN CD(s) to your hard drive, so you don't have to keep the MSDN CD(s) handy when programming with Visual Studio 6. Unless you have a great deal of free disk space, upwards of 700MB, this is not a practical solution.

After you have decided on an option, the appropriate portions of the MSDN Library will be installed on your PC and the installation process will terminate.

APPENDIX B

Tools of Visual Studio

There are many tools within the Visual Studio environment that do not relate to one specific programming topic. Such tools center more around easing the tasks that are common to application development, regardless of which language you are programming. This appendix covers these tools and presents some scenarios in which you may find them useful. If you are an experienced Visual C++ or Visual Basic developer, and therefore have experience with the Visual Studio IDE, you will already be familiar with the majority of these tools.

Using the Find Dialog

Visual Studio's Find dialog allows you to search for and replace a set of characters within a source file or collection of source files. To access the Find dialog, select Find and Replace from the Edit menu, or press Ctrl+F. Note that the Find and Replace selection under the Edit menu is always enabled in Visual Studio. The Find dialog is shown in Figure B.1.

> ### THE VISUAL STUDIO 6 FIND DIALOG
>
> In previous versions of the Developer Studio, there existed a Find dialog, a Replace dialog, and a Find In Files dialog. The Find dialog was only used for open files and could not be used to change occurrences of a set of characters. In Visual Studio 6, the functionality from the previous Find, Replace, and Find In Files dialogs is all wrapped up into the Find dialog.

FIGURE B.1

The Find dialog gives you many options to search for a set of characters within a file.

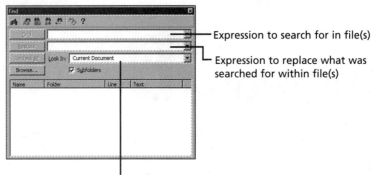

Expression to search for in file(s)

Expression to replace what was searched for within file(s)

Allows you to execute multiple-file searches

The simplest usage of the Find dialog is to search the current source file for a set of characters. To do so, you enter the expression to search for in the Find edit box and then select Current Document in the Look In combo box, as shown in Figure B.2. Repeatedly clicking the Find button, or pressing F3, will navigate the open document and sequentially highlight each occurrence of the expression being searched. When the entire document has been searched, you will receive a "No more occurrences" message box.

FIGURE B.2

The Find dialog allows you to sequentially view the occurrences of your chosen expression.

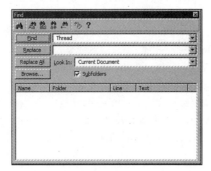

Other than simply entering in a sequence of characters and choosing the Find button to search the current document, you have many other options with the Find dialog. There is a collection of buttons on the Find dialog toolbar that allow you to modify your search criteria. These buttons are described in Table B.1.

TABLE B.1 BUTTONS ON THE FIND DIALOG TOOLBAR

Icon	Function	Description
	New Find	Clears all edit boxes in preparation for a new search
	Match Case	Case-sensitive search based on exactly what is entered in the Find edit box
	Whole Word	Delimited search requiring a space or special non-alphabetic character before and after each match of the entered expression
	Regular Expression	Default wildcard search returning all occurrences of the expression, in direct contrast to a Whole Word search
	Backwards	Executes the next search in the opposite direction
	Stop Search	Halts the execution of the current search
	Help	Help topics for the Find dialog

All of the buttons in the Find dialog can be used in conjunction with each other. A search for the expression int with both the Match Case and Whole Word buttons pressed will display each declaration of int variables, but will not stop for words like *paint* and *point*.

The Replace and Replace All buttons, along with the Replace edit box, allow you to substitute occurrences of one string for another within a single open source file. Choosing the Replace button will substitute the new expression for the Find expression and immediately search for the next occurrence. As shown in Figure B.3, you could use the Find dialog to replace the variable name *ThreadB* with *ThreadC* in the current source file. Each time a new occurrence of the expression is found, you can choose the Replace button to replace the string and continue to the next match, or press the Find button to leave the current line as is and continue to the next match. The Replace All button will replace all occurrences of the original expression with the new expression, and should only be used when you are absolutely sure that this is what you desire.

The Find dialog also allows you to search a collection of files. The Look In edit box, Browse button, and Subfolders check box allow you to specify which files should be searched. The matches from a multiple-file search, displayed in the list box in the Find dialog, can then be used to jump to each occurrence. To execute a search across multiple files, choose the Browse button to display the Look In dialog, as shown in Figure B.4. In the upper list box, navigate to the top-level directory you want to execute the search in, and choose the types of files you want to search in the Files of combo box. Choosing OK on the Look In dialog will redisplay the Find dialog with your options reflected.

FIGURE B.3

The Find dialog can be used to substitute one set of characters for a different set of characters within a source file.

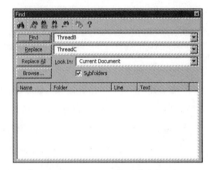

FIGURE B.4

The Look In dialog allows you to specify which top-level folder you want to begin your search in, as well as the file extensions that are applicable.

Select or deselect the Subfolders check box, and begin the search by pressing the Find button. All of the matches for your search will be displayed within the Find dialog list box, as shown in Figure B.5. Double-clicking on an entry within the list box will highlight the matched expression on the appropriate line within the edit window.

Finally, you should notice that when you use the Find dialog, the characters you're searching for stay in the Find combo box, and therefore can be selected from the dialog if you need to execute a search again. Additionally, the Find combo box may be displayed on the Visual Studio toolbar, and can be used directly for repeat searches.

FIGURE B.5

Results from a multiple-file search are written to the list box in the Find dialog.

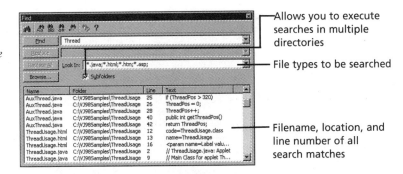

Allows you to execute searches in multiple directories

File types to be searched

Filename, location, and line number of all search matches

Using the Go To Line Dialog

Visual Studio's Go To Line dialog allows you to jump to a specific line number within a source file. To access the Go To dialog, select Go To from the Edit menu, or press Ctrl+G. The Go To Line dialog is shown in Figure B.6.

FIGURE B.6

The Go To Line dialog allows you to jump directly to specific locations within source files.

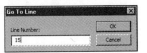

The Go To Line dialog is very easy to use and requires no further explanation. However, you should note that this menu item is only enabled when you are viewing a source file within Visual Studio.

Using the Advanced Menu

Visual Studio's Advanced menu contains six different items for editing a source file. To access the Advanced menu, select Advanced from the Edit menu. Note that the selections under the Advanced menu are only enabled if you have a source file opened within Visual Studio. The Advanced menu is shown in Figure B.7.

The selections in the Advanced menu are described in Table B.2.

FIGURE B.7

The Advanced menu provides additional flexibility for editing files within Visual Studio.

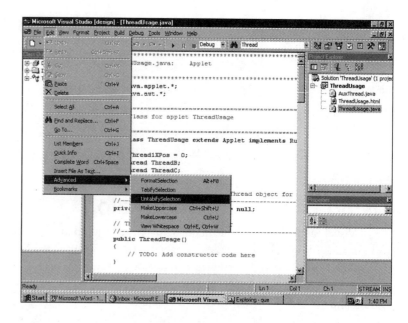

TABLE B.2   THE ADVANCED MENU

Selection	Shortcut	Description
FormatSelection	Alt+F8	Aligns selected code section in appropriate format
TabifySelection	None	Replaces spaces in selected code section with tabs
UntabifySelection	None	Replaces tabs in selected code section with spaces
MakeUppercase	Ctrl+Shift+U	Converts all characters of selected text to uppercase
MakeLowercase	Ctrl+U	Converts all characters of selected text to lowercase
View Whitespace	Ctrl+E, Ctrl+W	Displays spaces as "." and tabs as "->" within current module

The items in the Advanced menu provide basic editing functions, such as converting text to upper- or lowercase and inserting or removing tabs from a source line. Remember that before you can use one of the Advanced menu items, the line or area of text that you want to modify needs to be selected. You will often find that the Advanced menu items work best when included in macros, allowing you to convert an entire file at one time by recording some basic edit commands. An example of this, using the UntabifySelection menu item, is provided in the "Macros" section of this chapter.

Using the Bookmarks Menu

The Bookmarks menu allows you to create unnamed bookmarks within source files so that you can then easily return to specific file locations. To access the Bookmarks menu, select Bookmarks from the Edit menu. Note that the selections under the Bookmarks menu are only enabled if you have a source file opened within Visual Studio. The Bookmarks menu is shown in Figure B.8.

B

FIGURE B.8

The Bookmarks menu allows you to mark and jump to specific lines of code within Visual Studio.

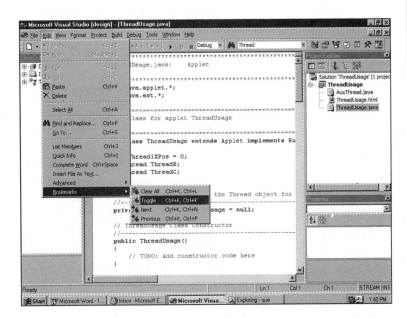

The selections in the Bookmarks menu are described in Table B.3.

TABLE B.3   THE BOOKMARKS MENU

Selection	Shortcut	Description
Clear All	Ctrl+K, Ctrl+L	Clears all bookmarks from the current source file
Toggle	Ctrl+K, Ctrl+K	Sets bookmark at the current line if one does not exist, or removes the bookmark from the current line if one does exist
Next	Ctrl+K, Ctrl+N	Navigates to the next bookmark within the current source file
Previous	Ctrl+K, Ctrl+P	Navigates to the previous bookmark within the current source file

Bookmarks serve as placeholders in code during the development phase. You may leave a section of code that you know you will have to return to as soon as you finish programming some required additional functionality. In this case, you should set a book-mark at the line of code that will require further changes and return to it when appropriate.

Using the Macro Dialog

The Macro dialog allows you to record and run macros on your Visual J++ source files. Visual Studio 97's Macro tool was not available in the Visual J++ 1 programming environment. To access the Macro dialog, select Tools, Macro from the Studio menu. If this is the first time you have selected the Macro menu option, a help screen, shown in Figure B.9, will appear to inform you how to terminate the operation of a macro.

FIGURE B.9

This help screen will not appear again if you uncheck the corresponding check box.

Next, the Macro dialog will appear, as shown in Figure B.10. Within this dialog, you can create and run previously created macros.

FIGURE B.10

The Macro dialog allows you to create new macros, as well as run any of the generic or personally created macros on your system.

Creating a Macro

Macros are an excellent method of handling repetitive tasks associated with your programming development. You can record the keystrokes needed to perform a task and have Visual Studio turn those keystrokes into a VBScript macro. Then, you can run this macro whenever you need to execute these steps again.

For example, when you run the Applet Wizard to produce a skeleton program, you will notice that Visual J++ provides code that is full of tabs. All of the to do and explanatory comments, as well as the code that they add within the methods, are preceded by a tab.

Many developers, myself included, hate tabs within their programs. You can ensure that tabs will not appear within your program by choosing this option in the Tabs page of the Options dialog, but the Applet Wizard code will not be affected. Therefore, you could create a macro that removes all the tabs from a Java source by executing the following steps:

1. Bring up the .java source code file that you want to modify.

2. Select Tools, Macro from the Studio menu to display the Macro dialog.

3. Click the Options button to display the complete Macro dialog, as shown in Figure B.11.

FIGURE B.11

Clicking the Options button will display the buttons needed to create a new macro.

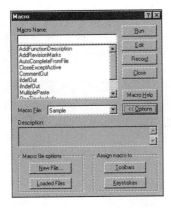

4. If this is the first macro you have created, you should first create a new file, as opposed to saving it in the sample macro file provided by Visual J++. To create a new macro file, click the New File button to display the New Macro File dialog. Create a macro file called Mymacros, as shown in Figure B.12.

FIGURE B.12

Use the New Macro File dialog to create a new, high-level macro file to hold the VBScript macros you create.

5. Press the Record button to start the creation of a new macro. Fill in the Add Macro dialog to create a macro called RemoveTabs, as shown in Figure B.13, and click the OK button to start recording.

FIGURE B.13

Use the Add Macro dialog to create a new VBScript macro that will remove all tabs from a Java source file.

6. Select Edit, Select All from the Studio menu to highlight all of the lines within the source file you want to modify.

7. Select Edit, Advanced, UntabifySelection from the Studio menu to replace all tabs in the source code with the equivalent number of spaces.

8. Click the stop recording button that appears below the Project Workspace window, as shown in Figure B.14. Visual Studio will now create a RemoveTabs() VBScript procedure within the MyMacros.dsm file, similar to what is shown in Listing B.1.

FIGURE B.14

While recording a macro, a stop recording button and a pause recording button will appear below the Project Workspace window.

Stop macro recording
Pause macro recording

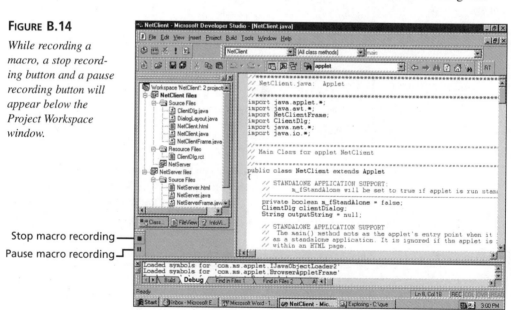

LISTING B.1   C:\PROGRAM FILES\DEVSTUDIO\SHAREDIDE\MACROS\MYMACROS.DSM—
THE RemoveTabs() PROCEDURE CONTAINS THE VBSCRIPT EQUIVALENT OF THE KEYSTROKES YOU
PERFORMED

```
1    '------------------------------------------------------------
2    'FILE DESCRIPTION: My personal macros.
```

```
3    '- - - - - - - - - - - - - - - - - - - - - - - - - - - - - - - - - - - - - - - - - - - -
4
5    Sub RemoveTabs()
6    'DESCRIPTION: Removes all tabs from a java source file.
7
8
9    'Begin Recording
10       ActiveDocument.Selection.SelectAll
11       ActiveDocument.Selection.Untabify
12   'End Recording
13   End Sub
```

B

Given the relative simplicity of this macro, this listing should be very easy to understand whether or not you are familiar with the VBScript language. Note that the ' character designates comment lines in VBScript. You can add additional macros to the Mymacros file by executing the preceding steps, or even create a new macro file that contains a completely different subset of macros.

Now that you have created a macro, you will open up a new source file and run the RemoveTabs macro on it to demonstrate how easy this formatting will now be.

Executing a Macro

The RemoveTabs macro will now replace all of the tabs within the active source file with the equivalent number of spaces. As was stated before, this is especially useful for classes that were created by the Applet Wizard because they are sure to contain tab characters.

To execute the RemoveTabs macro on a new source file, first bring the source file up in Visual Studio. Then, select the Tools, Macro menu item to display the Macro dialog. Highlight the RemoveTabs entry in the list box and click the Run button. Once again, the entire active document will be highlighted and all the tabs will be replaced with spaces.

There are two additional alternatives you may want to use for executing macros. Instead of bringing up the Macro dialog, you can add an icon to your toolbar or assign a keystroke sequence to start your macro. Both of these options can be initiated from the Macro dialog. To investigate both of these methods, bring up the Macro dialog and highlight the RemoveTabs entry in the list box. Bring up the additional macro options by clicking the Options button. Click the Toolbars button within the Assign Macro To group box to display the Commands tab of the Customize dialog. Notice how the Category combo box is automatically set to Macros and the RemoveTabs entry is selected in the Commands listbox, as shown in Figure B.15.

The Commands tab view of the Customize dialog allows you to create buttons on your toolbar, thereby allowing you to execute commonly used functions with a single click.

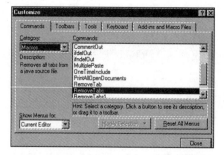

If you do want to create an icon on your toolbar for executing the RemoveTabs macro, click on the RemoveTabs item and drag your cursor to the desired location of your toolbar. The Button Appearance dialog, as shown in Figure B.16, will appear. This allows you to choose what the icon on your toolbar should look like. You can create a button with one of the images provided or with text. For the RemoveTabs macro, you would probably create an icon with the text "RT" on your toolbar.

The Button Appearance dialog allows you to set the appearance of a new button on the toolbar.

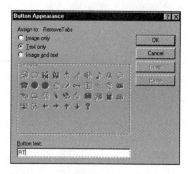

Aside from creating a button on your toolbar to execute your macro, you can also assign a key sequence. To show how this is done, bring up the macro dialog again, highlight the RemoveTabs entry, and click the Options button. This time, click the Keystrokes button to display the Keyboard tab of the Customize dialog. Notice how once again the Macros Category and RemoveTabs command is automatically selected. Record the shortcut key you want to assign to the RemoveTabs macro within the Press new shortcut key entry field, as shown in Figure B.17. Notice that if you use a key sequence that is already reserved, like CTRL+R, the dialog will inform you.

If you chose to execute all of these steps, you now have three different methods through which to execute the RemoveTabs macro. You should create additional macros for any tasks that you find yourself executing repeatedly during your development efforts.

B

FIGURE B.17

Use the Keyboard tab of the Customize dialog to assign a CTRL+T shortcut key to the RemoveTabs macro.

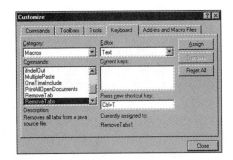

Using the Options Dialog

The Options dialog contains a tree view relating to several look-and-feel options for your Visual Studio platform. The six primary nodes of the Options dialog are Debugging, Environment, FormEditor, HelpSystem, HTML/Forms, and Text Editor. By using the top nodes of the tree view and their associated subnodes, you can specify the behavior of the HTML editor, the behavior of the source code editor, the output of the Visual J++ debugging windows, and so on. To access the Options dialog, select Options from the Tools menu. The Options dialog is shown in Figure B.18.

FIGURE B.18

The Options dialog contains numerous controls that can be manipulated to customize the behavior of your development platform.

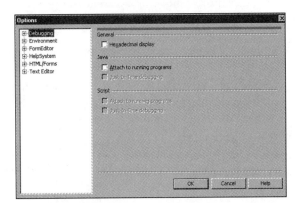

During the early stages of your Visual J++ development experience, you will probably find that the majority of the defaults provided to you in the Options dialog are sufficient. However, when you eventually want to alter something in Visual Studio, you will probably find the options associated with it in the Options dialog. Because there are so many options included in the Options dialog, it is best to take some time to browse through the various tab views and learn which options each one provides.

There are a few selections in the Options dialog that you may want to change before you begin using Visual J++ extensively. The first option is under the Environment, Saving node of the tree view. The option Save Changes under the On Run/Preview heading, as shown in Figure B.19, is highly recommended. Failure to set this option could result in a loss of code. If you had the Don't Save radio button selected and you ran your applet/application before manually specifying to save changes, an ABEND in the program, resulting in a necessary reboot, could cause you to lose all of the changes you had previously programmed.

FIGURE B.19

Saving all programming changes before executing the program will prevent loss of work due to faulty execution.

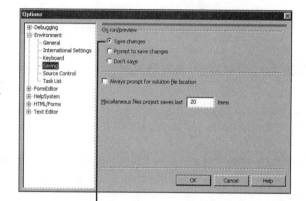

Code changes should always be saved before the project is executed

A second set of options that many programmers may want to change exist within the Text Editor, Tabs list. Under the Tabs node, you can specify how to treat tabs for HTML files, Java source files, and plain text files. If you are coding in a group environment where many programmers often edit the same programs, it will be beneficial if everyone chooses to either keep the tab characters within the source files or replace them with spaces, as shown in Figure B.20.

FIGURE B.20

Choosing a convention in your programming environment for dealing with tabs will prevent many headaches.

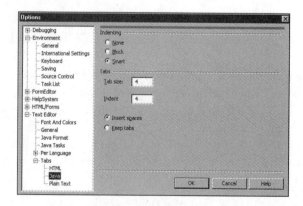

APPENDIX C

Visual J++ Programming Reference

Intrinsic Datatypes

Datatype	Size in Bits	Value Range	Default Value
boolean	8	true or false	false
byte	8	-128 to 127	0
char	16	\u0000 to \uffff	'\x0'
short	16	-32768 to 32767	0
int	32	-2147483648 to 2147483647	0
float	32	-1.40239846E-45 to 3.40282347E+38	0.0F
long	64	-9223372036854775808 to 9223372036854775807	0
double	64	-1.7E308 to 1.7E308	0.0D

Reserved Words in Java

abstract	else	interface	switch
boolean	extends	long	synchronized
break	final	native	this
byte	finally	new	
case	float	null	throw
catch	for	package	throws
char	false	private	transient
class	goto	protected	true
const	if	public	
continue	implements	return	try
default	import	short	void
do	instanceof	static	volatile
double	int	super	while

Comment Types

Syntax	Description
/* comment */	Multiple-line comment
// comment	Single-line comment
/** comment */	Java Documentation comment
/* TODO ...*/	Special comment for Visual J++ that will add a TODO task to the Task List Window for future reference

Special Character Literals

Description	Literal	Unicode Character
New line	\n	\u000A
Tab	\t	\u0009
Backspace	\b	\u0008
Carriage Return	\r	\u000D
Form Feed	\f	\u000C

Description	Literal	Unicode Character
Single quote	\'	\u0027
Double quote	\"	\u0022
Backslash	\\	\u005C

Operator Precedence

Precedence	Operators
1	. [ ] ( )
2	++ — ! ~ instanceof
3	* / %
4	+ -
5	<< >> >>>
6	< > <= >=
7	= = !=
8	&
9	^
10	¦
11	&&
12	¦ ¦
13	?:
14	= += -= *= /= %= >>= <<= <<<= &= ^= ¦=

Results of Mixing Datatypes in Expressions

Operands	byte	short	int	long	char	float	double
byte	int	int	int	long	int	float	double
short	int	int	int	long	int	float	double
int	int	int	int	long	int	float	double
long	long	long	long	long	long	float	double
char	int	int	int	long	int	float	double

continues

Operands	byte	short	int	long	char	float	double
float	float	float	float	float	float	float	double
double	double	double	double	double	double	double	double

Visual J++ Utilities and Help Screens

This section lists the utility programs that accompany versions 1, 1.1, and 6 of Visual J++, as well as the output you get when you invoke each with either no input or the /? option.

guidgen.exe—Create GUID Utility

FIGURE C.1

Front screen of the GuidGen utility. This interface can also be invoked in versions 1 and 1.1 of Visual J++ by selecting Tools, Create Guid from the studio menu.

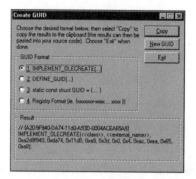

javaidl.exe—ActiveX Component Wizard for Java

FIGURE C.2

Front screen of the JavaIdl utility. This program can also be invoked in version 1.1 of Visual J++ by selecting Tools, ActiveX Wizard for Java from the studio menu.

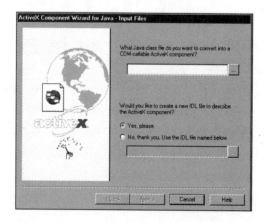

javareg.exe—Java/COM Registration Utility

FIGURE C.3

*Invocation information
for the JavaReg utility.
This utility was
shipped with versions
1 and 1.1 of Visual
J++.*

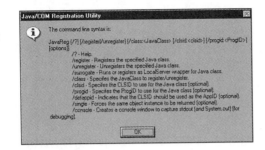

javatlb.exe—Java Type Library Conversion Utility

The javatlb.exe program was shipped with versions 1 and 1.1 of Visual J++.

```
Microsoft (R) Visual J++ Java Typelib Conversion Utility Version 1.01.7048
Copyright (C) Microsoft Corp 1996. All rights reserved.
Usage: JAVATLB [options] <filename>
 /d <directory>    root directory for class file output
 /p <package>      set package for types
 /p:b[-]           include basename as package <default=include>
 /X:m[-]           auto-marshal COM parameters <default=on>
 /U                unassemble class file
 /U:T              generate type library summary information
```

jvc.exe—Microsoft Visual J++ Compiler

Visual J++ 6 JVC Compiler Information

```
Microsoft (R) Visual J++ Compiler Version 1.02.7322
Copyright (C) Microsoft Corp 1996-1997. All rights reserved.
Usage: JVC [options] <filename>

 /cp <classpath>   set class path for compilation
 /cp:p <path>      prepend path to class path
 /cp:o[-]             print classpath
 /d <directory>    root directory for class file output
 /D <symbol>       define conditional compilation symbol
 /g[-]                full debug information (g:l, g:d)
   /g:l[-]            generate line numbers <default=none>
   /g:t[-]            generate debug tables <default=none>
 /nologo              don't display the copyright banner
 /nowarn              turn off warnings <default=warn>
 /nowrite             compile only - do not generate class files
 /O[-]                full optimization (O:I,O:J)
```

```
/O:I[-]                optimize by inlining <default=no opt>
/O:J[-]                optimize bytecode jumps <default=no opt>
/ref[-]                recompile referenced classes if out of date
                       <default=enabled>

/verbose               print messages about compilation progress
/w{0-4}                set warning level <default=2>
/wx[-]                 treat warnings as errors
/x[-]                  disable extensions <default=enabled>
```

Microsoft (R) Visual J++ Compiler Version 6.00.8052
Copyright (C) Microsoft Corp 1996-1997. All rights reserved.

Visual J++ 1 and 1.1 JVC Compiler Information

```
Usage: Jvc [options] <filename>
/?                list all options
/cp <classpath>   set class path for compilation
/cp:p <path>      prepend path to class path
/cp:o[-]          print class path
/d <directory     root directory for class file output
/g[-]             full debug information (g:1, g:d)
/g:1[-]           generate line numbers <default=none>
/g:t[-]           generate debug tables <default=none>
/nowarn           turns off warnings <default=warn>
/nowrite          compile only - do not generate class files
/O[-]             full optimization (O:I,O:J)
/O:I[-]           optimize by inlining <default=no opt>
/O:J[-]           optimize bytecode jumps <default=no opt>
/verbose          print messages about compilation progress
/w{0:4}           set warning level <default=2>
/x[-]             disable extensions <default=enabled>
'-'               turns flag off
```

jview.exe—Microsoft Visual J++ Command-Line Interpreter

Visual J++ 6 Jview Information

```
Microsoft (R) Command-line Loader for Java (tm) Version 4.79.2556
Copyright (C) Microsoft Corp 1996-1997. All rights reserved.
Usage: JView [options] <classname> [arguments]

Options:
/?                displays usage text
/cp <classpath>   set class path
/cp:p <path>      prepend path to class path
/cp:a <path>      append path to class path
/n                namespace in which to run
/p                pauses before terminating if an error
                  occurs
```

```
    /v                       verify all classes
    /d:<name>=<value>        define system property
    /a                       execute AppletViewer
```

Classname:
    .CLASS file to be executed.

Arguments:
    command-line arguments to be passed on to the class file

Visual J++ 1 and 1.1 Jview Information

Microsoft (R) Command-line Loader for Java (tm) Version 4.79.1515
Copyright (C) Microsoft Corp 1996-1997. All rights reserved.
Usage: JView [options] <classname> [arguments]

```
Options:
    /?                       displays usage text
    /cp <classpath>          set class path
    /cp:p <path>             prepend path to class path
    /cp:a <path>             append path to class path
    /p                       pauses before terminating if an error
                             occurs
    /v                       verify all classes
    /d:<name>=<value>        define system property
```

Classname:
    .CLASS file to be executed.

Arguments:
    command-line arguments to be passed on to the class file

midl.exe—Microsoft IDL Compiler

The midl.exe program was shipped with versions 1 and 1.1 of Visual J++.

```
-MIDL COMPILER OPTIONS-
                               -MODE-
/ms_ext           Microsoft extensions to the IDL language (default)
/c_ext            Allow Microsoft C extensions in the IDL file (default)
/osf              OSF mode - disables /ms_ext and /c_ext options
/app_config       Allow selected ACF attributes in the IDL file
/mktyplib203      MKTYPLIB Version 2.03 compatiblity mode


                               -INPUT-
/acf filename     Specify the attribute configuration file
/I directory-list Specify one or more directories for include path
/no_def_idir      Ignore the current and the INCLUDE directories


                       -OUTPUT FILE GENERATION-
/client none      Do not generate client files
/client stub      Generate client stub file only
```

```
/out directory       Specify destination directory for output files
/server none         Generate no server files
/server stub         Generate server stub file only
/syntax_check        Check syntax only; do not generate output files
/Zs                  Check syntax only; do not generate output files
/oldtlb              Generate old format type libraries
/newtlb              Generate new format type libraries
```

                              -OUTPUT FILE NAMES-

```
/cstub filename      Specify client stub file name
/dlldata filename    Specify dlldata file name
/h filename          Specify header file name
/header filename     Specify header file name
/iid filename        Specify interface UUID file name
/proxy filename      Specify proxy file name
/sstub filename      Specify server stub file name
/tlb filename        Specify type library file name
```

                      -C COMPILER AND PREPROCESSOR OPTIONS-

```
/cpp_cmd cmd_line    Specify name of C preprocessor
/cpp_opt options     Specify additional C preprocessor options
/D name[=def]        Pass #define name, optional value to C preprocessor
/no_cpp              Turn off the C preprocessing option
/nocpp               Turn off the C preprocessing option
/U name              Remove any previous definition (undefine)
```

                                -ENVIRONMENT-

```
/char signed         C compiler default char type is signed
/char unsigned       C compiler default char type is unsigned
/char ascii7         Char values limited to 0-127
/dos                 Target environment is MS-DOS client
/env dos             Target environment is MS-DOS client
/env mac             Target environment is Apple Macintosh
/env powermac        Target environment is Apple PowerMac
/env win16           Target environment is Microsoft Windows 16-bit (Win
3.x)
/env win32           Target environment is Microsoft Windows 32-bit (NT)
/lcid                Locale id for international locales
/mac                 Target environment is Apple Macintosh
/ms_union            Use Midl 1.0 non-DCE wire layout for non-encapsulated
unions
/oldnames            Do not mangle version number into names
/powermac            Target environment is Apple PowerMac
/rpcss               Automatically activate rpc_sm_enable_allocate
/use_epv             Generate server side application calls via entry-pt
                     vector
/no_default_epv      Do not generate a default entry-point vector
/prefix client str   Add "str" prefix to client-side entry points
/prefix server str   Add "str" prefix to server-side manager routines
/prefix switch str   Add "str" prefix to switch routine prototypes
/prefix all str      Add "str" prefix to all routines
```

/win16	Target environment is Microsoft Windows 16-bit (Win 3.x)
/win32	Target environment is Microsoft Windows 32-bit (NT)

-ERROR AND WARNING MESSAGES-

/error none	Turn off all error checking options
/error allocation	Check for out of memory errors
/error bounds_ check	Check size vs transmission length specification
/error enum	Check enum values to be in allowable range
/error ref	Check ref pointers to be non-null
/error stub_data	Emit additional check for server side stub data validity
/no_warn	Suppress compiler warning messages

-OPTIMIZATION-

/align {1¦2¦4¦8}	Designate packing level of structures
/pack {1¦2¦4¦8}	Designate packing level of structures
/Zp{1¦2¦4¦8}	Designate packing level of structures
/Oi	Generate fully interpreted stubs
/Oic	Generate fully interpreted stubs for standard interfaces and stubless proxies for object interfaces as of NT 3.51 release
/Oicf	Generate fully interpreted stubs with extensions and stubless proxies for object interfaces as of NT 4.0 release
/Os	Generate inline stubs
/hookole	Generate HookOle debug info for local object interfaces

-MISCELLANEOUS-

@response_file	Accept input from a response file
/?	Display a list of MIDL compiler switches
/confirm	Display options without compiling MIDL source
/help	Display a list of MIDL compiler switches
/nologo	Supress displaying of the banner lines
/o filename	Redirects output from screen to a file
/W{0¦1¦2¦3¦4}	Specify warning level 0-4 (default = 1)
/WX	Report warnings at specified /W level as errors

mktyplib.exe—Type Library Generator

The mktyplib.exe program was shipped with versions 1 and 1.1 of Visual J++.

```
Microsoft (R) Type Library Generator  Version 2.20.4048
Copyright (c) Microsoft Corp. 1993-1995.  All rights reserved.
Usage: MKTYPLIB <options> [inputfile]
Valid options are:
/help or /?        Displays usage.
/tlb <filename>    Specifies type library output filename.
                   Defaults to input name with extension
```

```
                        replaced by ".tlb".
/h [filename]           Specifies .H file output filename.
/<system>               Specifies kind of type library to make
                        (win16, win32, mac, mips, alpha, ppc or
                        ppc32). Defaults to win32.
/align <#>              Override default alignment setting.
/o filename             Redirects output from screen to
                        specified file.
/nologo                 Don't display the copyright banner.
/w0                     Disable warnings.
/nocpp                  Don't spawn the C pre-processor.
/cpp_cmd <path>         Specifies path for C pre-processor.
                        Defaults to CL.EXE.
/cpp_opt "<opt>"        Specifies options for C pre-processor.
                        Defaults to: "/C /E /D__MKTYPLIB__".
/Ddefine[=value]        Defines value for C pre-processor.
/I includepath          Specifies path for include files.
```

regsvr32.exe—Control Registration Utility

FIGURE C.4

The regsvr32.exe *application registers components and programs in the PC Windows Registry.*

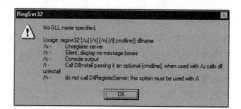

signcode.exe

The signcode.exe application was shipped with version 6 of Visual J++.

```
Usage:  SignCode [options] FileName
Options:
 -spc   <file>          Spc file containing software publishing
certificates
 -v     <pvkFile>       Pvk file name containing the private key
 -k     <KeyName>       Key container name
 -n     <name>          Text name representing content of the file to be
                        signed
 -i     <info>          Place to get more info on content (usually a URL)
 -p     <provider>      Name of the cryptographic provider on the system
 -y     <type>          Cryptographic provider type to use
 -ky    <keytype>       Key type <signature|exchange|<integer>>
 -$     <authority>     Signing authority of the certificate
<individual|            Default to using certificate's highest capability
commercial>
 -a     <algorithm>     Hashing algorithm for signing
<md5|sha1>.             Default to md5
 -t     <URL>           TimeStamp server's http address
```

-tr	\<number\>	The # of timestamp trial until succeeds. Default to 1
-tw	\<number\>	The # of seconds delay between each timestamp. Default to 0
-j	\<dllName\>	Name of the dll that provides attributes of the signature
-jp	\<param\>	Parameter to be passed to the dll
-c	\<file\>	X509 file containing encoded software publishing certificate
-s	\<store\>	Cert store containing certs. Default to my store
-r	\<location\>	Location of the cert store in the registry
\<localMachine¦ currentUser\>.		Default to currentUser
-sp	\<policy\>	Add all the certificates in the chain or add until one cert in the chain is from the spc store.
\<chain¦spcstore\>.		Default to spcstore
-cn	\<name\>	The common name of the certificate
-x		Do not sign the file. Only Timestamp the file

Note: To sign with a SPC file, the required options are -spc and -v if your private key is in a PVK file. If your private key is in a registry key container, then -spc and -k are the required options.

vstudio.exe

FIGURE C.5

vstudio.exe *is the main application of Visual J++ 6. This application will be added to the list of programs in the Start menu and launches the Visual J++ IDE.*

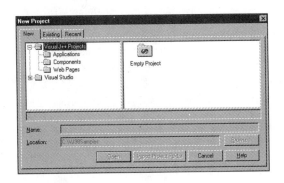

msjavx86.exe

FIGURE C.6

The msjavax86.exe *application was shipped with version 6 of Visual J++ and allows you to add Java support to Internet Explorer.*

spyxx.exe

FIGURE C.7

*The Windows Spy
debugging application
was shipped with ver-
sion 6 of Visual J++
and provides enhanced
message debugging.*

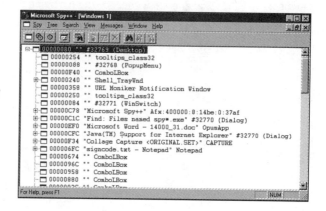

jactivex.exe—Version 6 Only

```
JActiveX [options] inputfiles...
```

Options:

```
    -TRANSLATION-
    /bx[+¦-][!]              expose OCX's as Bean (! == don't check for
                             control flag)
    /w                       disable all warnings
    /wec                     set exit code on warning
    /WX                      treat warnings as errors
    /X:m-                    disable automarshal (default=automarshal)

    -OUTPUT-
    /d <directory>           set output directory (default=%WINDIR%\java\trustlib)
    /e                       exclude output for typelibs not on command line
    /p <pname>               set root package (default=none)
    /p:b-                    don't include typelib name in package

    -MISCELLANEOUS-
    /?                       display this screen
    /javatlb                 JavaTLB compatibility mode
    /l <lstfile>             create list of all output files (default=none)
    /nologo                  don't show logo
    /r                       register type libraries
```

```
WARNING: Do not use Microsoft Visual J++ compilers prior to
   version 1.02.3920 to compile the files generated by this tool.
```

vjreg.exe—Visual J++ COM Registration Tool

The VjReg.exe application was shipped with version 6 of Visual J++.

```
Microsoft (R) Visual J++ COM Registration Tool Version 6.00.8055
Copyright (C) Microsoft Corp 1997-1998. All Rights Reserved.
Usage: vjreg [options] <class files>

Options:
 /nologo                      do not display the copyright banner
 /typelib <filename>          create type library with given name
   /name "<name>"             set internal name of type library
   /description "<desc>"      set description of type library
   /helpfile <file>           set type library help file name
   /helpcontext <number>      set type library help context id
 /regtypelib <filename>       register existing type library
 /cp:p "<path>"               prepend path to the classpath for typelib
                              creation
 /vbr <filename>              generate VBR (remote server info) file
 /noinvoke                    do not invoke user code during
                              registration
 /nowarn                      do not display warnings
 /unreg                       unregister classes and type library
 /unregclasses                unregister classes (leave type library
                              registered)
```

```
Microsoft (R) Visual J++ COM Registration Tool Version 6.00.8055
Copyright (C) Microsoft Corp 1997-1998. All Rights Reserved.

Usage: vjreg [options] <class files>

Options:
 /nologo                      do not display the copyright banner
 /typelib <filename>          create type library with given name
   /name "<name>"             set internal name of type library
   /description "<desc>"      set description of type library
   /helpfile <file>           set type library help file name
   /helpcontext <number>      set type library help context id
 /regtypelib <filename>       register existing type library
 /cp:p "<path>"               prepend path to the classpath for typelib
                              creation
 /vbr <filename>              generate VBR (remote server info) file
 /noinvoke                    do not invoke user code during registration
 /nowarn                      do not display warnings
 /unreg                       unregister classes and type library
 /unregclasses                unregister classes (leave type library
                              registered)
```

C

wjview.exe

FIGURE C.8

The wjview.exe *application was shipped with version 6 of Visual J++ and contains the same options as* jview.exe.

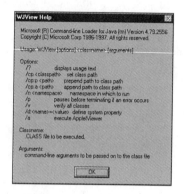

APPENDIX D

Other Sources of Information on the Web

As you have probably noticed, one of the largest sources of information on Java programming and related topics is the Web itself. There are countless sites that offer advice on Java programming, the Visual J++ programming environment, HTML files, ActiveX technology, and so on. In this appendix, I have listed some of the more popular sources for general information or asking a specific question of other users.

Newsgroups

comp.lang.java.advocacy

comp.lang.java.announce

comp.lang.java.api

comp.lang.java.databases

comp.lang.java.gui

comp.lang.java.help

comp.lang.java.machine

comp.lang.java.misc

comp.lang.java.programmer

comp.lang.java.security

comp.lang.java.setup

comp.lang.java.softwaretools

comp.lang.java.tech

comp.lang.javascript

livesoftware.javascript.developer

livesoftware.javascript.examples

microsoft.public.internetexplorer.java

microsoft.public.internetexplorer.java.cabdevkit

microsoft.public.java.activex

microsoft.public.java.afc

microsoft.public.java.cab

microsoft.public.java.sdk

microsoft.public.java.security

microsoft.public.java.visualj++

microsoft.public.java.vm

microsoft.public.visualj.com-support

microsoft.public.visualj.compiler

microsoft.public.visualj.debugger

microsoft.public.visualj.dev-environment

microsoft.public.visualj.discussion

microsoft.public.visualj.installation

microsoft.public.visualj.misc-tools

Web Sites

SiteBuilder Network Programming—`http://www.microsoft.com/workshop/prog/`

This site offers help on a wide range of Internet programming topics, including Java, ActiveX, cabinet technology, and security.

Cup O' Joe Java Shop—`http://www.cupojoe.com`

This site contains information on Java programming topics such as applets, applications, and JDK. The site also contains forums in which you can ask Java-related programming questions on topics such as applets, applications, threads, networks, databases, and so on, and receive answers from other Java developers.

Digital Espresso—`http://www.mentorsoft.com/DE/`

This site contains a weekly summary of information from various Java mailing lists and newsgroups.

Gamelan—`http://www.gamelan.com`

This site contains a great deal of Java programming information on topics such as JavaBeans, ActiveX, JavaScripts, and VRML. You can also send your Java development questions to some of the top Java experts around.

Welcome to JARS.COM—`http://www.jars.com`

Jars.com is a Java review service. This site lists some the Java applets that they feel are the best of their kind. Articles related to Java news are also listed.

The Java Developers Organizations—http://www.jade.org

This site claims to be trade association for Java developers worldwide. This site's goal is to provide a forum for Java developers to discuss their accomplishments and goals.

Java Home Page—http://java.sun.com

This is Sun Microsystems' official site for Java information. As you may have guessed, the site contains a large amount of information specific to the Java programming language, including documentation, JavaBeans, developer information, and products.

Java Developer's Journal—http://www.sys-con.com/java/

This site contains an online version of the Java Developer's Journal. This publication contains information on many Java programming-related topics, including development platforms, ActiveX, and security.

Javology—http://www.javology.com/javology/

This site contains a monthly online magazine with news related to Java development, and offers opinions on many of the numerous products available.

Visual J++ Web Page—http://www.microsoft.com/visualj/

Microsoft's Visual J++ Web site, containing information on all supported releases of the Visual J++ programming environment. A weekly tip related to Java programming is also provided, and can be very useful.

Microsoft Technologies for Java—http://www.microsoft.com/java/

Microsoft's Java Technologies home page. This site contains access to the tools, classes, and packages that Microsoft has developed to aid in your Java development.

Live Software: JavaScript Resource Center—http://jrc.livesoftware.com/

This site offers help with Java, specifically the JavaScript language. It contains many code samples written in Java and JavaScript, and provides links to other sites containing JavaScript documentation.

The JavaBeans Site—http://splash.javasoft.com/beans/

This site contains reference material about JavaBeans, billed as the only component architecture for Java.

ACTIVEX.COM—http://www.activex.com

This site contains a comprehensive library of ActiveX controls. You can download ActiveX component software, including freeware, shareware, and demos. It is an excellent place to see how ActiveX technology is being used.

D

Component Object Model—http://www.microsoft.com/com/

This site contains information about COM-based technologies, such as Distributed COM (DCOM), COM+, Microsoft® Transaction Server (MTS), and ActiveX™ Controls.

The Ultimate Resource for Java Developers—http://www.ibm.com/java/

This site includes information on many of the products IBM has produced to aid in Java program development, including BeanExtender, which builds and enhances JavaBeans components.

GLOSSARY

abstract For class methods, an empty method whose declaration is defined but whose implementation is not. All the methods of an interface are defined as abstract, leaving it the responsibility of the implementing class to provide the actual behavior of the method. Abstract methods are often referred to as incomplete methods.

abstract class A class that only contains abstract methods. *See* abstract.

accessor methods Methods of a class that return an otherwise inaccessible member. Accessor methods are generally public and return the value of class member variables that are private.

AFC (Application Foundation Classes) Developed by Microsoft as an alternative to the classes of the `java.awt` package. Each of these classes is developed in pure Java code, thereby providing another means of developing portable GUI interfaces in Java.

animation A programming topic relating to the presentation of a sequence of images and/or sound. Animation sequences are usually achieved in Java through multithreaded programming.

animation flicker The screen flickering caused by the repainting required to display an animation sequence. Concepts such as double buffering can be used to reduce animation flicker.

API (Application Programming Interface)   A set of functions provided by a library developer to give the programmer access to a specific set of features.

applet   A Java program that runs with the help of another program, typically a Web browser.

Application Wizard   Wizard application included with Visual J++ 6 to assist in the creation of Windows Applications. The Application Wizard is very useful in the creation of data-bound applications, allowing you to specify the database and tables the produced form should bind to.

array   A static data structure that places a single type of data in contiguous cells.

attributes   In HTML, the options that are available within each tag. *See* HTML and tags.

AWT   A collection of Java graphical user interface classes and interfaces provided by Sun with the Java Developers Toolkit.

builders   Applications included in the IDE that allow you to update existing classes based on options selected in a dialog. In Visual J++ 6, the J/Direct Call Builder and Class Builder are two such applications, allowing you to modify Java classes from a GUI interface.

bytecode   Instructions for the Java Virtual Machine, generated by the Java compiler and stored in the class file. *See* Java Virtual Machine.

CAB   In Visual J++, one of the options for Distribution Unit projects. A CAB file is a compressed collection of bytecode class files, usually used with an applet to reduce the download time required. Additionally, CAB files can be digitally signed, producing applets that can perform more operations than are normally allowed within the Java sandbox. *See* Java sandbox.

character literals   In Java, a 16-bit unsigned integer with a value from 0–65535, or a Unicode character. In the source code, a character literal is placed within tick marks (` `` `).

class   A template for objects, typically modeled from real-world entities.

class libraries   A collection of classes and interfaces logically packaged together for use by other programmers. In Java, class libraries are referred to as packages.

client/server application   Term used to describe a distributed programming solution. The client application, run by the user community, communicates with the server application, which generally houses the data repository required by all users.

CLSID   Class Identifier, or the GUID that represents a COM class viewable in the Windows Registry. In Visual J++ 6, the CLSID is automatically assigned by the Visual Studio platform.

coclass   Another term often used for a COM Class. *See* Component Object Model.

code block   In programming terms, a section of code usually surrounded by curly brackets ({ }). The area of code placed within the curly brackets is often referred to as a code block.

Code-behind HTML projects   One of the project classifications supported in Visual J++ 6. These projects are created with a single HTML file and a single Java source file. The HTML file loads the COM object produced from the Java source file. The COM object can add and manipulate controls on the HTML Web page.

COM   *See* Component Object Model.

COM DLL   One of the project classifications supported in Visual J++ 6. A COM DLL project is compiled as a COM object that is registered in the Windows Registry and is therefore usable from other applications.

COM integration   *See* Component Object Model.

comments   Text included in a Java source file that describes how a piece of code executes. In-line comments appear after a "//" entry, while multiple-line comments, also called traditional comments, usually appear within a "/* */" section.

Component Object Model   A standard developed by Microsoft to provide a seamless mechanism for software components to provide services to each other. COM provides a common paradigm for interactions among applications.

Console Applications   One of the project classifications supported in Visual J++ 6. Console applications start out as fully portable Java applications that are launched by the Java Virtual Machine, or `Jview.exe` for Windows developers.

constants   A value used in a computer program that is guaranteed not to change at run-time. The guarantee is often enforced by the compiler. In Java, constants are declared `static final`.

constructor   The first method of a class called when an object of the class is created with the new operator. The constructor method has the same name as the class itself, can receive any combination of input parameters, and is always declared as returning no value.

context menu   Also known as a pop-up menu. A context menu for a component appears when the component is selected and the right button of the mouse is pressed.

decrement operator　An operator that reduces the value of a variable. The operator is referred to as the decrement operator in Java.

Design Time Properties　The properties that can be applied to a control in the Form Designer. Contrast this with Execution Properties, which are the properties of a control changed during the execution of the program. *See* Properties Window.

distributed　A type of application that contains both a client and a server component. An application that is distributed contains multiple application components, often running on different systems, all developed to meet a specific need in an expedient manner.

Distribution Unit　A high-level project classification in Visual J++ 6 that includes Self-Extracting Setup programs, ZIP files, and Cabinet (CAB) Files. Distribution Unit projects give you enhanced capabilities and flexibility in the area of applet and application distribution to your user community.

DLL　*See* Dynamic Link Library.

Document Outline window　One of the windows included with Visual Studio 6. The Document Outline window is dynamic in nature, in that it changes to the Class Outline window when a Java class is being viewed and to the HTML Outline window when an HTML file is being viewed.

Dynamic HTML model　A feature of IE 4.0 that gives Web developers the ability to dynamically update the content, style, and structure of Web-based content, while providing them with detailed control over the appearance, interactivity, and multimedia elements required for the application.

Dynamic Link Library (DLL)　Compiled files that are generally not directly executable, and they do not receive messages. DLLs are separate files containing functions that can be called by programs and other DLLs to perform certain computations or functions.

encapsulation　In object-oriented programming, a feature that allows you to hide the data elements of a class from other classes that access it.

equality operators　Operators that compare the value of two variables or expressions.

escape characters　A character used in a Java source file to inform the compiler that the next character is special. The backslash (\) is a commonly used escape character.

Exceptions　Events that occur during the execution of a program that disrupt the normal flow of instructions. Methods in Java that are declared as potentially throwing an exception must be called in a `try-catch` code block.

extends   Keyword used in the declaration of a Java class to achieve inheritance. *See* inheritance and inherited members.

floating point literals   A literal with a whole-number part, a decimal point, a fractional part, an exponent, and a type suffix. The exponent, if present, is indicated by the ASCII letter *e* or *E* followed by an optionally signed integer. A floating-point literal is of type `float` if it is suffixed with an ASCII letter *F* or *f*; otherwise its type is double, and it can optionally be suffixed with an ASCII letter *d* or *D*.

floating-point number   A number that can have its decimal point in any position. Internally, the computer usually stores these numbers using scientific notation, so that the number of digits of precision is separate from the exponent. For example, $.234 \times 2^4$ is a floating-point number equal to 3.744.

fully trusted   A classification of Java applets where the normal security restrictions no longer apply. A fully trusted applet exists within a digitally signed CAB file where the signature is flagged by the user as being completely trustworthy.

garbage collector   In Java, the mechanism by which the memory associated with unused objects is reclaimed and freed.

Graphical user interface (GUI)   A human/computer interface such as Microsoft Windows, the Mac OS, or the X Windowing System, which relies upon a high-resolution display, a graphical pointing device such as a mouse, and a set of onscreen controls that the user manipulates directly.

GUID (Globally Unique Identifier)   A 128-bit unique identifier associated with a COM object stored in the Windows Registry to assist COM clients in locating COM servers.

HTML (Hypertext Marked Language)   A tag-based language used in the creation of Web pages.

HTML Authoring tool   The GUI-based HTML editor included with Visual J++ 6. This tool allows you to create sophisticated Web pages used in the Java applets, and occasionally Java applications, that are developed in Visual J++.

HTML intrinsic components   Components that can be added to an HTML file, including buttons, radio buttons, and text fields.

hyperlink   An area of text within an HTML file that, when selected, will point the browser to a different URL.

hypertext   Text that can be clicked on to jump to another URL or HTML file.

IID (Interface Identifier)   The GUID that represents a COM interface viewable in the Windows Registry. In Visual J++ 6, the IID is automatically assigned by the Visual Studio platform.

implements   Keyword used in the declaration of a Java class to implement a Java interface. *See* interface.

import   Keyword used in a Java source file to import a Java class or entire package of Java classes. *See* packages.

increment operator   Add to the value of a variable. The ++ operator is referred to as the increment operator in Java.

inheritance   A fundamental concept of object-oriented programming that allows one class to inherit behaviors from an existing class. The base class is often referred to as the superclass, and the class that inherits from it is known as the subclass. *See* subclass and superclass.

inherited members   The methods and variables a superclass exposes to its subclasses. *See* subclass and superclass.

inner classes   *See* nested classes.

instance   A software object made from a class. *See* object and class.

instantiated   Term used when an object of a class is created. When an object of a class is created with the new operator, it is also referred to as instantiated.

integer literal   A number that may be expressed in decimal (base 10), hexadecimal (base 16), or octal (base 8).

Integrated Development Environment (IDE)   A development environment that supports the development, debugging, and execution of an application. Visual Studio 6 is the IDE for Visual J++ 6.

IntelliSense   A technology designed to ease the process of writing syntactically correct code. These features are included in Visual J++ 6 and provide developers with instant syntax reference and object model assistance to reduce programming time and ensure syntactically correct code.

interface   In Java, a mechanism for telling the compiler that you intend a specific set of methods to be defined in certain classes. Those classes are then defined to "implement" the interface. The methods included in the interface are abstract and empty.

interpreted   In programming terms, a language is classified as interpreted if the instructions the compiler outputs are then interpreted by the operating machine. Java is considered an interpreted language because the bytecode class files are examined and interpreted by the Java Virtual Machine on varying platforms.

intranet A network that exists exclusively within an organization and that is based on Internet technology. It can have thousands of users across many locations and still be private.

IP addresses A 32-bit number that uniquely identifies a computer, printer, router, or other device on a TCP/IP network. TCP/IP addresses are normally expressed in dotted-decimal format, with four numbers separated by periods.

J/Direct A Microsoft technology that allows the Java classes you develop to call native methods, often in the Windows API. Additionally, J/Direct can be used to create structures and constants used in external DLL files.

J/Direct Call Builder Dialog GUI interface in Visual J++ 6 that allows you to invoke the J/Direct Call Builder to include the required directives in your Java class to access native methods, often in the Windows API.

Java Applet Wizard A wizard application included in Visual J++ 1 and Visual J++ 1.1 that allows you to develop applets and applications specifying options such as multi-threading, animation, and input parameters.

Java Archive (JAR) File A file that contains Java components, such as class files, and optional supporting resources, such as sounds and images.

Java class A Java-developed class. *See* class.

Java Developers Toolkit *See* JDK.

Java Native Interface (JNI) A method developed by Sun that allows Java methods to be implemented in a native language such as C or C++.

Java Resource Wizard Wizard application included with Visual J++ 1 and 1.1 that converted a dialog drawn within a resource editor to fully portable Java classes. This wizard does not exist within Visual J++ 6, making the development of portable GUI-based applets and applications more difficult.

Java Sandbox A set of security restrictions designed to keep Java applets from accessing system resources.

Java Virtual Machine (JVM) The Java interpreter that executes the bytecodes on a particular platform. *See* bytecode.

java.net One of the packages of the JDK that supports the creation of distributed applets and applications in Java.

JDK (Java Developers Toolkit)   The packages containing classes and interfaces developed by Sun, used as the basis for the development of fully portable applets and applications in Java.

JNI   *See* Java Native Interface.

Just In Time (JIT) compilers   Java compilers that create binary executables from the bytecode class files. The binary executables execute much faster than the bytecode class files because the interpreted layer is removed, but they are not portable to other platforms.

life cycle   Describes the processes employed by a Web browser from the beginning of the applet's execution through termination.

logical expressions   Expressions in a programming language that equate to one of two Boolean values, true or false.

members   The methods and variables of a class. *See* class, methods, and variables.

method signature   Term used to describe the syntax of a particular method, including the input parameters and the returned value. Also referred to as the method definition.

methods   In object-oriented design, the functions that are associated with a class. *See* class.

modifiers   The scope in which a Java class, a method, or a class variable can be referenced. Examples of modifiers include public, private, and protected.

modular   Term used to describe the type of programming employed in object-oriented solutions. Through concepts such as inheritance, classes are developed as building blocks based on existing superclasses, thereby achieving a modular design.

modulus   Mathematical operator that returns the remainder of a division operator. The modulus operator in Java is %.

multi-project solutions   A solution, in Visual J++ 6, that contains multiple projects. This type of solution can be very beneficial when multiple projects require a great deal of interaction with each other. Also highly recommended for an application and its corresponding distribution unit project.

multithreading   In programming terms, separate threads of execution can be created to perform multiple operations simultaneously.

native method   A method that exists in an external file, such as a DLL, that you may want to call from a Java program. The J/Direct technology assists Java developers in accessing the native methods of the Windows API, and other third-party DLLs.

nested class A class declared within the scope of another class. Nested classes, also known as inner classes, are considered to be within the scope of the enclosing class and are available for use within that scope.

network The collection of computers, printers, and routers available within your organization. The Internet itself is a very large-scale network.

object The implementation of a class. Objects are created by the new operator for a given class.

object-oriented In programming terms, the idea that classes that often emulate real-world items are used as the fundamental building block of all programs. Java is a strict object-oriented language because all code exists within a class.

override In object-oriented programming, a method created in a subclass that has the same method signature as the superclass. The new method overrides the implementation of the method contained within the superclass by providing more specific functionality. *See* polymorphism.

packages The name of a class library in Java. *See* class libraries.

parameters Values or objects passed between a subroutine and a calling routine. Also used to describe the values passed from an HTML file to a Java applet class.

pointer A variable that holds the address of another software entity. Pointers are not supported in Java, but are commonly referred to within J/Direct.

polymorphism In object-oriented design, the ability to use the method of a subclass in place of its superclass method. *See* override.

primitive type In Java, a datatype that is not an object. Primitive types include characters, integers, floating point numbers, and Booleans.

priority For threads, the priority determines which thread should receive processing time. The priority of a thread can be retrieved and modified.

project In Visual J++, the primary container for a Java application or applet. Several different types of projects can be created in Visual J++ 6, including Applet on HTML projects, Code-behind HTML projects, Windows Applications projects, and Console Application projects. Projects themselves are contained with solutions. *See* solution.

Project Explorer window One of the main windows of the Visual Studio 6 platform that displays the Visual J++ solution currently being worked on. Within this solution will be one or multiple projects, with the source files contained within each also being displayed in the Project Explorer window.

Properties window   One of the main windows of the Visual Studio 6 platform, primarily used during the HTML and Form design process. For example, while using the Form Designer, the Properties window displays all of the properties of the selected WFC control and allows the users to change each.

Raw Native Interface   An alternative to J/Direct, used to create Java classes than can communicate with native methods.

relational operators   Operators that compare the value of an expression or variable to a value of another expression or variable.

Resource Editor   In Visual J++ 1 and 1.1, a drag-and-drop–based editor that allowed you to create fully portable GUI applications in Java. The Java Resource Wizard would convert the Resource Template file produced from the Resource Editor into portable Java classes.

RNI   *See* Raw Native Interface.

Sandbox   *See* Java sandbox.

scope   The region in a program in which a variable exists. Variables can be declared within a particular method, meaning they have local scope to only that method. Class variables have a scope relating to all methods of the class.

self-extracting setup   In Visual J++, one of the options for Distribution Unit projects. A Self-Extracting Setup project produces an executable that, when executed, installs the Java application on the user's PC.

solution   The top-level item in Visual J++ 6 programming. A solution contains one or multiple projects, which themselves contain Java source files, HTML files, image files, and so on.

SPC   The file extension for a digital signature file. These certificate files are often referred to as SPC files.

static   In object-oriented design, of or pertaining to the class as a whole, rather than an instance.

string literals   Literals that have zero or more characters enclosed in double quotes. These quote-enclosed characters can include escape sequences.

structs   *See* structures.

structures   In programming languages, a datatype that is the combination of other, often varying datatypes. Structures are not supported in pure Java programs, but are often required when accessing native methods using J/Direct.

stub out In programming terms, omitting the operation of a section of code. For example, the area of code that must perform interaction with a separate application that is not yet available is stubbed out.

subclass A class that extends from another class. The class the subclass inherits from is known as the superclass.

superclass The class a subclass extends or inherits from. The superclass is often referred to as the base class.

tags In HTML, the acceptable marks that produce the desired HTML components.

Task List window One of the main windows of the Visual Studio 6 platform, which contains all of the compiler errors encountered during a solution build. Additionally, programmers can add tasks to the Task List window as a reminder of future programming needs.

this Keyword used for a special variable that refers to the current object.

toolbar A GUI control traditionally containing image buttons displayed on the upper portion of the dialog.

traditional comment A comment in a program that exists within a "/* */" construct.

unary operators Operators that act on one operand with one expression. The increment and decrement operators are examples of unary operators. See increment operator and decrement operator.

URL (Uniform Resource Locator) A compact representation of the location and access method for a resource located on the Internet. Each URL consists of a scheme (HTTP, HTTPS, FTP, or Gopher) and a scheme-specific string. This string can also include a combination of a directory path, search string, or name of the resource.

variables In Java, a primitive or reference datatype container. Variables defined within a Java class outside of one specific method are often referred to as class variables.

Visual InterDev An additional Microsoft development platform that uses the Visual Studio 6 IDE, along with Visual C++, Visual Basic, and Visual J++.

Visual J++ Solution *See* solution.

Web browser Software that allows a user to connect to a Web server by using the Hypertext Transfer Protocol (HTTP). Microsoft Internet Explorer, Netscape Navigator, and Sun's HotJava are all popular Web browsers.

WFC *See* Windows Foundation Classes.

Windows API   A set of DLLs containing methods that can be used to achieve the graphical and non-graphical components prevalent in the Windows Operating System. The J/Direct technology and the Windows Foundation Classes both allow Visual J++ developers to exploit the power of the Windows API within Java programs.

Windows applications   One of the project classifications supported in Visual J++ 6. Windows application projects are GUI-based projects that use the WFC to create a user interface. As the name suggests, the applications can be run only in the Windows environment.

Windows Foundation Classes   The application framework included with Visual J++ 6 that accesses the Windows API. With these classes, Java developers can develop fully featured Windows applications.

Windows Registry   The storage location used by the Windows NT, Windows 95, and Windows 98 operating system where programs can maintain state information and register themselves with the system. You can use the `regedit.exe` application to view your Windows Registry.

wizard   An application that can be executed to create new files for your development efforts. For example, Visual J++ 6 includes an Application Wizard that can be executed to greatly ease the processes in creating a data-bound GUI application.

workspace   Term used in Visual J++ 1 and 1.1 for what is now known as a solution in Visual J++ 6. The Project Workspace was the container for one or multiple Visual J++ projects.

ZIP files   In Visual J++, one of the options for Distribution Unit projects. A ZIP file is a compressed collection of multiple files that can be unzipped by a user.

INDEX

SAMS
Teach Yourself
in 21 Days

Sams Teach Yourself in 21 Days *teaches you all the skills you need to master the basics and then moves on to the more advanced features and concepts. This series is designed for the way you learn. Go chapter by chapter through the step-by-step lessons or just choose those lessons that interest you the most.*

Sams' Teach Yourself Java 1.2 in 21 Days

Laura Lemay
Date Published: Jun 23, 1998
ISBN: 1575213907
Retail Price: $29.99 US / $42.95 CAN
Category: Web Development
Topic: Java

Other Sams Teach Yourself in 21 Days Titles

Sams Teach Yourself Visual InterDev 6 in 21 Days
Michael Van hoozer
Date Published: Aug 24, 1998
ISBN: 0672312514
Retail Price: $34.99 US / $50.95 CAN
Category: Programming
Topic: Visual InterDev

Sams Teach Yourself More Visual Basic 6 in 21 Days
Lowell Mauer
Date Published: Aug 14, 1998
ISBN: 0672313073
Retail Price: $29.99 US / $42.95 CAN
Category: Programming
Topic: Visual Basic

Sams Teach Yourself Access 97 in 21 Days
Craig Eddy;
Paul Cassel
Date Published: Jun 24, 1998
ISBN: 0672312980
Retail Price: $34.99 US / $50.95 CAN
Category: Database — Client/Server
Topic: Access

Sams' Teach Yourself Visual Basic 6 in 21 Days

Greg Perry
Date Published: Aug 13, 1998
ISBN: 0672313103
Retail Price: $29.99 US / $42.95 CAN
Category: Programming
Topic: Visual Basic

Sams' Teach Yourself Visual C++ 6 in 21 Days

US*Davis Chapman*
Date Published: Aug 4, 1998
ISBN: 0672312409
Retail Price: $34.99 US / $50.95 CAN
Category: Programming
Topic: C++

SAMS

www.samspublishing.com

Other Related Titles

Using Java 1.2
Michael Morgan
ISBN: 0789716275
$29.99 US/$42.95 CAN

JFC Unleashed
Mike Foley and
Mark McCully
ISBN: 0789714663
$39.99 US/$57.95 CAN

Using Visual J++ 6
Scott Mulloy
ISBN: 0789714000
$29.99 US/$42.95 CAN

Java 1.2 Unleashed
Jamie Jaworski
ISBN: 1575213893
$49.99 US/$71.95 CAN

Java 1.2 Class Libraries Unleashed
Krishna Sankar
ISBN: 078971292x
$49.99 US/$71.95 CAN

The Waite Group Java 1.2 How-To
Steve Potts
ISBN: 157169157x
$39.99 US/$57.95 CAN

Special Edition Using Java 1.2
Joe Weber
ISBN: 0789715295
$39.99 US/$57.95 CAN

Sams Teach Yourself Java 1.2 in 21 Days
Laura Lemay
ISBN: 1575213907
$29.99 US/$42.95 CAN

SAMS

www.samspublishing.com

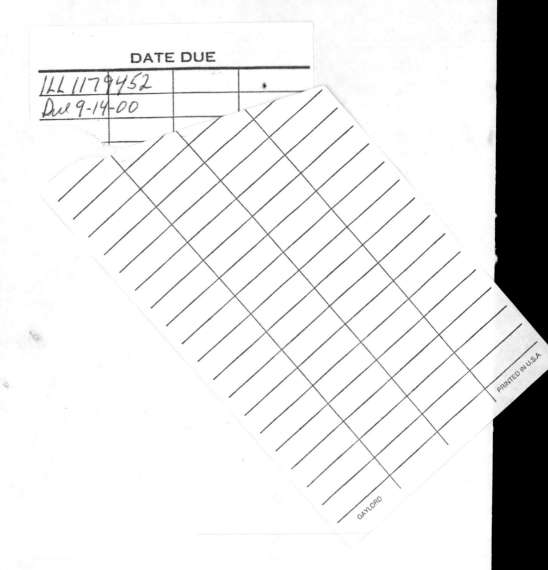